GW00994422

Information Resource Management

INFORMATION RESOURCE MANAGEMENT

OPPORTUNITIES AND STRATEGIES FOR THE 1980S

WILLIAM R. SYNNOTT

The First National Bank of Boston
Boston, Massachusetts

WILLIAM H. GRUBER

Research & Planning, Inc.
Cambridge, Massachusetts

A WILEY-INTERSCIENCE PUBLICATION

JOHN WILEY & SONS
New York • Chichester • Brisbane • Toronto • Singapore

This publication is designed to provide accurate and
authoritative information in regard to the subject
matter covered. It is sold with the understanding that
the publisher is not engaged in rendering legal, accounting,
or other professional service. If legal advice or other
expert assistance is required, the services of a competent
professional person should be sought. *From a Declaration
of Principles jointly adopted by a Committee of the
American Bar Association and a Committee of Publishers.*

Library of Congress Cataloging in Publication Data:

Synnott, William R.
  Information resource management.

  "A Wiley-Interscience publication."
  Includes index.
  1. Management information systems.   I. Gruber,
William H., 1935–   II. Title.

T58.6.S846   658.4′0388   81-11388
ISBN 0-471-09451-X   AACR2

Printed in the United States of America

10 9 8 7 6 5 4 3 2 1

FOREWORD

Information is an ingredient vital to good management. The sharply reduced cost of computer technology and the rapid improvements in the availability of useful new technologies in the telecommunications and office automation arenas have created a very real opportunity to improve the effectiveness of corporate and nonprofit management through improved use of information by management. However, this opportunity has not been easy to exploit in the past two decades. If anything, it is becoming more difficult.

The problems today in the information systems field are legion, but I cite only a few: the need to prioritize the huge resources that are being pumped into information systems development; the need to integrate the various pieces; the difficulties that nonspecialists are finding in working with new technologies; the conflicts between the information specialists and the users of information; and the lack of education of top management as to the key opportunities. One could go on and on.

In every organization there is a need to assist key users to ascertain information requirements, to plan for systems development, and to monitor the status of both the development and the ongoing status of information systems. In short, there is a need for someone to act as the architect of the organization's information capabilities. This is what William R. Synnott and William H. Gruber call "Information Management." Historically, for the first 25 years of the computer revolution, the focus has been on the individual parts of the whole field that Synnott and Gruber have defined as Information Management. Information technology and practice have changed very rapidly, and this has encouraged specialization in hardware, software, operating systems, management information systems, telecommunications, office automation, systems analysis, programming, and so on. This book puts it all together from the viewpoint of the top information officer of the firm.

The strength of the book comes from the experience of the authors. Bill Synnott has provided a wealth of day-to-day "gut feel" for the operating environment of the information manager together with the wisdom derived from years of experience. The strategies suggested are those that have been tried and found effective in actual operation. Bill Gruber has added the conceptual insights gained from many years as a researcher, professor, and consultant in the information systems area.

This book thus provides an answer to a need that has only recently become recognized. There are hundreds, even thousands, of books about various facets of the field, but no other book provides such a pragmatic, organized focus for the total field of Information Management from the viewpoint of the top information managers. This book may be used as a handbook of strategies that are useful in improving the effectiveness of specific facets of Information Management. Thus the reader can turn directly to strategies on hardware capacity planning, user service contracts, programmer productivity, or executive information systems. One way of looking at the book is as a "how-to handbook."

The book is more than a collection of strategies for improving the effectiveness of various specialized facets in the field of Information Management. It provides a cohesive approach that integrates the field of Information Management.

Synnott and Gruber hold strong opinions about how to manage information resources. They have little patience for the amateurishness which too often comes with decentralization of information activities. A strong centralized Information Management function sharing power in the management of information resources is an important theme of their book. They make a strong case for the creation of the role of Chief Information Officer in the firm. They argue that effective Information Management can be best performed through adoption of the centrally oriented Management by Strategies (MBS) technique described in this book. Some will argue that their views are too centralized. So be it. The case is made with vigor and has much to recommend it.

I believe the book succeeds in documenting the extraordinary opportunities managers have in the 1980s for improving the effectiveness of Information Management. The importance of Information Management as a critical success factor in the achievement of high business performance is also documented. The uniqueness of this book is not only that it addresses the neglected management side of Information Management, but that it is written from a practitioner's point of view. The strategies discussed represent techniques and ideas that have been used successfully. Thus, this is a timely and useful book for information managers, users of information services, and professors who want to expose their students to the current issues and opportunities in the field and some of the management strategies being used by leading companies to effect strong Information Management leadership.

JOHN F. ROCKART

MIT Sloan School
of Management
Cambridge, Massachusetts
June 1981

PREFACE

Despite the extraordinary progress made in information management practices during the 1970s a dichotomy still exists between producers of information services and users of information. Most of the literature in the field is concerned with technical details and fails to make the connection between the information resource and the overall goals of the organization. *Information Resource Management* was written to bridge this gap. Our major goal is to deal with information resource management from the general management perspective: to show the information specialist how to work effectively with users, senior management, and staff professionals in the overall management of information resources.

Our methodology in writing *Information Resource Management* has been to organize the book around a series of strategies that have helped to produce the progress of the 1970s. These strategies have not been drawn from out of the blue. They work. They are the result of our work in and experience with several industries—banking, insurance, pharmaceuticals, petroleum, transportation, and publishing.

The more we thought about and studied these successful strategies the more we could see the necessity for users to better understand the field of information management in order to take full advantage of the opportunities it presents for improving organizational productivity. These new capabilities demand the involvement of all who are concerned with the information needs of their organizations. Our experience demonstrates that both users and producers of information services must be jointly involved in any program to improve the effectiveness of information processing and utilization.

We benefited from the careful editing of Alice Falk and Naomi Rosenberg. The many drafts were produced with patience and dedication by our secretaries, Mary Gail Barberio and Joyce FitzGerald. Warren MacFarlan, Richard Nolan, Paul Strassmann, Jack Rockart, and others provided many useful suggestions. Our Wiley editor, John Mahaney, and his staff ably guided our efforts to transform our draft manuscript into the document which was published.

Executives and managers at the First National Bank of Boston and client companies of the Research and Planning Institute contributed their perspective on strategies for information management and have been involved in implementing many of the strategies cited for improving its effectiveness. Of course, we would like to thank our wives Suzanne and Lucretia, without whose patient support and understanding we could not have devoted the time, labor, and lost evenings, weekends, and holidays to this effort.

WILLIAM R. SYNNOTT
WILLIAM H. GRUBER

Boston
Cambridge
October 1981

CONTENTS

Information Resource Management

The New Management

Information in the Practice of Management

The organizations that will excel in the 1980s will be those that manage information as a major resource.

John Diebold[1]

A quiet revolution is occurring in the data processing industry. The computer era of the 1960s and 1970s is giving way to the information era of the 1980s. The emphasis on hardware and software of the computer era is shifting toward a focus on information management as we enter the first decade of the information age.

This difference in focus is significant because it emphasizes the quality and the value of the output of computers rather than the quantity, "by-the-pound" approach of the past. The data processing industry has demonstrated its capacity to produce huge outputs of paper—literally billions of pages every working day. What is needed, however, is not more paper or raw data, but distilled, summarized information that can be accessed, assimilated, and used more effectively, particularly by managers. In a recent speech, Robert M. Price, president of Control Data, questioned the need for even larger volumes of computer outputs:

> On the one hand, American business is inundated with information about itself, its products and the economic environment. On the other hand, business is experiencing stagnation of productivity that threatens its very ability to compete.[2]

And John F. Rockart, director of the MIT Center for Information Systems Research, cited the typical experience of a company president:

> I think the problem with management information systems in the past in many companies, has been that they are overwhelming as far as the executive is concerned. He has to go through reams of reports and try to determine for

himself what are the most critical pieces of information contained in the
report, so that he can take the necessary action and correct any problems that
have arisen.[3]

The data processing industry has experienced a remarkable growth since
1960. But for the most part, the quantity of output has outstripped the quality
of output. This is not to say, however, that great strides have not been made
in improving the quality of these products, in increasing the productivity of
the firm, and in developing more effective information systems and services
in support of business activities. In fact, both the quality and the quantity of
data processing—or, more aptly stated, *information resources*—now provide
an opportunity to move from the computer orientation of the recent past to
the information orientation of the 1980s.

Executives in the best-managed companies achieved impressive progress
in information management and utilization during the 1970s. From this progress in leading companies, it is now possible to set standards for effective
information-management practices in the 1980s. John Diebold has stated this
challenge for corporate management very clearly:

> Information, which in essence is the analysis and synthesis of data, will
> unquestionably be one of the most vital of corporate resources in the 1980's.
> It will be structured into models for planning and decision making. It will be
> incorporated into measurements of performance and profitability. It will be
> integrated into product design and marketing methods. In other words, infor-
> mation will be recognized and treated as an asset.[4]

The information age revolution represents new opportunities for data
processing managers, directors of management information systems, and
system and programming managers to extend their career paths into the new
world of information resource management. This new role of information
resource manager, or simply, information manager, as we refer to it throughout the book, as director of the *information management (IM) function* in the
organization, offers an opportunity to migrate away from the technocratic
image of the past and to establish a new image as a business manager, a
general manager, and an information manager.

The low cost of computers is giving increased impetus to the distributed
processing movement, with its attendant physical control of computer resources moving into the hands of users. This new development creates the
need for an entirely new way of thinking about and managing distributed
information resources in the organization, another new challenge to today's
information manager.

In *The Third Wave,* Alvin Toffler painted a powerful picture of the world
of the next few decades and suggested that the new civilization and the
computer revolution (the third wave) will follow the industrial revolution
(the second wave) as one of the most potent forces in our society.[5]

We can see how dramatically our society has changed from an agricultural society to an information society by noting the change in the deployment of human resources in the last century. In 1890, 46% of the working population was deployed in agriculture, and only 4% in the information business; by 1979, these statistics were reversed, with only 4% in agriculture and 46% in information services.[6]

The traditional responsibility of information managers will change with this revolution to that of control over information resources, rather than control over physical computing resources. The new challenge of the 1980s for information managers is to understand that this revolution is occurring, to understand how it is changing the role of information managers, and then to rise up and *lead* that change. Those who do this successfully will become the new breed of EDP managers; and those who do not will remain as part of the old breed—who will probably be working for the new breed.

TRANSACTION VERSUS INFORMATION PROCESSING

For over 20 years, we have been developing systems for clerks. It is time we began putting computers to work for managers. During the 1960s and even during most of the 1970s, the primary responsibility of the corporate EDP function was to reduce the clerical costs of producing ever-larger volumes of paper output. The typical corporate EDP function was the manufacture of paperwork. It processed the transactions of operating a business. The processing of transactions is, of course, important in the operational or lower-level control of business activities, and computers have made possible important improvements in the productivity of these clerical workers. However, the processing of transactions from operations, no matter how effective, rarely reaches into the offices of corporate management. Thus the role of the IM function beyond simple transaction processing is not even considered by too many corporate managements.

Transaction processing was, and still is, the prevalent use of computers in business, but this is changing. In a survey of 81 user managers in six major corporations, Dr. John Rockart and his associates at the MIT Center for Information Systems Research reported that over 90% of the installed computer applications in those companies were transaction-processing systems.[7] On the other hand, Rockart also reported the trend toward management information systems, noting that the development backlog showed that only 60.6% of new systems requests were for transaction processing, the remaining 39.4% being for on-line inquiry/analysis-type systems. Moreover, the backlog of inquiry/analysis systems was more than four times greater than the present installed base of such applications.

These findings highlight both problems and opportunities. Large backlogs of computer systems continue to exist in many firms, and users are impatient with the IM's function's lack of responsiveness to their systems

and information needs. On the other hand, as basic transaction systems
become automated, the demand begins to shift to management and inquiry
systems, providing a greater opportunity for information managers to direct
more of their resources to management assistance rather than operations and
clerical support. Management systems tend to require more advanced
technologies, such as interactive systems, data-base management systems,
high-level user languages, computer models, minicomputers, and telecommunications networking. Management systems also require greater user-
management involvement than traditional record-keeping and transaction-
based systems. Thus the frontier for information managers in the decade
ahead will very likely be greater information-systems involvement in programs that improve the effectiveness of management functions in the corporation, as well as greater user involvement in the management and use of
information resources. Direct user interfaces with information data bases
will also help to address the system's backlog, particularly the maintenance
of existing systems, much of which is devoted to information extraction and
reporting. As users begin to bypass the need for programmer intervention,
more resources will be freed for new development work.

The challenge for information executives will be to define their responsibilities more broadly to include the full scope of all facets of information
management. Paul Strassmann, vice-president of Xerox, with worldwide
responsibility for administrative and information systems, defined this challenge and the new scope of opportunity as follows:

> Once we accept the notion that the top information executive's job encom-
> passes much more than managing data processing expenses, we still have to
> articulate, in terms of precise objectives, just what the job calls for in today's
> business environment. In my view, the new job definition would include the
> following objectives:
>
> Ensuring the integration of data processing, administrative processing, and
> office labor productivity programs.
>
> Instituting accounting, cost-control, and budgeting innovations that will sub-
> ject all information systems overhead activities to the disciplines traditionally
> applied to direct labor.
>
> Subjecting office labor automation programs to analyses comparable to those
> applied to all other forms of capital investment.
>
> Conceiving organizational designs that will permit information to be handled
> as a readily accessible and easily priced commodity rather than as a bureau-
> cratic possession.
>
> Creating within the organization an internal market for alternative informa-
> tion systems products, so that trade-off decisions, even technologically com-
> plex ones, can be decentralized into the hands of local user management.
>
> Fostering a technique of pricing that will allow decisions on introducing new
> technology, or abandoning obsolete technology, to be made on a decen-
> tralized basis.

Installing and monitoring measurement methods that will protect improvements in productivity achieved by automation programs.[8]

INFORMATION AGE INTEGRATION

In the 1960s, the data processing manager presided over the company's computer programmer resources like a high priest over his subjects. No one in "user land" or management understood much about the "technical back shop." They only knew that it was a powerful, though esoteric, tool that was incredibly fast and could do the work of a great many people. They told the DP manager what they needed and he or she went about doing it, one day appearing on the doorstep to announce that the new system was ready to be converted. Because of inexperience and the state of the art, considerable ups and downs occurred as systems were installed and shaken down. Also, because of inadequate specifications and lack of user involvement, these systems often performed well short of expectations even after being shaken down.

Nonetheless, the practice of systems management gradually improved, user involvement as a requisite for success became more recognized, and hardware and software became more reliable. By the late 1970s, many a DP department had matured to become an efficient, controlled, and vital support function of the organization. Costs were coming under control, systems were performing as expected, and reliable and valuable services were provided by data processing departments.

Just as it appeared that data processing was reaching a stage of maturity, major technological developments entered on the scene to shake up the data processing world once again. The spread of minicomputers and telecommunications began to break up data processing and the centralization–decentralization issue heated up anew. Richard L. Nolan described this process in his well-known *Harvard Business Review* article, "Managing the Crises in Data Processing."[9] He described six stages of EDP growth, as illustrated in Exhibit 1-1.

Stage 1, *Initiation,* marks the installation of the firm's first computers and the introduction to automation; Stage 2, *Contagion,* marks the rapid proliferation and growth of computer systems in the organization as automation spreads; Stage 3, *Control,* marks management's attempt to contain the rapidly rising costs of computing services and to bring data processing growth under control; Stage 4, *Integration,* marks the transition point for renewed but controlled growth as diverse systems and technologies are integrated into cohesive systems; Stage 5, *Data Administration,* marks the conclusion of the development and implementation of a completely integrated data-base system; and Stage 6, *Maturity,* is the final stage of data processing maturity in the firm.

Most well-run DP organizations have now been through the *computer era*

Exhibit 1-1   Six stages of data processing growth.

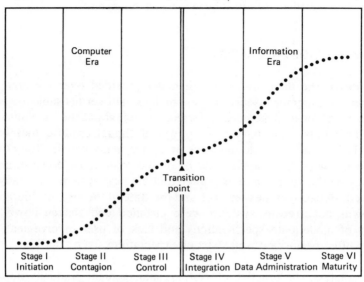

characterized by the first three stages of growth and are now at the transition point of moving into the *information management* era, characterized by Nolan's last three stages of growth. The early 1980s will see many of these organizations struggling with the *integration* of diverse systems and distributed resources as they strive toward the totally integrated-data-base administration stage in the latter part of the 1980s.

Information resource management, in our view, involves the integration of diverse disciplines, technologies, data bases, and other information-handling resources. We see this integration stage as a particularly challenging aspect of IM in the 1980s. Integration will take many forms. To be successful, it must necessarily involve the people side of management as well as technology management. We see at least three dimensions in 1980s integration: *planning, people,* and *technology.* On the *planning* side, there will be a need to carefully integrate business and systems planning so that they jointly address the objectives of the firm. Long-range strategic planning of this kind is still done only rarely by most companies. On the *people* side, it will be absolutely mandatory that the various management groups in the organization (i.e., corporate senior management, user management, and information management) be integrated through the shared management and control of tomorrow's distributed information resources. On the *technology* side, not only will the technical delivery systems (i.e., computers, terminals, communications, and data bases) have to be integrated, but also the diverse information systems that have been built over many years must be integrated into more meaningful, useful information resources and management information systems.

In *Managing in Turbulent Times,* [10] Peter F. Drucker provided guidance for information managers who see the opportunities in the information age. Drucker noted the importance of concentrating resources on results and a "sloughing off of the resource-devouring and unproductive past" (p. 45). Turbulent times provide an opportunity to move ahead of competitors. Drucker noted that leading companies tend to operate at about twice the productivity of other companies in their industries (p. 19). William H. Gruber and John S. Niles[11] also evaluated this disparity between leaders and followers in the utilization of new management technologies. They analyzed trends in the utilization of more effective management practices and forecast the best management practices in the mid-1980s as a "future-firm" status of management competence. We believe the image of a future-firm level of competence in the management of information is a useful standard for planning the transition from the computer era to the information era.

SYNOPSIS OF THIS BOOK

This book has been written as a guide to opportunities and strategies for information managers in the 1980s. Effective leadership of the IM function in this decade will require different strategies than those used in the past. The strategies which have been brought together in this book have been used successfully by leading well-managed companies. They work! Therefore, they can serve as useful guides to information managers in the changing times ahead.

Not all strategies will fit all organizations. All companies are different and require different solutions to problems. But many of the problems, opportunities, and strategies presented can be applied in many company situations. The reader can pick and choose from this collection of ideas and tools to solve specific problems in his or her own environment.

Part 1: The New Management

Following this introductory chapter, we begin by examining the importance of strategic planning as the first step toward integrating corporate objectives, individual business unit needs, and information management goals. Leading companies practice various planning techniques to achieve the integration of business and information systems activities. The unique methodology which we have developed is the management by strategies (MBS) concept introduced in Chapter 2. MBS serves as the framework of the book, which sets forth a series of strategies that can be applied to specific information management situations. MBS should be an adjunct to a management by objectives (MBO) program. Whereas MBO defines *objectives,* MBS defines *strategies* for reaching those objectives—strategies that can be customized to fit a specific company and its problems and needs. The cumulative effect of an MBS program is, in itself, a powerful integration mechanism for effective information management. Effective information management, in turn, is a desirable goal because it leads to better support of the business activities and information needs of the corporation.

The transition from data processing to information management will present new role opportunities for alert information managers in the years ahead. To avoid falling into the "marketing myopia" experienced by the railroad business, which failed to realize that it was not in the railroad business but in the broader business of transportation, we need to understand that the data processing business is evolving into the broader information management business. Change occurs rapidly in a revolution. The information age is opening new opportunities for information managers. In this first part of the book, we evaluate these new opportunities for information managers and recommend a major new perception of the scope of information management in the 1980s. A number of role strategies are discussed to help information managers recognize and capitalize on the opportunities now available to them.

Part 2: Management Integration

The human relations and political dimensions of information management are the subject of Part 2 of the book. The critical interrelationships among the three management groups described earlier (corporate management, user management, and information management) will probably be the single most critical success factor in the effectiveness of IM functions in the future firm. This is true because top managers are becoming research-based managers, looking more to analytical–statistical–quantitative tools to manage the business, as opposed to the experience-based managers of the past, who relied heavily on verbal inputs. Users are also becoming more sophisticated in computer literacy and, because of declining costs in computers, are becoming more involved in the management and control of the computer resources used to support their business activities.

Part 2 examines ways and means of increasing the influence of IM in the organization. Influence is important because it has to do with strong leadership, and leadership is needed both to obtain and to direct the resources needed to support corporate goals and business activities, which, in turn, lead to increased productivity, new computer-based revenue services, and higher profit contributions. The IM function's location in the hierarchical structure, the nature of its management and control of corporate information resources, and its success in automation penetration in various parts of the firm, all contribute to the degree of influence, the leadership ability, and the effectiveness of the IM function. Two chapters are devoted exclusively to specific strategies aimed at improving *user relations* and increasing *top management* involvement in information management activities. The importance of this facet of information management cannot be overemphasized.

Richard L. Nolan noted that "When you look at the actual amount of contact that the CEO had with MIS, it generally could be measured in minutes per year. MIS managers are not given much guidance."[12] Perhaps this is why there has always been a communications gap between senior managers and information managers. Strategies are needed to increase this exposure and to effect meaningful and continuing communications with senior users and corporate management. Most users and senior managers want improved relations with the IM function but have always had a difficult time dealing with what they view as a technical world. The time has come for information managers to change that state of affairs. The time has come to shed the mystique of information processing and to become effective business managers, lifting the IM function out of its technical back-shop image and eliminating the "we–they" syndrome of the past. Part 2 suggests 24 strategies for dealing with this increasingly important facet of user relations in information management.

Part 3: Information Resource Management

Whereas Part 2 deals with the management aspects of the exogenous forces surrounding the IM function (e.g., users and corporate management), Part 3 focuses inward, on the management of internal resources. It logically begins with the management of human resources, the most important resource in any firm. The strategies for attracting and retaining valuable people cover career pathing, motivation analysis, job enrichment, and others.

The hardware/software management chapter which follows explores a variety of strategies for improving the efficiency and productivity of these basic and traditional technical resources. Capacity planning, computer performance evaluation, programmer productivity, software aids and tools, data base systems, and data security are some of the strategies covered.

Because of the rapid advances in telecommunications and office automation, each of these important areas deserves and receives a chapter. The *telecommunications* chapter covers new technical advances, network developments, and communications services. Here, we examine strategies for accomplishing the integration of computers and communications, as well as of voice and data networks. *Office automation* is on its way, with its pioneers forging ahead in all directions. An organizational and leadership strategy is suggested for achieving the successful implementation and integration of diverse office systems as they emerge in this decade.

Finally, the continuing problem of managing major systems projects on time and within budget is treated with, an extensive list of strategies linked to stages in the project life cycle, focusing particularly on the user's involvement in *project management*. This comprehensive review covers the entire

cycle, from project initiation, through project development and implementation, to project management and tracking, to postaudits.

It should be noted that we do not include a chapter on the management of
the administrative and operating resources which make up the clerical and
administrative overhead (and costs) of a total information-resource-
management program. The reason is that in most companies, these resources
are not under the direct management and control of the information manager
(with some notable exceptions). Thus, while we have included no strategies
for managing these resources, it should be recognized by the reader that they
represent the major input- and output-handling side of information resource
management and thus must be included in any evaluation, compilation, or
planning activities involving the coalescence of corporate information resources.

In the closing chapters, we look at some of the problems and opportunities of information management in the future firm.

Distributed processing is no fad; it is here to stay. And as the cost of
computing continues to decline, we will see intelligent terminals (microprocessors) used throughout future firms. While mainframe computer growth
will triple in the next decade, microprocessors will grow by a factor of 150
times today's installations. Managing this change will represent a major
challenge to information managers. The role of a distributed processing controller, matrix management arrangements, and the importance of establishing policies, standards, and procedures for distributed processing are some
of the strategies presented as food for thought for tomorrow's information
managers.

The final chapter revisits *management by strategies* as a strategic planning
technique by illustrating the synergistic effect of building on strategies that
cumulatively increase IM effectiveness. The cases used to illustrate this
synergism demonstrate how an MBS program of innovation in information
management can work to increase the influence and effectiveness of the IM
organization in the future firm.

Inventory of Strategies

Information management in the 1980s is similar to drinking out of a fire
hydrant. The flow of new information technologies is so strong that it is
difficult to control consumption. There are large numbers of serious issues in
the management of information resources, and the length of the list of difficult problems is increasing rapidly. Responding to these rapid changes in
the information age will require information managers who can manage by
plan rather than by crisis.

The speed of change in technology, the increase in user expectations, the
shortage of skilled professionals, and other problems of information management have created a work over-load condition for many information
specialists. In this context, this book can be used as a handbook of strategies

for more effective information management. Sixty-eight strategies for improving the effectiveness of information management are summarized in the "Inventory of Strategies" which follows. This inventory of tested strategies can produce improved performance in the management of information resources.

The strategies are organized by chapter and by major topic within each chapter. Thus, a reader concerned with teleprocessing can turn to Chapter 9 for a review of the role of telecommunications in the overall management of information resources; to Chapter 10 for a discussion of an office automation strategy; and so on. Each strategy's location (chapter and page number) in the book is given for easy reference, and a checklist is provided for use by the reader in appraising the status and/or the applicability of these information management strategies in his or her own organization. In this context, it must be noted that although a number of the case examples used are from the banking industry, most deal with management strategies that are general enough to be applicable to a wide variety of companies and industries. In Chapter 13, cases from The First National Bank of Boston's experiences are, in fact, deliberately used in order to illustrate the synergistic effect which obtains when a program of management by strategies (MBS) is applied to a specific company situation.

The "Inventory of Strategies" allows this book to be used as a handbook of strategies. Pick an opportunity, select a relevant strategy, and implement. This is management by strategies. The example below illustrates how the "Inventory of Strategies" is organized.

		Current Status in Company			
	Location in Book				
S-50 Computications	(Chapter/Page)	O	P	I	NA
A merger of data processing and telecommunications within the IM function to achieve single-mind planning and implementation of tomorrow's communications-based computer systems.	9/000			X	

The code letters for current status are defined as: O = operational; P = plan; I = investigate; NA = not applicable

Readers are encouraged to use the inventory as a worksheet for scoring the status of needed strategies in their companies. From our experience in working with information managers, there are many strategies which can be useful in their companies but are not currently utilized. The "Inventory of

Strategies" provides a worksheet for setting priorities in the implementation of more effective information resource management.

Additional suggestions for the implementation of the 68 strategies recommended in this book will be found in Chapter 2. Some readers will find it useful to read introductory Chapters 1 and 2 and then move directly to a chapter which covers problems of greatest current urgency.

NOTES

1 John Diebold, Foreword to the Diebold Group Special Report, "IRM: New Directions in Management," *Infosystems*, October 1979, p. 41.

2 Robert M. Price, keynote address at the 12th Annual Meeting of the Society for Information Systems, quoted in John Whitmarsh, "Productivity Linked to Knowledge Nuggets," *Computerworld*, September, 29, 1980, p. 1.

3 John F. Rockart, "Chief Executives Define Their Own Data Needs," *Harvard Business Review*, March–April 1979, p. 82.

4 Diebold, "IRM: New Directions," p. 41.

5 Alvin Toffler, *The Third Wave*, New York: William Morrow, 1980.

6 Marc Uri Porat, "The Information Economy," Stanford University thesis. As reported in the *Wall Street Journal*, February 23, 1981, p. 1.

7 John F. Rockart *et al.*, "User Needs Survey: Preliminary Results," CISR Working Paper Draft, September 1978, p. 9.

8 Paul A. Strassmann, "Managing the Costs of Information," *Harvard Business Review*, September–October 1976, pp. 134–135.

9 Richard L. Nolan, "Managing the Crises in Data Processing," *Harvard Business Review*, March–April 1979, pp. 115–126.

10 Peter F. Drucker, *Managing in Turbulent Times*, New York: Harper & Row, 1980.

11 William H. Gruber and John S. Niles, *The New Management: Line Executive and Staff Professional in the Future Firm*, New York, McGraw-Hill, 1976.

12 Richard L. Nolan, quoted in Martin Lasden, "Should MIS Report to the President?" *Computer Decisions*, August 1980, p. 59.

INVENTORY OF STRATEGIES

Strategy (Number and Name)	Location in Book (Chapter/Page)	Current Status in Company*			
		O	P	I	NA
Part 1 The New Management					
Chapter 1 Information in the Practice of Management					
Chapter 2 Management by Strategies: A Strategic Planning Concept					

* Code: O = operational; P = plan; I = investigate; NA = not applicable

Strategy (Number and Name)	Location in Book (Chapter/Page)	Current Status in Company*			
		O	P	I	NA
S-1 Management by Strategies (MBS). Organized and formal program for identifying strategies designed to increase the effectiveness of the IM function in the organization.	2/000				
S-2 Strategic IM Planning. The linking of corporate, business, IM, and individual objectives into a cohesive integrated action plan which maximizes IM effectiveness.	2/000				
Chapter 3 Changing Roles for Information Managers S-3 Role Identification. The migration from data processing to information management in the 1980s will create new roles for information managers. Those who successfully identify and manage these new roles will rise in the organization.	3/000				
S-4 Proactive Change Agent. Discovers opportunities for improving the effectiveness of information utilization and "sells" those options where appropriate and beneficial to the company.	3/000				
S-5 Coalescence Planner. The information manager identifies, coordinates, and coalesces information resources throughout the corporation, managing information as an integrated corporate resource.	3/000				
S-6 Integrator. The new breed of information managers will wear business suits, not technical cloaks, as they learn the business					

* Code: O = operational; P = plan; I = investigate; NA = not applicable

Strategy (Number and Name)	Location in Book (Chapter/Page)	Current Status in Company*			
		O	P	I	NA
and successfully integrate business and information resources.	3/000				
S-7 Chief Information Officer. Senior executive responsible for establishing corporate information policy, standards, and management control over all corporate information resources.	3/000				
Part 2 Management Integration Chapter 4 Increasing the Influence of the IM Function S-8 Distributed Data-Processing Standards. Corporate standards for the management of information resources wherever located in the corporation.	4/000				
S-9 Trojan Horses. IM promotes user penetration by placing systems professionals as "gifts" in user divisions. Trojan horses quickly learn the business and promote systems solutions to business problems.	4/000				
S-10 Business Information Planning. Structured planning strategy for working with users to identify new ways to apply systems solutions to business problems and needs.	4/000				
S-11 Technology Forecasting. A formal approach to the identification of technical trends and their likely impact on the organization.	4/000				
Chapter 5 Effective User Relations S-12 Inventory of Users. A market-research information system for better understanding of					

* Code: O = operational; P = plan; I = investigate; NA = not applicable

Strategy (Number and Name)	Location in Book (Chapter/Page)	Current Status in Company*			
		O	P	I	NA
the user community and identification of problems and/or service opportunities.	5/000				
S-13 User IM Penetration. The status of current user applications compared with the best practices of leading organizations in implementing operational, management, and strategic planning systems.	5/000				
S-14 User Satisfaction Surveys. Program for monitoring user satisfaction with IM services.	5/000				
S-15 Backlog Task Force. Users and IM staff form a task force to determine the magnitude of systems backlog, the adequacy of IM resources, and priorities for backlogged projects.	5/000				
S-16 Foot-in-the-Door. IM provides simple, low-cost, rapid response for users in order to demonstrate the costs and benefits of IM services.	5/000				
S-17 Joint Systems Development. User involvement in the planning, development, and implementation of new systems to assure systems success.	5/000				
S-18 Information Resource Product Managers. Shared management of dedicated information resources gives users greater control without their having to become data processing experts.	5/000				
S-19 Perception Management. Reconciliation of user perception of IM performance relative to the actual service provided.	5/000				

* Code: O = operational; P = plan; I = investigate; NA = not applicable

Strategy (Number and Name)	Location in Book (Chapter/Page)	Current Status in Company*			
		O	P	I	NA
S-20 User Service Contracts. Agreements with users on IM performance objectives and measurement, and reporting of actual performance compared with objective.	5/000				
S-21 Customer Service Center. Provides users with a single service facility for two-way communications about user complaints, service status, downtime, and other problems.	5/000				
S-22 Information Centers. User and/or systems groups specially trained in the use of query language/report writer to provide fast turnaround for user requests for information, data analyses, special reports, and other one-shot information needs.	5/000				
S-23 User-Oriented Charge-Out System. IM charge-out system based on user-understood business units rather than on technical computer-resource units of little value to users.	5/000				
Chapter 6 Top Management: Closing the Communications Gap S-24 Critical Success Factors. Identification of the small number of factors critical to successful performance, and the implementation of executive information systems to monitor activity on the critical factors.	6/000				
S-25 Decision Support Systems. Computer programs, models, and data organized to provide quick response to analyses or informa-					

* Code: O = operational; P = plan; I = investigate; NA = not applicable

Strategy (Number and Name)	Location in Book (Chapter/Page)	Current Status in Company*			
		O	P	I	NA
tion requested by executives to support decision making.	6/000				
S-26 Business Graphics. Pictorial representation of business data represents a powerful new executive information systems tool.					
S-27 CEO Briefings. Periodic scheduled meetings with senior corporate executives for carefully prepared presentations on issues, trends, plans, opportunities, and problems in the world of information management.	6/000				
S-28 Year Plan. Preparation of a year plan in support of the annual IM budget helps to win top management support for needed resources.	6/000				
S-29 Information Resources Management (IRM) Committee. Coordinates and monitors major investments in information resources and sets priorities for the allocation of IM resources to user divisions and functions.	6/000				
S-30 Performance Reporting. Measures the contribution of IM to the corporation in a variety of ways and demonstrates productivity and performance to senior management.	6/000				
S-31 IMPRES. An information-management performance-reporting and evaluation system (IMPRES) for monitoring the efficiency and effectiveness of the IM function.	6/000				
Part 3 Information Resource Management					

* Code: O = operational; P = plan; I = investigate; NA = not applicable

Strategy (Number and Name)	Location in Book (Chapter/Page)	Current Status in Company*			
		O	P	I	NA
Chapter 7 Human Resources Management					
S-32 Staff Management Systems. A set of integrated building blocks used to attract and retain qualified professionals that spans recruitment, skills identification, job assignment, staff development, performance evaluation, and remuneration.	7/000				
S-33 Psychometricians. A programmer-screening tool which helps identify good talent without bias or discrimination.	7/000				
S-34 Human Motivation Seminars. A technique for guiding staff members to a better understanding of themselves and others to improve interpersonal work relations.	7/000				
S-35 Mentors. Experienced IM professionals assigned responsibility for the assimilation and early career growth of new IM staff members.	7/000				
S-36 Career Pathing. An organized multipath structure within IM used to provide broad career-advancement opportunities for motivated staff members.	7/000				
S-37 Systems Interns. A horizontal entry-level training strategy used to upgrade the quality of the IM staff and improve user service levels.	7/000				
S-38 Eagles. Identify, motivate, and effectively utilize the high achievers in the organization.	7/000				

* Code: O = operational; P = plan; I = investigate; NA = not applicable

Strategy (Number and Name)	Location in Book (Chapter/Page)	Current Status in Company*			
		O	P	I	NA
S-39 Gatekeepers. Identify individuals with unique technical talents and abilities who can be called upon by staff members with difficult technical problems.	7/191				
S-40 Consultants. Management strategy for the effective utilization of consultants.	7/192				
S-41 Time Management. Twelve tested time tips for getting more done in less time.	7/194				
Chapter 8 Hardware and Software S-42 Productivity Management. IM role in the planning and implementation of new information technology to improve the productivity of business operations.	8/202				
S-43 Capacity Planning. Management procedures for the balancing of existing IM work loads and the forecasting of future work loads through analytical modeling.	8/206				
S-44 Computer Performance Evaluation. New tools and techniques used to effect management control over computer performance.	8/209				
S-45 Programmer Productivity. A carefully prepared menu of programmer productivity tools and aids can result in dramatic gains in applications software development with the existing staff.	8/216				
S-46 Package Programs. Search and evaluation steps for acquiring package programs which are a good "fit" for the organization, as					

* Code: O = operational; P = plan; I = investigate; NA = not applicable

Strategy (Number and Name)	Location in Book (Chapter/Page)	Current Status in Company*			
		O	P	I	NA
well as service tips on contract negotiation.	8/221				
S-47 Data-Base Management System (DBMS). A prudent strategy for moving into data-base systems.	8/224				
S-48 User Roundtables. Participation with a small number of other organizations in a program of information exchange on issues of common concern.	8/227				
S-49 Security. An access control strategy over a company's vital data resources.	8/230				
Chapter 9 Telecommunications: The Enabler					
S-50 Computications. A merger of data processing and telecommunications within the IM function to achieve single-mind planning and implementation of tomorrow's communications-based computer systems.	9/246				
S-51 Telephone Network Control. Computer-controlled telephone accounting and control systems used to reduce telephone costs and improve service to telephone users.	9/247				
S-52 Diagnostic Center. A centralized capability for communications-systems failure diagnosis and maintenance in a complex multivendor data-communications equipment environment.	9/251				
Chapter 10 The Office Automation Frontier					

* Code: O = operational; P = plan; I = investigate; NA = not applicable

Strategy (Number and Name)	Location in Book (Chapter/Page)	Current Status in Company*			
		O	P	I	NA
S-53 Office Information Systems Strategy. IM leads the firm into the office of the future through proactive leadership and phased planning to increase office and managerial productivity in the organization.	10/259				
Chapter 11 Project Selection and Management S-54 Project Life Cycle. The systems-development life cycle, from project selection to post-audit, as a shared systems/user process.	11/276				
S-55 Project Selection. A process for identifying and selecting new systems projects.	11/283				
S-56 Project Estimating. By combining experience-based with research-based estimating techniques, better project cost estimates are possible leading to fewer project overruns.	11/286				
S-57 Cost–Benefit Analysis. A practical guide for determining the value of investments in information systems.	11/289				
S-58 Standards Manuals. Help to assure success in IM management by consistently applying past successful practices to future activity.	11/291				
S-59 Icebergs. The one-year iceberg rule can be effective in breaking down large tasks into easy-to-manage subprojects.	11/293				
S-60 Project Control System. Four types of project control systems are options for assuring proj-					

* Code: O = operational; P = plan; I = investigate; NA = not applicable

Strategy (Number and Name)	Location in Book (Chapter/Page)	Current Status in Company*			
		O	P	I	NA
ect target dates and avoiding overruns.	11/295				
S-61 Quality Assurance. Quality assurance in the IM function is all too rarely used, yet it can be an excellent early-warning system for the information manager.	11/299				
S-62 Project Implementation. Standards and procedures for full implementation of new systems capability, including postsystem propagation.	11/302				
S-63 Postaudits. The comparison of actual capabilities developed in a systems project and the actual costs with project objectives and budget.	11/305				
Chapter 12 Managing Distributed Processing Resources S-64 Distributed-Processing Controller. Centralized management control over corporate information resources which are distributed throughout corporate divisions and functions.	12/324				
S-65 Matrix Management Strategy. Multidimensionality of large complex organizations is recognized through the assignment of shared responsibility for specializations which cross divisional or geographic borders.	12/325				
S-66 Corporate Policy. Issuance of corporate policies is an appropriate service of the IM function.	12/329				
S-67 Vendor Policy. Centralized IM control over major hardware and software acquisitions, as well as vendor contacts and contracts.	12/332				

* Code: O = operational; P = plan; I = investigate; NA = not applicable

Strategy (Number and Name)	Location in Book (Chapter/Page)	Current Status in Company*			
		O	P	I	NA
Chapter 13 Management by Strategies in Action S-68 MBS Synergism. A program of management by strategies produces a synergistic effect that can greatly increase the overall effectiveness of individual management strategies.	13/340				

* Code: O = operational; P = plan; I = investigate; NA = not applicable

2

Management by Strategies: A Strategic Planning Concept

Strategic planning is the process of deciding on objectives . . . and establishing policies for the attainment of the objectives.

Robert Anthony[1]

If we substitute the word *strategies* for *policies* in the above definition, we will have captured the essence of this chapter.

Given the quiet revolution which is moving data processing from the computer age to the information age, it is now time for information managers to develop strategies to address specific new situations. This is the concept of management by strategies, which is the subject of this chapter and a powerful strategy in its own right. Management by strategies can, in fact, be a useful supplement to Drucker's management by objectives, as we will illustrate.

MANAGEMENT BY OBJECTIVES (MBO)

One of the truly great innovations in the practice of management is the MBO concept first recommended by Peter Drucker in 1954.[2] When implemented *effectively,* an important condition, MBO creates a contract between managers and their subordinates which specifies the objectives to be achieved during the coming year. The relative importance of each achievement is specified in the MBO contract. Procedures for performance reporting and employee evaluation are also specified in a well-designed MBO program. MBO provides an opportunity for employees to participate in the setting of their own objectives. It creates a mission statement against which performance can be evaluated—thereby reducing the arbitrariness of many employee evaluations.

MBO has worked well in some organizations and has been a failure in others. We refer to organizational units as the location for success or failure of MBO rather than companies because MBO can be very effective in one division and a gross failure in another division of the same company. One frequent weakness in MBO programs is a *failure to build into MBO contracts the strategies for meeting objectives*. A second common weakness of MBO programs is a failure to specify achievements in improved management practices. That is, it is common to set targets for sales, costs, profits, and other such bottom-line objectives without also setting objectives for longer range improvements in management practices. Although there are many categories of management practices that should be part of an MBO contract, greater effectiveness in the management and use of information resources is the category on which we focus in this book. The successful implementation of a variety of strategies for improving the effectiveness of information resource management will contribute to performance on the more traditional bottom-line objectives which tend to dominate MBO contracts.

How does one go about developing such strategies?

MANAGEMENT BY STRATEGIES

> **S-1 MANAGEMENT BY STRATEGIES (MBS)**
>
> **Organized and formal program for identifying strategies designed to increase the effectiveness of the IM function in the organization.**

Any planned improvement in the effectiveness of the information management function of an organization demands careful planning and implementation. Management by objectives provides the methodology for the *planning* of goals and objectives; management by strategies, likewise, provides a useful methodology for the *implementation* of strategies designed to attain goals and objectives. In this chapter we introduce the management by strategies, or MBS, concept. The matching of management strategies to the solution of specific problems represents a unique way of approaching information management throughout the rest of the book. Various strategies are suggested to deal with the various management problems inherent in managing an IM function so as to improve the effectiveness and contribution to the organization. Whenever a strategy that is presented in the book is mentioned, its strategy number will be noted in the text for ease of reference.

Many of the strategies presented in this book have been used in companies with very strong IM functions. They are user-tested. On the other hand, we are careful to note that not all of these strategies will fit every business environment because every company is different, and each has different needs and problems. In fact, the very essence of an MBS program is that it is tailored to the environment in which it must work. This custom tailoring is accomplished by an analysis of the environment for which the program is to be designed; the development of goals and objectives based on the problems, needs, and opportunities discovered in the analysis; and then a search for the appropriate strategies to realize these objectives. This concept of management by strategies (MBS), first described in an article by one of the authors in *Infosystems* magazine, October 1979, is restated in the following pages.[3]

STRATEGIC PLANNING FOR INFORMATION MANAGEMENT

A more descriptive term would probably be *strategy planning* rather than *strategic planning,* because the emphasis is more on strategy formulation than on planning per se. That is, what is described is a planning process which we call *management by strategies* (MBS).

MBS, using a process described as *situation analysis,* recognizes that corporations, like people, are all different and that different strategies are needed for different environments. It's all a matter of proper fit. MBS, then, is a holistic strategy for planning in the business environment which recognizes that results-oriented information management and optimal IM effectiveness can be attained only through a proper "fit" with the organization. *Fit,* in this sense, then, means (a) understanding your environment; (b) defining your role within that environment; and (c) developing strategies that fit the two together. The process can be reduced to three questions: What are the needs of the organization? What is the technology available to meet those needs? What can the management information function do to match these up? Strategic planning must pull together four things:

Corporate objectives.
User needs.
Technological trends.
IM role in the organization.

Let us illustrate this process using some factors common to all businesses.

ENVIRONMENTAL FACTOR 1: THE COMPANY

Some important factors to consider in the company environment include organizational style, objectives, and political makeup.

Organization

The information management organization should follow the company organization. If the company is centralized, centralize IM; if it is decentralized, IM follows. The First National Bank of Boston, for example, is a centralized institution in Boston, but it is decentralized internationally. Information resource management does likewise. Computer, systems, and telecommunications services are centralized in Boston, but a distributed processing network is in operation overseas, with regional data centers serving the UK, Brazil, and Argentina, and distributed minicomputers operating in other countries where automation is warranted. This strategy of following the bank's organizational style helps to integrate the IM function more smoothly and effectively into the bank's organization.

Another important organizational point is the location of the information management function in the company hierarchy. It is important that it have a position in the organization of equal stature with other major functions of the business. Why? Because IM is a corporatewide activity, and making it subservient to another function could deprive the company of the real potential of its scarce (and expensive) resources.

Objectives

IM objectives should also follow corporate objectives. You can't plan in a vacuum. If the company does formal long-range planning, information management should participate in it; if it does not, don't stop there. IM can be a catalyst for planning: by conducting executive interviews, determining long-range business plans and needs, and formulating its own objectives around them. Systems planning must be done with corporate input; otherwise, you are shooting without aiming.

In establishing objectives and developing action plans, our motto is "Keep it simple." Many plans fail because there is no commitment from the top, the wrong people are doing the planning, and/or too much time is demanded of the planning participants. All of these pitfalls can be avoided if the planning process is kept simple. It doesn't take a lot of people to plan—just one or two right people, preferably someone high enough and knowledgeable enough to know the business and its needs so that he/she (a) need not demand too much of anyone's time; (b) can put together an action plan which will achieve results and not just push a lot of paper; and (c) can get the commitment of top management because of (a) and (b).

One needs only a simple five- or six-page management summary, followed by a few pages of appendixes. It could begin with a short discussion of important technical trends and their potential impact on the company, then (re)state its information management objectives (these are short "momentum-type" strategy statements), and then recap major accomplishments (during this year) and plans (for next year) toward those objectives. One-page appendixes might graph some or all of the following: a projects plan, manpower plan, a technology (hardware/software) plan, a budget plan, an organization plan, or an education plan. An easy-reading 10 or 12 pages is likely to be read and acted upon. (This year-plan strategy is discussed in more detail in Chapter 6.)

Political

The political realities of life—the people, power, and policies of an organization—can and must be channeled into a supportive rather than an opposing force. This channeling takes planning. Political strategies are of two types: direct control and indirect influence. We recommend both. Here is an example of each:

Direct Control   The issuance of corporate policy in any organization is a form of direct control. While management creates policy, the writing and dissemination of that policy in an organization can be a responsibility of the information management function—because it's a management information service that crosses divisional lines. This can be a very effective strategy for controlling such things as major spending, equipment acquisition, and use of outside services. This strategy will be explored further in Chapter 12.

Indirect Influence   An influential strategy, on the other hand, uses more subtle means of influencing actions or events. This strategy often requires more time and patience, but the results can also be more permanent since the actions are taken and the decisions are made by the user. A systems coordination strategy is a case in point. This strategy involves the "gift" of systems people to users, especially where users are unaware of the potential benefits of automation to their business activities. In such cases, our systems coordinators can be instrumental in letting in automation, designed to help the user do his job better and more profitably. The key to this strategy lies in first enlisting the support of top management. With their endorsement and support, systems-trained people can be transferred into user areas—either as resident systems planners or as line managers—to the benefit of all concerned. These "Trojan horses" are treated in more depth in Chapter 4.

ENVIRONMENTAL FACTOR 2: THE USERS

Once tuned in to the company—its organization, objectives, and political makeup—we are ready to turn our attention to the next environmental factor: the users. Two important considerations here are the backlog of systems work and the level of user satisfaction.

Backlog

The use of a high-level priorities or steering committee can be effective in preventing cries of unresponsiveness, because it means that information management never turns down a job. That is, as projects are identified, IM estimates costs, users give the benefits, and the priorities committee (i.e., management) makes the decision.

Systems backlog can be determined by a business systems planning group. This small group of systems specialists establishes corporate needs through extensive executive interviews, defines priorities based on some criterion (such as staff reduction or return on investment), and matches needs with the available IM resources, assuming the projects are all approved. This procedure quantifies the backlog, and the result is an annual projects manpower plan which can be presented to the priorities committee every January. If the work/manning balance results in too heavy a backlog (say, over three years), we can ask that they either increase the supply (add staff or outside resources) or reduce the demand (establish priorities based on the work load). Thus information management can rarely be accused of being unresponsive, since they are simply providing a service based on management's priorities. This backlog strategy is also discussed in Chapter 5.

User Satisfaction

The most important thing to users is good service, which is measured in terms of responsiveness, the availability of resources, and the quality of the work performed. Thus an effective user-satisfaction strategy is one that places greater emphasis on service and effectiveness (results achieved, value of product) than on efficiency (cost control).

One way to assure effectiveness is to have the user create his own product, through heavy user involvement in all phases of systems activity. We can do this as follows: first, establish as company policy that no major systems project shall be undertaken without the joint participation of the user. This does not mean assigning the latest management trainee to the project; it means assigning a high-level user representative who has a thorough grounding in the business of the user. His assignment is not part time in conjunction with other duties but full time for the duration of the project. The user's representative should be one of the division head's chief lieutenants, if not a key manager. (In fact, if the user screams at the very suggestion of the name, you know you have the right person.)

Users should be involved in four areas of systems activity: systems planning, project team organization, system development, and postaudits. Systems planning starts with the business systems planning process described earlier: systems people working with users to identify systems needs. (This phase might be more accurately described as systems involvement with the user rather than the other way around.) Project team organization, as a matter of corporate policy, should be comprised jointly of systems and user personnel: the systems people are responsible for the efficiency of the system, and the users are responsible for its effectiveness.

The user determines what is to be done; we should suggest how. Systems development should not be left entirely to the systems people; it is a user responsibility as well. Standards should define both systems and user responsibilities throughout the life cycle of the project. Finally, a postaudit should be conducted following the completion of every major project—and this is a team effort involving not only the user but representatives from finance, audit, and other functions as well.

The real benefit of a user involvement strategy is that it helps insure that users get what they want and thus assures success because the users feel it is THEIR system. This whole issue of user involvement in the systems development process is covered in detail in the project-life-cycle strategy presented in Chapter 11.

ENVIRONMENTAL FACTOR 3: TECHNOLOGICAL TRENDS

Up to now, we have considered internal environmental factors. Now let us look at some external considerations—in this case, technical trends such as advancing technology, distributed processing, and office automation.

Advancing Technology

Continuing cost/performance gains and declining computing costs are important because IM is one of the few disciplines successfully fighting inflation today through increased productivity. We need to educate management and potential users in how to exploit this technology, and we need to aggressively seek out new automation opportunities within the companies served. Productivity measurement strategies are needed which communicate to management the fact of automation's productivity.

Typical productivity measurement strategies include equipment utilization/optimization measures, programmer productivity measures, the use of transaction-based charge-out systems which illustrate declining unit costs over time, before-and-after measures of single-system automation (revenue, costs, staff), and measures of automation impact on the total enterprise's cost trends. The important thing is to give top management something by which they can measure the contribution of automation in general and the information management function in particular so that they can justify the needed support for the continued advance of technology in the organization. Further ideas along these lines are contained in Chapter 6.

Distributed Processing

The old centralization/decentralization issue seems to be giving way to distributed processing, probably because it appears to offer the advantages of each without the disadvantages of either, that is, low cost, central management control, and local operational autonomy. But distributed processing is not without its problems. Uncontrolled, redundant automation can lead to higher (not lower) costs; a lack of standards can result in splintered operations; and user inexperience can lead to big mistakes, loss of control—even self-destruction! In the authors' opinion, distributed processing should not mean distributed control. With control, you have distributed processing; without it, you have decentralized processing or perhaps distributed incompetence. We think central management control is what makes the difference between distributed and decentralized processing.

A strategy for achieving some degree of corporate control over distributed resources is the issuance of distributed processing standards. These cover such areas as control over major spending, hardware/software selection criteria, data communications network protocols, physical facilities (security and control over computer operations), vendor contracting and corporate data standards. Several strategies dealing with the management and control of distributed processing resources are presented in Chapter 12.

Office Automation

The office of the future is one of the remaining automation frontiers. Most authorities agree that this is an area that has been consuming more and more of the expense dollar while showing little improvement in productivity. Most IM functions currently have both the computer resources for office automation, and the systems skills to do the job. Not all are providing the leadership, however, to carry it out. A long-range phased implementation plan is needed to guide this important effort.

The first phase in the evolution of the office of the future began some time ago, with distributed-text-processing work stations replacing typewriters. We are now moving into the second phase: electronic mail/filing, which will reduce paper and the need for file cabinets. The resultant proliferation of systems will, in the third phase, require the integration of these independent elements and systems into a single office system. But the real productivity gains in the office will come from fourth phase: the computerization of office processes and procedures, which will free up secretaries AND managers so that fewer of both will be needed to manage the offices of the future.

This phased approach has been described by Zisman[4] as being a corollary of Nolan and Gibson's well-known hypothesis on the stages of DP growth; that is, office automation will also follow the stages of initiation, contagion, formalization, and maturity. The point is that most IM functions have the resources and the opportunities to lead the way to the office of the future, if they can provide the leadership, get management support, and also develop a sound strategic plan to get there. More importantly, if IM people don't do it, someone else will, perhaps with less effective results. This whole planning process is the subject of Chapter 10.

ENVIRONMENTAL FACTOR 4: INFORMATION MANAGEMENT ROLE

The role of the IM function in the organization of the 1980s will represent a radical change from the early days of data processing. We see at least three important roles for ourselves as future information managers: we see ourselves as proactive change-agents, as coalescence planners, and as integrators.

Proactive Change-Agents

Through business systems planning, we have adopted a proactive, rather than a reactive, role in searching out opportunities to apply technology to the solution of business problems. To be simply reactive is to abdicate to the users the decisions on how best to put computers and other information technologies to work for the company. Why should these decisions be the user's responsibility? We think information managers should assume greater responsibility in helping to decide the application of technology on the basis of what's best for the company, not simply on who "squeaks" the loudest. If the company has no priorities committee to deal with projects competing for scarce resources, perhaps the information manager can help to form one. There must be a conscious effort to allocate scarce resources where they will do the most good for the company. Users who have learned how to tap this resource will continue to do so; those who have not will not, thus making permanent an imbalance between profit contributors and the allocation of scarce computer and other information resources in the organization. We describe this idea in more detail in the next chapter.

Coalescence Planners

In turbulent times, in an age of discontinuity, as Peter Drucker has noted, we must ask: "What business are we in?"[5] Today's astute manager realizes that it is no longer the data processing business; it is the information management business. What does this mean? It means that we have a new identification and a new set of responsibilities. Let's start with identification.

"Data processing" is a limiting title! For example, the issuance of corporate policy can be a responsibility of the IM function. This is logical because the issuance of corporate policy and instructions is, in fact, *an information service*. On the other hand, it would make no sense to say: "Corporate policies will be issued by the data processing division." *Data processing* connotes a technical limitation that is considerably broadened when changed to *information services* or *information management*. Thus, it is important that the right identification be established before one can embark on a program of coalescing the information resources in the organization. As the IM function, we can begin to define appropriate responsibilities that "fit" the organization of the 1980s. With the right identification, the coalescence of information resources can begin. This subject, too, is covered further in Chapter 3 and involves bringing together the important information resources of the company in question.

Integrators

Above all, the information manager of the future must be an effective integrator—of the IM function with the business and with users, of the decentralized pieces, and of corporate information resources. It will be his or her job to close the communications gap with senior management. How? By shedding the technical mystique and getting to know the business to be served. The integration role focuses on bringing together the different management groups and working with their people to define information and systems needs. This will be the challenge to information managers in the 1980s. This new role is expanded in Chapter 3 as well.

This strategic planning process is designed to channel information managers into thinking about their environment, assessing effective roles within that environment, and then developing strategies that effectively "fit" the two together. The factors discussed, as summarized in Exhibit 2-1, are ger-

Exhibit 2-1 Strategic planning (situation analysis.)

Environment	IM Strategies
Company	
Organization	IM organization
Objectives	IM objectives
Political	Influence/control techniques
Users	
Backlog	Priorities committee
Satisfaction level	User involvement
Technical trends	
Advancing technology	Productivity measurement
Distributed processing	Control standards
Office automation	Phased integrated plan
IM role	
Proactive change agent	Business systems planning
Coalescence planner	Chief information officer
Integrator	Technical cloaks

mane to every company. The reader will think of others of your own to add, particularly those applicable to your company. But beyond the efficacy of the individual strategies of this method, one will get a bonus through the synergism which comes from combined strategies.

In the fast-changing world of information resource management, we must know how the DP manager's role is changing—because it is up to all of us to lead that change. We must shed our technical cloaks and become a part of the mainstream of the business. It has been said, "There are only three kinds of people in the world: those who make things happen, those who watch things happen, and those who don't know what's happening." Management by strategies is a planning concept designed to stimulate information managers to think about how to reach their objectives. If it succeeds in doing that, we will have achieved our objectives in the writing of this book.

THE IMPORTANCE OF PLANNING

Before planning can occur, there must be a commitment to planning. If planning is not viewed as important, it will not be done. Is planning important? We think it is, for a number of reasons.

Planning is the key to success.   To paraphrase Arnold Glasgow, "Management without planning is like shooting without aiming." Planning is the only way to manage change effectively. If the IM function is truly to be an agent of change, then it must plan for change. As far back as 1968, a McKinsey survey showed that of the more successful companies surveyed, 75% conducted long-range planning, compared with 14% that did not.[6]

Planning leads to better resource management.   If resources were not scarce, then perhaps there would be no need to plan. Because computer and human resources are not unlimited, they must be allocated to the right priorities, to doing those things that will bring the greatest benefit to the company. Priority setting requires planning.

Planning improves communications.   A survey by McLean and Soden[7] showed that the two primary long-range objectives of the information managers surveyed were (1) to improve user communications and cooperation and (2) to improve top management communications and support. Planning helps to close the communications gap with users and top management as discussed in Part 2.

Planning brings control.   Management by objectives beats management by crisis. Control beats chaos. Planning helps to bring about control, control buys time in which to plan, and planning leads to more control—a nice fire-prevention cycle.

Planning influences the future.   You must invent the future, not just let it happen; shape it, don't wait for it. Long development and lead times in the

IM world dictate the need for long-range planning. Long-range planning, in turn, improves short-term decisions and starts the action of molding the future toward the achievement of objectives.

How Not To Plan

Many plans fail simply because they get off to the wrong start. It's just as important to know what to avoid in planning as it is to know how to plan. Here are some things to avoid:

No support.   It is the responsibility of the information manager to support the corporate business plan. If there is no corporate plan, a supporting IM plan would be most difficult to prepare. So, if there is no corporate plan, don't stop there. Interview users and top management to learn their long-term plans and needs, and build the IM plan around these. Management and user involvement is mandatory for successful IM planning.

No real plan.   Often, what passes for a plan is not really a plan at all. A budget is not a plan, it is a forecast—and forecasts are not strategies. A collection of systems projects is not a plan, it's a resource allocation system—it's part of a plan, not the plan itself. Moreover, it's responsive, not innovative. One survey of 35 large-scale organizations (median budget, $20 million) showed that the plans of one-quarter of the companies were simply budgets and half were a collection of ongoing and proposed projects; most of the rest had no plans at all. Only 3 of the 35 companies had plans and/or policy statements describing long-range DP-resource objectives.[8]

No action plan.   Planning does not involve future decisions; it involves decisions today. Long-range strategic objectives must be converted into current tactical decisions and action steps. Plans that do not translate into action fail. They become an exercise in paper pushing instead of setting real objectives and prescribing actions to achieve those objectives.

Bad Plans

McLean and Soden described six examples of bad planning, which we summarize as follows:[9]

Squeaky wheel.   No plan at all. Crisis management, pumping water (resources) to wherever the fire is.

Straight-edge approach.   A linear extrapolation of past data-processing expense trends (like putting a straight edge over a chart and extending the trend line into the future).

Ivory tower plan.   IM forecasts human and equipment needs based on its own guesses of what is needed. No top management or user input.

Silver platter plan.   Corporate management demands an IM plan but offers no guidelines. IM develops a list of projects, perhaps resource requirements. Still no user involvement and no priorities.

Smorgasbord method.   Recognizing the need for user involvement, IM develops a "smorgasbord" list of needs, prepared with no real idea as to costs, benefits, priorities, risks, or "fit" with corporate objectives. Since it is not an integrated plan, management cannot properly evaluate it.

Tinker toy plan.   A grandiose architectural design for a total corporate management information system. Multiyear, large general funding is sought. The plan is represented by "charts depicting numerous data base circles, interconnected with information flow arrows, and interspersed with transaction boxes and report wingdings" and is so highly complex and interrelated that no one understands it (including the architects). Sounds great but is impossible to achieve. After much planning and resource expenditure, nothing comes out the other end, and the plan falls on its face. (An all-or-nothing approach usually leads to nothing.)

Probably the single most important ingredient in successful planning is *commitment.* Strategic planning deals with long-range corporate objectives, which can be set only by chief executives who know what businesses they want to be in and what results they want from these businesses and from the corporation as a whole.

Some CEOs, of course, do establish clearly defined goals and support the implementation of those goals through rational tactical business plans. Too many companies, however, simply establish general growth goals, such as earnings per share (EPS) growth, price–earnings ratios, and return of investment on capital or assets, without any specific plan for getting there. And some, of course, establish no corporate goals at all but simply assign resources in support of individual business-unit objectives.

If the corporation has clearly defined corporate objectives, then the information manager's job is made easy: IM goals are simply matched to corporate goals. Where such goals are not clearly set out, however, the task becomes more difficult. In such a case, the IM manager can attempt to elicit top management's goals and objectives through executive interviewing or go instead to the heads of the individual business units which comprise the company and learn their objectives. The IM managers can also help users by teaching them how to plan or provide resources to them that would allow them to plan. In this way, the information manager can develop a strategic plan based on corporate goals and/or on the goals of the various business units of the company. In point of fact, IM plans can often be formulated *only* in support of individual business-unit objectives because sometimes corporate objectives are simply the unification of the plans of the individual business units. Thus, it is the individual systems and services developed for the business units that make up much of the IM plan.

STRATEGIC PLANNING

> **S-2 STRATEGIC IM PLANNING**
>
> The linking of corporate, business, IM, and individual objectives into a cohesive integrated action plan which maximizes IM effectiveness.

The first step in management by strategies (MBS) should probably be the development of a program for strategic planning to identify and respond to the corporate business environment. This strategic-planning strategy is designed to accomplish this purpose.

Successful planning always requires interaction with users and top management, so that a meaningful and useful IM plan evolves, with goals consistent with the goals of the corporation, accompanied by an action plan to carry out those goals. We would like to review a six-step IM strategic-planning strategy designed to achieve an integrated planning effort.

Step 1   Corporate (Strategic) Objectives

Strategic planning often begins with the adoption of a "mission" statement:

"Maximize long term EPS in the conduct of an ethical financial business."
"Expand all existing business units without unrelated diversification."
"Move the company into the Fortune 500 list within five years."

Corporate objectives can then promote the *mission* of the company. As indicated previously, these mission statements often range from well-thought-out and well-articulated entrepreneurial-type goals, to simple "wish" statements, to none at all. Corporate objectives are really a set of "momentum" statements which provide the necessary stimulation to the individual business units in setting their own subobjectives for corporate goals. Some strategic objectives often work well even without specifics on how they are to be accomplished, simply because they are simply stated and easy to communicate:

"Increase return on capital to 15%."
"Increase EPS growth 20% per year over the next five years."
"Increase share of market in X product lines."

Contrarily, a voluminous long-range-planning document runs the risk of being relegated to desk drawers, with no real action plans motivated.

Strategic corporate objectives can serve simply as directional statements which give stimulus to the setting of supporting subobjectives by the individual business units of the corporation.

Step 2 Business Unit Objectives

Business objectives often revolve around product development and/or promotion. (In a service industry, the products are services.) Preferably, they should result from marketing research, that is, an analysis of business trends and conditions, changing markets, consumer attitudes and needs, competitive considerations, economic forecasts, etc. More and more, in these times, this kind of analysis involves the use of sophisticated techniques such as computer modeling (see Exhibit 2-2). Here is where the IM organization may have its first opportunity to support the business planning effort.

Exhibit 2-2 Future planning models.

A *Business Week* article described computer planning models as follows:

> The hottest planning tool around today is computer modeling, in which planners construct sophisticated business models to test hypotheses on a wide range of decisions at much lower cost and at greater speed than ever before. Programmed into a computer, typically, are the historical data on a business—the "what happened and how" information of the past—along with specific assumptions for the future. Against those data, planners can play "what if" games covering nearly any contingency. Complex software is now available for the basic modeling job, as well as programs that pinpoint the issues that ought to be addressed for each industry. The goal is to be able to measure in advance the effect on the business of any decision and to react rapidly in a changing environment.[10]

The article went on to warn, however, that such models are only as good as the people who create them and the information they contain. Hence, rather than attempting to develop their own models, many businesses perfer to use professional planning consultants who have developed sophisticated computer models. There are also a number of outside proprietary data bases containing much industry and econometric information which it would be impractical for individual companies to put together themselves.

Using such computer models and commercial data bases, companies today can simulate any number of planning strategies and thus minimize business risks from faulty planning. *Business Week* noted, for example, "Inland Steel Corporation credits modeling with saving it from embarking on a $1.5 billion expansion program that would have proved to be a financial disaster."[11]

Step 3   *IM Objectives*

The IM organization also needs a mission statement, for example:

"Support business objectives through operational, management control, and planning systems so as to increase effectiveness and profits." (Dupont).

"Ensure that divisional business needs are satisfied by working with divisional personnel in concert with each divisional business Systems manager." (Norton Co.)

"Produce services and products related to the electronic handling of information, and market them to the Sun Co. and others at sustainable profit levels. Become an attractive holding in the Sun Co.'s portfolio of diversified businesses." (Sun Information Services)

Like the corporate mission statement, the IM mission statement's purpose is directional. It is a policy statement which serves to support the corporate mission. In support of the general mission statement, again, a series of simple IM objectives can be drawn up to serve as momentum statements that support corporate objectives. These should be long-range (say, five-year) objectives dealing with broad goals such as (1) the use of new technologies (hardware/software migration plans, data-base-systems implementation, the building of a distributed processing network) or (2) supporting company goals and directions (proactive automation efforts, productivity improvements, support of new product development, management information systems, and computer-based research). Such policy statements are usually enough to give general direction to IM staff. For example, a corporate objective to "increase net profit 15% per year" could be met by an IM objective to "increase productivity through proactive automation efforts." Such a goal would aim at planning new projects which contribute to profit goals by cutting operating costs. The actual projects so identified would be not part of the strategic goals but part of the tactical plan to carry out the broadly defined objective.

Earlier, we suggested that strategic objectives should be long-term. Why? Because the evolution of information programs are measured in years. Major systems development and hardware and software generations span years. It's like turning an aircraft carrier. It's not a rowboat—it takes time. Some managers find this hard to understand, especially those that are accustomed to working on problems and solutions which are short-range; they are concluders, finishers—such managers may not realize that information management never finishes. New systems are born, and old systems become obsolete and must be replaced. To end, or finish, systems work would, in fact, be to fail. Because most managers can't see beyond the horizon, there is often a tendency to assume that the future will need fewer resources. History has proved this to be not the case. Thus, without long-range planning, we move into the future inadequately prepared (from the standpoint of resources) to respond quickly and effectively to user needs.

Step 4   IM Tactical (Action) Plan

The tactical, or action, plan represents the specific actions to be taken toward accomplishing the strategic objectives which have been established. This plan is essential since objectives which are not converted to decisions and actions today will remain unfulfilled objectives. The tactical plan usually has a one- to three-year horizon, simply because some projects and lead times take that long. However, it should be updated annually as a year plan (see S-28) that reflects changes in and additions to the previous annual year plan. User involvement is a must in determining needs and systems projects which represent the action part of the plan. Thus, user interviews and re-planning and prioritization of tasks should take place annually, preferably before budget review time so that the tactical (year) plan can be incorporated into the budget review process for resource approval purposes.

Emphasis in the year plan ought to be concerned with the *new*, not the old. There will always be those who simply want to do more of what they already do. Maintenance and enhancements are necessary, of course, but the purpose of planning should be to serve the future. To be a leading-edge competitor, one needs *new* products and services, not just a patching up of the old. To do too much of the latter is to become a maintenance shop, which is contrary to the purpose of planning.

Drucker suggests that abandonment should be part of future planning: "What is crucial . . . [is] that planning start out with a sloughing off yesterday, and that abandonment be planned as part of the systematic attempt to attain tomorrow; . . . look for new and different ways to attain objectives rather than believe that doing more of the same will suffice."[12]

Step 5   MBO Contracts

The action steps spelled out in the tactical (year) plan can next be assigned as specific tasks to specific individuals, through the setting of individual MBO goals. An effective way to do this is through the use of MBO contracts between employee and boss: the MBO contract is a mutual agreement between boss and employee about what the employee's contribution will be in the coming year toward the attainment of company objectives, on the basis of reasonable and doable assigned tasks. Individual goals, if achieved, ensure the attainment of company goals. Once a task has been agreed upon between boss and employee, it can be reduced to a written contract. To be effective, successful achievement of MBO contract goals should be built into the salary review procedure. If a person's salary depends on achieving goals, they will have meaning; otherwise, they may be just an exercise in paperwork. MBO allows objectives to be filtered down into the organization, with each successive level breaking down the objective into subtasks. Everyone thus contributes to the division's objectives. In fact, if anyone's individual objectives cannot be matched to a division objective, either IM has the wrong objectives or the IM staff is working on the wrong things. In many organizations, corporate and division objectives are not widely known. (Ask your staff members what your own are.) With MBO contracts, everyone knows the objectives.

Step 6   Management Feedback

The final step in this planning strategy is to develop an appropriate management-control process to track achievements against the plan and to report progress back to management. The year plan mentioned earlier is one form of this reporting process. So are oral reports made at user management meetings, or before the information resources management committee (see S-29), at annual budget review meetings, or CEO briefings (see S-27). What-

Exhibit 2-3   Strategic planning steps.

Steps	Bank Example
(1) Corporate Objectives	Expand services to Multi—national corporations
(2) Business Unit Objectives	Coordinate worldwide loans to MNCs
(3) IM Objectives	Proactive support of International services
(4) IM Tactical plan	Build consolidated worldwide Management Information System (MIS)
(5) MBO Contracts	MIS targeted for 1/1/82 — goal of P. Smith
(6) Management Control Process	Project Control reports — Quarterly updates to Management

ever the process, feedback is a very important part of the planning process. Without it, objectives—and accomplishments—will be forgotten.

The strategic-planning steps logically move from top to bottom, as summarized in Exhibit 2-3, with the establishment of the general mission of the corporation.

NOTES

1   Robert N. Anthony, *Planning and Control Systems: A Framework for Analysis,* Studies in Management Control, Harvard Business School, 1965, p. 24.
2   Peter F. Drucker, *The Practice of Management,* New York: Harper & Row, 1954, pp. 121–136.
3   William R. Synnott, "Strategic Planning for Information Management Effectiveness," *Infosystems,* October 1979, pp. 70–82.
4   Michael D. Zisman, *Office Automation: Revolution or Evolution?*, CISR Report 34, Sloan WP 986-78, MIT, April 1978, pp. 2ff.
5   Peter F. Drucker, *Managing in Turbulent Times,* New York: Harper & Row, 1980, p. 65.
6   *Unlocking the Computer's Profit Potential,* McKinsey and Company, New York, 1968, pp. 16–20.
7   Ephraim R. McLean and John V. Soden, *Strategic Planning for MIS,* New York: Wiley, 1977, p. 66.
8   Survey done by McCaffrey, Seligman and Von Simson (N.Y. consulting firm), 1974.
9   McLean and Soden, *Strategic Planning,* pp. 80–82.
10   "The New Planning: Computer Games that Planners Play," *Business Week,* December 18, 1978, p. 66.
11   *Ibid.,* p. 66.
12   Peter F. Drucker, *Management: Tasks, Responsibilities, Practices,* New York: Harper & Row, 1974, p. 128.

3

Changing Roles for Information Managers

Business needs a new breed of EDP manager.

Richard L. Nolan[1]

Data processing managers need a new image. No longer technical back-shop wizards running arcane machines in support of a company's clerical record-keeping and/or transaction-based systems, today's new breed of EDP managers are moving out of the back shop and into business manager roles. They are taking on new and broader responsibilities and repositioning EDP in the organization so as to be more influential, more participatory, and more responsive to users' business systems needs as well as to executive information needs. Those who are succeeding in this transition are migrating from being the data processors of the past to being the information managers of the future. Those who are not are seeing a massive decentralization of power over the allocation of computer resources to users.

This chapter urges data processing managers to reconsider their changing role in the information era, to reassess their self-image, and to consider what their image is in the minds of others in the corporation. The "new breed" of information manager will be assuming greater responsibility as the manager of corporate information resources in the 1980s. Let's review some of the ways the manager will do this through a strategy of *role identification*.

ROLE IDENTIFICATION

> **S-3 ROLE IDENTIFICATION**
>
> The migration from data processing to information management in the 1980s will create new roles for information managers. Those who successfully identify and manage these new roles will rise in the organization.

The strategy of creating an information manager rather than a data processing manager in the company's organizational structure is an important primary role for data processing managers to assume in the decade ahead. However, it is not the only role that is changing the DP manager's job. There are a number of roles that are possible to adopt to enhance the effectiveness of the information manager. The process of identifying these roles is, in itself, a useful strategy.

Let us consider the distributed processing world of the 1980s to put some perspective on the changing role for information managers. As distributed processing penetrates faster and deeper into the organization, the integration of diverse systems into a cohesive information infrastructure will become increasingly important.

We will not only see data processing resources distributed into user areas in the decade ahead, but along with that movement, we will also see continued expansion in the size and power of central data centers as well. The

Exhibit 3-1   Future-firm distributed networks.

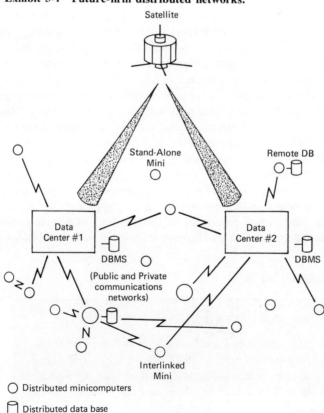

central data center will likely house the corporate data-base system and will handle the heavy transaction-based systems and perhaps some management control systems. Inexpensive broad-band communications will allow the ''central'' center, however, to be split into two or more physical locations, for security reasons, sharing the work-load and application interdependencies via very-high-speed computer-to-computer transmission. Distributed mini- and microcomputers will be located in all parts of the organization, not just in geographically dispersed units, but within departments in the same building. Some will stand alone, others interlinked, some with their own data bases, perhaps shared by others in the chain. More and more people will do their work with the aid of computers through intelligent terminals at their desk, accessing computers and data bases, both local and remote. This environment, as depicted in Exhibit 3-1, is an environment that links a variety of emerging technologies: host computers, distributed computers, data-base systems, and high-speed public and private satellite and terrestrial communications networks. This is a vastly different world than the one faced by the DP managers of the 1960s and 1970s, and that is why the management of such a plethora of information systems will demand new roles for information managers, roles that will enable information managers to design and manage complex computer and communications systems that are spread throughout the organization and even throughout the world.

One must think about one's own environment, of course, in choosing new roles appropriate to that environment, but there should be a shifting emphasis toward *business* management. This does not mean that technical competence will no longer be needed. Quite the contrary, the complex distributed-processing world depicted in Exhibit 3-1 will require an even greater grasp of emerging and merging technologies than was ever needed in the past. But to those skills must be added *business* skills that make the information manager a part of the senior management of the firm. What are these business roles? Here are some examples:

Planner.
Change agent.
Information manager.
Proactivist.
Businessman.
Politician.
Integrator.
Information controller.
Strategist.
Staff professional.
Manager.
Futurist.

Planner

The very nature of information management requires that information managers be planners. Long lead times for equipment deliveries, systems development, and hardware/software migration require advanced systems planning. Dovetailing systems planning with corporate long-range planning necessitates wide horizons. Even developing strategies to increase IM effectiveness means planning. In the 1980s, it will not be enough just to be a systems expert. If technology will be a prime factor affecting how corporations are managed in the 1980s, information managers will have to become the *catalysts* for planning in the organization, taking the initiative to do business information planning, to participate in corporate planning, and even to become part of the corporate planning team—a new and logical role for information managers in an age when information will play an increasingly important part in management decision making.

Change Agent

Systems people have always been agents of change. Their very work dictates that change will take place. The new continually replaces the old, and with it, new methods, concepts, technologies, and ideas for improvement are introduced. To many, change is upsetting because it introduces the unknown and disrupts the status quo. Therefore, change should be introduced with care, patience, and sensitivity. At the same time, change is necessary. In our fast-moving world, to stand still is to quickly fall behind. Information managers cannot simply sit back and react to requests for service. They must actively ''sell'' technology, and where it will do the most good for the firm, not just where the discord is most vocal. The change-agent role starts with business information planning (S-10), extends to technological forecasting (S-11) as input to corporate planning, involves the users in any systems changes to minimize the fear of the unknown, and works continuously to lead positive change in the organization. A major role of IM in the years ahead will be to be a change agent, an innovator, a planner, and an exponent of needed change, so as to ensure that the firm will get the best that technology can offer—to keep it ahead of competitors and running at peak efficiency.

Information Manager

The evolution from data processing to information management represents a merger of different fields that will change today's conventional organization charts. The information manager must take the initiative in leading the merger of the firm's information resources before someone else does it. He or she should serve as a consultant to operating divisions, operating under a matrix management arrangement for the IM function. Planning will be needed to move into this new role (see coalescence planner, S-5, to determine what activities should be part of the information function (e.g. word processing, administration, telecommunications), and to initiate information coalescence, either through reorganization or gradually, in pieces, as circumstances warrant. It is important that this new role be taken on, because someone in the future firm is going to run the information business; if it is not the DP manager, then it will be the senior executive to whom he reports.

Proactivist

It will not be enough simply to be responsive to user needs in the future. Information managers will have to be aggressive—in taking the initiative to guide the firm's use of technology, in seeking out opportunities to apply systems solutions to company problems, in seeing that information resources are properly managed. Information will become the heart of management in the information age; hence, its management cannot be left to chance. Nor can the application of technology be left to users to determine how, when, and if it is to be used. Information managers understand the technology; users understand their business needs. Only by working together will they achieve the best match up of technology to business needs. A proactive product-planning role will necessarily involve such strategies as business information planning (S-10) for the identification of user information needs and critical success factors (S-24) for the identification of executive information needs.

Business Manager

The previous discussion brings us to the business role of tomorrow's information manager. Information managers will need a solid understanding of both business and technology in the future if they are to be effective in integrating IM and the business, the decentralized pieces, technology and information needs. To do this, they will need to rid themselves of their technical image—not their technical expertise, only the aura of mysticism associated with the DP managers of the past. Management must be able to deal with them as with managers of every other aspect of the business. Only in that way will meaningful user participation occur, leading to successful systems projects. And only in that way will top management involvement be secured for the needed resource planning. Information technology is becoming increasingly important to managers in all aspects of business. The information manager who learns the business and understands its needs will be the one who is most successful in the years ahead. Being a successful businessman is what will bring the DP manager out of the back shop and into the executive suite in the 1980s.

Politician

As discussed under management by strategies (S-1), political strategies are
an important part of turning the power structures of organizations into a
positive supportive force for the spread of technology. Thus, among his
many other capabilities, the information manager must be a good politician
as well. A good politician can influence users and top management people
and lead them through the maze of technology to the acceptance of information and systems planning for the organization. This political side of information management requires such skills as the ability to recognize power bases;
the development of awareness, sensitivity, and communications skills; and
the interpersonal skills needed to "win friends and influence people in the
corporation."

Integrator

The integration stage of EDP growth described earlier will require information managers to take a broader corporate view of systems development in
order to envision how diverse systems should be brought together in ways
that will make sense of the corporation's information structure. The integrating of distributed systems, of office automation systems, of electronic information and service systems, and of management planning and control systems will require an integrator of the corporation's information resources.
The integrator role will merge computers, communications, and data bases
into effective delivery systems that will bring information resources to managers and staff throughout the organization, when and where needed.

Information Controller

The spread of sophisticated and expensive technical resources throughout
the company will require extra care in the management of these resources.
Operations can be distributed, even systems development can be distributed,
but management control must never be distributed because such distribution
would create decentralized chaos. The result could be more than just costly
and inefficient operations; it could be loss of control. Computers are fast all
right, but when they go awry, errors pile up just as fast. In the information
age, firms will have an information controller over distributed information
resources just as they now have financial controllers over accounting and
financial activities. This information controller will preside over information
management, exercising the three Cs of control—coordination, consistency,
and compatibility—to ensure efficiency and effectiveness in the use of the
information resources distributed throughout the firm.

Strategist

The information manager's role as strategist in the firm is amply demonstrated by the theme of this book. Management by strategies (S-1) is a new

and unique way of looking at information resource management. A management-by-objectives program can be effective in establishing objectives, but strategies are then needed to meet those objectives. Management by strategies (MBS) provides a methodology for increasing the effectiveness and the influence of the information management function in the organization. Any information manager who adopts MBS, either by using the strategies in this book or by developing strategies of his or her own, will be fulfilling the role of strategist.

Staff Professional

The information manager is generally recognized as a staff professional in the organization. As such, he or she is expected to provide technical guidance, technological forecasts, decision support systems, researched-based information, and computer-based systems of all kinds in support of company activities and management. If the information manager is to maintain respect and credibility as a staff professional, however, technical knowledge and education must be continuous. Allocating a percentage of one's time to trade association conferences, subscribing to research services, reading extensively, and exchanging information everyday are important to maintaining the role of staff professional in information management. Otherwise, an information manager will not only sacrifice the role to others but will become completely obsolete within five years.

Manager

In addition to being staff professionals, information managers are also just that: managers. They don't just manage technology. They manage people, equipment resources, systems projects, user relations, management interfaces, budgets and capital expenditures, *and* technology. Anyone who manages all of these things successfully (especially in a multi-million-dollar shop) is not just a technician; he or she is a *manager*—a manager with a technical specialty, but a general manager nevertheless. Consider, for example, how systems are woven throughout a business. There is almost no aspect of a company's business today that is not affected by systems, manual or computerized. Information managers, thus, are actively and continually involved in all aspects of the company's business, often with more knowledge of the intricacies of its operations than the business' unit managers themselves. To be sure, they are applying their specialty to the business, but their broad knowledge of and exposure to the business itself makes them generalists, not specialists. The role of information managers as general managers is often obscured by the technology which surrounds them. Therefore, the information manager must make every effort to demonstrate her or his management role, not only to avoid being stereotyped, but to avoid being overlooked when a promotion opportunity occurs for a top executive *general manager*.

Futurist

Under technological forecasting (S-11), we discuss the importance of the futurist role. Technical trend analysis is a vital input into corporate planning. The information manager must follow closely the trends that are occurring and their likely impact on the business. This requires constant research, exploration, and analysis—and a very long-range view; thus, the importance of the futurist role in business planning.*

ROLE STRATEGIES AT WORK

Our role identification strategy (S-3) suggests the importance of thinking of the information manager as a business manager as well as a staff professional. There are three role strategies which we would like to suggest as being vital to the changing role of information managers. As we present each one, we cite case examples of how they have been applied in actual situations.

PROACTIVE CHANGE AGENT

> **S-4 PROACTIVE CHANGE AGENT**
>
> **Discovers opportunities for improving the effectiveness of information utilization and "sells" those options where appropriate and beneficial to the company.**

Improved information management is built on a *mental set of proactive management.* A common complaint of information specialists is that they are unappreciated. Their companies have serious information problems, yet senior corporate, division, and functional management do not beat a path to the information manager's door.

A proactive change agent is quite different from the more traditional reactive approach followed by most systems organizations today. The difference is important. In a reactive role we say, "What can we do for you?" In a proactive role, we say "Here's what we can do for you." To be simply reactive is to abdicate to users the task of how best to put computers to work for the company. Why should this be a user responsibility? In their survey of

* Security Pacific Bank, Los Angeles, recently actually created the position of *futurist* as part of their operational planning department—it was the first bank to do so to our knowledge.

a group of information managers of large corporations, McLean and Soden reported the following:

> Participants saw two quite different roles for themselves—the "reactive" service role and the "proactive" change-agent role. The reactive participants took a largely defensive posture, justifying their lack of regard for the strategy of the overall enterprise by stressing the importance of being responsive to users' immediate requirements. Their major problem ironically was a lack of credibility and confidence on the part of their respective user communities. On the other hand, the proactive group sought ways of actively interacting with the strategic planning effort of the host organization. Almost without exception, the more advanced planners were proactive and the novice planners were reactive.[2]

A proactive change agent, for example, is one who not only causes change, but does so in an active and innovative way, seeking out ways and places to apply information technology to the solution of business problems and seeking to allocate resources where they will do the most good for the company.

This is a most important role that all too few information managers take on. Most are content to be reactive, to wait for project requests and to respond to them as they come, perhaps leaving someone else to worry about priorities. In any event, they seldom go out seeking new automation applications on the basis that they are already overloaded with work and that such a proactive posture would only result in bigger backlogs of work that can't be handled. Nonsense! It is not a matter of trying to do everything, it's a matter of doing the *right things*. Without a proactive posture, the information manager does only what is asked, not necessarily what is truly *best* for the company. Each functional area of the company is involved with its own work; none can provide the corporate overview or the trade-off considerations needed to balance conflicting demands for resources. This is the role of the corporate steering committee, of course, but the information manager must also play a role in assessing the alternate uses of scarce resources that will best serve the company.

Proactive information managers are in the minority today. However, in our opinion, the increasingly complex business climate ahead and the increased need for technology and improved information systems and services will create an increasing demand for such managers in the decade ahead. The fast-track information managers will be imaginative and aggressive in applying technology to the solution of business problems in the future and in applying systems resources where they will do the most good for the company. They will be the managers who will be finding their way into the executive ranks of the company. They will be involved in corporate planning, policy formulation, and executive decision-making because they will be recognized as business managers who can contribute to growth and profits, not just as people who provide a necessary staff support function which is perceived to be out of the mainstream of the business. Consider these examples taken from The First National Bank of Boston.

Case 1   Automated Financial Analysis   New management trainees in the credit area of the bank were routinely assigned for some period of time to the "spreading" of corporate financial statements, that is, the listing of balance sheet items and operating statements and the calculation of traditional financial ratios. Such work was an important, but time-consuming, part of the training. Unfortunately, the time spent in mechanical calculations was taken away from the more important task of *analyzing* financial statements. Recognizing that this could be a logical computer-assisted application which could help managers to make better credit decisions, to lower losses, and to monitor credit expenses, the information systems manager approached the credit department management with a proposal to automate the financial analysis work that was being done manually. The credit management immediately accepted the suggestion, stating that they, in fact, had already done some work on their own in this area, attempting to develop some financial analysis aids on a time-sharing system. The information systems division assigned to the project a systems analyst who had had some background in corporate finance, and ultimately the system was brought up on the bank's mainframe computers. It consisted of capturing five years of financial data for corporate customers in various industries, calculating key financial ratios, and performing cash flow projections based on this data. At this point, the automated-financial-analysis system was a historical type of system. Not stopping there, the information systems manager went back to the credit manager and suggested that the mainframe COBOL programs be converted to a large scale minicomputer located in the credit department, so that a pro forma forecasting capability could be added to the system for the projection of financial ratios and cash flow five years *into the future,* based on changing assumptions (economic conditions affecting sales, changing interest rates on debt, etc.). The suggestion was accepted, and the system is now in successful operation and has gone a long way toward bringing a true decision-support system to the lending side of the bank, an area which, outside of routine record-keeping, had previously had little to do with automation. It is important to note that this system resulted from a *proactive* information manager's initiative, bringing closer together computer technology and the lending function, which generally contributes the highest profits of any area of a commercial bank. Its enthusiastic acceptance by the users is best illustrated by this statement by one of the lending officers:

> . . . the ultimate benefits to the user can be significant to the bank's bottom line. The end result of this system, properly used, is to give the commercial lending officer a dynamic and more accurate tool with which to analyze a

credit. Such analysis should result in a more appropriate structuring and pricing of a loan, a more efficient monitoring of a company's performance and ability to repay borrowed funds, an earlier recognition of bad credits, and, ultimately, a reduction in that all-important loan loss account.[3]

Case 2   Total Customer Relationship   The international division of the bank was experiencing a growing problem of how to control the flow of vital management information, both customer and financial. The data processing manager approached international management with the suggestion that a task force be appointed consisting of representatives from the IM division, the international division, and the domestic banking division. Their task was to address the feasibility of developing a worldwide total customer relationship (TCR) system, which would consolidate information from both the international and the domestic offices. Their objectives were described as follows:

> The objective of TCR was to provide management with easily accessible, comprehensive information on worldwide dealings with large, multi-national corporate customers, as well as to be able to examine cross sections of business by countries, industries, banking offices, etc. The prospect of being able to get, at the touch of a button, the total deposit and loan arrangements in effect for, say General Motors, and any of its subsidiaries doing business with the bank around the world, was exciting. The value to marketing officers having such a consolidated picture was immediately perceived as an invaluable aid to customer servicing.[4]

The task force submitted a proposal document for TCR implementation which was approved late in 1976. TCR became operational early in 1978. Today, on-line and printed reports on customer borrowing arrangements, customer profitability, total customer relationships, and cross-industry data are conveniently available to bank officers via terminals located in appropriate places in the organization. The idea for the system was reasonably simple. Through the leadership of an appointed task force, a master file of significant corporate customers would be created. The data base would consist of summarized information on deposits and loans, fees, interest rates, and other banking business, stored by month for one year. Data would be gathered from in-place domestic and international systems once a month. Report programs would produce a variety of regularly scheduled and "on-request" reports, for both domestic and overseas managers and calling officers. Terminals would allow quick and easy access to consolidated customer data for managers at the head office in Boston and regional offices. Thus, once again, through the exercise of a *proactive change-agent* role, the bank now has for the first time ever, through TCR, the nucleus for a truly worldwide management information system.

Coalescence Planner

> **S-5   COALESCENCE PLANNER**
>
> The information manager identifies, coordinates, and coalesces information resources throughout the corporation, managing information as an integrated corporate resource.

With the right responsibilities in the organization, information managers can begin to plan for the coalescence of information resources. In many ways, this is a senior-management-level issue. *In well-managed companies in the 1980s, senior corporate executives will recognize that the essence of management is, in fact, the effective utilization of corporate information.* These senior managers in well-managed companies will set the standards for the development and utilization of these important corporate information resources.

Unfortunately, we believe that the importance of managing information as a resource will probably be slow to be recognized and will, in fact, be practiced by only a small number of firms in the immediate years ahead. Therefore, there is an opportunity for information managers to lead this movement toward the more effective utilization of information in the firm. One way to begin this process is through the adoption of a coalescence planning strategy.

Coalescence planning starts with getting the right identification—an identification which is broader in scope and function than the traditional data processing manager. The information manager must be viewed not as a technician who runs computers, but as a business manager who provides information needed to run the business, as the information architect of the organization, and, ultimately, as the chief information officer. Coalescence planning involves bringing together the diverse information resources of the firm so that they can be used when and if needed by all levels of management and staff. This requires identifying these resources, building the technical delivery systems that will transport them where needed, and putting together organization structures designed to permit better information flow in the organization. Coalescence planning also involves determining what functions in the organization are properly a part of the information-handling business and then setting about coalescing these functions into a single total information resource. What are these information functions? They might include the coalescence of such functions as:

Data and word processing.
Telecommunications.
Manual systems and procedures.

Management science.

The issuance of corporate policy and other corporate instructions.

Administrative services.

Paperwork management (records, forms, reports).

Printing.

Micrographics.

Libraries.

Office automation.

Mail services.

Distributed data processing.

The list can be as limited or extended as the information manager's imagination. These are primarily the tasks that provide or deal with information. To this, we must add all of the people in the organization who deal with creating, moving, manipulating, extracting, or changing the information (the maintenance of the information base) as well as those who use the information to serve customers, control activities, manage their own affairs, and make decisions (the users of the information base). Thus the information resource in most companies is vast, explosive, and critical to the very existence of the firm. Coalescence of these resources into more useful, accessible information is, then, an important activity of the information manager.

Please note that we are not necessarily suggesting that all of these functions should be merged under the management of the IM function. In some cases, such a reorganizational alignment might make sense and lead to more efficient information management. In other cases, for a variety of organizational, management, or political reasons, this realignment might not be feasible. No matter. The important thing is to embark on a formal program of identifying corporate information resources and then bringing them together through systems integration efforts, data base management, communications planning, or any other ways that lead to a better use of corporate information by those who need it, when they need it, and in whatever form they need it.

Paul Strassmann, head of information and administrative services at Xerox Corp., said:

The investment in information systems for increased profitability relates to the systematization of all new investments needed to improve the productivity of people engaged in information processing. To understand this investment process requires insights that stretch beyond computer technology. Telecommunications, word processing, administrative systems, decisions systems are some of the classifications. . . . As advanced stages of growth are attained, the EDP executive will be left to grapple with technology. His boss—the Information Systems executive—will manage the new investment opportunities leading to dramatic improvements in overall organizational profits and performance.[5]

C. W. Getz, as Commissioner of Automated Data and Telecommunications Services (Region 9), General Services Administration, said:

> The coalescence or merging of different functional fields is progressing at McLuhan's electric speeds. It is straining the confining lines of conventional organization charts. . . . From these technological ashes of confusion shall arise a new Phoenix of organization—the data resources management organization. The manager of this new area will be a generalist with a solid understanding of technology but a better understanding of business conditions and needs . . . all of these predictions will be accomplished within the next decade. Coalescence is the inevitable fate of data processing. . . . The message is quite clear; either the MIS manager will take the initiative to lead this merger of the firm's data resources activities and make some sense of their management, or a manager outside of the MIS organization will do it for him.[6]

A plan is needed to accomplish this coalescence—it will not happen by itself; it must be carefully managed. The following may serve as a guide:

1 Start with a determination of what the various information resources are in the organization.
2 As part of the "integration" stage of IM growth, begin to plan the logical integration of diverse functions which process information into cohesive systems.
3 Establish corporate policies for information management, corporate data base standards, etc.
4 Identify the organizational rearrangements necessary to manage information resources effectively.
5 Implement these changes slowly, one logical step at a time, but all as part of an overall coalescence planning strategy.

Coalescence planning may well be one of the most important roles of information managers in the 1980s, because it could form the foundation for the transition from DP manager to information manager. The following case studies offer two examples of coalescence planning.

Case 3 Telecommunications Merger   Implementation of The First National Bank of Boston's first on-line real-time system created the need for a data communications specialist in the telecommunications department. As more and more communications-based systems were added over the years, the data processing department was also required to build up its own expertise in this area to provide the needed planning and service capability to on-line users. The problems that arose with these two departments reporting to

different corporate division heads increased proportionately with the growth
in on-line systems. Data processing felt that it could not be held responsible
for on-line services when it controlled the computer at one end and the
terminals at the other, but not the lines in between. Telecommunications felt
that it could not adequately perform its function when much of the network
planning and many of the diagnostic capabilities were assumed by data processing. At first, the DP manager attempted to resolve the problem by asking
that the responsibility for data communications be transferred from the telecommunications department to the DP department. The telecommunications
manager's response was that often the same lines are used for both voice and
data; therefore, responsibility for the two could not logically be separated. It
soon became evident that the computer and communications technologies
had, in fact, come together and should be treated, like Siamese twins, as a
single technology (see computications strategy, S-50). Thus, the groundwork
for the ultimate coalescence of telecommunications and data processing was
laid with senior management, so that when it became organizationally practical to do so, the telecommunications function was merged into the information systems division. The coalescence of planning for computer and communications systems now produces more effective management, improved
integration, and better service to users.

Case 4 Office Automation Coalescence can also be accomplished without
organizational change, as this case illustrates. With the first stirrings of the
office-of-the-future movement, the bank's IM division took a proactive step
to initiate a corporate project to investigate the potential impact of office automation on the bank. The results of that early study indicated that considerable potential existed for office automation, especially in a service industry
such as banking. In the conduct of the study, the surveyors, noting that
administrative services was a completely decentralized function, suggested
that an administrative services department might be formed to which all
secretaries and administrative help might report. This attempt at organizational coalescence was met with great resistance, so great that it was aban-
doned. The second attempt was much more subtle. It was determined that
coalescence of the offices could—and probably should—be effected *without*
organizational change. The IM division established an internal office systems
group which was given the responsibility of implementing *distributed* word
processing in departments that expressed interest in using these new tools.
IM would therefore select the equipment, install the system, train the user
personnel, and provide technical support. Users would operate the equipment as tools added to their present environment—no organizational changes
would be made. This time, the concept was met with enthusiasm, and a
number of departments elected to install the equipment. By word of mouth,
the success of office automation spread, and it was off to a fine start.

Why did the first attempt at coalescence fail and the second succeed?
One might say that the first approach was organizationally disruptive. It was

threatening, and it invaded sensitive organizational arrangements that permeated the corporation, not just an isolated department. To introduce technology *and* drastic organizational change, especially without strong top management support, is not the way to "win friends and influence people." The second approach involved less organizational disturbance, was implemented first where interest was strongest, and let success breed itself.

Coalescence in this case of office automation was accomplished through central planning and control, but with no organizational realignment and a minimal impact on people—considerations which are too often glossed over, but which can sabotage a program before it gets off the ground.

Integrator

> **S-6   INTEGRATOR**
>
> **The new breed of information managers will wear business suits, not technical cloaks, as they learn the business and successfully integrate business and information resources.**

The third role for the information manager in the 1980s will be that of integrator. While the coalescence planner role concentrates on organizing the information resource functions of the organization, the integrator role focuses on the integration of the people side of information management. Information technology and the needs of business users must be brought together by effective personnel management. This is mandatory for the successful integration of the many specialized divisions and functions that exist in many corporate organization structures. The job of information managers will be to finally close the communications gap with top management. To do this, they will have to become both business-oriented and technically-oriented. They must learn the business—understanding its problems and its needs—and then apply their tool in trade, technology, to the solution of business problems, not just technical problems. Robert E. Umbaugh, vice-president and head of data processing (and five other divisions) of Southern California Edison, advises the DP manager to become a business manager first, an entrepreneur second, and third, if at all, a technician:

> I think that if you were to analyze the successful data processing shops, you'd find that the successful ones have good working relations with the top management, not because top management understands computers, but because the data-processing manager understands business.[7]

The business-oriented information managers of the future who successfully cross over this technical bridge and integrate DP technology with business will find themselves, like Mr. Umbaugh, promoted to top executive roles in their companies.

The integrator role also carries with it the responsibility of providing the corporate overview. That is, whereas specified areas of the company can formulate plans for systems and services to satisfy their own needs, only a corporate staff function like IM can provide the overall viewpoint of the corporation in terms of the technological impact and/or systems integration benefits of separate, but related, systems.

An effective integrator strategy will require the shedding of technical cloaks. It is significant to note that many information managers have, in the past, been passed up for top executive jobs because they were perceived narrowly as technical specialists, not as general managers. In fact, in many cases, information managers are being replaced by managers from the business side of companies rather than by technically trained managers.

What this means is that top management wants business managers, not technicians, heading up the information function, in the same way that business managers run all other functional areas of the business. They want people who understand the business, who can be effective in solving business problems, and to whom they can relate in a straightforward business manner.

Top management wants to deal with someone who can speak business English. Unfortunately, the information manager's biggest roadblock can often be his very expertise, which can become a dead end. Technical excellence does not a manager make; it only brings one to the management door.

There are both image and self-image problems; therefore, information managers must work all the harder at being general managers, at participating in the decision making on company policies and corporate long-range planning. In the 1980s, those who succeed will be much more likely to be reporting directly to the office of the chief executive as members of top management. As Mr. Umbaugh suggested, the successful information manager of tomorrow will develop good working relations with top management not because top management will understand computers, but because the information manager will understand their business.

In Part 2 we discuss a variety of strategies for dealing with the vital integration of the IM function with the various management groups within an organization. Because of the extensive treatment of the subject given, we will leave this aspect of the integrator role for the present.

Another task of the integrator role is to provide the needed technical delivery systems to move information around the firm and make it accessible to the appropriate people. This involves integration of computers, communications, and data bases, when appropriate and needed. The information manager must always be alert to overall corporate needs and promote this type of integration wherever and whenever it is deemed advisable.

Here are two examples involving the integration of delivery systems: the first involves communications networks; the second pulls together diverse data bases into a management information system.

Case 5   Electronic Banking   Three different areas of The First National Bank of Boston offered related but separate on-line services. The first served a network of point-of-sale terminals located in supermarket chains. The second served the bank's branch office network of manned teller terminals and unmanned (automated) teller machines. The third network served a large number of correspondent banks for which data processing services were being performed, which also included on-line teller support. From a corporate point of view, the systems division saw these as overlapping systems resulting in excessive communications and software costs. For example, duplicate telephone lines covered the same geographical areas; utilization of System A was heavily a daytime operation with little traffic at night, while System B was just the opposite; a customer cashing a check, whether in a bank branch, a supermarket or a correspondent bank, had to access the same balance file in order for the tracking of funds to be current. The IM division determined that a much more efficient system could result from integration of these separate networks into one common network, accessing a common data base.

Different software could support each system to keep services unique and distinctive, but the systems integration of common networks would result in lower costs, greater efficiency, and better customer service. To "sell" this corporate view, the information manager arranged a series of technical presentations for interested parties and senior management describing the proposed integrated systems approach and delineating the expected benefits. The individual user's marketing views were thus expanded to include a technical view, so that the merits of the proposal were unanimously accepted by all—an example of the integrator role in successfully applying the corporate view to the building of integrated systems solutions. (This is also an example of a proactive management style, S-4).

Case 6   Lending MIS   The First National Bank of Boston's 10-year-old commercial loan accounting system was about to be rewritten so that it could be brought into a generation-later style of business. The objective was that the new system should better serve senior lending management than had the old system. The old system was developed as an underlying record-keeping system, and as such, it was more oriented toward operational needs than management needs. Management reports were provided as a by-product of the accounting system. The IM division felt that this kind of bottom-up systems development would not be adequate to address senior management's information needs this time around. A top-down approach would be needed instead. This approach would involve learning the lending business from the viewpoint of *senior* lending management rather than from lower-level credit personnel. In addition, information management knew that higher-level information needs would not be entirely satisfied by the commercial loan system alone but would require tapping other credit-related data bases as well. In other words, only *integration* of the various credit sources would produce the information needed to satisfy the various senior lending management perspectives.

Spurred by the head of the loan review division, a senior (high-level lending management) user committee was formed for the purpose of reviewing the plans for the new commercial loan system. At the outset, information management encouraged the committee to think in terms of a broader data base; that is, to think beyond the commercial loan system and to view all credit-related systems as if they were a single data-base system. (This single system was, in fact, the ultimate aim, and although it would take a number of years to become reality, the independent application files could be regarded as one for information purposes; the IM function would bridge the gap by extracting data from various sources through report generators to produce the desired management information and reports in a way that would be transparent to the users.) A list of all credit-related systems was prepared, and the initial meetings of the committee were concerned with understanding the data base concept and reviewing the major underlying credit information sources.

Next, it was decided to use the critical success factors (CSF) (S-24) method as a top-down approach to learning senior lending management's needs. Dr. John Rockart of MIT's Center for Information Systems Research, developer of the CSF concept, was brought in to assist in this effort. Interviews were conducted with a number of members of senior lending management, including the president of the bank. In this process, a number of critical success factors were elicited, which, highly summarized, came down to three major factors:

1 *Quality staff.* The acquisition and development of lending officers was the key to successful lending management. Measures of the quality of the staff might include business development efforts, loan losses, and profitability of business generated.
2 *Quality loans.* An effective loan-approval process and loan-monitoring system was paramount to quality loan assurance. Possible measures were loan approval, review procedures (rating system), and exposure data, that is, an early warning system based on key indicators.
3 *Effective business development.* A general marketing plan could be coupled with specific account strategies to develop business potential (measures of service [marketing] data, account profitability data, and the like).

The lending management information system (LMIS) envisioned from this exercise is illustrated in Exhibit 3-2. In order to address the specific measurements and reports needed to satisfy these CSFs, and to make recommendations to the senior users' committee, two sub-task-forces were formed: the first consisted of key systems people familiar with the underlying credit-related systems; the second was composed of one representative from

Exhibit 3-2   Future-firm lending management information system: total corporate integration achieved.

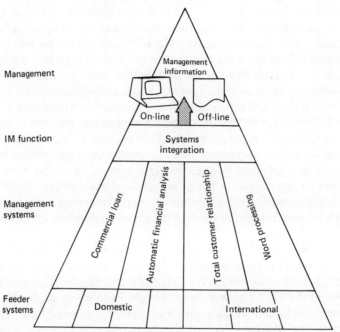

each lending division. The combination of these two groups resulted in bridging the knowledge gap between systems technology and lending management for purposes of addressing both information needs and implementation. The recommendations of this combined group were presented to and approved by the senior users' committee. Thus, through a strategy of learning the business from the top down, of integrating systems and business planning, and of integrating diverse credit-related systems into a single data base, the basis for subsequent LMIS planning was formed, which now provides senior lending management with total credit information with which to manage a multi-billion-dollar global loan portfolio.

THE NEW BREED

The new breed of information managers will, among other things:

Learn the business.   The very nature of their work keeps information managers in broad contact with all facets of the business. There is almost no area of business today not affected by the computer in some way. Thus, information managers have more opportunity to gain a wider knowledge of the totality of the business than most executives in specialized functions. They need to take advantage of that edge.

Get involved in corporate planning.   The very nature of their business (long development time and long equipment lead times) forces information managers to do long-range planning. As a result, they are probably more experienced at it than most executives. Why not use that experience to become more active in the activities of the firm? The information manager should get involved (or even lead) corporate long-range planning—it's an excellent way to demonstrate knowledge of the business and general management capabilities to senior management.

Demonstrate management ability.   The successful management of a complex computer operation, budgeting, a body of knowledge workers, and major project development over a period of time will demonstrate management capability, not just technical ability.

Redefine their roles.   Information managers should extend their function by going beyond DP into telecommunications, office automation, corporate records management, reproduction services, management services, corporate planning, and corporate development, as coalescence planners (see S-5). Their chances of rising in the organizational hierarchy are better if they are known as information managers, or corporate planning officers, or corporate development officers, or other such titles, than if they are known merely as DP managers.

Communicate with top management.   Information managers should try to get more of top management's time in setting priorities for systems throughout the organization and to involve them in IM planning and major decisions. Two strategies for doing this are CEO briefings (S-27) and the information resources management committee (S-29). Effectiveness means making sure that management is involved in IM and vice versa, and that IM is successfully integrated with the company. Information managers should penetrate user areas with systems personnel (see Trojan horses, S-9). They should also make information management and general management styles compatible by developing a strategic planning approach which fits the company (see management by strategies, S-1).

Develop performance evaluation measures.   Developing meaningful performance measures for the IM function is not just desirable, it is imperative. Budget performance and user feedback are the management measures of the IM function today. DP expense as a percentage of sales or total expense is usually a weak measure that does not offer meaningful ratios. Competitive bidding against outside sources can sometimes be used to test IM efficiency, but this is often impractical. Unfortunately, no reliable industry standards exist, so other ways must be found to compare automation benefits and costs so that IM is seen not as a big cost operation but as a contributor to profits; not as a clerical cost-control mechanism, but as a new income-producing function and as a management control and decision-making tool. In our performance reporting (S-30) strategy in Chapter 6, we present a variety of performance measures used by leading companies as a guide to stimulate the reader's thinking on this key point.

The new breed of information manager characterized by the various new roles we have been discussing is far different from the DP manager of the past. More and more top managers are seeking an individual to fill their company's top EDP slot who will be a true participant in their decision-making process. This concept of participation in management is the key to the distinction between the old and the new breed, which Halbrecht defined as follows:

> The "new breed" understands and has shown that he knows how to manage management information systems efficiently, but, more importantly, how to manage them effectively.
>
> He understands he is not managing technology as much as he is managing change, change of the decision-making process as well as change of the way in which a company is run. He should be a participant in top management decisions from the outset, responsible for identifying the systems required as well as the costs of implementing these systems and their implications for the entire organization. . . .
>
> Accordingly, he must have the perception of a general manager, be ready not only to "sell" EDP, but also to develop and sell the logic and discipline of how one does business in a particular technological environment. He must be able to develop in other top executives an appreciation of the value of the systems function and a perception of the requirements for implementation.[9]

CHIEF INFORMATION OFFICER

> **S-7 CHIEF INFORMATION OFFICER**
>
> **Senior executive responsible for establishing corporate information policy, standards, and management control over all corporate information resources.**

The ultimate goal of the new breed of information resource manager in the 1980s should be to become recognized by top management as the chief information officer (CIO) of the firm. This is the culmination of all of the new roles for information managers discussed thus far. The CIO of the firm will be responsible for establishing corporate information policies, standards, and procedures for information resource management in the corporation and will identify, coalesce, and manage information as a resource. Because information is a necessary and important ingredient in corporate and business planning, decision support systems, and control activities, the CIO will necessarily be involved in these activities with senior managers throughout the firm.

The CIO role does not yet exist except in the minds of imaginative leaders today. It remains to be created by information managers committed to harvesting the management of information as a resource in the years ahead.

The CIO concept should not be very hard to sell. Top management certainly understands the role of the chief executive officer (CEO) and the chief financial officer (CFO). Why not a chief information officer? What needs to be sold is not the CIO role but an understanding and acceptance of the fact that information is a valuable corporate resource that must be managed as a total entity, and that the role of the manager of information resources must be that of chief information officer in order to exert a broad corporate perspective and a leadership role in bringing together and managing information as a corporate resource. The job of the information manager is to educate senior management as to what can be done to make more effective use of information resources through the development of technological delivery systems to bring needed information quickly to those who need it, when they need it, and in the form they need it. The CIO in the corporate organization structure should be able to provide centralized management and control over information processing and utilization, even though it may be distributed geographically and functionally throughout the organization.

The chief information officer will *share power* with the managers responsible for the control of information in the divisions and functions (see Davis and Lawrence[10] for a description of shared resources, shared power, two-boss managers, and matrix processes, and see our S-65, matrix management strategy).

The speed of change in the technology of information processing and utilization has made it very difficult for an adequate level of competence to be maintained in the many divisions and functions into which most large companies are subdivided. Thus, the chief information officer has as a primary function the responsibility of providing consulting services to the operating divisions and functions. The corporate finance/accounting function and the corporate certified public accountants audit the *accuracy* of financial records. Similarly, the chief information officer should be responsible for *audits of the effectiveness and efficiency* of information processing and utilization. Audits focused only on accuracy are an inadequate measure of information management.

The CIO is a concept whose time has come. Leading-edge information managers will gradually evolve into that role during the 1980s as they integrate technology more effectively with user and senior management business and information needs.

Business needs information managers who can play a larger role in helping managers plan, can participate in decision making, and can help lead the corporation to continued growth. Today's information managers have the resources and the opportunity to broaden their role in the company, to produce more and better management systems, and to participate in corporate strategic planning, in alternative investment decisions, in new product research, in marketing analysis, perhaps even in acquisition analysis (modeling). They are challenged to build a corporate communications network and a compatible data-base architecture that will integrate the entire organization. Performance is the key! There is still a large gap between what is produced and what is expected of information managers.

As we move into the information age of the 1980s, the new breed of information managers will become integrated into the businesses they serve by working more closely with users and senior management in solving their problems and serving their needs, will marshall their information resources for the solution of business problems and in support of management, and will move up the corporate ladder as their firms' chief information officers.

The role strategies suggested in this chapter are aimed at helping information managers to focus on the quiet revolution that is occurring as data processing evolves into information management. The trend from the computer age to the information age is now a reality in the best-managed companies. This focus, in turn, leads to a consideration of how this change will affect the information manager's roles in the organization. We have suggested a number of these roles; the reader will find others on thoughtful reflection. The important thing is to recognize that times are changing and that the information manager must change with them. The ability to overcome the counterproductive technical image held by user management and top management is the key to success in the increasingly decentralized information era ahead.

In Part 2, we consider strategies aimed at increasing the effectiveness of the information management function in the 1980s.

NOTES

1 Richard L. Nolan, "Business Needs a New Breed of EDP Manager," *Harvard Business Review,* March–April 1976, pp. 123–133.

2 Ephraim McLean and John Soden, *Strategic Planning for MIS,* New York: Wiley, 1977, p. 65.

3 David Coit, "Automated Financial Analysis: A New Tool for Commercial Lending," *Journal of Commercial Lending,* March 1977, p. 53.

4 William R. Synnott, "Total Customer Relationship," *MIS Quarterly,* September 1978, p. 16.

5 Paul Strassmann, personal communication.

6 C. W. Getz, "Coalescence: The Inevitable Fate of Data Processing," *MIS Quarterly,* June 1977, p. 28.

7 Robert Umbaugh as quoted by Gene Bylinsky, "EDP Managers Put on Business Suits," *Fortune,* November 6, 1978, p. 69.

8 John F. Rockart, "Chief Executives Define Their Own Data Needs," *Harvard Business Review,* March–April 1979, pp. 81–93.

9 Herbert L. Halbrecht as quoted by Richard L. Nolan, "Business Needs a New Breed of EDP Manager," *Harvard Business Review,* March–April, 1976, p. 133.

10 Stanley M. Davis and Paul R. Lawrence, *Matrix,* Reading, Mass.: Addison-Wesley, 1978, pp. 69–101.

Management Integration

Increasing the Influence of the
IM Function

Outstanding EDP professionals . . . devote effort to keeping up-to-date, react
quickly to new technology . . . and build a good track record within their organization. The dilemma for such individuals is that they can easily reach a well-paid dead
end.

Keen and Scott Morton[1]

OPPORTUNITY FOR INFORMATION MANAGERS

In this chapter, we recommend several strategies for increasing the influence
of the IM function. We see an opportunity in the 1980s for information
managers to reverse a trend in which influence over information activities is
migrating toward the users of information resources.

During the early years of the computer age, the corporate EDP function
dominated data processing because of the high cost of computers and the
great technical difficulty of computer operations.

The early ADP, DP, or EDP functions were created primarily to process
accounting transactions. Most of today's *management* applications have
been implemented in the best-managed companies only in the last decade.
For example, computer-assisted strategic planning models, decision support
systems, marketing models, and sales force information systems are management capabilities of relatively recent origin in even the best-managed
companies.

Senior corporate executives and managers in line divisions in most companies have often experienced difficulties in working with their corporate DP
functions in the implementation of management systems. The basic skills in
the DP function in the past tended to be used in transaction-processing
systems. In many firms, the disparity between the business needs of management and the technical focus and skills of DP professionals has gradually
decreased the influence of DP managers in the management of corporate

information. Users in line divisions and functions are more and more often electing to buy their own computers or to contract directly with outside time-share vendors rather than attempt to work with what appear to be unresponsive corporate DP functions.

WHY IM INFLUENCE ENHANCEMENT?

We suggest that it is important to reverse the trend of declining influence in order to reach one of IM's primary goals in the organization; to increase its effectiveness and ability to properly support the business activities of the company. Without a position of some power and influence in the organization, the IM organization will not be able to accomplish this goal. We see an opportunity to reverse this trend of declining influence in the 1980s through a greater *sharing of power and management* over information resources between the IM function and user management as illustrated in Exhibit 4-1.

Note in Exhibit 4-1 that we do not see information managers regaining the same level of control over information-processing activities that was once held by DP managers in the early days of the computer age. Instead, we see a *sharing of influence* between information managers and managers in the user divisions and functions. The importance of shared control can be seen by some of the problems that can arise when data processing is simply distributed into user areas that do not have adequate technical expertise on their staff to manage it:

1 Serious technical errors can result from inadequate knowledge of data processing.
2 Redundancy of information resources is likely.
3 Failure to utilize information technologies as a source of the integration of company organizational units.
4 Failure to achieve an integration of information technology.

INTEGRATION OF INFORMATION RESOURCES

Given the costs of the declining influence of the traditional DP function, it is useful to develop a strategy for the repositioning of information management in the organization. Nolan's EDP growth-stages concept is a good beginning for the implementation of strategies for increasing the influence of information management.

Nolan characterized the fourth stage of growth as an integration stage. *Integration* means many things. It means technological integration of computers, communications, and data bases; it means systems integration of diverse but interdependent applications; and it means people integration—

Exhibit 4-1   The relative influence of traditional data processing versus 1980s information management.

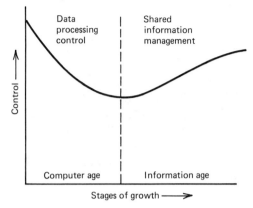

bringing together information management, user management, and top management in the shared control and management of information resources. *The successful integration of these three management groups is the answer to increasing the influence of the IM function in the 1980s.* Information management goals and strategies must be carefully structured to match user needs and corporate (top management) objectives if integration is to be realized.

Part 2 of this book deals with the all-important *organizational behavior* side of information management; that is, the successful integration of information management with the user management and the top management of the firm. This integration is important not just to increase the influence of IM in the company, but to ensure that these valuable resources will be utilized optimally to promote continued growth, competitiveness, and profitability in the increasingly complex business environment in which all companies find themselves. In such an environment, companies will need all the help they can get. The IM side of the house is in a unique position, through its productivity tools, its management support tools, and its accelerating technological progress, to provide a lot of this help—if it is managed appropriately.

Each company's uniqueness, of course, requires customized strategies aimed at integrating the IM, user, and senior management groups. Nevertheless, there are some general strategies that can be followed by every IM organization bent on increasing its influence and effectiveness in the organization. These strategies include the following:

Adopting new roles.
Developing IM policy.
Penetrating the organization.
Planning proactively.

Extending the IM function.

Keeping users happy.

Focusing on top management.

ADOPTING NEW ROLES

Chapter 3 discussed a variety of new roles beginning with the change from a technically oriented data processing manager to a business-oriented information manager. The importance of adopting such specific roles as proactive change agent (S-4), coalescence planner (S-5), and integrator (S-6) were also treated in some detail, and the suggestion was made that the most important role objective, that of the *chief information officer* (S-7), should be the ultimate aim of 1980s information managers.

DEVELOPING AN IM POLICY

If knowledge is power, then *information is power,* because knowledge is information. Companies can't run without it; managers can't manage without it. Yet, organizations are only just beginning to recognize the value of their corporate information resources. The information manager is the logical person to stimulate that awareness and to educate management on what that resource truly is and how to use it to maximum advantage. The information manager is also the one with the technological tools (computers, communications, data base systems) needed to provide the delivery systems for corporate information. In fact, the information manager will probably not even have any competition for this role, since the management of information resources has not been given serious attention by senior executives in most companies. Information is in no single domain. It exists throughout the firm, and the managers in each area use it as needed to run their aspect of the business, with little thought as to the corporate value of consolidated information. This situation represents a perfect opportunity for information managers to step forward and take the lead to establish corporate policy (see corporate policy, S-66), for the identification, coordination, consolidation, control, and utilization of information resources. The information manager must educate management as to the value of managing information as a resource and establish the IM function as the logical *manager* of information resources. He or she must also get top management to recognize, understand, and support this activity early and build from there.

Corporate IM policy should include the development of standards, procedures, protocols, and systems that tie diverse information resources together. A logical place for the information manager to start is with the development of standards for distributed processing resources. Distributed resources need coordination and control to ensure compatibility, consistency, efficiency, and effectiveness. This will enable information to be more easily transmitted and consolidated. The issuance of distributed processing standards logically belongs to the company's chief data processing officer (the future chief information officer).

Distributed Processing Standards

> **S-8 DISTRIBUTED DATA PROCESSING STANDARDS**
>
> **Corporate standards for the management of information resources wherever located in the corporation.**

A major New York corporation had a policy which allowed individual department heads to authorize expenditures up to $500,000. Because of the backlog of work in the central data processing group, the department heads were finding it hard to get small systems approved and implemented, so they began to turn to minicomputers. These minicomputer systems were often cheaper to develop than equivalent systems designed to run on their mainframe computers and could be implemented more quickly. Since it was not necessary to go through any management committees for the approval of minicomputer systems under $500,000, these systems proliferated. The problem, however, was that all of this activity was "growing like Topsy," with no central management control to assure the compatibility of the systems and the effective use of the distributed resources. By the time the company woke up to the need for some central management control over its growing minicomputer complex, it discovered that it had already installed 40 head office computers dedicated to single applications, 61 computers in its international offices, and 16 other special-purpose computers, a total of 117 minicomputers from some two dozen vendors, using a multitude of software languages and operating systems under maintenance contract, and none of them planned to be compatible under a corporate master plan.

What this case illustrates is that distributed processing is a new world that must be *managed* and not simply allowed to grow into distributed ignorance. Information resources can be distributed effectively only if they are planned and controlled through the issuance of corporate policies, standards, and procedures governing the use of such resources. One way to begin is to gain top management agreement to place the responsibility for the issuance of such distributed processing standards in the hands of the IM function in the organization. Given this responsibility, the information managers can issue a corporate policy establishing the ground rules for the use of distributed computers in the organization, indicating the conditions under which computers can be acquired, approvals that are necessary, and setting up

Exhibit 4-2   Distributed processing standards

Introduction
Distributed processing overview
Equipment selection/acquisition
Systems software selection/acquisition
Application software selection/acquisition
Feasibility studies
Requests for proposals—software development
Contract negotiations—general
Contracts—hardware acquisition
Contracts—hardware maintenance
Contracts—package program acquisition
Contracts—package program maintenance
Contracts—systems development
Organizational issues
Use of consultants/contract personnel
System/program implementation
System/program documentation
System/program controls
System/program testing
System/program changes
System (control) program changes
Use of text processing/administrative terminals
Computer operations control
Data security
Physical security—site
Physical security—equipment
Physical security—media
Software security
Backup and recovery
Insurance
Use of outside computing services
Data communications protocols
Planning/installing voice communications systems
Planning/installing data communications systems
Corporate data standards
Data privacy
Software protection
Personal use of computers

standards to which distributed resources must adhere. This phase could be followed by the preparation of a manual of distributed processing standards to be issued to all users or potential users of minicomputers. These standards should be written in such a way as to ensure that distributed processing resources are compatible with corporate long-range planning, are secure, and are being used efficiently and effectively throughout the corporation. Distributed processing standards might serve simply as guidelines (e.g., contract negotiation guidelines) or might also establish rules or "thou shalt not's."

The standards should specify such things as the responsibility of the IM function for automation master planning and coordination, the criteria for an application's going on a minicomputer versus centralized main-frame, and the responsibility of the user for the operation and control of the minis in user areas. They should cover such things as hardware and software selection criteria, security over physical facilities (site and computer media), contract negotiation guidelines (especially for "turnkey" development), data communications network protocols, corporate data standards, organizational issues, use of outside resources (time sharing, service bureaus, consultants, contract programmers), and systems implementation guidelines. A list of possible distributed processing standards is shown in Exhibit 4-2.

The standards could be prepared by the IM function and then approved by other management-designated key executives, such as the company's physical plant officer, auditor, security officer, and comptroller. Once issued to every minicomputer user, they could then be tested for adherence as a part of the central audit of a user's operations, with copies of audit comments relating to standards forwarded to the corporate information manager.

The use of corporate distributed-processing standards governing the acquisition and use of information resources throughout the organization will become increasingly important as the trend toward distributed processing accelerates in the years ahead. The company that gets control over this diverse resource early in the game will ensure that its future information network function is a fully integrated set of systems, able to pass information around the firm easily and quickly for improved management information and control. A strategy for developing and disseminating distributed processing standards should be implemented before decentralization goes too far, creating a problem of diverse, uncoordinated, and incompatible systems, such as was experienced by the New York corporation cited earlier.

PENETRATING THE ORGANIZATION

The demand for automation and systems projects continues to outstrip the supply of systems resources in most organizations. Thus it would seem that we need not be concerned with spreading automation and technology within the firm. Yet high demand does not necessarily mean that we are always doing the right thing, nor does it mean that some important areas of the company are not being overlooked. New roles for the information manager—and the extension of IM into new areas such as office automation—can increase IM effectiveness through the assumption of new responsibilities.

Another way to be influential is not to add new responsibilities but to add *new customers*. In most organizations, there are certain departments that have always been heavy users of IM services. Conversely, there are functional areas of the business that have used few, if any, even though they might be able to benefit greatly from such services. Part of the reason is that automation was first applied to the labor-intensive areas—operations, record keeping, transaction processing—and these have remained heavy users of IM resources. Specialization areas and professional and managerial areas, on the other hand, have been slower to move heavily into automation. If we are to be successful in bringing systems and computing to bear on management and other areas of the business that contribute significantly to profit but are not "demanders" of systems services, we will need some penetration strategies to make meaningful inroads into these areas. We want to employ information resources where they will do the most good. Thus, we must plan their activity and not just react to demand. This is important because not all IM activity contributes equally to corporate objectives.

Some functions and user divisions will implement IM activities to management's benefit. Other functions and divisions will remain very backward users of IM capabilities. Operations activities are usually big IM users, whereas high-level management decisions involving hundreds of millions of dollars are usually made with little or no information or support from IM resources. Aggressive information managers are needed to identify those functions and divisions that are inadequately supported by IM resources. The IM function, even if overloaded with work, will be more effective if it maintains a strategy that reallocates scarce resources to the user(s) with the greatest potential contribution to corporate performance. Thus, penetration strategies can be used to achieve this objective. One of the most successful penetration strategies we have found is called the *Trojan horse strategy*.

Trojan Horse Strategy

S-9   TROJAN HORSES

IM promotes user penetration by placing systems professionals as "gifts" in user divisions. Trojan horses quickly learn the business and promote systems solutions to business problems.

In Greek mythology, the Trojan War between the Greeks and the people of Troy raged for nine years, with the Greeks being unable to conquer the well-fortified city of Troy itself. Finally, the Greeks built a large hollow wooden horse in which were concealed a small group of warriors. The Greeks then appeared to sail home, leaving behind the horse, which the Trojans took within the city walls. At night, the Greeks returned; their companions crept out of the horse and opened the city gates, and Troy was conquered.

Taking an author's license, we use the term "Trojan horse" to describe this next strategy as a positive rather than a negative action. The Trojan horse idea is a way of building rather than destroying as in the myth, as the "gift" of systems professionals to users is a positive way to increase automation penetration in user areas where automation can be beneficial.

The Trojan horse strategy does involve a gift—the gift of systems people to users. Systems people are transferred into departments where automation has met with lack of interest, with reluctance, or with resistance, but where the application of systems technology is sorely needed. In this case, our Trojan horse soldiers let in automation designed to help, rather than conquer, the user. The key to this strategy is first to enlist the aid of top management. If they are sold on the efficacy of the strategy, convincing target division heads to take on a needed resident systems person is relatively easy. The information specialist may be assigned to head systems planning for that division or may, in fact, take on direct line-management responsibility. Either way, his or her systems training provides a capability that quickly results in the application of technology to the division's activities—to the benefit of the user, the company, and the IM function. It's hard to beat a strategy where everybody wins, but not everyone is convinced of that at the beginning—and that's why the Trojan Horse strategy is needed. Now, one might say, "Yes, but once an information specialist is transferred, the allegiance will move to the user, so how can you be sure he or she will fulfill the mission you set out to accomplish?" We have found that motivation is determined by career interests. Once trained in computer technology and knowledgeable about the benefits it can provide, a systems person will promote it wherever feasible, not simply because he's a believer, but because the benefits of automation accruing to the department will be attributed directly to the information specialist. "Spreading the faith" promotes growth even though the "Trojan horse" no longer works for the IM function.

The above notwithstanding, we do caution against the "black holes." In space terminology, this phrase refers to giant stars which have collapsed in upon themselves with such energy that nothing can ever leave them—not even light. They sit in space acting as giant vacuum cleaners, sucking in anything that comes their way. This can happen when a Trojan horse is moved into an area fraught with such problems that he or she immediately gets sucked in and disappears forever. If this seems likely, one can either forget the Trojan horse strategy or keep a tie through continued reporting to the IM function, even though the systems specialist is assigned full time and indefinitely to the user department.

The Trojan horse concept can be a powerful "influence" strategy. We have seen it used with great success to automate major divisions which previously had little or no interest in automation, but which ultimately ended up among the staunchest supporters of the IM function.

Some further user penetration strategies are discussed in Chapter 5, and some case examples are presented in Chapter 12.

PLANNING PROACTIVELY

The adoption of a management-by-strategies (MBS) program will, in itself, result in proactive planning. The establishment of objectives and of strategies to meet those objectives requires a considerable amount of strategic planning. Getting involved in corporate planning is another good way to promote the IM function. However, this is not always within the control of the information manager. A planning strategy that *is* within the information manager's control, however, is the planning of business information systems with user managements. We view proactive business information planning as involving the following strategy:

> **S-10   BUSINESS INFORMATION PLANNING**
>
> **Structured planning strategy for working with users to identify new ways to apply systems solutions to business problems and needs.**

In Chapter 3, we discussed the merits of adapting a proactive change-agent role. One cannot be active in identifying opportunities for systems solutions to user problems, or in getting technology working for the good of the corporation, without also being active in the company's business planning. A strategy for promoting this involvement with users and top management is the formulation of a business information planning (BIP) activity within the IM organization.

In a small company, this strategy could involve one person; in a larger company, several. The function is the same: to work with management personnel to identify and give birth to new business systems projects. The planning process is simply a structured way of involving systems planners with top management and users to identify overall information and systems needs and to define the requirements of the highest-priority areas. It is, thus, an ongoing systems support to user business plans, both long- and short-term, as prioritized by the user. The cornerstone of the philosophy is that systems are more effective if they are planned by and for the managers who will use them. Therefore, a BIP study is a user study assisted by IM, not the other way around.

BIP methodology involves a combination of top-down analysis and bottom-up development strategy. Top-down analysis identifies needs through executive interviews, defines priorities (ranking systems in terms of some criteria, such as return on investment), and determines systems support availability. Bottom-up development identifies information data-base needs, develops systems solutions, and establishes implementation goals (scheduling tasks and manning requirements). The basic steps of BIP are:

1   Determining the scope of BIP planning.
2   Selecting the BIP team (or starting with a task force, see S-15).
3   Beginning the search to identify new project opportunities (i.e., learning the user's business, needs, opportunities, and top priorities).
4   Defining the highest-priority systems (rough requirements and preliminary cost–benefit analysis).
5   Getting initial systems studies approved and turned over to systems development.
6   Beginning the planning of the next level of systems needs.

BIP objectives are to establish a long-range plan for IM development and a short-range plan for implementing the highest-priority systems first. BIP is active in the planning phase only. Its relationship to development is illustrated in Exhibit 4-3.

BIP activities usually constitute only 5% of an entire project. Once the planning group identifies and develops a first-draft project definition, the project is turned over to the development group to carry on. This procedure keeps the planning group focused on business systems planning and out of the technical details of systems development.

This accent on project identification and definition only allows the BIP group to be kept small. But although small in number, the planning staff must be a very-high-level group of experienced professionals, individuals who possess a broad understanding of both technology and business needs. Their ability and opportunity to participate in proactive planning within the corporation will be heavily dependent on the general recognition by users and man-

Exhibit 4-3   Business information planning in the project life cycle.

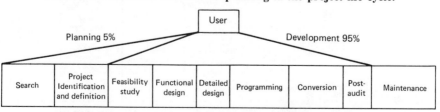

agement of their level of competence and experience. This fact becomes more apparent when we examine the types of project identification approaches open to BIP (Exhibit 4-4) as it attempts to move up the scale from reactive to proactive involvement in corporate business planning activities.

At the reactive end of the scale, systems planning simply meets the mandates of new regulatory and other requirements. The next step up the scale involves the rewriting of existing systems (usually because they have become obsolete). A bit more proactive, but still not involving users or top management, is the step of searching out and emulating successful new systems installed in other companies. The realization that user involvement is needed eventually leads to user interviews and the development of a laundry list of needs (which may or may not be prioritized). The next stage is an extensive analysis of the company's needs made through financial analysis and a study of trends, environmental considerations, etc., which is participated in by other staff support functions, such as the finance division of the corporate planning staff. The integration grows greater when formal corporate long-range plans are reviewed for the purpose of identifying system projects in support of those plans. Total integration is reached when the BIP staff actually participates with senior management in the formulation of corporate long-range plans and a determination of the systems support required.

From this stage analysis, we can see that in order for business information planners to function at the upper level of effectiveness, they must be a highly respected group of systems professionals, recognized as competent business and technical consultants who can help solve business problems with modern systems solutions. (Some typical responsibilities of such a group are outlined in Exhibit 4-5).

Finally, to be most effective, regardless of the charge-out system used, the BIP function should be treated as a corporate research group, whose time is charged to corporate overhead and not to the users. This approach will encourage their use as business systems planners by users who might other-

Exhibit 4-4 Business information planning (BIP) project identification approaches.

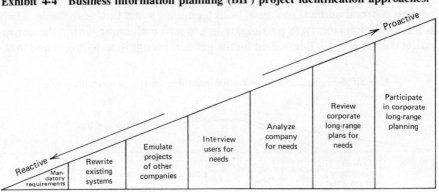

Exhibit 4-5   Business information planning (BIP) job responsibilities.

The BIP group has responsibilities in four areas: information systems planning, user consulting, new project identification, and the development of long-range systems plans.

Information systems planning requires keeping abreast of technological developments in order to anticipate, develop, and maintain the skills needed to perform current and future systems consulting assignments at a high level of expertise and effectiveness. The planners should be aware of systems developments within the industry in order to recognize and pursue new opportunities leading to new systems projects, application expansion, or automation penetration into additional areas of the company, which will have a significant and positive impact on users' business opportunities and profitability.

User consulting involves working closely with high-level user management in the area of business systems planning directed toward long-range technical and application solutions and strategies for leading-edge product development. The BIP consultant's knowledge and experience should lead to recognition and acceptance by the user, who seeks his advice, counsel, and assistance on all *major* systems planning activities. User acceptance should manifest itself in a high level of confidence in and satisfaction with the planning support provided by the BIP consultant.

New project identification means conducting, preparing, and presenting initial systems surveys, preliminary feasibility studies, and recommendations for the development of leading-edge *major* systems projects. Such recommendations should recognize and present solutions and plans for new or expanded systems and services, often involving sophisticated automated systems in complex user environments. Included in such proposals should be initial rough cost–benefit analyses of the proposed systems. Proposals prepared by the BIP consultant should demonstrate a broad understanding of the user's business objectives and the impact of his systems plan on those objectives.

A long-range systems plan should be drawn up by BIP as a result of their individual planning efforts. This plan should cover systems project work planned over a three-year time span. The plan should include, at the least, a projects plan, identifying and scheduling all major new development efforts, and a manpower plan, identifying and scheduling the manning resources needed to support the projects plan. The plan should be updated each year, following extensive executive-interview planning sessions held each fall.

---

wise be turned off by the prospect of internal consulting charges. The formulation of a BIP group, if implemented properly and manned with high-caliber consultants, not only can foster good systems planning within the company but can be an excellent user-relations tool as well.

EXTENDING THE IM FUNCTION

It will be mandatory to reposition EDP in the organization of the 1980s. The right image, the right name, and the right responsibilities will be needed to go with the transition from EDP to Information Management. The right image can be brought about through "selling" the information resource management concept and the chief information officer concept to users and senior management. The right name is important to this image. Shakespeare said, "What's in a name?" In this case, a lot. You are what you are called. In the early days of computing, *automatic data processing* (ADP) was the common label attached to this function. As we moved more from punch cards and electromechanical devices to electronic processing, the label changed to *electronic data processing* (EDP), and later, in some cases, to *management information systems* (MIS). Recognizing the movement toward information processing, many today have the word *information* in their titles, for example, information systems and information services. We refer to this function as the *information management function*. The important thing is to have a name that fits the responsibilities that are appropriate to an information era. That is why more and more industry leaders are dropping technical labels like *EDP* and *data processing* and going to broader information management titles. *Information* is data massaged with intelligence; *management* is a broader concept than *processing*. Therefore, we prefer the term *information management* to describe the new image and role of this function and *information manager* as the name of the director of this function in the 1980s. With the right identification, the assumption of new responsibilities that extend the function beyond its present scope of activities is made easier. The coalescence of information activities under the umbrella of the IM function becomes easier and more logical.

There are two different ways to extend an IM function: direct and indirect. The direct way is to coalesce under the IM function the *existing* information activities in the organization. We suggested a number of these in our coalescence planner (S-5) strategy. Two of these are telecommunications and office information systems. Telecommunications is an obvious candidate because of the merging of the computer and communications industries in recent years. These will be inseparable in future years, and thus, there is logic in their being under the same management. This idea is discussed in more detail in our computications strategy (S-50). Office information management is also a good candidate simply because it involves several information management disciplines—computers, communications, systems, and information processing—and all need leadership and direction. We believe these areas offer an excellent opportunity for the extension of the IM function in the organization in the 1980s. We present our case in the office information systems (S-53) strategy in Chapter 10.

The indirect way to extend the IM function is to create *new* opportunities for automated products and services which will increase the contribution of the IM function in the firm. This approach requires imagination and planning. A good strategy for developing new ideas and opportunities that can result in extending IM effectiveness is technological forecasting.

Technological Forecasting

S-11 TECHNOLOGY FORECASTING

A formal approach to the identification of
technical trends and their likely impact on the
organization

One of the important inputs into the corporate planning process, but one
which is rarely included, is an assessment of the impact of technology on the
company. It is necessary to forecast the impact of change on the organization
so that it can plan to advance that change and take advantage of what that
change can do for the company economically and competitively. This approach provides protection from obsolescence and protection from competitive inroads. How does one go about assessing the impact of technical trends
on the organization? We suggest the following five-step technological forecasting strategy:

1 Identify key technical trends.
2 Analyze industry impact.
3 Analyze company impact.
4 Determine the information manager's role as a change agent.
5 Develop appropriate strategies.

We can perhaps best illustrate this five-step process by describing its
application to the current trend toward *electronic banking* in the banking
industry.

Electronic Banking: Trend Analysis

Step 1   Trend Identification

Back in 1966, the term *checkless society* came into being. The impetus
came from the fact that banks were being inundated by a rising tide of
checks: then some 20 billion a year were going through the banking system.
And check processing is a labor-intensive activity because of the archaic
laws that require the physical presentation of paper (checks) to finalize payment. Everyone had visions of replacing paper with electronic payments.
After some frustrating years, it became apparent that while automation could
speed up check processing and that electronics could provide new modes of
payment, checks would still not be eliminated, and the checkless society
began to be referred to as the "less checks" society, implying a slower rate
in check growth. By 1980, the annual check volume was over 30 billion with

a projected rise to 47 billion by 1985. Eventually, both terms were replaced by the now common term for the trend toward electronic banking, EFTS (electronic funds transfer systems). EFTS, however, is only part of what we perceive to be a broader trend toward *electronic banking,* which we identify as (a) electronic money cards, (b) funds transfer systems, (c) automated clearinghouses, (d) automated tellers, and (e) home banking. We will evaluate each of these in turn in Step 2.

Step 2   Industry Impact

Some examination of these five components will make it clear that the impact of electronic banking on the banking industry in the 1980s will be profound. Banks today are faced with rising service costs and with increased competition from other banks as well as from other financial and nonfinancial (e.g., Sears, Merrill Lynch) institutions—in the face of rising customer expectations of better service. Electronic delivery mechanisms offer the most apparent answer to these problems. Let's examine the industry impact of our five components to see why:

Electronic Money Cards   These, of course, started with bank credit cards some 10 years or so ago with the introduction of Bankamericard (now VISA) by Bank of America, soon followed by Master Charge from a consortium of competing California banks. These two bank-credit-card systems today have issued over 152 million cards worldwide, with $25 billion of credit outstanding. However, credit cards do not replace paper; they simply substitute one kind of paper for another (transaction slips for checks). Credit cards are now being followed by *debit* cards. (While credit cards create loans, debit cards substitute for checks and withdrawal orders in getting money out of checking and savings accounts.) We predict that in the 1980s, credit and debit cards will merge into full-transaction electronic money cards. To prepare for this eventuality, Master Charge has in fact already changed its name to Master Card. This electronic money card allows customers to borrow money, move money around, and do just about everything that can now be done in a bank—without having to go to a bank to do it.

EFTS   Although almost all aspects of electronic banking are called EFTS, for purpose of this discussion we will confine ourselves to two basic aspects: retail and wholesale. On the retail side, most of the activity to date has consisted of check verification/authorization systems through point of sale (POS) terminals in supermarkets and other retail outlets. The conduct of banking transactions through remote POS terminals is still illegal in many parts of the United States, since they are considered bank branches and therefore run afoul of restricting branch-banking laws. Enabling legislation is coming—in some states has arrived—but it will take time.

The recent U.S. Federal Court of Appeals ruling that certain regulation-approved EFT experiments were, in fact, illegal under present banking laws has underscored the technology that EFT has made obsolete concerning the nation's present banking structure.

We believe that the legislation issue will be resolved in the next few years and that this resolution will give rise to an exploding market of electronic banking located in shopping outlets throughout the country. The impact on branch banking laws, interstate banking, and the broadening of markets served by banks will completely change the way retail banking is conducted in the United States.

There is also a wholesale side to EFTS: automated money-transfer systems and corporate cash management—for corporations. Despite the 30 billion checks written annually, some 95% of all money exchange in the United States is done by wire transfer (telephone or telex). This is a clumsy process, prone to error. As a result, many banks are switching from paper-tape telex systems to minicomputer-based electronic systems. These systems are connected to all wire services—bank wire, fed wire, SWIFT (the international network), TWX, telex, etc.—so that all incoming and outgoing transfers are handled automatically. Incoming messages are subjected to test-word validation and then passed on to terminals or printers located in receiving departments. Outgoing messages are entered over on-line terminals, verified, and electronically routed to the appropriate wire services. This method is resulting in greatly improved service, a fast turnaround of money, and lower operating costs.

Another form of corporate EFTS is cash management services. Through electronic mail boxes and computers, banks are helping corporations to make more efficient use of cash funds. In an electronic mailbox (or lockbox) system, a company has customers mail payments to a special lockbox number at its bank's post office. As mail arrives, the bank collects and processes it, immediately crediting the receiving corporation's account for all monies received. The result is a reduction in the processing "float," or uncollected funds, which in turn permits the company to reduce short-term borrowing or to increase short-term investments, as well as to reduce the clerical handling of accounts receivable. Another facet of this service is cash concentration, by which payments collected at various locations are accumulated daily into a special central corporate account through wire transfers. This procedure again enables corporate treasurers to get funds working faster. Some companies even have terminals in the corporate treasurer's office, allowing the treasurer to assess her or his company's cash position quickly at the start of the day and to get funds to work quickly and efficiently. These systems are offered by banks and nonbanks—for example, Info-Cash (Chase Manhattan Bank, New York), Chemlink (Chemical Bank, New York), Spacifics (Security Pacific Bank, Los Angeles), NDC Service (National Data Corp., Atlanta), and Cash Management Services (Phoenix-Hecht, Chicago). These services are likely to continue to spread through competition and more corporate pressures in the 1980s.

Automated Clearinghouses (ACH)   A bank clearinghouse is where banks in a given city go each day to exchange checks drawn on each other. An automated clearinghouse does the same thing electronically, that is, by tape-to-tape exchange. This method is cheaper and faster, particularly for handling preauthorized transactions. Preauthorized transactions include automatic credits to accounts, like the direct deposit of one's paycheck from one's employer to one's bank or the direct deposit of dividend checks, and automatic debits on one's account for the payment of preauthorized bills like a mortgage payment, a car payment, and utility bills. The movement to ACHs is relatively new—less than 10 years old. But by the mid-1980s, there will be ACHs in all major U.S. cities, linking up banks throughout the country for the transmission of billions of transaction dollars daily. (Note that instantaneous transmissions of money will mean fewer "float" dollars in the banking system. Speeding up the collection of checks by one day would result in $50 billion less of float dollars, which, at 10% interest, would save $5 billion in the lost availability of funds to banks today.)

Automated Tellers   Both manned and unmanned automated-teller systems are developing rapidly in a number of major U.S. banks today. Many of the manned systems are minicomputer-based, with minis in individual branches supporting teller-operated terminals for transaction processing, account balance inquiries, and cash control and settlement procedures. These systems speed up transaction processing and result in shorter customer lines, and fewer tellers are needed. On the unmanned side, automated-teller machines (ATMs) are also becoming more popular. There are about 15,000 units installed in the United States today. About one-third of all banks have installed at least one unit, and for large banks (over $1 billion), the percentage is 85%. Thus, ATMs are offering a visible demonstration of the trend toward self-service electronic banking, and rapid expansion is expected in the next few years.

Home Banking   The height of convenience banking has to be the ability to bank right out of one's own home. Telephone bill-paying, the first stage of home banking services, is currently offered by some 250 financial institutions in the United States. Here's how a bank-by-phone system works: A customer calls the bank, using a touch-tone phone, and enters his account number and secret code (personal identification number). He can then initiate a variety of transactions; for example, transferring funds, getting balance information, activating credit or pay bills—in fact, most of what can be done in a bank. (No one has yet found a way to send dollar bills over phone lines, though.) The customer's account is charged for the bills paid, and the merchant receives the credit, either by check or through credit to his account. If desired, the customer can also talk to a person, by entering a special code, in order to get detailed information on checks paid, to add merchants to the bill-paying list, to ask advice, etc. An audio response program verifies all transactions received and gives the customer a reference number (audit trail), which later appears in his statement, which lists all bank-by-phone transactions for the month (who paid, amount, date). Only about 20% of all banks offer bank-by-phone services today, but if it evolves, as we think it will, into bank-by-TV in the next few years, then it promises to become one of the fastest-growing electronic banking services of the 1980s.

One of the drawbacks of bank-by-phone is that there is no visual display of data, and an audio response must be relied on. Bank-by-TV, on the other hand, provides visual feedback. Bank-by-TV is based on videotext technology. It can provide a variety of information services, including banking services, over the home TV. Arch L. Madsen, whose television station KSL in Salt Lake City is testing a videotext system, recently told an Associated Press annual meeting that within five years, Americans should be able to ask their TVs for a bank statement, a new recipe, a stock market report, news, or weather. He said that videotext systems are a totally new form of communication that will become the primary home data center in the information age. In fact, viewdata has been in use in Great Britain for some time and has fueled interest in a number of other countries watching its development. Started by the British post office, it now calls its service Prestel; in France, the PTT (postal telephone and telegraph) is working on a system called Antiope; similar systems exist in some form in Japan, West Germany, the Netherlands, and the United States. In the United States, GTE has obtained the rights to use Canada's Telidon videotext system. Viewdata Corp. of America is also running a pilot teletext system in Miami, which provides weather, news, sports, adult education courses, movie schedules, and calendars of local events. Other U.S. firms interested in getting into teletext include AT&T, IBM, CBS, Western Union, Viewtron, Cabletext, and Microbaud. Mutual Institutions National Transfer System (MINTS) in New York has a working model that offers bill-paying services, airline reservations, bank information, retail-catalog ordering, and home-alarm monitoring.

One of the most advanced bank-by-TV systems, however, is one being experimented with by Barclays Bank, London, over Britain's Prestel service. Customers gain access over a specially equipped TV. An attached entry-key-pad station provides interactive capability as well as information. The information provided by Barclays includes explanations of bank services, locations of banking offices and ATMs, foreign exchange and money market rates, advertising of less-known banking services, and financial advice. The interactive services include an experimental loan-application form which can be filled in on the customer's TV screen and transmitted to the bank directly. (Someday we may see a credit-scoring system added to this service so that customers can approve their own loans.) Other services being considered include preauthorized bill-paying (simply enter the variable amount to be paid), payment for goods and services by credit card charge, and balance inquiry (or even a full bank statement displayed on the screen). Last year, Bank One (a Columbus, Ohio bank) began a 200-house test of an in-house bank-by-TV service. This service enables customers to pay bills, review the status of deposit accounts, and get other banking services by using viewdata technology to provide two-way communications through the home phone and TV set.

Step 3   Company Impact

The industry impact of electronic banking is clear. The impact on any individual bank will vary depending on its own circumstances, its competitive market, and its management goals. Many leading banks today are moving aggressively on all these fronts. For example, many issue electronic money cards (both debit and credit cards); many have installed POS terminals in retail outlets for check authorization and the conduct of banking transactions where legal; and many of the major banks have developed minicomputer-based money-transfer systems for the transfer of both domestic and international corporate funds, are actively marketing cash management services, and are participating in automated clearinghouse arrange-

Exhibit 4-6   Technological forecast #1: electronic banking.

Step 1
```
┌─────────────────┐     Components:
│     Trend       │        Electronic money cards
│ identification: │        EFTS
│   Electronic    │        ACH
│    banking      │        Automated tellers
└─────────────────┘        Home banking
```

Step 2
```
┌─────────────────┐     Potential:
│                 │        Dramatic growth expected
│    Industry     │        Structure of banking changing
│     impact      │        Implications to branch banking laws
└─────────────────┘
```

Step 3
```
┌─────────────────┐     Planning:
│                 │        Debit/credit card expansion
│    Company      │        EFT point of sale banking
│     impact      │        Automated wire transfer systems
│                 │        Branch automation & ATMs
└─────────────────┘        Bank-at-home system
```

Step 4
```
┌─────────────────┐     Leadership:
│                 │        Leading-edge position
│     IM role     │
│                 │
└─────────────────┘
```

Step 5
```
┌─────────────────┐     Implement:
│                 │        Self-service banking systems
│    Strategies   │        Systems integration planning
│                 │
└─────────────────┘
```

ments. The installation of automated-teller systems and automated-teller machines in banking offices is becoming widespread. And some banks are even experimenting with bank-at-home services. Banks that choose to ignore these electronic banking trends may soon find themselves at a severe competitive disadvantage.

Step 4   *Role*

We suggest that an appropriate role for IM in the trend toward electronic banking might be to serve as a leading-edge developer of electronic banking systems. Electronic banking has the potential to increase productivity, to lower costs, to improve customer service, to increase share of the market, and to provide a competitive advantage to those banks that are in the forefront of this trend, which we believe will revolutionize banking in the decade ahead.

Step 5   *Strategies*

In our view, the above discussion suggests two strategies: (1) the support of self-service banking systems and (2) the integration of diverse electronic banking systems:

1 *Self-service banking* leads to productivity because it squeezes the labor costs out of the delivery of banking services. At the same time, electronic delivery systems bring banking services more conveniently to customers—where they work and shop, and even at home.
2 *Integration* of diverse systems is needed to bring cohesiveness to the electronic banking movement. Customers view banking as a *package* of financial services, not as a bunch of individual stand-alone services. Hence, it will be important to build these systems under a coordinated master plan that assures standardization, compatibility, and consistency. A bank's services should be consistent and should look alike at all its entities: branches, subsidiaries, even international offices.

Technological forecasting is a further extension of the situation analysis method in an MBS program. The stepped process described above is summarized in Exhibit 4-6. As input into the corporate and business planning process, a similar technological forecast and trend analysis can be made for each technical trend that is identified for its possible impact on the company.

KEEPING USERS HAPPY

Keeping users happy is the real key to success for any information management organization. User service is the *raison d'être* of its existence. High user satisfaction will most assuredly increase an IM function's influence in the organization; high user discontent will assure fast management action to replace the information manager with someone who can keep users happy. Favorable user feedback is still the most common method by which top managements measure IM performance, so it is vital for information managers to make sure that user satisfaction is high. Now, the reader is probably saying, "Of course, but how do we do the impossible? Too many demands, too few resources, unrealistic expectations. When we do things right, we hear nothing; when anything goes wrong, we hear about it immediately—and so does top management." The information manager cannot win as long as it's a "we–they" situation. It has to become a collective "we" situation. If we are to be successful, there has to be joint management of information resources by IM and users. User involvement has been discussed for years as the key to the success of systems projects. But in a world of distributed information resources, it will become paramount to have shared management over *all* information resources. If this can be successfully accomplished, there will be no such thing as user complaints to top management and their resultant negative effect on the IM function. If resource management is shared, then *both* parties (users and IM) are responsible for success or failure. Users are not going to complain that *they* have failed. Joint management completely defuses this entire problem. It ceases to exist!

How do we accomplish this? Two strategies that deal specifically with the issue of shared management of information resources are information resource product managers (S-18), which addresses data processing service, and joint systems development (S-17), which addresses systems projects.

In Chapter 5, we discuss these two strategies and a number of others designed to promote the all-important integration of the IM function with user management.

FOCUSING ON TOP MANAGEMENT

To increase its effectiveness in the organization, the information management function must finally close the communications gap with top management, demonstrate solid performance, and begin to apply the power of computing and information systems to the managers of the firm instead of to the clerks. Clerk-oriented, record-keeping, transaction-based systems have been the primary thrust of most data processing organizations for the past two decades. The 1980s must see a shift in emphasis to *management* information systems if we are to succeed in repositioning EDP into a more influential IM role.

This projected repositioning will require, first of all, that information managers *learn the business* they are serving. It will not be enough to know technology in the future. Information managers will have to know the business as well, because only by knowing what the real needs of the business are, only by knowing its priorities, its goals, its competition, will information managers be able to provide useful information systems (not just raw data) to help managers to manage and control their business activities better, to be more competitive, and more successful.

Second, information managers will have to *become business managers* first and staff professionals second. Too often, technical executives are seen as technicians rather than as managers. This kind of mentality can be extremely damaging to the career path of the information executive and perhaps is why EDP managers have experienced such high turnover in the past. Top management must be shown that EDP executives can be as effective in management as are executives in any other part of the organization. For the information manager who has come up the technical route and has never been exposed to management courses and techniques, this is the place to start. She or he should take some management courses (corporate finance, marketing, organizational behavior, organizational development, personnel management, effective communications); learn management styles and techniques (Theory X and Theory Y, Blake's managerial grid, force-field analysis, decision analysis); learn about leadership styles and effective presentations; and learn the chief executives' language, their business arena—their *business.* Look, act, and talk like a manager, and you will be a manager!

Third, the information manager should work toward becoming not the chief data processing officer, but the *chief information officer,* and should start educating management to view corporate information as a resource, a resource that must be coordinated and managed, that requires technological integration to achieve, and, most of all, that should be the domain of the information manager, the chief information officer of the future firm.

Finally, the information manager should *do something for top managers,* not just build systems for clerks. The failure of EDP in the past to do something directly useful to chief executives is the reason for their low interest in EDP. In Chapter 6, we discuss some techniques for building executive information systems and some strategies designed to close, once and for all, the communications gap with top management.

NOTES

1 Peter G. W. Keen and Michael S. Scott Morton, *Decision Support Systems: An Organizational Perspective,* Reading, Mass.: Addison-Wesley, 1978, p. 53.

Effective User Relations: The Care and Feeding of Users

If the masses who are potential users of technology are not educated sufficiently to appreciate what it can do for them, you will find it going to waste.

Dixon Doll[1]

In the previous chapter, we suggested that one of the critical keys to the success of any information management function lies in the effectiveness of its user relations. In this chapter, we examine a number of strategies aimed at improving this all-important facet of information management.

There was a time when data processing was esoteric and clouded in mystique. Computers were huge and difficult to utilize. Outside time-sharing vendors, systems application packages, and minicomputers were not as available. Users knew little about computers, and the technical cloak was a source of power for data processing professionals. In the 1980s, the IM function faces a user community that is less intimidated by computer technology. The mystique is slowly dissolving as alternative sources of information services, minicomputers, outside time-sharing vendors, and DP service bureaus offer solutions for many user needs.

More knowledgeable and involved users in the 1980s will either cause an increase or a loss of power for the corporate IM function, depending on the effectiveness of user relations in this period of expanded use of technology.

Many organizations do an excellent job of managing technical resources while doing a dismal job in user relations. The inadequacy in this area has, in fact, caused the demise of many an information manager over the years. It is one of the most difficult challenges faced by information managers the world over. Why? The answer is not simple, by any means. High demand and expectations, a shortage of resources, the rapid pace of technological (and business) growth, the long lead times needed for equipment planning and systems development, constantly changing requirements, technical obsolescence, communications problems, interpersonal relationships—all of these are contributing factors. We believe that part of the answer must lie in a better understanding of each other's business problems and opportunities. Information managers need to understand the user's business needs; user managers need to understand more about data processing and systems work. Learning more about each other requires more involvement in each other's business. The successful marriage of business and technology in the 1980s will require participatory management by information managers and user managers.

It is possible for information management to be mediocre in the management of internal resources, yet still have a high level of user satisfaction. Why? Because IM has done a better job in servicing the user's needs. Attitude, sensitivity, and good communications, rather than technical competence, are what impress users about information managers. Thus, if there is a trade-off between competence in the management of technical resources and skills in user relations, top management in many companies decides in favor of effectiveness in user relations. *Business Week,* for example, concluded:

> Although they possess strong technical expertise, the computer specialists who supervise data processing systems at most companies often lack the business background that is needed to determine just how those systems can best be used to improve the operation of their companies. In recent years nearly 100 major companies have filled that void by taking computer management out of the hands of technicians and putting it into the hands of management information systems (MIS) teams, headed by high-ranking executives who are just as comfortable talking about profits and losses as they are about bits and bytes.[2]

This *Business Week* quote suggests that there are executives who are knowledgeable in both business and computer use. In point of fact, executives with this combination of skills are very rare. In this chapter, strategies designed to integrate the IM function with user businesses more effectively are examined from the following viewpoints:

User measurement strategies.   We must first know who our users are and how well we are doing in both service and responsiveness to the needs of the organization.

User involvement.   Picking up on the notion that *shared* management will probably be increasing through the 1980s, we look at some ways to augment user involvement in information resource management.

User service.   Finally, we focus on several techniques aimed at improving user service levels and performance.

USER MEASUREMENT STRATEGIES

We start our user assessment with an inventory of users, an analysis of user automation penetration, user satisfaction surveys, and a determination of the backlog of work to be done.

Inventory of Users

```
┌─────────────────────────────────────────────────┐
│  S-12   INVENTORY OF USERS                        │
│                                                   │
│  A market research information system for better  │
│  understanding of the user community and identifi-│
│  cation of problems and/or service opportunities. │
└─────────────────────────────────────────────────┘
```

The IM function sells services to corporate and division users. In inventory-ing users, we have discovered a wide range of user characteristics. There are *passive users* who will almost never ask for assistance from the IM function regardless of the opportunities for improved management effectiveness or operational efficiency that can be achieved with information systems applica-tions. There are *overly active users* who want IM to produce systems solu-tions even when such applications cannot be cost-justified. This kind of user tends not even to think about costs and benefits when requesting such ser-vices. Then there are the *semi-informed users* who consider themselves systems-wise and tend to insist on their right to make decisions about infor-mation services and equipment, a frequent cause for the serious difficulties that have given information systems a bad reputation in some companies.

Note that users can range from the chief executive officer to an assistant controller to a junior clerk. Often, systems professionals spend most of their time serving junior-level people, neglecting the needs of top management. An inventory of users provides an important guide for assessing just who is being served in the organization. This user inventory might include such information as:

1   Current level of automation relative to state of best business practices.
2   Competence of user staff in utilizing information services; evaluation of key people in a user division.
3   Attitudes toward future systems opportunities.
4   Satisfaction with current IM services.
5   Actual quality of services, as defined by information managers (which may vary significantly from user perception).
6   Degree of business systems planning performed in the user division.

Inventories of users frequently provide such important information for IM management as:

The users who contribute most to corporate profits are receiving very little from the IM function.

Users who contribute little to corporate performance may be consuming the bulk of the IM budget.

Users who are receiving high-quality services may be unaware of their good fortune and may be dissatisfied with IM performance (a perception control problem).

IM may be delivering poor service to important users who may not (yet) be aware of this weak performance.

The evaluation of IM performance and plans for improved user relations clearly should begin with a current status user inventory.

This inventory can be maintained in an on-line computer system or in a simple user-inventory notebook. It can be expanded to include information developed in several of the other strategies presented, such as business information planning (S-10), perception management (S-19), user satisfaction surveys (S-14), and user IM penetration (S-13). An example of a user inventory form is presented in Exhibit 5-1.

User IM Penetration

> **S-13   USER IM PENETRATION**
>
> **The status of current user applications compared with the best practices of leading organizations in implementing operational, management, and strategic planning systems.**

A question that should be asked more frequently by senior corporate executives and even members of corporate boards is: How adequate are the information services provided for this company, division, department, or function? The answer to this kind of question is that everything is relative. "Adequate" compared with what? For example, consider information services received by today's corporate controller. The typical controller in a large company receives a wide range of IM services in 1981 which were not provided ten years earlier. "Progress" in the utilization of IM services during the last decade is a positive sign, but it is no guarantee that a company or a division has an adequate level of competence in information management. Instead, we feel that a hard look must be taken at IM utilization relative to the problems to be managed.

This user penetration strategy suggests procedures for the development of a long-range plan for future information utilization at the corporate, division, and function levels of management. The specification of future services is then based on the dynamically changing state of best business practices.

In Exhibit 5-2, we present Richard Nolan's estimates of the penetration of IM by category of management function in each of his six stages of EDP growth. Initially, according to Nolan, all of EDP activity is operational,[3] primarily the automation of accounting transactions. As progress is achieved

Exhibit 5-1 Sample user inventory form.

1 User division (filing system will frequently be coded by user divisions).
2 Name, position, address, and phone number of user.
3 IM representative (an IM representative should be assigned to all senior-level executives in user divisions).
4 Key user-division staff people involved with IM: name, position, address, phone, and relationship to user.
5 IM systems/services currently provided.

System/ Service	Perceived Satisfaction of Users		Quality of Systems/Service (IM Judgment)	Date System Installed	Last Major Upgrade	Est. Future Life
	System Design Features	Operations				

6 Overall potential contribution of IM to this user (summed across several key users to produce potential IM contribution to the user division). This would include potential for cost reduction through automation, better decisions, etc. Perhaps a simple coding for Items 6 and 7 could be used, such as high–moderate–low.
7 Over-all actual contribution of IM to this user.
8 Relative importance of this user in division and company (key measures include user responsibility for dollars of sales and profits, number of people reporting to user).
9 User IM knowledge and experience.
10 User attitudes about IM potential (range from a user who enthusiastically seeks opportunity to utilize new IM capabilities to a strong rejection of all suggestions for additional IM activities).
11 Quality of in-division IM support (could range from a strong IM professional, to the user division that actively supports this user, to no in-division IM competence directly relating to systems professionals in the IM function).
12 Ratings user gives to IM function:

Rating	1 (low)	2	3	4	5 (high)
Overall evaluation					
Timeliness of reports					
Accuracy					
Cost					
Responsiveness to requests for assistance					

Exhibit 5-2 **Nolan's six stages: mode of IM penetration by category of management function.**

	Operational Systems	Management Control Systems	Strategic Planning Systems	Total Systems Resources
Initiation	100%	0%	0%	100%
Contagion	85	15	1	100
Control	80	20	1	100
Integration	65	30	5	100
Data Administration	55	35	10	100
Maturity	45	40	15	100

Source: Richard L. Nolan, "Managing the Crisis in Data Processing," *Harvard Business Review,* March–April 1979, p. 123. © 1979 by the President and Fellows of Harvard College; all rights reserved.

in the sequential implementation of Nolan's stages, operational systems become less important than systems for management control and strategic planning. Progress in the productivity of paperwork processing is obviously an important dimension of the corporate information function. However, as Gorry and Scott Morton[4] and Keen and Scott Morton[5] have clearly documented, the IM function contributes to company performance most through decision support and other executive information systems. These assist senior management in evaluating long-range strategic options to position corporate resources in markets and products.

The major computer hardware and software companies have off-the-shelf systems for supporting many business applications, and there is a sizable literature on systems applications. Seminars and management consultants are other sources of information on the available software to support business activities.

There are advantages for a company that lags behind the vanguard in business computer applications: as in product R&D, running a quick second is frequently more profitable than running the risks of being first. Because of the huge increase during the 1970s in the demands of managers for improved information services, "better" does not mean "adequate." However, it is important to assess the degree of penetration, by division, in operational, management, and planning systems, not simply so as to determine what stage the company is in relative to Nolan's percentages (Exhibit 5-2), but especially so as to determine where the company should be in relation to potential and where efforts and resources must be exerted to move IM penetration in that direction.

Business information planning (S-10) provides a procedure for the specification of cost-effective advanced systems applications relevant to a given business function. These user-division application opportunities should be monitored as part of the inventory of users (S-12). The monitoring of a backlog of such potential systems applications not yet implemented is then a useful practice. A backlog which is large, relative to the systems applications which have been implemented, provides strong evidence of low user penetration, which should be questioned in the review of management practices for that division. Thus, a user penetration strategy can provide a basis for communications between IM and user management as to how well the division is doing in relation to potential.

User Satisfaction Surveys

S-14   USER SATISFACTION SURVEYS

Program for monitoring user satisfaction with IM services.

What is the perceived image of IM in the organization? Is it a cost service bureau? A dictatorship? Or an enlightened instrument of change? How can an information manager—and more importantly, top management—find out for certain how users view the service and the support received? By asking them! This can be done informally, of course, but it can also be done through a formal user-satisfaction survey. The survey can be conducted by the IM division itself, but this approach might tend to inhibit frank and candid responses. As an alternative, management can initiate such a survey, through either some other function (like auditing) or the appointment of an ad hoc committee. Or, finally, the survey can be conducted by an outside consulting firm. The value of the latter approach is that it assures objectivity and, in some cases, allows outside comparisons. That is, if the consulting firm has done similar surveys for other companies, it can provide a general indication of how one company compares with other companies similarly surveyed. Obviously, a positive report validates user satisfaction ratings and is meaningful feedback to top management.

The findings from a user satisfaction survey performed for a commercial bank are presented in Exhibit 5-3. This survey provided a benchmark for measuring future performance in achieving user satisfaction. One by-product of this survey was the discovery that divisions which had some in-division systems capabilities had a higher level of satisfaction with the corporate IM function than the divisions without even one systems staff professional. User satisfaction surveys should provide guidance for actions to improve the effectiveness of IM utilization. User satisfaction is also an input to the inventory of users (S-12).

Exhibit 5-3   Satisfaction by users as perceived by data processing users in divisions of a large commercial bank with and without an in-division systems capability.

Question	Average Satisfaction Scores from Users in Divisions	
	With an In-Division Systems Capability	Without an In-Division Systems Capability
Overall evaluation	4.3[a]	2.4
Accuracy	3.6	3.5
Timeliness	3.9	3.2
Ease of use	4.1	3.1
Responsiveness to requests for change in functions, outputs, etc.	3.9	2.0
Support by data processing— answers to questions, user assistance	3.1	3.4
Integration with other applications	3.1	2.2
Average all questions for each application	3.7	2.8
Number of responses	7	18

Source: A report to the senior management committee of one of the largest commercial banks in the United States. W. H. Gruber and J. S. Niles, *The New Management: Line Executives and Staff Professionals in the Future Firm,* New York: McGraw-Hill, 1976, p. 123.

[a] There were 8 user divisions with a systems capability and 12 user divisions without a systems capability. The findings are based on a calculation of the average scores in the two categories of user divisions. A score of 5 is very satisfied, 4 is satisfied, 3 is neither satisfied nor dissatisfied, 2 is dissatisfied, and 1 is very dissatisfied.

Backlog Task Force

> **S-15   BACKLOG TASK FORCE**
>
> **Users and IM staff form a task force to determine the magnitude of systems backlog, the adequacy of IM resources, and priorities for backlogged projects.**

As noted earlier, most IM organizations are already overloaded with work. If the user penetration strategies suggested here are successful in allocating scarce IM resources where they will do the most good for the company, then it stands to reason that the work load must be given priorities. Some users should get more resources, some less, some none. Yet, this very allocation process is likely to result in cries of unresponsiveness in management's ears. These are likely to have an adverse effect on user relations and on the influence of the IM function. How then, are we to manage this problem? By taking the monkey off the information manager's shoulders and putting it on management's through a backlog task force.

Task force management and ad hoc task forces, formed to address specific problems, are well-known techniques which have been used successfully in business for some time. One application of this technique which we have found particularly effective has been a task force organized to address the "user backlog" problem. A task-force backlog study involves extensive interviews with all users to determine what work is currently outstanding, what is pending, and what is planned or needed in the future. Thus, the task force pulls together in one place *all* existing and future systems work loads. This evaluation can then be matched up with the available manpower to calculate the total systems backlog. A backlog goal can be established (e.g., one rule of thumb for backlog goals might be three to six months for existing systems and two to three years for new development, depending on the industry). If the task force comes up with a work load exceeding this goal, a case is built for additional resources or, at the very least, for a reprioritization of the work load. A task force can give such a study greater credibility and legitimacy than would be the case if IM were to make one alone.

A study team including people from outside the IM function is likely to be viewed by management as being more objective and as having no vested interest in systems per se. To be effective, the task force should probably be kept small, perhaps to five or six people, at least half from outside of the IM function. The participants should preferably have a broad knowledge and understanding of the business, should be capable of assessing needs and priorities in a broad context, and should have the respect of management. This respect is important because their recommendations to management should not only be an accumulation of the systems backlog, it should also include an assessment of the urgency, the criticalness, and the priorities on which resource allocations are to be based. The task force report can establish the total systems backlog, identify the priorities within the organization of the user divisions competing for systems resources, and contain specific recommendations as to supplemental staff needs, the use of outside resources, the suggested allocation of resources, and the cancellation of low-priority projects, if appropriate. *Management* can then make the decisions on staffing, prioritization, and resource allocation. The task force, called into being either on a one-time basis or every five years or so, can be an effective agent for focusing management attention on user needs, resource needs, and the balancing of supply and demand through the maintenance of a proper work-load/manning ratio in the systems organization. At the same time, the task force can take the onus off the IM function, which cannot be accused of unresponsiveness, because management is deciding what's best for the company, and IM is only responding to management's direction.

USER INVOLVEMENT STRATEGIES

If shared management of information resources will be the trend in the 1980s, we will need some strategies to get IM involved with users and users involved with IM. The following strategies cover this process, from getting started, through systems development, to the entire information management activity of the user.

Foot in the Door

> **S-16   FOOT IN THE DOOR**
>
> **IM provides simple, low-cost, rapid response to users in order to demonstrate the costs and benefits of IM services.**

Sometimes, through business information planning (S-10) or some other planning activity, one uncovers an opportunity to get into an area where there has been low use of IM resources. At this early stage, something of value must be demonstrated quickly to convince the potential user of the merits of a proposed system or project so that the user will continue to use IM services. One way to do this is through the foot-in-the-door strategy.

Many of the applications of modern IM resources could be useful to executives who have demonstrated little interest in the utilization of IM to improve the effectiveness of their management practices. In some companies, decisions involving the management of huge amounts of money are made with information technology that is little different from practices of 50 years ago.

It is frequently a strategic error to attempt a major improvement in the utilization of IM resources when the potential user has had little experience with modern technology. Such a user is ill prepared to cope with a massive infusion of new technology. Even if IM specialists see a very favorable benefits-to-cost ratio for a big investment in IM technology, a cautious strategy may be warranted for several reasons: a big proposal may frighten management in the user division; the user may not be prepared to assimilate a major change in its way of doing business; and the user's lack of knowledge of systems and technology could result in communications difficulties and misunderstandings. In such cases, a foot-in-the-door strategy might be useful. Let us cite two examples to illustrate.

Case 1   Foot-in-the-Door Proposal   In this first example, the IM function was interested in finding ways to provide support to a multi-national corporation's fast-growing international activities. The company had three data centers overseas, but no master plan for central automation was being prepared to coordinate growth. The IM organization called management's attention to the need for such a master plan to avoid splintered, incompatible, and redundant operations, and it proposed conducting a simple front-end study to address this issue at a cost of $10,000. The modest funding involved was the foot in the door which lead to approval of the study. Result: the company ultimately implemented a distributed international system in their overseas offices, providing local automation coupled with central control and consolidated management information on overseas activities. The simple foot-in-the-door proposal resulted in an automation master plan, as well as major systems support and penetration in a previously low user of IM services.

Case 2   Quick Prototype   In another example, the IM function wished to extend its support to the marketing managers of the company, which had traditionally been a low user of IM services. The IM people began by interviewing marketing managers to learn their information needs. Rather than attempting to patch up systems to provide this information, or building a major new information system, it was decided simply to draw on various information sources to produce several quick prototype reports as a first step in addressing these managers' information needs. Because these reports were assumed to be throwaway programs requiring several iterations, they were produced through an information center (S-22) using a report generator language. Result: the managers were delighted with this quick promise–deliver approach. They became more interested, participation increased, and a good working relationship was fostered. Here again, a small and experimental foot-in-the-door approach was successful in promoting penetration into the managerial ranks of the company.

Joint Systems Development

> **S-17   JOINT SYSTEMS DEVELOPMENT**
>
> **User involvement in the planning, development, and implementation of new systems to assure systems success.**

Involvement of users in their own projects has been a demonstrated success strategy for years. As far back as 1965, McKinsey & Co. reported on user-involvement in a study of successful and not so successful computer users. The study showed that companies that involved line managers in project planning and development were more successful than those that did not by a factor of 3 to 1. This joint systems development strategy includes the involvement of users in the following four facets of systems projects:

1   Planning.
2   Project team organization.
3   Systems development.
4   Postreview.

An action plan for the implementation of this strategy in each of these four facets of systems development is described below.

Planning   The planning phase deals with business systems planning; that is, the determination of needs and the identification of systems projects that will solve the users' business problems. This phase would be more accurately described as systems involvement with the user, rather than the other way around. See business information planning (S-10) for a more in-depth look at this strategy.

Project Team Organization   We suggest that in every organization, it should be a matter of company policy, endorsed and supported by top management, that high-level user representatives with a thorough grounding in their business should be assigned full time to every major systems project for the duration of the project. The user's representatives on the project are responsible for ensuring that the system delivered is, in fact, what is wanted and needed. This means they are responsible for defining the functional requirements of the system, not the technical development.

Systems Development   As noted above, the user should be committed throughout the project. User management must also be involved in periodic project reviews and approval processes. The user's representatives on the project look out for the user's interests by seeing that systems specifications accurately match needs. Systems development must not simply be left to the systems people; it is the user's responsibility as well. For a detailed discussion of project team organization and user tasks and areas of responsibility throughout a systems project, see the project life-cycle strategy (S-54).

Postreview   Finally, when the project is completed, a postreview (or postaudit) should be conducted to determine whether the project met its goals and projected benefits, what problems were encountered, what lessons were learned, etc. Once again, the user can participate in this review process, as described in postaudits (S-63).

The real benefit of heavy user involvement from the genesis of a systems project through its postaudit is that (1) it ensures that the users will get what they want, and (2) it ensures success. It ensures success because the users feel that it is *their* system—the users, through their representative, have designed and created the system—and creators rarely criticize their own work. Because the users feel that it is their system, they will make a good system work better; and because it is their system, they will even make a *bad* system work. The synergy that results when systems and user personnel work together to provide balanced efficiency (cost-oriented) and effectiveness (results-oriented) can be illustrated by an analogy to Blake's managerial grid as shown in Exhibit 5-4. In this analogy, our vertical scale represents the effectiveness orientation of systems, and the horizontal scale represents the efficiency orientation. The grid suggests that a system developed by a technical group is likely to be highly efficient but may not be effective in terms of the users' needs. Conversely, left to themselves, the users could dream up a utopian information system that produced exactly what was needed (i.e., effectiveness in serving user needs), but with unacceptable costs (i.e., low efficiency). Our recommended strategy of user involvement with systems professionals in joint development efforts fosters the achievement of a balance between the advantages of efficiency and of effectiveness.

Exhibit 5-4   The user and systems relationship: trade-off between efficiency and effectiveness in systems development projects.

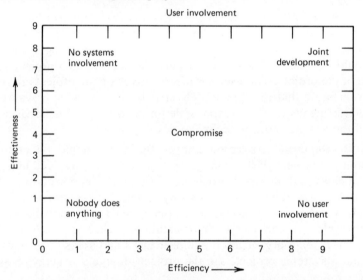

Information Resource Product Managers

S-18   INFORMATION RESOURCE PRODUCT MANAGERS

Shared management of dedicated information resources gives users greater control without their having to become data processing experts.

The ultimate in user involvement is the information-resource-product-manager approach to information management. For years, users have become increasingly frustrated by their inability to control the data processing and systems resources which have become all-important to their business activities. The shortages of analysts and programmers and the prioritization of requests for systems services have often meant that desired projects could just not be done. In fact, in anticipation of rejection, many have not even been requested. On the data processing side, users are often frustrated victims of missing or late reports, computer downtime, or poor response time—none of which they can do anything about. Moreover, they are at the continued mercy of conversions to new systems software or new applications, which again can adversely affect their service levels. The monolithic data center of centralized data processing has many corporate advantages, but users often find it unresponsive to their needs and frustrating to deal with as a service provider.

The great interest which users have shown in distributed processing in recent years (i.e., having their own computers dedicated to only their work) has largely come about because of these frustrations (coupled, of course, with the low cost of minicomputers). However, distributed processing is not without its problems either. Today's minicomputer has more power and complexity than the data center mainframe of just five years ago. Putting this power and sophistication into the hands of inexperienced users, unless they are carefully managed and controlled, can lead to higher costs, loss of control, and chaos. We discuss a strategy to deal with this problem in Chapter 11. For now, we would like to suggest yet another alternative. One might call this approach *centralized processing with dedicated resources* (as opposed to shared resources). This alternative amounts to dedicating both computing and systems resources to a given user's information systems needs, with technical management by the IM function, more or less as a facilities manager. This approach gives users three processing choices: (1) centralized processing with shared resources; (2) centralized processing with dedicated resources; or (3) distributed processing (managing their own resources).

Under a dedicated-resources arrangement, what we have dubbed an *information resource product manager* is appointed to serve as the user's information-processing manager. The product manager is given computing resources, an analyst/programmer team, and whatever else is required for total support of the user's information resource needs. The organizational arrangement is one of matrix management (see S-65). The product manager continues to report administratively to the IM function but also reports functionally to the user function head (i.e., solid line to IM, dotted line to user). A product manager with dedicated resources promises the benefits of both centralization and decentralization without the disadvantages of either. Central IM continues to provide technical direction, professional management, and corporate control over information-processing policies, standards, and procedures. Users get independence, greater responsiveness, and more control over their information resources, without having to become data processing experts in the process. Thus, *a product manager strategy can provide the ultimate in user involvement in the shared management of information resources.*

As central data centers become increasingly large and complex in the years ahead, and as computers become less and less costly, we believe that we will see users increasingly agitating to spin off on their own. One way they will be doing this is through distributed processing: running their own computers. Another way, which we believe will increasingly gain favor in the 1980s, will be centralized processing-dedicated resources, using the product manager/user shared approach to the information-processing resources.

The product manager concept can, in fact, be applied to the full spectrum of information resource management. At one end of the spectrum, we have, as described above, product managers who have all resources dedicated. In another option, product managers would have their own systems and programming resources but would continue to "buy" their computing services from the central data center. Note that the user in such cases would continue to look to the product manager, however, for *all* service. That is, problems with data processing service levels would be taken up not with data processing but with the product manager; hence, there would be *no direct user contact with the data processing department.* Even further along the spectrum would be the users that are too small even to have their own programming team. They could still have a product manager who buys both data processing and systems services from the central IM function, that is, who buys all *shared* resources. Finally, there are the really small users who cannot even afford to have their own dedicated product manager and, in fact, would *share* a product manager with one or more other users.

The options, then, can be summarized as follows:

	Resources		
	Product Manager	Computer(s)	Programmers
Fully dedicated	Dedicated	Dedicated	Dedicated
Partially dedicated	Dedicated	Shared	Dedicated
Product manager dedicated	Dedicated	Shared	Shared
Fully shared	Shared	Shared	Shared

Thus, it can be seen that the product manager approach can work for *all* users, providing a single interface between the user and the IM function for

Exhibit 5-5   Horizontal information management organization.

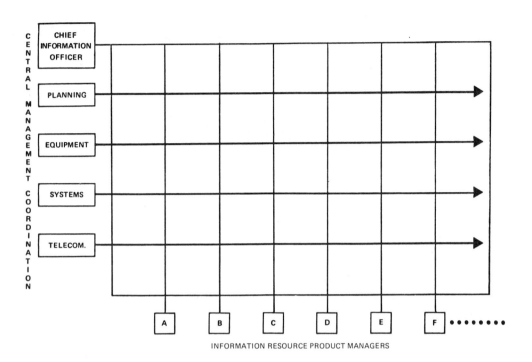

INFORMATION RESOURCE PRODUCT MANAGERS

all user service needs and problems—an arrangement which we believe users would enthusiastically prefer over their present plight of having to deal with a myriad of data processing and systems people to get a response to their needs.

The user-dedicated product manager approach to information management offers an opportunity to adopt a completely different organizational approach to information management. Traditionally, IM has been a *vertical* management scheme, the pyramidal hierarchy. Using product managers, the central IM function manages technology *horizontally*. Central staff responsibility for various technical disciplines (e.g. hardware/software planning, systems, telecommunications) crosses through all IM departments and product managers. The latter, in turn, have line responsibility to run their own operations. This organizational setup is illustrated in Exhibit 5-5. It can be seen that under this arrangement, any number of product managers supporting new services and users could be added without disturbance to other users while IM still retains central coordination and control over technical management disciplines. Best of all, product managers provide true participatory management of information resources between users and the IM function.

USER SERVICE

In this final section on user relations, we present several ideas on how to improve user service levels or, at the very least, to put users and IM on the same wavelength in assessing true performance.

Perception Management

> **S-19 PERCEPTION MANAGEMENT**
>
> Reconciliation of user *perception* of IM performance relative to the *actual* service provided.

We live in an imperfect world. In the words of Gilbert and Sullivan, skim milk frequently passes as cream. Good performance may be unrecognized and unrewarded. Poor performance may also not be recognized. A high-performance IM function should include the measurement of the *actual delivery* of IM services relative to senior management's and other users' perceptions of the quality and usefulness of these services. Performance standards and performance objectives should be established against which users can compare the quality of delivered services.

Winning over users to the belief that the IM function has quality management is a matter of attitude and perception formed through positive feedback and good communications. In other words, it's not enough simply to perform well; one must also publicize that performance. That it is important to control perception can be illustrated by the actual/perceptual relationships in Exhibit 5-6. The goal should be always to have users and senior management in Zone 1; that is, where IM is providing good service and it's perceived that way. If a slip in service moves IM to Zone 2, the tendency will be for management to continue to perceive service as good—for a short time. If there is a good performance reporting (see S-30) system in place, IM will be able to perceive the dropoff in service in time to take immediate corrective action and, thus, keep management in Zone 1. Zone 3 simply means that IM is giving poor service and everyone knows it—corrective action is indicated (a new manager?). Zone 4 is what perception control is all about. IM is giving good service, but it's not perceived that way. How do people fall into Zone 4? Poor communications! If all management ever hears is the bad news and never the good, they will end up with a negative image. For instance, every time the computer goes down, user management hears about it, but when it's up, users hear nothing. (No news is good news?) The fact is that when the

Exhibit 5-6   IM service versus user perception.

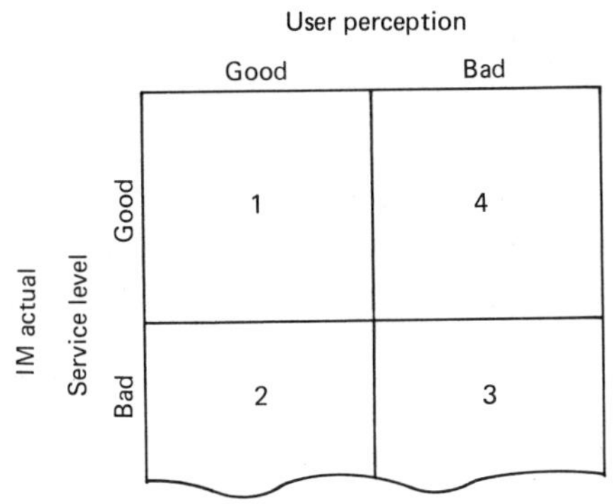

User perception

	Good	Bad
Good	1	4
Bad	2	3

IM actual Service level

computer has been 2% down for the month, it has also been 98% up! Users often prepare internal trouble reports for their management which list every incident of down time but say nothing about the 98% up time. That's why every DP shop needs its own performance measurement reports (see performance reporting, S-30), so that the *total* performance picture can be communicated, both the 2% down and the 98% up.

The second reason that IM falls into Zone 4 is unrealistic expectations. If IM is providing a 98% service level but the user is expecting 100%, he will consider service poor. Some perception control should be applied in the form of education in the realities of service level versus cost trade-off, as discussed under user service contracts (S-20). If a user perceives that the service he or she has paid for is, in fact, 98%, then this becomes the standard, not 100%. All performance measurement reports can then measure actual service against this standard, and realistic expectations will once again bring about proper perception.

Perception management is such an obvious strategy for self-survival that one might question the need for our attention to this facet of management. We have observed too many examples of executives in Zone 4 to treat perception management as an inconsequential factor in success. In fact, we have observed that many executives in Zone 4 complain about service levels while other executives in Zone 2 do not. The *Wall Street Journal* (January 22, 1980, p. 1) reported the findings of an executive placement survey: 83% of fired executives responded that "They didn't aggressively call their superiors' attention to their achievements, preferring that they be rewarded without doing so." Too bad! That's the real world.

User Service Contracts

S-20 USER SERVICE CONTRACTS

Agreements with users on IM performance objectives and measurement, and reporting of actual performance compared with objectives.

Establishing a service contract between data processing and users is another useful strategy for creating a proper perception of DP service levels. What is a user service contract? It is a three-step process:

1 Negotiation of mutually agreed-upon performance objectives, or standards of performance.
2 Development of appropriate tracking tools for measuring performance.
3 Implementation of a reporting system showing how performance measures up to standard.

The *negotiation of standards* begins with a definition of what constitute good data-processing service levels. As a minimum, this definition might include (1) a deadline for the delivery of standard reports; (2) the turnaround time needed for special requests; (3) system availability (downtime, response time); and (4) the quality of the work (reruns, errors).

In connection with deadlines, one should distinguish between critical and noncritical reports. These should have different performance objectives, such as 100% of critical reports, 95% of noncritical delivered on time. Also, the actual time the report is needed should be established. Not all reports are needed at 8:00 A.M. every morning; some can wait until 10:00 A.M., noon, or later. Establishing realistic delivery times also helps immeasurably with production scheduling.

Standards should be agreed upon for the other service functions, such as 2% downtime, 3-second response time 95% of the time, 12-hour turnaround for special request reports, and 2% reruns. Different standards will also apply to different users; since their requirements are not the same, response times may differ by transaction type, for example. This negotiation of standards takes a lot of initial education, discussion, and negotiation, but cooperation with users is usually good because it is being done for the purpose of improving their overall service levels.

Developing tracking tools may initially be a manual effort, particularly the recording of the numerous regular and special reports by function, time of delivery, etc. We cannot offer much on this point, as data tracking is unique to each installation's operating problems. However, once established, the data can usually be collected semiautomatically through established logs and other records and can often be automated, if desired. Systems downtime and response-time records are often maintained anyway, for internal purposes, reducing the amount of collection work necessary to produce the reports.

Implementing the reporting system follows the establishment of standards of performance and the tracking of performance. In general, the simpler the reports, the more useful and effective they will probably be. People turn off on too many numbers. In Exhibit 5-7*a,b,* we show a sample two-page performance report which is probably self-explanatory. As long as IM meets its performance objectives, it has satisfied its user service contract. If it fails to do so, it must take immediate remedial steps to get back to its service goals. What remedies do users have for breech of contract? The usual: appeal to a higher court (i.e., complaints to senior management). But if and when the user does complain, it will be no surprise, since everyone will be working with the same facts. The advantages of a user service contract are as follows:

It promotes better service to users by focusing attention on service and on negative trends.

It aids production scheduling by establishing more realistic report deadlines.

It creates more realistic expectations from users and hence better perception of service level.

It establishes total performance over time, rather than focusing on specific service problems (they see the 98% up, not just the 2% down).

Priorities are known and agreed on ahead of time.

Everyone deals with the same facts and figures; no misunderstanding or misinterpretations.

It provides useful management information.

Another interesting example of an IM performance-measurement system is one marketed by Mathews & Company, Stamford, Connecticut, called Performance Appraisal Reporting Service (PARS). PARS provides a systematic and objective rating of DP performance. A subscriber distributes performance appraisal forms to each user department to complete each month. Users grade IM performance from poor to exceptional in eight different categories: accuracy of reports, timeliness of reports, distribution of reports, meeting implementation schedules, on-line availability, response time, solution of problems, and attitude and cooperativeness. After the user departments complete their appraisals, the appraisals are forwarded to a liaison officer who tabulates and summarizes the ratings and comments. These can then be measured against predetermined objectives as well as against the ratings of other subscribers to the service. The price of the service is a one-time fee of $75 to set up a PARS user on the system, and $500 for a

Exhibit 5-7a User service contract report.

Data Center Performance Summary
On-Line System

December 1980

System Availability

```
         S S       S S        S S        S S  H    S S
Days              1 1 1 1 1 1 1 1 1 1 2 2 2 2 2 2 2 2 2 2 3 3
of the   1 2 3 4 5 6 7 8 9 0 1 2 3 4 5 6 7 8 9 0 1 2 3 4 5 6 7 8 9 0 1
Month    ----------------------------------------------
100          *     *      *   * *     * *  * *      * * *     *
 —                                      *                          Performance
 —       ------------------------------------------------------- Objective    98%
 —          *    *      *                                          Actual
 95                                                                Availability 97.0%
A —
V —
A —
I —
L 90
A —
B —
L —
E —
 85
 —
 —          *
 —
 80              A                    B
```

Code: A = 74% avail on the 11th
Code: B = 77% avail on the 24th

On-Line System Start-up
No. Proc. days   20
No. days up on time   19

On-Line System Outages
Recovery Time:
  1–15 mins   4
  16–30 mins   6
  31–60 mins   0
  61 or more   2
Total outages   12

User Response Time

Application	% of Trans Less than 3 Seconds	Perf Obj	% of Trans Less than 5 Seconds	Perf Obj	% of Trans Less than 10 Seconds	Perf Obj
International						
December	60%	60%	85%	88%	96%	97%
November	61%	60%	86%	88%	97%	97%
October	55%	60%	81%	88%	95%	97%
September	55%	60%	81%	88%	95%	97%
August	62%	60%	88%	88%	97%	97%
July	62%	60%	83%	88%	97%	97%

Exhibit 5-7b User service contract report.

Data Center Performance Reports
Overnight Batch Production
Commercial Banking

December 1980

	Input		Reports Distributed									Reprints		
Application	No. Rcvd	% Late	No. Sched	No. Req	Tot Repts	Crit Repts	% On Time	Perf Obj	Other Repts	% On Time	Per Obj	No.	%	Per Obj
Affl loan	1	0	2	0	2	0	—	—	2	100%	95%			
Cml loan	20	0	383	7	390	359	96%	100%	31	100%	95%	1	0.2%	.5%
Collat loan pri	5	0	20	0	20	0	—	—	20	100%	95%			
Data sec & priv	2	0	14	0	14	4	25%	100%	10	100%	95%	1	7.1%	.5%
Dep acctg hist	1	0	16	0	16	8	100%	100%	8	100%	95%			
Factoring	86	0	666	20	686	337	93%	100%	349	94%	95%	5	0.7%	.5%
Fed tax deposit	8	0	11	0	11	0	—	—	11	100%	95%			
Tot cust relat	Online	—	357	3	360	0	—	—	360	99%	95%	1	0.2%	.5%
Lease acctg sys	20	0	23	0	23	23	95%	100%	0	—	—	2	8.6%	.5%
Division totals	143	0	1,492	30	1,522	731	%	100%	791	97%	95%	10	0.6%	%

12-month subscription for in-house (or off-premise) service ratings. This fee entitles the subscriber to three comparative performance reports each month. A sample PARS report is shown in Exhibit 5-8.

The comparative performance report is prepared monthly by Mathews & Company for each PARS subscriber. It is designed especially for IM managers and other corporate managers in the subscriber organization.

Exhibit 5-8   Comparative DP performance report.

Comparative DP Performance Report

Ms. Mary Smith   *January, 1980*
Liaison Officer   Period covered
New Town Bank & Trust Company
One Main Street
New Town, TX 10001

Percent of Performance Objective Attained	*Our Organization*	*Similar Organizations*	*Number of Subscribers*
This month	90%	93%	44
Average for prior three months	88%	91%	
Average for prior six months	86%	89%	

Comparison of User Satisfaction
(Rating of 1–3, with 1.0 being Poor
and 3.0 being Good.)

Performance Criteria	*This Month's Ratings*	
1. Accuracy of reports	3.0	2.9
2. Timeliness of reports	2.7	3.0
3. Distribution of reports	3.0	3.0
4. Meeting implementation schedules	2.5	2.6
5. On-line availability	3.0	2.9
6. Response time	2.9	3.0
7. Solution of problems	2.5	2.7
8. Attitude and cooperativeness	2.5	2.6
Average rating	2.7	2.8

User Participation
Number of service appraisals distributed   24
Number of service appraisals included   22

Copyright © by Mathews & Company 1980

Customer Service Center

> **S-21   CUSTOMER SERVICE CENTER**
>
> **Provides users with a single service facility for two-way communications about user complaints, service status, downtime, and other problems.**

A simple strategy for improving user satisfaction is the establishment of a customer service center within the data processing department. It works the same way as the complaint department in a department store or as making service calls to a vendor to report hardware problems. The responsibility of the service center is to keep apprised of both production and output distribution problems so as to keep users informed when downtimes, reruns, or backlog problems will affect on-line operations, report deliveries, and the like. The service center gives users a single telephone number to call about service problems. A specific individual can be left in charge of the service phone, with backup as necessary to cover lunch hour and other absences. If there is a quality assurance function (S-61) in place, the service center could be part of that function, or the people who prepare user service reports might also staff the service center. It's not important who does it; it can even be a part-time assignment, depending on the size of the organization. The important thing is to give users a single place to call for information on production status or problems which are affecting them, or simply to register complaints about service, late reports, etc.

Channeling service calls in this manner provides a central log of user complaints and problems so that they can be more efficiently followed up and resolved. It is less frustrating to users than being shuffled around from place to place trying to get answers, and it is less disturbing to the data processing staff, who can concentrate on solving problems rather than on handling phone calls about them. When one calls the telephone company to report a problem, it's nice to have one service number to call, and even nicer to know the individual to whom one is reporting the problem; one gets answers and feels she or he is getting service responsiveness. The customer service center can do the same thing for users. The benefits include:

Higher user service levels through an increased services orientation.

Quick response to and resolution of user problems.

Provision of a single data-center interface for users with service problems.

Assistance to users so that they use the data center more efficiently.

A note of caution, however; the customer service center cannot be an ineffective user interface. It needs a good, in-place information system that provides intelligent answers to users' inquiries. If the customer service center really has no information and must chase it down in every instance, users will soon lose confidence in its efficacy. So, an information system must be developed and put in place *before* the customer service center is established, so that responses to customers will be rapid, accurate, and creditable. If the center works in this manner, it will very likely be welcomed by users as an aid to the resolution of service problems.

Information Centers

> **S-22   INFORMATION CENTERS**
>
> User and/or systems groups specially trained in the use of query language/report writer to provide fast turnaround to user requests for information, data analyses, special reports, and other one-shot information needs.

Information centers can do two valuable things: (1) they can provide quick response to special information requests from users; and (2) they can reduce maintenance programming. Both of these are highly desirable goals. Our information center strategy suggests combining two ideas into one: quick-response reports and user information centers.

The *quick-response-report* (QRR) group is an information center established within the IM function. It can be either a team of systems professionals or a single individual on each project team trained in the use of query language/report writer capability. There are a number of these languages around today (DPL, QBE, RAMIS, FOCUS, etc.) that could be selected as an installation standard for this purpose. The function of the QRR people would be to handle one-time requests for information, data analyses, special reports, etc., that are contained in data files maintained on the company's *mainframe* computer.

Today, there are many huge systems-application data bases. The standard reports from these application systems frequently do not provide answers to the current problems of users. The modification of a large application system is often a tedious task that requires days, weeks, and sometimes even months to program. When a user has a problem that is not solved by a standard report, the IM response can frequently be a QRR program that produces a specific analysis from data stored as part of an existing application system.

High-level query languages and report writers enable quick response to special user requests for information. These high-level languages frequently combine report writer, query, analysis, and data-base management capabilities. They are very effective when programmed by competent IM professionals who have been trained to use them. These high-level programs tend not to be as efficient in the production of ongoing systems, which are usually written in more standard computer languages such as COBOL. However, for quick-response, one-of-a-kind reports requested by users, these high-level programs provide an extraordinary resource for fast IM responsiveness, usually an overnight turnaround.

A *user information center* is a similar idea, except that here, the QRR capability is placed directly in the hands of users. That is, one or more users are trained in the query language/report writer capability so that they can provide the same quick extraction and/or manipulation of data for themselves without requiring IM function intervention. Separate information centers could be established in as many user areas as desired. To the extent that users are able to satisfy their own information needs, the maintenance programming burden on the IM function is obviously relieved. The main distinction between QRR groups and user information centers is that the former generally resides in the IM function and uses a standard query language to access mainframe data files to satisfy quick turnaround information needs. The latter resides in a user area and usually works with extract files that have been down-loaded from the company's central mainframe computer to a minicomputer located in the user area. The query language/report writer capability is usually a utility program provided by the minicomputer vendor. Other than this difference, the function of the information center is the same as that of the QRR group. In fact, the QRR group can be used as a backup to the information center in that it can be called upon whenever the information desired is not contained in the user's minicomputer, or whenever a more complex program is needed than can be provided by the information center. In this way, the QRR group can serve as consultants, advisers, and professional programmers for user information centers. The combination of *user* information centers and *IM* QRR people can provide a very powerful quick-turnaround information response to management information requests.

At a recent GUIDE meeting (IBM users group), the authors were struck by the number of companies discussing their use of information centers and the excellent response of the management people who were the beneficiaries of this quick-response capability.

Performance sells, and senior executives and other users can be astounded at the fast response time that is possible with such high-level report generation groups. We expect such centers to grow rapidly in the next few years as more and more companies acquire minicomputers in user areas that come with built-in query language utilities.

Charge-out System

S-23   USER-ORIENTED CHARGE-OUT SYSTEM

IM charge-out system based on user-understood business units rather than on technical computer-resource units of little value to users.

The other side of the delivery of services is the payment for such services. There is nothing worse than to be perceived as providing poor service and overcharging for it as well. It helps if the user at least understands the charges for data processing services. The problem is that most charge-out systems for DP services are based on computer-resource pricing; that is, all costs are reduced to unit rates expressed in CPU seconds, memory occupancy (bytes/sec.), tape and disk I/Os (input-output operations) etc. The main problem with such systems is that they are expressed in data processing terms and not in user terms. Hence, users do not really understand the charges and find that it is difficult to forecast their costs. Frequently, users distrust the fairness of the charge algorithm. *For a charge-out system to be truly effective, it must be easy to communicate and easy for a user to understand.* From a user standpoint, this means stating DP costs in familiar terms. A user-oriented charge-out system, then, is one which translates DP costs from computer-resource pricing to transaction pricing.

One advantage of a transaction-pricing, user-oriented, charge-out system is that the user can understand the basis for assessments for DP services. A second advantage is that productivity improvement from one year to the next can be measured in terms that have meaning for users.

Transaction pricing converts DP costs to some unit of measurement which is appropriate to the users' business. For example, charges may be based on number of accounts (checking account application), number of employees (payroll), number of checks written (accounts payable), number of items in inventory (inventory control), etc. If users know that their charge will be 50 cents per account, a forecast of charges can be made with reasonable accuracy just by projecting expected business volume—something the user can certainly understand and do. The standard cost to be applied to unit pricing, however, should be established once a year (preferably at budget time) and should not be adjusted each month. That is, the total charge to the user should vary only with the volume processed, not with changes in the cost per unit. For example, a checking account application in a bank being charged 50 cents per month per account would vary according to the number of accounts on the file each month, but the 50 cents per account would remain unchanged for the year, even if actual costs were different. This procedure is consistent with most standard cost systems in manufacturing. Given an estimate of standard costs and a forecast of sales volume, companies then set a price which will return the desired profit margin. If, after some period of time, the profit margin proves unsatisfactory, the company may choose to increase the price, but usually it will not increase the price from month to month just because manufacturing costs fluctuate. In the same way, the price per unit given the user for DP charges should be established at the beginning of the year based on estimated costs and usage rates, and then it should be left undisturbed until the following year. If total costs are not recovered, the rate can be adjusted upward next year.

The main weaknesses of this strategy are that (1) not all applications are easily adaptable to unit pricing, so some combination of units may have to be used; (2) some applications may require establishing both a fixed charge (where costs are insensitive to volume) and a variable charge, complicating the charging system; and (3) unit pricing is not entirely accurate since it does not charge for the actual work done (e.g., on-line inquiries, special report requests, and transactions of varied complexity). On the other hand, the benefits of a charge-out system in user terms include these: (1) the user is better able to forecast DP costs and to rely on the charges for the entire year; (2) because the system is simple to understand, there will be fewer complaints and less user dissatisfaction with the charge-out system; and (3) productivity gains can be more easily demonstrated when the unit price is later lowered (with improving power/cost ratios, this should be the case, over time). We believe the benefits outweigh the weaknesses, and thus, a user-oriented charge-out strategy warrants careful consideration. A simplified example of such a system is reviewed in the appendix at the conclusion of this chapter.

For a discussion of a more complex but highly accurate and fair system of DP costing, we refer the reader to the Bank Administration Institute publication "EDP Facility Accounting, Implementation," by Kenneth W. Kolence,[6] which is an attempt to establish an industry standard for banking. Mr. Kolence has since joined the Institute for Software Engineering, where he has expanded the publication for EDP organizations in general; it is available from that source. In this publication, the author presents the concept of *software work* in DP costing. Software work represents a common unit of computer usage (defined as the alteration of a byte of media by a processor) which enables repeatable measures of usage and, therefore, repeatable charges (the lack of which is one of the weaknesses of most computer-resource pricing systems). Since most DP accounting systems measure usage in terms of CPU seconds, K-seconds, I/Os, etc., these must be converted to software work. To put the results into user terms, software work is then converted to transaction pricing. For readers interested in the accuracy and the consistency of costs, this publication is probably the most exhaustive treatment available.

Appendix A   A How-To on Transaction Pricing

TRANSACTION PRICING SYSTEM

The following process describes a relatively simple and straight-forward computer resource cost recovery system converted to standard cost transaction pricing, in user terms.

Step 1 *Allocate DP Expenses to Hardware Classes*

All DP costs are allocated to hardware classes used in the pricing algorithm as in the example shown in the following table.

Estimated Expenses, Coming Year	Allocation CPU	Memory	Disks	Tapes	Printers	Card R/P Paper	Special Purpose Equipment
Salaries and benefits	Production salaries allocated as relevant, e.g., computer operators to CP, printer operators to printers, etc.						
Equipment	Specific annual cost of each hardware item (rent or depreciation and maintenance)						
Occupancy	Based on square feet occupied by total computer room divided by *all* occupancy costs						
Insurance	Premium, by device						
Forms and supplies	Specific to hardware items, but bulk allocated to paper costs, which is a direct charge to users						
Special purpose equipment	Direct charge to users						
Allocated charges Total	—————	Allocated, based on previously distributed expense					

Step 2   *Calculate Unit Device Cost*

Determine the standard cost for each hardware class based on the total cost for that class (from Step 1) divided by the usable capacity, for example:

$$\text{Unit device rate} = \frac{\text{Total cost, hardware class}}{\text{Usable capacity}}$$

or in the example below:

$$\frac{\$657,000}{18,869,760} = \$.0348 \text{ per CP second}$$

Hardware Class	Total (From Step 1)	Usable Capacity*	Unit Device Rate	Unit Expression
CPU	$657,000	18,869,760	.0348	CP sec
Memory				Ksec
Disk				I/Os
Tape				Allocated seconds
Printer				Lines printed
Card R/P				Cards processed

In this case, the standard cost for each CP second would be $0.0348. Repeat for each hardware class.

* Usable capacity in this case was arrived at as follows:

Annual hours of operation × % usage × units per hour × # devices
7.488   ×   70%   ×   3600 sec.   × 1 = 18,869,760 CP sec.

Annual hours of operation assumes 26 days per mo. × 24 hrs. per day × 12 months.
Percentage usage assumes 30% is lost to preventive maintenance, reruns, downtime, etc. (This will vary by device, by installation experience, and by the method of treating reserve capacity) (see Step 3).

Step 3 *Calculate User Charges*

The unit device rates (from Step 2) are next multiplied by actual device utilization, by application, to obtain monthly user charges. Actual usage data is derived from system measurement data (e.g., IBM's System Measurement Facility (SMF)) massaged by some sort of job accounting system.

$$\text{Unit device rate} \times \text{actual device utilization} = \text{User charge}$$
$$\$0.0348 \times 154{,}167 \text{ CP sec} = \$5{,}365 \text{ month (CP charge)}$$

Repeat for each hardware class to accumulate total user charges, for example:

Hardware	Monthly Charge
CP charge	$ 5,365
Memory	—
Disk	—
Tape	—
Printer	—
Card R/P	—
Other	—
Total	$15,000

Except for month-end processing, a month's activity is probably sufficient to establish average costs. However, the results of several months, or several runs in the case of month-end runs, can be used if it is felt that a better averaging is needed.

Note: In Step 2 we deducted reserve capacity in arriving at usable capacity. The problem with this method is that it penalizes current users by making them pay for the corporation's reserve capacity and discourages usage, leaving the remaining users with even higher unit costs. This is known as the capacity/price spiral. An alternative is to assume no reserve capacity (in Step 2) and to charge the difference between capacity and actual utilization to corporate overhead. This method results in lower unit rates to users and thus lower rates.

Step 4 *Convert to User Transaction Pricing*

The user's transaction prices (charges) are the total charges (from Step 3) divided by the appropriate unit of measurement agreed upon for each application:

$$\text{Transaction price} = \frac{\text{Total monthly charge}}{\text{Number of transaction units}}$$

Example

$$\frac{\$15,000}{30,000 \text{ accounts}} = 0.50 \text{ per account}$$

The standard cost in user terms is thus established as 50 cents per account per month. To forecast annual DP costs, the user need now only estimate the number of accounts to be serviced and multiply by 12. However, several other points bear noting:

High fixed overhead costs might suggest the need for two charges: a fixed charge based on total accounts plus a variable charge based on transaction volume.

A differential charge (premium) may be desired to influence user behavior (e.g., acceptance of overnight or longer turnaround times).

It may be desirable in some cases to carry a separate charge for special-report requests.

On-line device usage may be difficult to get, necessitating the use of a flat percentage charge rather than a measured use charge.

These exceptions do not necessarily create problems if appropriate adjustments are made to accommodate them. For instance, the use of penalty rates differential and special-report charges will result in a profit for the data center (may be desirable?) unless the rates are adjusted downward for regular production—that is, to increase the reserve capacity (Step 2)—thus providing a lower unit-device rate for regular production. If detailed device-usage data are not available for on-line systems, one can usually find a way to estimate the percentage of each resource used by each application, then extrapolate CP seconds, K-seconds, device I/Os, etc., from these.

NOTES

1 Dixon Doll as quoted by Brad Schultz in "Interview with Dixon Doll," *Computerworld,* March 18, 1981, p. 14.

2 "Solving a Computer Mismatch in Management," *Business Week,* April 2, 1979, p. 77.

3 Richard L. Nolan, "Managing the Crises in Data Processing," *Harvard Business Review,* March–April 1979, pp. 116, 118.

4 G. Anthony Gorry and Michael S. Scott Morton, "A Framework for Management Information Systems," *Sloan Management Review,* Fall 1979, pp. 55–70.

5 Peter G. W. Keen and Michael S. Scott Morton, *Decision Support Systems,* Reading, Mass.: Addison-Wesley, 1978.

6 Kenneth Kolence, *EDP Facility, Accounting: Implementation,* Bank Administration Institute, 1975.

Top Management: Closing the Communications Gap

The by-product approach is undoubtedly the predominant method in determining executive information needs. . . . It has the paper-processing tail wagging the information dog.

John F. Rockart[1]

TOP MANAGEMENT INVOLVEMENT

Just as user involvement is indispensable to successful project management, so management involvement with IM will be a critical success factor in achieving IM effectiveness in the organization of the 1980s. This fact was underscored at the 1978 SMIS conference by A. Jackson Forster, who said:

> The importance of top management involvement and input must be considered by the Management Information Systems (MIS) professionals as critical to the success of the MIS activities. The rationale is simple and basic: without management support and input, a companywide commitment to MIS will not exist . . . this lack of commitment will be significantly detrimental in terms of the development and approval of an MIS master plan as well as the availability of adequate budget and resources.
>
> It is essential, therefore, that the MIS executive clearly understands the proper role and relationships between top management and MIS and, most importantly, identifies those strategies and techniques that will result in effective top management input into the master MIS plan.[2]

William Woodside, president of American Can, speaking on the necessity for top management involvement in information planning had this to say:

> Taking this kind of strategic look at our information capabilities and needs was not a minor undertaking. It required, of course, my own commitment, but more importantly included extensive involvement of virtually all the execu-

tive and senior management in our entire corporation. I believe this level of involvement is absolutely essential for the success of any company's information function.[3]

In setting the direction for their information-planning activities, Woodside reported that American Can took three basic steps:

1 The first step was to revise the organization of the information management group. Centralized management and direction of all information activities was placed under a single unit to ensure that systems would be developed in a professional manner, and that critical data about profitability and productivity would be provided consistently across all business units.

2 Second, to close the communications gap between line management and technical information people, they upgraded the business quality of the information organization by placing people there who were equally proficient as businessmen and as systems people. They were expected to contribute more than just the technical answers to business unit management.

3 The third major change was the establishment of management advisory committees in the key business areas. Each committee was composed of business unit managers and key resource heads. Committee members were charged with the responsibility for establishing priorities, approving systems plans, and monitoring all information programs.

Woodside went on to say:

. . . the executives who will manage corporations in the future must include the ability to manage information as an essential skill in their management portfolio. I believe that no company will be able to ignore information as a resource, and that resource requires the same level of management attention and control as other assets in order to be successful in today's fast-moving business environment.[4]

The strategies discussed in this chapter have one thing in common: they focus on improving communications with top management. It is the information manager's job to promote this improvement, not top management's. We have found that surprisingly few information managers make a strong effort to get time with senior management in order to help them understand the issues, trends, and problems of information management, perhaps because few information managers, as yet, report directly to the top. This is gradually changing, but in the meantime, there is no reason not to be active with top management. Executive information systems can be developed, and top management support can be enlisted—if information managers can learn to communicate with the top and close the dysfunctional communication gap which has plagued DP managers since the introduction of computers more than 25 years ago.

EXECUTIVE INFORMATION SYSTEMS

John F. Rockart, director of the Center for Information Systems Research at MIT, has documented the peculiar willingness of information mangers to neglect the needs of senior corporate executives.[5] Efforts to provide information services to senior corporate management can provide a far greater contribution to corporate performance and higher rewards for information management than the use of resources to serve lower-level managers and clerical staffs. Yet, despite the obvious differences in contribution, information managers and staff professionals in many companies tend to devote most of their time and energy to serving the lower end of the corporate hierarchy.

Computer outputs produced by the IM function are only rarely used directly by senior corporate executives. Instead, if there is relevant information in IM reports, it is discovered by people in other corporate functions, who then reorganize the data for presentation to top management.

Rockart has made an important contribution in this regard in pointing out the way for IM functions to meet specific executive information needs. His methodology for accomplishing this is the critical success factors (CSF) method.

James Rude, of Rude, Harvey Schwartz and Associates, says there are five types of executive information needs: comfort information (state-of-the-business data); problem information (project progress or problems); outsider information (sensitive data for outside consumption, e.g., earnings data for stock analysts); external intelligence information (competitive and business environment data); and internal operating information (key indicators of business health).

One of the realizations to come from a number of research efforts devoted to executive information needs, however, is that most of these top management data are soft data rather than hard data. That is, the sources of most executives' information is verbal and short (telephone and personal conversations) and comes mainly from trusted associates and advisers. Such information has the advantage of being received more quickly and of being timelier and probably more relevant than hard data.

Very little executive information today comes from computer-based systems. Even computer-prepared financial data are usually reformulated before they get to the executive level. Why is this so? Because most hard information going to top executives is usually a by-product of underlying record-keeping systems which were designed for another purpose. A true executive information system (EIS) should be a *top-down system* rather than a bottom-up system. This means starting at the top, with the executives themselves, to find out what information they need to do their jobs. This is what Rockart's CSF method does, so it's a good place to start in closing the communications gap with senior management.

CRITICAL SUCCESS FACTORS (CSF)

> **S-24   CRITICAL SUCCESS FACTORS**
>
> **Identification of the small number of factors critical to successful performance, and the implementation of executive information systems to monitor activity on the critical factors.**

In the 1960s and 1970s, most organizations concentrated on automating their labor-intensive operations. Now that this has been done, we finally have the opportunity in the 1980s to address the information needs of *managers,* not just clerks. If we are to be successful, however, we must improve the quality of the information that managers receive. How should we go about learning what information managers need? In Chapter 4 we discussed business information planning (S-10) as a technique for determining user needs and identifying new systems projects. While this technique is particularly useful for projects, Rockart's critical success factors method is even better suited to identifying the important information needs of top executives.

Rockart identified four popular techniques for determining management information needs. These he called the *by-product* approach, the *null* approach, the *key indicator* system, and the *total study* process, which we summarize as follows:

In the *by-product* approach, the primary emphasis is on developing applications systems. As a *by-product* of these systems, reports are made available to management. This is by far the predominant approach to information management needs today.

The *null* approach suggests that since executives receive the bulk of their information informally and verbally from trusted advisers, no attempt should be made to provide computer-based (hard) data to top management.

The *key indicator* system is based on the premise that a set of key indicators can be used to get a picture of the health of the business and that exception reports based on these key indicators should be produced only when performance is significantly different from expected results.

The *total study* approach is, in fact, based on IBM's planning methodology, which was described under business information planning (S-10) in Chapter 4.

Rockart suggested that all of these methods have their shortcomings. One is that they do not provide the full range of information needed by senior management; that is, they may be limited to financial data or application systems data, not the total of hard and soft data needed. Another shortcoming is that they are not tailored to the information needs of individual managers. They aim more at organizational positions than at the individuals who occupy those positions. To overcome these shortcomings, Rockart proposed the use of the CSF method for identifying executive information needs, which he described as follows:

> Critical success factors are, for any business, the limited number of areas in which results, if they are satisfactory, will ensure successful competitive performance for the organization. They are the few key areas where "things must go right" for the business to flourish. If results in these areas are not adequate, the organization's efforts for the period will be less than desired.[6]

CSF depends on the use of short interview sessions with top executives that focus on the few key areas of the business where things must go right. Usually any one executive should monitor only six or eight of these factors. When these factors have been identified, measurements can be devised and reports produced to provide the monitoring and control process. The four sources of these factors are (a) the industry (i.e., each industry has critical success factors that are relevant to any company in it); (b) the company (i.e., the dominant companies in the industry generally provide factors significant to smaller companies in the industry); (c) the environment (e.g., consumer needs, the economy, political factors in the countries where the company operates, resource problems); and (d) temporal organizational factors (i.e., areas of company activity that normally do not warrant concern, but that are currently unacceptable and need attention; for example, loan losses in a bank).

Critical success factors generally vary from organization to organization, from time period to time period, and from manager to manager. The steps involved in CSF are to:

1 Identify the objectives of the organization.
2 Determine those few factors critical for accomplishing those objectives.
3 Determine a few prime measurements of those factors (both hard and soft data).
4 Develop appropriate management reports of those measurements.
5 Provide follow-up activities to improve results.

While the CSF analysis process should begin at the top of the organization, CSF can also be used to zero in on specific functions of the organization. For example, one of the authors used the CSF method in addressing the information needs of the senior lending management of his bank. Through interviews with top management and several lending division heads, it was determined, in summary, that the three most critical factors in successful loan management were (a) quality loan officers; (b) quality loans; and (c) effective business development. These factors were divided into various subfactors so that measurements could be developed. For example, a measurement of the quality of loan officers might be their loan loss record, or the new business generated. Quality loans can be measured through a rating system (on a scale of 1 to 10, for example) and then determining the percentage of the loan portfolio that falls in each class. Business development can be measured by the number, size, and profitability of new accounts or loans generated over time, by geographic region, etc. With these measurements in hand, systems can be developed to produce reports that compare performance with expectations.

CSF was also applied to help measure the effectiveness or performance of the IM function in the organization. The critical success factors in this case were developed from these viewpoints: top management, user management, and the information manager. As shown in Exhibit 6-1, these might be summarized by four critical success factors in the performance evaluation of the IM function: (a) management and user satisfaction; (b) quality IM people; (c) efficient use of resources; and (d) good service. Having established these as the critical success factors for the IM function with senior and user management, one must then determine the current status of these factors in the organization, take steps to make improvements where needed, find ways to measure these factors, and, finally, communicate CSF to senior and user management.

Exhibit 6-1   The IM function: critical success factors.

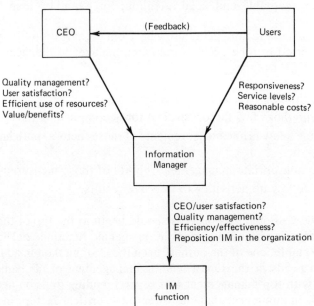

Measurement techniques for IM performance have always been seriously deficient in the eyes of top management. Since top management thinks in terms of business performance, sales, new business, earnings, and key business indicators, it has always been difficult to develop rational standards of measurement of the performances of IM to produce information on their business indicators by identifying the key elements of data most important to monitor. CSF can work in a variety of ways. We saw it used to identify management's concerns with IM so that performance measures could be devised to address them. We saw it used to help define the information needs of a specific function in the organization, and we can see that, similarly, it could do the same for top management's information needs as well. Once executive information needs have been identified, computer-based hard data *can* be put together to supplement the executives' soft data input, and these data, too, can be quick, timely, and relevant. Quick and timely data can be provided in a variety of ways through computer systems tools such as on-line query systems, report generators, computer graphics systems, analysis-type systems (such as IBM's Trend Analysis/370), and decision support systems. Two of these particularly (decision support system and graphics systems) represent, in our opinion, two underutilized, high-potential strategies for serving senior executives and thus we include them here as suggested strategies to serve top management's information needs.

DECISION SUPPORT SYSTEMS (DSS)

> **S-25 DECISION SUPPORT SYSTEMS**
>
> **Computer programs, models, and data organized to provide quick response to analyses or information requested by executives to support decision making.**

As indicated earlier, the 1960s saw computers put to work largely in the batch processing of huge volumes of transactions, bringing productivity to bear on clerical operations. In the 1970s, as most of these clerical systems were automated, some attention began to be given to putting these machines to work for managers, and not just clerks. Progress, however, has been slow, primarily because automating the work of managers requires a real understanding of what managers do. Technologists have been slow to learn and understand the needs of their business. Yet here is where the real productivity benefits of automation can be made to pay off, in helping managers to make better decisions, to control their business better, and to have information at their fingertips when they need it.

Putting the computer to work for managers will be the real challenge for information managers in the 1980s. We discussed one way of addressing this challenge: through the CSF strategy. Another is through the development of more decision support systems (DSS). A DSS is an interactive computer system which is used directly by a manager to help improve his or her judgment and decision making in a semistructured environment. Traditional computer systems take on structured tasks in ways that increase efficiency. A DSS works in a semistructured environment in ways that increase the effectiveness of the decision makers. Developing such systems for management, however, is a difficult task because it requires two-way education. The information manager has to learn a great deal more about the business and the decision-making process of the managers, and the managers need a better understanding of how the computer can help them to do their job better.

Many managers do not believe the computer to be of any value to them because they do not perceive how the computer can help them make better decisions. Another problem is the backlog of work in most organizations. Lack of resources often prevents experimentation and research into management decision systems. Cost-justification concerns also work against experimentation with high-risk and unquantifiable benefit systems, such as a DSS. A DSS is complex, costly, high-risk, and not easily cost-justified, and it requires a unique blending of technical capability and managerial decision analysis—the manager learning what a computer can do, the systems developer learning the business and the decision-making process. For these reasons, the use of DSS has been slow to develop. Practically all of the experimental development work has been done either in universities or by consultants, as Keen and Scott Morton observed:

> None of the DSS with which we are familiar have been built within the main EDP department. In fact, in several of the systems, the organization's EDP group was seen as the enemy. S. A. Alter's survey of 56 systems (1975) reaches the same conclusion. . . . One implication of Alter's study, which found that not one of the 56 systems studied was developed within the corporate data processing group, is that innovations in the use of computers are increasingly initiated by line departments, drawing on outside consultants.[7]

While Keen and Scott Morton have documented the dismal history of the IM function in developing and implementing decision support systems, we believe this history is not due to any shortcoming in ability or resources. Rather, we suggest it has been due to an unfortunate preoccupation with clerical systems in the past. Concentration on the labor-intensive automation opportunities in the company has, up to now, kept most IM functions busy trying simply to keep up with demand and get the daily product out the door. On the other hand, consultants and university people have had more time to do the research necessary and to work with managers to understand their business, their decision-making processes, and their information needs.

Thus, most DSS departments have been created in this way, and the work along these lines done by in-house IM organizations has been small. Now that much of the clerical automation is done, many companies are beginning to pay more attention to higher management's needs, and DSS services are beginning to be developed in-house by the IM function, whose staff members have learned the business and are making a greater attempt to emphasize the development of management systems.

As an example, in critical success factors (S-24), we showed how the CSF concept was used in senior management interviews at The First National Bank of Boston to learn their information needs in relation to the management of the bank's loan portfolio.

The DSS that resulted from that exercise was reviewed in Case 6 of Chapter 3 (p. 62). It will be recalled that a number of existing systems were integrated into a new minicomputer data-base system called the *lending management information system* (LMIS). Here is an example of a DSS *created by the IM function,* which—through the combination of a dedicated minicomputer, a query language/report writer utility program, existing information systems, and a greater knowledge of the business information needs of credit managers—enabled the building of a very powerful management decision-aid system with a minimum of resources in a very short time. Given today's technology aids, a DSS does not have to be a major, multiyear systems effort. To show the reader how this decision support system can be used, let us run through the hypothetical scenario of a loan manager who has just received a request for additional credit from a large corporate customer.

The manager goes to the terminal outside his office, which is shared with one or two other loan managers (in some cases, administration assistants might actually operate the terminal). The first three questions he has are: What is the current indebtedness of this company? What other business do we do with this company? What is its financial condition? To get the answers, he first calls in the commercial loan file, which lists the details of any outstanding loan. Next, the total customer relationship file gives him information on any other loan arrangements made with the company or any of its subsidiaries around the world, as well as information about other business the company maintains within the bank. Then, the automated financial analysis file is requested to produce a financial analysis of the company, consisting of a printout of its latest balance sheet and operating statement, a calculation of financial ratios, and a cash flow projection. He now adds new data which assume approval of the current loan request—that is, loan added to balance sheet, and interest burden and sales projection (based on new loan) added to operating statement—and produces new pro forma statements, ratios, and cash flows five years into the future based on these new data. He now calls in the credit file to read over comments and notes which have been added to the file from previous dealings with the company. Having decided to present this new loan report to the bank's senior credit committee, he now requests that a loan request form be printed. This request produces a stan-

dard form with fields completed with the data previously extracted as to
current loans outstanding and worldwide business relationships. He fills in
the terms and conditions of the current loan request and adds free-form comments as desired (word processing merged with data processing). The completed loan request form is then printed. He adds the financial analysis
reports previously calculated, and the package is ready to go to the credit
committee. Note that all of the above can be done from a single terminal in a
matter of minutes. This decision support system has gone a long way toward
promoting closer working relationships between the IM function and senior
management, because it has put technology to work for managers who are
solving business problems and making business decisions. LMIS serves as a
customer control information file, a management information system, and a
decision support system for the management of a multi-billion-dollar loan
portfolio.

It is our belief that DSS such as the one described above will become
more common in the 1980s as imaginative information managers increasingly
recognize the importance of putting their technology to work for managers
and as the technological tools (microprocessors, query languages, graphics
systems, etc.) become more widespread and easy to use. The provision of
decision support systems for senior managers will be one of the more important responsibilities of the chief information officer (CIO) of the firm in the
decade ahead.

MANAGEMENT GRAPHICS

> **S-26 MANAGEMENT GRAPHICS**
>
> **Pictorial representation of business data repre-
> sents a powerful new executive information
> systems tool.**

Management graphics is another form of decision support system. Executives today are buried in paper and detailed data. The problem is a shortage
not of data but of *information*. What is needed is not more raw data contained
in mountains of paper, but fewer data and more summary information. Information is data massaged into intelligence. Executives need only a small
amount of critical information to do their jobs. But the data must be distilled,
encapsulated, and presented in concise, summary fashion to become intellig-
ible and useful information. Graphics has the ability to synthesize data into a
powerful visual representation that conveys the value of the data and is
easily grasped. Computers can be used to convert columns of numbers into
charts, graphs, and maps that allow managers to make an easier and quicker
interpretation of trends, relationships, and rates of change, to identify prob-

lem areas through key indicator charts, to make better decisions and to control business activities more effectively. Graphics can increase a manager's effectiveness and thus his productivity (the return on investment of a manager). Valid, timely, and concise information results in better decisions. Better decisions, in turn, lead to increased executive productivity. Just as word processing can increase the efficiency of a secretary, so management graphics can increase the effectiveness of an executive. Therefore, management graphics deserves careful consideration as a powerful new strategy for executive information systems in the 1980s.

The power of visual depiction of data is indeed great, as the ancient Chinese proverb declares: "A picture is worth 10,000 words." According to one study, it may be worth even more. As reported by Joel Orr, president of Orr Associates: "A Hewlett-Packard study indicates we communicate with words at 1200 words per minute and with pictures at the equivalent of 40 million words per minute."[8]

Perhaps this is why management graphics is now moving into business offices explosively, as *MIS Week* reported: "This wave of change is spreading like prairie fire through the MIS departments of the Fortune 1000 companies, but it is also likely to spread to smaller firms."[9]

Clearly, management's use of computer graphics will be an important new information strategy for satisfying executive information needs in the 1980s. Traditional approaches to decision support will give way to easy-to-use colorful graphics systems that will take the mystery out of computers and put meaningful information at the executive's fingertips. In this strategy, we discuss the trend toward management graphics to instill a general awareness in information managers of the potential of a management graphics strategy in their stable of top-management communications strategies. It also provides the most viable method of putting computing power directly on the desks of executives.

Business Graphics

Over the past 10 years, graphics have been used primarily for manufacturing, scientific, and military purposes. Computer-aided design (CAD) and computer-aided manufacturing (CAM) still make up the bulk of the graphics systems which are supplied by industry leaders such as Computervision, Calma Co., and Applicon. Only about 10% of graphics systems today are business graphics, but this percentage is growing rapidly and it is predicted that business use of graphics will constitute 50% or more of new installations within the next few years. One reason is that there are about four times as many computers in business than there are in the scientific community.

Two developments are basically driving this change: *cheaper hardware and better software*. Graphics hardware today can be purchased for as little as $2,000 (Apple Computer). An IBM 3279 graphics CRT is in the $4,000 price range, and a large number of middle-market vendors are selling systems ranging from $10,000 to $50,000. This is a big change from the six-figure CAD/CAM systems used in manufacturing.

Software, however, has been the real key to the intense interest in business graphics in the last few years. Up to then, not only was hardware rather expensive, but little in the way of packaged software was available to support business systems. Most manufacturing CAD/CAM systems were turnkey systems designed for specific functions. Business systems need more flexibility to do a variety of things; they even need "what if?" capabilities. The availability in the last year or two of versatile business-computer graphics packages has caused a dramatic turnaround from almost a total lack of interest in the business community to a literal stampede for management graphics.

There are three components that must be researched in acquiring a management graphics system: hardware, software, and data bases. Let's consider each briefly.

Hardware

There are at least five hardware options:

1 *Central computer.* IBM's introduction of the 3279 color graphics CRT terminal has given impetus to the central mainframe alternative. As more software becomes available from the vendor, this is likely to grow as a relatively easy way to get into graphics because of the obvious support of the vendor. (It can also chew up an awful lot of computer overhead.)

2 *Service bureaus.* A number of these today sell graphics services. Again, this can be relatively painless since the hardware and software expertise is simply bought. (But it can also be expensive.)

3 *Time-sharing vendor.* Same as the service bureau except that in some cases, only the operations of a terminal/printer are done in a company, with other operations done by the service bureau. This is often linked to other time-sharing vendor services, such as models and data bases.

4 *Turnkey.* Some systems houses sell "turnkey" packages consisting of both hardware and software which they will modify to the buyer's needs. They can also maintain and support the system once it is installed.

5 *Graphics processors.* Stand-alone graphics microprocessor work stations are sold by a number of vendors, ranging from Apple Computer ($2–3M price range), to Integrated Systems Corp. ($5–10M), to Chromatics and Ramtek ($20–25M) for the base computer. Output devices such as printers and plotters, cameras, and other "bells and whistles" can double the cost of the system. Yet, hard-copy output is probably a necessary requirement of executive information systems. (One way to get

around this is to bring the graphics floppy disk to a service bureau to have hard copies made.)

There are many advantages and disadvantages in all of these options. Therefore, a graphics consultant may be useful to help select the right system to fit your needs.

Software

What has spurred the major interest in business graphics is the greater availability of software packages that massage data into graphics form, available from vendors such as Integrated Software Systems (ISSCO), SAS Institute, AUI Data Graphics, Boeing Computer Services, and Tymshare. Graphics software is sophisticated and complex in order to be user-friendly; thus, it is difficult to develop and maintain. For this reason, few organizations develop their own graphics software. Our advice is don't write your own. It is not only difficult, but programmers with graphics experience are quite scarce. General-purpose packages can provide a ready-made product that is relatively easy to learn to use. Examples are TEL-A-GRAF and DISSPLA (ISSCO), SAS-GRAPH (SAS Institute), TREND-SPOTTER (Friend Information Systems), and ODYSSEY (Harvard Laboratory for Computer Graphics and Spatial Analysis). Moreover, such packages often provide interfaces with the available government and public data bases needed to provide the raw information for the graphics. If current needs cannot be met by an existing general-purpose package, there are systems houses and time-sharing vendors such as GE Information Systems, Data Resources Inc., and Service Bureau Corp. that will develop a customized program under a turnkey contract. Other software sources can be found through software service companies like Datapro, Auerbach, and ICP.

Graphics software provides managers with visual statistical tools that ease information absorption. These tools generally consist of pie/line/bar charts, graphs, maps, and even three-dimensional data representations, as illustrated in Exhibit 6-2. Some of the techniques commonly used are:

Smoothing. Moving averages that "smooth" out highs and lows; for example, an average of the last three months' sales plus the current month as a trend line provides more information than one month's sales figures alone.

Forecasting. Regression analysis is performed on historical data to extrapolate a best "prediction" trend line into the future.

Ratios. The relationship between two variables at various points in time, differences and rate of change in key business indicators.

Mapping. Cartographic data provide demographic information for marketing and other business analyses.

Exhibit 6-2   Types of graphic representations.

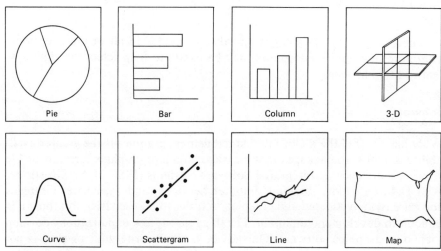

Presented in color visuals, such management information can be a powerful tool for executives to use in spotting trends and relationships that would otherwise be difficult to pull out of masses of data and columns of figures.

Here is a nine-step process for installing a management graphics system:

1 Identify the graphics audience (select a high-visibility high-intent candidate to start with).
2 Determine the candidate's functional needs (in writing).
3 Survey potential systems solutions (hardware and software).
4 Arrange vendor presentations so as to compare capabilities, costs, constraints, and the support available for the different options.
5 Assess the flexibility and expansibility of the system to handle changes and growth.
6 Select hardware and software (and data bases, if appropriate).
7 Prepare an implementation plan, including management presentations and user training.
8 Install the system.
9 Demonstrate it to potential graphics candidates (and repeat Steps 1 through 9).

Data Bases

The data bases needed to supply the raw data for a graphics management information system can come from a variety of sources. In-house computers can provide most of the company data needed to analyze and monitor corporate progress. Outside commercial data bases (Dun & Bradstreet, DRI, AC Nielson, Census Bureau) can be used to provide the noncompany data needed to analyze markets, competitive forces, economic impacts, and other external factors affecting the company. The effectiveness of managers will very likely be in inverse proportion to the size of their personal data base; that is, the larger the data base, the less accessible is the information to managers. The objective when dealing with management information systems should be *simplicity*. Managers need highly summarized information, not an information overload. The key to a successful personal data base for a corporate executive, then, is information synthesis. Managers don't need short-term accounting or transaction detail. Managers need long-term perspective, a "big picture," an overview, highly summarized information. This is, in fact, what they get when they receive soft data (verbal) from trusted associates, the most common source of executive information. Other executive information sources include reading (periodicals, internal and external reports), outside contacts (including consultants), personal intuition, and corporate computer output. Of these, corporate computer output has been shown usually to be *last* in order of impact on an executive's information input, because it is usually in the wrong form for executive ingestion. For the most part, it is as described above: detailed, short-term accounting data rather than summarized, long-term, "big-picture" information. Management graphics, on the other hand, can take that same data base and put it into executive form. This is why it has such potential as an executive information system strategy. Creating an executive data base involves working directly with the executive through six action steps:

1 Identifying the executive's current information sources.
2 Determining the executive's critical success factors (see S-24).
3 Locating the crucial information needed to satisfy those factors.
4 Identifying gaps (missing data) that must be filled in.
5 Testing each information item for relevance to the executive's decision-making needs.
6 Gathering the information items into a personal executive data base.

A Case Study   The economics department at The First National Bank of Boston subscribed to an outside service organization that prepared and maintained numerous economic charts for use by the bank's economists in briefing management, staff, customers, and the community at large on economic trends, issues, and forecasts. When the service was discontinued, the bank's IM function was approached for an alternative solution to the preparation of the charts. The charts were not to be done manually, and slides of each chart would be needed for mobility of presentation. Graphics was felt to

be a good answer to the problem. After some research into the three resources needed (i.e., hardware, software, and data bases), the following
solution was offered to the bank's economist.

It was determined that all of the data needed to produce the econometric
charts were, in fact, available from an outside data base service, Data Resources, Inc. (DRI), on a time-sharing basis. The analyst suggested the use of
a stand-alone graphics station (microprocessor) consisting of a Chromatics
CG 1999 system, with an attached Dunn Instruments Model 631 camera to
produce the needed slides and glossy hard copy of the screens. The machine
would be resident within the economics department and would be used by
them directly. The graphics software package was jointly designed by the
bank and MVE Spectragraph from Mystic Valley Engineering Co., Winches-
ter, Massachusetts. The proposal was accepted and the system installed.

Here is how it works: The econometric data used to prepare the charts is
transmitted from DRI on a time-sharing basis and is stored directly in the
Chromatics floppy disk. An operator creates the graphics from these data,
which are then stored for later retrieval and periodic update. The charts can
be displayed on the CRT screen, projected onto a larger screen TV for easier
viewing, or reproduced in 8 × 10-inch color glossy photographs and/or 35
mm slides. The system uses raster scan technology that is capable of providing the full spectrum of graphic imagery. The camera is cabled to the terminal, enabling it to accept the video signal of the display for output on an
8 × 10-inch glossy photograph or the slide camera. Two software modules
were developed to enhance ease of operation and standard chart production.
The first module is an English-language, menu-driven program allowing
operators to produce approximately 15 types of charts on-line with an absolute minimum of training. A second software module provides the system a
telecommunications interface with DRI. In addition, operators can access
the full generalized graphic capabilities of the package as they become more
proficient.

The graphics station itself is housed in a presentation facility adjacent to
the economics department. The room seats approximately 35 people and
contains a multiprojector system. The cost of the complete graphics system
was $45,000. The displaced annual cost of the old service ($15,000) produced a three-year payback. More importantly, the bank's economist is
delighted with the system and the quality and ease of its graphics capabilities. A by-product of the system is that a number of bank managers are
beginning to use the system to produce 35-mm slides from charts, which are
easily prepared on the graphics terminal, to be used for speeches and presentations, in and out of the bank.

The Future

The system described above is just one example of the use of business
graphics. Other systems today are providing graphics representation of such

things as balance sheet and operating statements, cash flow projections, comparative data, key ratios, financial trends, sales forecasts, production statistics, performance reporting, and operating measures. Also produced are breakeven charts, Gantt charts, PERT/CPM charts for project tracking, investment decisions, resource allocations, and even "What if?" capabilities that allow executives to insert changing assumptions and see the results projected in graphics form as a decision support system.

Management graphics is just beginning to get off the ground as a new and exciting form of executive information system. As hardware costs continue to decline, as more business graphics packages become available, and as commercial data bases proliferate, we believe it will see explosive growth in the future as a management information tool. Graphics systems will be built to be user-friendly, but this does not mean that all an executive will need to do is punch a button and get a graph. Training, knowledge, and expertise will still be needed to create graphics displays. Thus, it is likely that executives will continue to delegate the actual use of the machine to others. Executives are probably no more likely to create their own graphics than they are to type their own letters. This is an opportunity, therefore, for information managers to work more directly with top executives in the creation of personal executive information systems, showing them how computers can be put to work for managers and helping to close the communications gap with top management.

The next 10 years may become the decade of the user, employing user-friendly intelligent desk-top computer systems such as graphics work stations to improve information flow for better decisions and executive productivity. Management graphics is a powerful and largely untapped strategy for bringing information and managers together in a more efficient manner—not data overload, but information utility in a highly effective visual form. A picture may well be worth 10,000 printouts.

TOP MANAGEMENT SUPPORT

Under critical success factors (S-24), we talked about the need for demonstrating the value/performance of the information management function to senior management. This is an area in which few senior managements have much experience; thus, it is hard for them to understand and participate in the problems, issues, and decisions that must be made by the IM function. It is even harder for them to evaluate IM performance in the absence of industry standards for performance measurement. Effective communication between the IM function and top management, as well as participation by senior management in information management decisions, is important to the success of the IM function in getting top management's support for needed action and resources. In this section, we present four strategies for communicating with top management.

CEO Briefings

S-27 CEO BRIEFINGS

Periodic scheduled meetings with senior corporate executives for carefully prepared presentations on issues, trends, plans, opportunities and problems in the world of information management.

"I have had less than two hours with my CEO in the last year and only a little more time with the executive vice president that I report to."[10] This is a quote from an information manager that illustrates the problem of getting chief executive officers (CEOs) involved with the IM function. The truth of the matter is that it is not uncommon for top management to spend very little of their time on this area. Why? Is it because it is not significant or important enough to deserve their time? Hardly! The amount of resources and budget consumed, and the high dependence of most companies today on their information management function, would belie that contention. We believe it is due to two things: (1) CEOs, by and large, do not understand the information management business and find it hard to communicate with those who do, and (2) information managers really do little to actively involve top management and break down the communications barrier. We believe it is the information manager's job to do something about this, not the CEO's! CEOs are usually willing to participate in any facet of the business where they can contribute to the good of the company. However, unlike other areas of the business where the CEO may have direct experience to draw on, he usually has no technical experience to help him to understand IM problems. Therefore, the place to start is education. Not technical education about computers and the like; CEOs do not need to know about bits and bytes. What they need to know are the business problems, the management problems, and the key decisions to be made in the IM area; the issues, the trends, and the impact of technological forecasts on the business of the company. They need to know the "what and how" of the resources needed to support company needs. Most of all, they need to know that they are getting good mileage for the DP dollar. A strategy which has been used by information managers to get more of top management's time in order to address issues of this kind is CEO briefings.

CEO briefings are meetings scheduled with top management—chairman, president, executive vice-president, whoever makes up the top rung of the hierarchy—on some scheduled basis, for purposes of briefing them on what is happening in the world of information management. The meetings should be carefully planned presentations, brief and businesslike; technical jargon avoided. Presentation aids should be professionally done, not thrown together. The quality of an IM presentation must be equal to the quality of the presentations received from other areas of the company (advertising presentations, architect's plans, and other polished presentations). The information manager can use graphics to advantage, especially with public relations' help, to tell the story succinctly and convincingly. These meetings shouldn't be scheduled just for the sake of having a meeting, however. Top management's time is valuable, so a meeting should be held only when there is something important to communicate. Five or six meetings a year may be enough, each scheduled for 1½–2 hours, covering a variety of issues. The benefits can be many:

1   Top management becomes better informed about IM plans, decisions, and issues.
2   The IM function gets top management feedback as to direction, priorities, and reactions to plans.
3   Short, carefully prepared presentations by staff members crystallize their thinking as well as help management to get to know a number of key staff members.
4   Improved perception, understanding, and involvement of top management create support for the programs and resources required to support company needs.

CEO briefings are a relatively simple strategy, yet curiously, few IM organizations use them. They can be an effective way to get top management more involved, to help close the communications gap, and yet demand relatively little of their time. Six 1½-hour meetings a year add up to less than half of 1% of a CEO's time, yet, like a leveraged investment, the return can be tenfold in terms of management understanding and support for information management activities and plans.

Year Plan

> **S-28   YEAR PLAN**
>
> **Preparation of a year plan in support of the annual IM budget helps to win top management support for needed resources.**

In Chapter 2, we alluded to the year plan that is prepared annually by the information management function at The First National Bank of Boston. This year plan is an important medium of communication with senior management. It is prepared as an adjunct to the budget review process as a means of communicating to senior executives the current technological issues and trends of which they should be aware, together with their likely impact on the bank. It also shows how IM objectives are tied to corporate objectives, and it discusses major accomplishments toward those objectives in the year just past as well as plans to meet objectives in the year coming. All of this is summarized in an easy-reading management report of just a few pages, which is usually followed by (largely) one-page appendixes outlining a projects plan, a manpower plan, a budget plan, and as appropriate, a technology plan, an organization plan, and an education plan. The year plan's objective is to produce a short, nontechnical, informative management report that shows in a nutshell what the IM function is doing, what resources it needs, where these resources will be allocated in the coming year, and what support resources—people, machines, and money—are needed to accomplish its goals. The year plan goes not only to the chief executive officers but to the executive directors of all user divisions as well. Although a simple device, it can be an effective communications tool if kept short, concise, and business-oriented. More importantly, it can help gain senior management support for needed resources.

To illustrate the contents of this summary management report, we reproduce in Exhibit 6-3 an actual year plan.

Exhibit 6-3

To: The Office of the Chief Executive

From: The Information Systems and Services Division

Subject: **1980 Year Plan**

I CORPORATE AND SYSTEMS GOALS

Corporate goals calling for the development of new non-asset-based services and increased control over costs offer this division the opportunity to be proactive in business systems planning to identify new computer-based revenue-producing services and to apply the productivity of automation to reduce operating expenses.

Declining computer and communications costs will continue to promote the increasing use of technology in business activities of the 1980s. James Martin, the world's leading systems author, says: "The single factor most affecting how corporations are managed in the 1980s will be technology." There is little doubt that technological trends such as electronic banking systems, office automation, distributed minicomputers, and worldwide telecommunications networks will dramatically impact how we do business, the markets we serve, and the services we offer in the years ahead. Thus, the impact of technology will be an increasingly important input to corporate planning, and business and systems planning will need to be carefully dove-tailed to gain the full benefits of this technology and remain a leader in state-of-the-art banking systems and services.

Information is becoming a more important ingredient in the effective practice of management, and the need to manage information as a corporate resource is only

Exhibit 6-3 (*Continued*)

beginning to be recognized by the best-managed companies. The evolution in technology in the 1980s will call for a transformation in management perspective, from that of the management of electronic data processing to one of information resource management. John Diebold has suggested that: "the corporations that will excel in the 1980s will be those that manage information as a major corporate resource."

As we enter the decade of the 1980s, then, we need long-term objectives geared to corporate goals, to the technological evolution that is taking place, and to the increasing information needs of the organization. During the last half of the 1970s, our goals were to provide *service assurance* (stable and reliable computer services), *product planning* (new ways to serve the bank), and *corporate support* (EDP support to international banking and corporate entities). While we continue to be concerned with these activities, service levels are now consistently high, business systems planning with users is a continuing formal process, and international automation efforts are well under way.

For the first half of the 1980s, then, we will be changing our focus somewhat with the following new long-term objectives:

1 *Proactively plan new services* to generate new revenue, lower costs, and increase productivity. Being proactive rather than reactive means we will seek out automation and new service opportunities rather than waiting for users to come to us.

2 *Integrate systems* to increase management effectiveness through the coordination of diverse systems and better communications among distributed resources. Our role here will be to continually project the corporate view and need for information beyond the interests of individual user perspectives.

3 *Automate office systems* through expanded text processing, electronic mail and filing systems, the merger of text and data processing, and a focus on ultimately automating *managerial* functions. This new automation frontier offers a significant potential for productivity gains.

4 *Improve access to corporate information* through distributed-processing management, corporate data-base management, and communications network management. New information delivery systems will be developed and managed to make needed information conveniently available to those who need it when they need it.

II MAJOR 1979 ACCOMPLISHMENTS

Highlights of our efforts in support of bank systems and data processing services in 1979 were as follows:

A Systems

Rewrite of the 10-year-old commercial loan system was begun, with considerable work done documenting new systems functions and information needs appropriate to today's sophisticated lending practices. Likewise, the automated financial analysis minicomputer system in the credit department was expanded to add a pro forma forecasting capability, and a bankruptcy prediction formula was also added to the system this year.

Exhibit 6-3 (*Continued*)

In the commercial finance area, much work was done in connection with the rewriting and expansion of the aging factoring system. At nearly $5 million in development costs, this effort promises to be the largest single systems project ever undertaken by this bank. The leasing system acquired from Wells Fargo bank, after considerable difficulties and modifications, was also finally installed.

The Sanders-based minicomputer systems in Europe have been replaced by IBM S/34 minicomputers to provide better service and support, added features, and growth potential. This effort was done by London with participation from Boston. The new system is called DIBS (distributed international branch system). The Nassau operation has also been converted to DIBS by the Boston systems staff. Further letter-of-credit system developed by TMI was nearing completion by year end.

In trust, the main preoccupation in 1979 was development of the systems specifications for the trust information management system (TRIM), which will put trust officers on-line to both the trust-accounting and portfolio management systems for on-line query, direct transaction entry, and trust management support. Trust fees were also automated and added to the trust accounting system.

The investment-division automation system began conversion of assets late in 1979. Liabilities were converted a year-and-a-half ago, but loss of key personnel prevented completion of this system conversion until now.

A major effort was made to build the Lloyds data-base system for the purpose of tracking Lloyds insurance exposure and the remarketing of insured IBM 370 computers around the world.

The retail division conducted a successful pilot branch-automation study early in the year, and conversion of all branches to this on-line teller system was well under way by year end. The finance division upgraded and expanded the financial control (responsibility accounting) system during the year. Personnel replaced its personnel/payroll system with a new package program, and changes in the thrift incentive program accommodating new employee options were also implemented by year end.

The supplies accounting system was replaced with a broader-based supplies and inventory control system. Rewrite of the mutual funds system was begun in 1979, international collections were added to the newly automated collection system, and an on-line travel-department reservation system was installed.

The wire room system represented a major development effort, providing a "wholesale" funds transfer system, minicomputer-based, for corporate money movements in and out of the bank, between all wire services. This joint effort between systems, TMI, and Freyberg Associates brings to the bank the very latest in state-of-the-art electronic funds transfer, competitive with the largest New York banks.

Our office automation efforts during 1979 resulted in installation of distributed text-processing systems in 12 bank departments and the addition of a number of administrative functions to increase productivity in the office. Planning for an entirely new telephone system at Columbia Park was also carried on during the year, with installation planned for early 1980.

Finally, we assumed responsibility for two ACS data centers during the year, the first from Framingham Trust early in the year, and the second from Itel late in the year. While these added 40 new banks to our correspondent bank processing systems, both centers suffered from considerable control problems at the time of the takeovers. We

Exhibit 6-3 (*Continued*)

are pleased to report that these problems have been corrected and that good customer relations have been restored at both sites.

B Data Processing

Major changes at the data center in 1979 involved the addition of a second IBM 3032 computer and the sale of two IBM 370/155 computers. Additional memory was also added to the 3032s (to 6 megabytes) to improve system response time. A second IBM 3800 high-speed laser printer was installed, and major peripheral upgrades of high-density tape and disk drives were undertaken during the year. The Qantor computer output microfiche (COM) units were replaced with higher-capacity Komstar machines from Eastman Kodak.

On the software side, three major undertakings were carried on in 1979: conversion to a new operating system (MVS), replacement of our teleprocessing system (RTS), and acquisition of a data-base management system (IDMS). Our conversion to the MVS operating system is now 70% complete. RTS was converted to MVS for existing on-line systems; however, all future on-line systems will be supported by the new INTERCOMM system. The data-base management system (IDMS) is currently being used for the new commercial finance system and the Lloyd's project.

Servicewise, data processing production volume in 1979 was up 40% while costs rose 20% over a year ago. Substantial progress was made in user service levels and in development of a DP-performance reporting system to users. A new user chargeback system was also instituted for 1980, which relates charges much more realistically to costs than was previously possible. A great deal of work was also done to elevate the quality of staff at the data center to keep abreast of fourth-generation technology.

A number of software aid packages were acquired during the year to help in capacity planning and problem resolution efforts, and the communications diagnostic center was upgraded to allow for faster on-line problem diagnosis. Finally, the split operation at the data center was consolidated by year end onto Floor 2 of the building at Columbia Park for a more efficient operation.

III MAJOR 1980 PLANS

A Systems

Commercial banking systems activities in 1980 will include continued rewrite of the commercial loan system, expansion of the automated financial analysis system to include quarterly (rather than only annual) data and new industries (e.g., banking), semiautomation of the credit files, and development of a lending management information system (LMIS) to provide instant support information for the initiation, monitoring, and management of all lending activities.

In this connection, the total customer relationship (TCR) system, serving both domestic and international banking, will also be expanded to add missing entities and services in order to make the system more complete, current, and accurate for the overseeing of global loan exposures and business development efforts.

Also in the international area, the DIBS system will be installed by Boston in Panama and Tokyo during 1980 as part of our ongoing plan for automating international

Exhibit 6-3 (*Continued*)

offices. Data transmission of timely financial, TCR, and other data from the European and U.K. offices to Boston is also planned for 1980. The BBI N.Y. CHIPS system will be replaced by a new minicomputer-based money transfer system, and a new project will be started for the development of an international cash management system.

The retail banking side will see completion of the branch automated teller machines (ATM) with debit card support tied in to the new MONEC system. MONEC itself will be developed as a full-fledged electronic banking system.

The first phase of the trust information management (TRIM) system, on-line inquiry, will be operational in 1980 and Phase 2, on-line transaction processing, is expected to be well under way by the end of the year. Tax cost accounting will be added to the trust accounting system; the pension trust minicomputer will be upgraded, enabling discontinuance of outside service bureau processing; and index systems will be contracted to make some major improvements to the IMDS portfolio management system.

The personnel/payroll system will see the addition this year of human resource management functions such as skills inventory, career pathing, and historical data. The overseas payrolls will also be studied for possible conversion to the domestic payroll system.

Office automation expansion is expected to continue throughout 1980 with new installations as well as added administrative functions such as an electronic mail pilot study and electronic filing (computer information storage and retrieval) adding to office productivity. The economics chart room will be replaced with an on-line graphics terminal display capability, and automation of the bank's library is under study.

Finally, a number of telecommunications projects will be completed in 1980, including the conversion to the new Dimension 2000 telephone system at Columbia Park, expansion of the microwave system to handle data transmission growth between Columbia Park and the head office, and installation of PBX telephone systems in corporate locations such as Worcester, BBI New York, and BBI Miami. Two telecommunications networks are also planned for 1980. Domestically, we will consolidate the various networks now serving our various on-line banking services (e.g., Money/One, branch automation and ATMs, and correspondent bank networks serving Boston, Wellesley, Framingham, and White Plains). By combining these networks into a single electronic banking network, a more efficient, low-cost, and high-service-level network will result. Internationally, a master plan for connecting our worldwide facilities' needs for voice, data, and record (telex) communications will be put together to better serve our growing communications needs abroad.

The demand deposit system will be split in 1980 into two systems separating commercial and retail accounts. Savings will also be combined with checking to produce a single-statement account. Also, bulk filing (of checks) for commercial accounts will follow the successful introduction of bulk filing for retail accounts introduced last year. Further expansion of cash management services is also planned.

The new mutual fund system should be operational by mid-year permitting the release of the IBM 360/40 stand-alone computer, which has become obsolete and unreliable. Also, the correspondent bank-teller inquiry and data entry system (TIME) is expected to be converted to the IBM mainframe computers, permitting the release of the Burroughs 3700 at a savings of $120,000 per year. Automated Corporate Services will be installing a new version of the corporate payroll service.

Exhibit 6-3 (*Continued*)

Support of all ACS banking services now serving 135 banks will continue in 1980, and the Framingham and Wellesley data centers will be combined into a single servicing facility, with White Plains continuing as an on-line remote satellite center.

B Data Processing

The major objectives of the data center in 1980 will center on further equipment upgrades, improved staff quality, and better user service. The only major equipment change planned is replacement of an IBM 370/158 with an IBM 3033 computer late in the year. Peripheral changes will be aimed primarily at improving the cost–performance ratios of the existing configuration. Increased promotion of conversion from tape to disk processing, use of microfiche, and high-speed (3800) printing will combine to lower user charges. The actions taken to charge out 90% of our DP costs in 1980 caused a large increase in charges to users in 1980. This will not be repeated in 1981. Next year should see only a slight increase in user charges over 1980.

The extensive work done to upgrade the DP staff and to provide extensive cross-training and career pathing should begin to pay off in 1980 with more highly trained, versatile employees more attuned to the fourth-generation technology being employed at the data center.

Service levels will be helped by the initiation of a 24-hour customer service center troubleshooting problems for users, and by the physical joining of the diagnostic center with computer console operations overseeing on-line operations.

CONCLUSION

The above represents an enormous amount of work being done in support of corporate business needs and goals. The resources under our management (including the ACS data centers) for 1980 total $23.8 million annually, and we have been growing the last few years at a compound growth rate of 20% a year. Nevertheless, our biggest problem in meeting our objectives continues to be the gap between supply and demand. The continuing need to attract and retain quality resources, coupled with rapidly advancing technology, represents a considerable management challenge. We must be sure that we do not lose control because of too-rapid growth. It will be our intention to continue to support the bank's systems and information needs within the bounds of careful management and controlled growth.

The 1980s promise to be the information age. Good and accurate information will be ever more important in running our businesses, controlling our activities, and servicing our customers. Our new long-term objectives are designed in part to help us to better manage information as a corporate resource—through data-base management, integration of separate systems, and easier access to corporate information throughout the organization. We will continue to apply our tool in trade, technology, toward the furtherance of business goals wherever possible in 1980 and beyond. We appreciate the support we have received from senior management in providing us with the resources needed to do the job. Attached is a summary of our projects and manpower plan for 1980 and our 1980 budget.

Following this highly condensed management report were one-page appendixes consisting of a manpower plan (a listing of anticipated manpower allocations for the coming year, by bank function); a projects plan (a graph showing the division of labor between the maintenance of existing systems and new major project activities, by project); and a budget plan (a comparison of the prior year's budget with the current year's forecast, by major categories of expense). The entire report consisted of only 10 pages, even though the effort which it summarized was obviously major. Backup material, in greater detail, was also supplied to each user division head. This material summarized the results of the business information planning (S-10) interviews conducted prior to the preparation of the year plan. These interviews served to guide the systems development process during the ensuing year.

Information Resources Management Committee

> ### S-29 INFORMATION RESOURCES MANAGEMENT (IRM) COMMITTEE
>
> **Coordinates and monitors major investments in information resources and sets priorities for the allocation of IM resources to user divisions and functions.**

Most IM organizations today have some sort of priorities or steering committee. (We prefer the term *Information Resources Management Committee*.) Some of these committees are more successful than others. Much has to do with how and why they were formed and how they function. More than one information manager has been known to express the feeling that they are nothing but a necessary evil, just one more piece of bureaucratic nonsense to get through: "They approve everything anyway, so why have them?" Properly handled, however, we believe an IRM committee *can* be a useful aid to the information management function. Here is a 12-point strategy for the effective use of an IRM committee:

1 *Prepare the way.* Have a long-range IRM plan in effect, including the projects plan and the manpower plan discussed under business information planning (S-10). Have a standard project-management and control system in place which makes consistent project monitoring possible. Enlist top management support for the establishment of a top-level committee.

2 *Get the right people.* The main reason for having an IRM committee is to get senior management involved in setting goals, priorities, and the allocation of information resources. Just as user participation is impor-

tant to project development, senior management participation is even more important to project *selection*. Who knows more about what business the information manager should be in, what products and services are most needed, what the real priorities are, than top management? Therefore, start at the top—with the CEO as chairman of the committee, if possible. Work down, not up! The committee should be composed of senior management people, representing a good cross section of the company, who can act on a "What's best for the company?" basis. The only IM member of the committee should probably be the information manager himself. The smaller the committee, the better: 6–8 members is good; 15–20 is bad. Effectiveness generally works in inverse proportion to size.

3 *Have the right charge*. The main function of the IRM committee should be to evaluate alternative investment proposals and to approve projects on a prioritized basis consistent with the available resources and the needs of the company. The emphasis is on priorities, not on steering (managing?) the IM function. This is why we prefer the term *information resources management committee* to *steering committee*. (If management supervision over IM is required, it isn't a committee that's needed, but a new information manager.) The responsibilities of the committee might include:

Evaluating investment proposals.
Mediating competing user priorities.
Allocating scarce resources.
Exercising a funding discipline over major expenditures.
Providing better communications between IM and top management.

4 *Establish realistic funding limits*. These limits will, of course, vary according to company policy. We have seen approval limits on major expenditures ranging from $10,000 to $500,000. While one wants to avoid wasting the IRM committee's time on trivial matters, the funding limit ought not to be so high as to defeat its purpose. For example, minicomputers today can be purchased and installed for $50,000 or less. Thus, a funding limit above this amount could result in the loss of central IM control over minicomputer installations. If this loss of control is not desired, what is needed is either a lower funding limit or a requirement that *all* computers, regardless of cost, must be approved by the IRM committee. Two things must be decided in advance about the purview of the committee: the item classes to be approved and the corporate entities involved. Items to be approved might cover all projects involving systems resources above a given dollar limit, all equipment acquisitions above a given amount (whether purchased or leased), the retention of consultant and/or contract services, time-sharing services, purchased

programs, building alterations resulting from new systems installations, etc. The entities to be involved may range from headquarters only, to corporate divisions, to international subsidiaries.

5 *Have a year plan.*   To get an overall "feel" for total requirements and manpower needs, the committee might review a list of all existing and proposed projects and manpower requirements and assignments at the start of each year. General direction and priority setting could result from this review. As individual projects are presented during the year, the plan can be updated so that the committee knows who is doing what at all times. Without such a plan, projects will tend to be approved singly, without regard to alternative investment opportunities, without regard to capital and resource limitations, and without regard to priorities. This approach makes the committee more of a rubber stamp than a true information-resources allocation committee. For ease in allocating priorities, a simple classification can be used. Consider the following list of priorities:

All major, compulsory, and critical projects.

Important, but not qualified for A status.

Worthwhile, but neither critical nor essential (do as time permits).

Nice to have (lowest priority—often not done.)

6 *Hold meetings only when needed.*   A regular time for a monthly meeting is fine, but if the material is light, skip it. It's better to wait than to waste the time of high-level committee members. Worthwhile meetings hold member interest and encourage participation; trivial meetings dilute interest and effectiveness.

7 *Involve users.*   User beneficiaries of proposed systems should be asked to come before the committee, not the information manager, to "sell" their projects. IM may be responsible for developing costs, but the users are responsible for defending needs and benefits. They could, in fact, be asked to "sign off" on proposed savings as their endorsement of the project (which the committee can validate later through a postaudit).

8 *Standardize the meeting agenda.*   Be consistent in presenting meeting documentation, the same for all projects; for example, a formal request-for-information-management form, containing a short explanatory letter, a standard cost–benefit analysis form, and any other appropriate supporting material. The material could be sent out one week in advance to give the committee members time to read it, ask questions, hold premeeting briefings if necessary, and/or do whatever preliminary investigation (or political jockeying) is deemed necessary.

9 *Talk business, not computerese.*   To communicate best with senior management, always talk their language. Meetings should be free of all technical jargon and discussion. Deal in straight business terms only. If

technical explanations are necessary, define all terms and acronyms and keep the explanations as short as possible.

10 *Establish preapproved maintenance levels.*   Since maintenance and enhancement of existing systems typically consume a large portion of systems resources, it is useful to establish a resource limit for these activities; for example, "A limit of 60% of total systems resources will be devoted to maintenance/enhancement, broken down by percentage into the following divisions: . . . " The allocation to each division could then be made on the basis of past experience and current needs and business priorities. Within its allotment, a division could prioritize its requests as it sees fit. If and when the backlog resulting from the preapproved limit becomes excessive, an appeal would have to be made to the IRM committee to adjust the allocation. This technique allows general control over the resources devoted to the maintenance of existing systems without burdening the committee with a myriad of minor requests.

11 *Provide feedback.*   Make periodic status reports on major projects which have been approved, allowing the committee to reaffirm the decision to go ahead, especially if facing a project overrun. Have all project add-ons and enhancements which will significantly increase costs approved as addenda to the original project. Conduct postaudits after the completion of every major project to verify the objectives met, the benefits realized.

12 *Increase senior management awareness.*   One of the most important, but often overlooked, benefits of an IRM committee is its use as a vehicle for improving communications between IM and senior management. Be sure that meeting minutes are circulated to the members of top management not on the committee. Conduct periodic briefings, presentations, system demonstrations, etc., to promote increased awareness and understanding of the information management function in the organization.

Performance Reporting

> **S-30 PERFORMANCE REPORTING**
>
> **Measures the contribution of IM to the corporation in a variety of ways and demonstrates productivity and performance to senior management.**

One of the persistent problems which information managers have always had is the inability of top management to evaluate and measure the contribution of the information management function to the organization. Although computer and systems services benefit the users of those services, it is not always easy to demonstrate the productivity and the project contribution which the IM organization makes possible for the corporation. Performance reporting is required if IM is to gain top management support.

The performance reporting strategy is concerned with measuring the contribution of IM to the organization. Information managers buy new computers not in order to have the latest toy but to obtain the benefits of improved cost–performance gains from new technology, which translates into increased productivity for the corporation. But measuring improved productivity has not always been easy. Why? Because there are no industry standards against which to measure. Thus, there are no easy ways for management to evaluate the true contribution of IM to the organization. Evaluation is made even more difficult because few top managers understand enough about the data processing business to be able to make intelligent judgments about its performance. Hence, information managers are left with the task of finding ways to demonstrate the value of their contribution and performance, if for no other reason than to get needed resources approved. In Chapter 11, we discuss the costs–benefits dilemma of EDP; that is, automation's benefits accrue to the users, while the associated costs (programmers, computers, operators) add to IM budgets. We discuss how to associate benefits with costs by summing the benefits from all the projects undertaken in any given year and comparing them to the costs of development. This is a useful exercise, but it is weakened by the fact that not all projects have quantified benefits or calculated returns over the life of the system. Moreover, this procedure addresses only development costs, not ongoing operating costs. What is often needed is a broader measure of productivity to assess the value added by the IM function to the organization. Especially difficult to measure are missed opportunities, better and more timely management information, and improved utilization of information resources. In the performance-reporting strategy, we present a variety of performance measures which have been used by organizations to demonstrate the value of investment in the information management function. From these measures, readers will perhaps gain some ideas for developing an effective performance-reporting strategy of their own.

Company versus IM Measures   Here are some gross performance measures common to all business activities compared with their counterparts in IM:

Company	IM
Sales growth	Budget growth
Profitability	Productivity
Return (ROI, ROA)	Return (ROI)

Sales growth (in a bank, deposit growth) is probably the most widely used measure of company progress. In an IM organization, however, this translates into budget growth. Is budget growth good or bad? That, of course, depends on whether it reflects increased output or only increased cost. Budget growth alone does not measure anything unless increased output (productivity) can be demonstrated. As to the profitability measure, most IM functions are cost centers, not profit centers; hence, emphasis is usually placed on demonstrating *cost reduction* rather than revenue generation (which is credited to the IM users, in any event). As we atttempt to move the computer more and more into the executive suite, how do we justify management systems (which usually do not cut costs)? In the area of return on investment, we can demonstrate return on many systems projects (other than nonquantifiable systems, as noted). Yet, this demonstration addresses only the systems development side of the house. How do we demonstrate return on investment on information resources per se? In general, we can perhaps conclude that systems development is normally justified on the basis of *return on investment,* while data processing's contribution is most often demonstrated by increased *productivity* measures.

Global Measures   Global measures of performance can be demonstrated in a variety of ways. These can take the form of IM measures, overall company measure, or simply broad technology measures. Examples of IM measures might be:

IM expense to company expense, sales, and assets.
IM staff to company staff.
IM equipment to total assets.

Such measurements are usually made in comparisons with the competition. The problem with these kinds of measurements is that they are often comparing apples with doughnuts; that is, companies are rarely alike. Much will depend on whether the company concentrates on the retail (consumer) side of the business or on wholesale business, as the latter generates far less data processing volume. Another important factor is whether the geographic spread of the company is local, regional, or international.

In some cases, performance can be demonstrated for the company as a whole. Let us consider the following cases.

Case 1   Using the chart shown in Exhibit 6-4, Citibank successfully demonstrated an improvement in their overall productivity from their operating group's multiyear cost-cutting program. The chart shows that operating expenses had grown at a compound growth rate of 15.2% per year between 1962 and 1970, when the cost-cutting program was put into effect. In the ensuing five years, the total-expense line remained almost flat. By extrapolating the expense trend line into the future (dotted line), they were able to make a case for effected savings of $160.3 million before taxes, or $80 million after taxes, because of the cost-cutting program—a most impressive performance.

Exhibit 6-4   Citibank performance in EDP function: measurement of total productivity improvement.

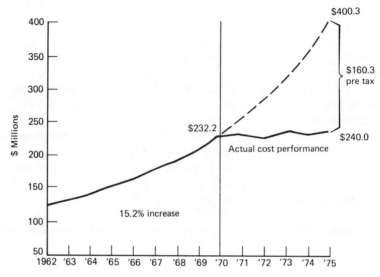

Case 2   The Occidental Life Insurance Co. has a "total-cost" system of productivity measurement, which was described by William W. Marks, Vice President, at a recent SMIS Conference. Exhibit 6-5*a* shows the growth in the number of claims processed from 1970 to 1976. The administrative costs per claim basically held steady until 1975, when costs-per-claim then dropped markedly as the program took effect over the next two years. In Exhibit 5*b*, we see several operating measures rising faster than staff size. From this chart, the following operating productivity indexes were drawn:

Measure	1970–1976
Increase in staff	+12.6%
Increase in earnings	+59%
Increase in insurance in force	+73%
Increase in premium income	+80%

Finally, per employee indexes were calculated that showed varying levels of productivity improvement related to staff, as follows:

Measure	1970–1976
Premium income per employee	+62%
Insurance in force per employee	+54%
Underwriting earnings per employee	+41%
Claims processed per employee	+194%

Exhibit 6-5   Occidental Life Insurance productivity measures (a) Administrative costs per claim. (b) Comparison of home-office staff size with revenues and insurance in force.

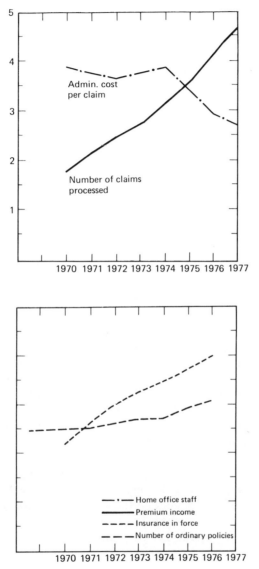

Marks summed up his company's productivity measurement method as follows:

> The indices which have been discussed are the key measurements used at Occidental to judge the operational benefits realized from management actions. Our company has an aggressive and healthy MIS effort in order to offset

the pressures of competition and inflation. This effort has resulted in a general upgrade in the level of our staff and a constant productivity improvement. The changes are often difficult to measure on a specific product or organizational unit, but can readily be demonstrated for the total enterprise.[11]

Case 3   At a recent meeting of security analysts in New York City, a large midwestern bank demonstrated its productivity using these seven global performance measures over time:

1 Total assets per employee, measured on the basis of a constant dollar to factor inflation out.
2 Gross revenue per employee, also on the basis of a constant dollar.
3 Noninterest operating expenses per employee, with a base year used as an index of 100 and projecting forward several years.
4 Net operating earnings per employee; the same index was used as for Item 3 but compared with selected competing banks.
5 Noninterest operating expenses as a percentage of gross revenue; again, compared with those of the competition.
6 Noninterest operating expenses as a percentage of total assets, as compared with those of the competition.
7 Rate of annual staff growth over several years, compared with staff growth at competing banks.

Again, these are all global performance measures which are attributable to overall operations management, including automation. Hence, the contribution from automation alone is not easily demonstrated from these measures.

Finally, there has been ample evidence of cost–performance gains through the use of technology; last, however, have been indirect measures of productivity. They do not necessarily translate directly into in-company performance gains (though these are implied).

Systems Development Measures   Systems development performance can be demonstrated through such gross measures as average lines of code per programmer or total lines of code in the program library. Most often, however, return on investment is the basic criterion for the value of systems projects (management systems notwithstanding). Here are three examples of such measures:

Case 4   Postaudit (Single-System Measurement)   If a system can be isolated, very often it can be measured, either in dollars or in head count. Take the example in Exhibit 6-6. The chart shows an operation with a staff of 500 people that is losing money at the rate of $3.3 million before automation. Following automation, business growth is accommodated with fewer people and lower overall costs. By 1978, the profit is $1.3 million—a total gain of

Exhibit 6-6   Operating expense, revenue, and IM staff size in a division of a large institution.

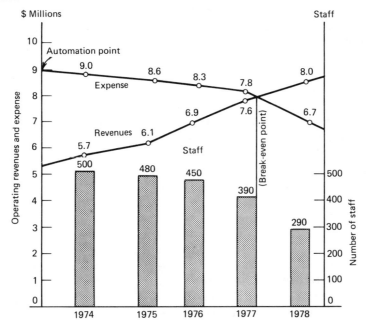

$4.6 million over a five-year period. While automation may not be able to claim full credit for a gain such as this, it can certainly be credited with the lion's share of improved performance.

Case 5   CBA Approach   In Chapter 11, we describe a cost–benefit analysis (CBA) strategy (S-57) which compares the projected and proposed costs of undertaking a systems project over the anticipated life of the system. In Appendix B of Chapter 11, a completed sample CBA form shows the return on investment of the project in terms of present volume. This can be an excellent methodology for demonstrating the value of investment in systems project. It loses its effectiveness when the benefits of the project are difficult or impossible to quantify (in management systems or because of competitive forces or regulatory requirements). In such cases, the "value of information" approach suggested in our costs–benefits strategy (S-57) may be useful; that is, "backing in" the amount of revenue needed to recover the company's desired hurdle return-on-investment over the life of the project. If the perceived value of the system is at least equal to or greater than that amount, the system can be considered justified. Although this method is merely judgmental, it can be an effective way of demonstrating value for projects with unquantified benefits.

Case 6   Value-of-Investment Approach   Gerald Matlin has described an approach used by his company, Land O' Lakes, to measure the value of investment in systems projects.[12] Matlin suggested three techniques for demonstrating the value of an investment in information systems: the assignment of dollar values to information systems benefits; the arrangement of expenditure data so that it is easily understood; and the measurement of user satisfaction with performance. The primary issue, according to Matlin, is *placing dollar amounts on intangible benefits.* It was not clear from the article exactly how he does this. However, we concur that this kind of evaluation is, indeed, the key to demonstrating return on investment for new systems development projects. If it can be done successfully, management will have an absolute measure of the value of investment in all systems projects and will moreover be able to weigh one investment against another in allocating scarce resources to competing user divisions.

Data Processing Measures   Most DP departments maintain charts on workload growth; for example, the number of jobs run daily or monthly, the number of lines of printing, the number of characters in the data base, or the number of on-line terminals served. These charts can show *why* additional resources are needed, but they do not necessarily prove productivity. The real question is: Are unit costs going down? Ways must be found to demonstrate unit cost reduction, not just increased work load. Exhibit 6-7 shows

Exhibit 6-7   A large midwestern bank's major operating units: cost containment experience, 1975–1979.

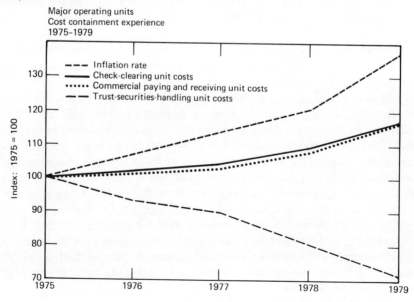

such a measurement as presented by a major midwestern bank at a recent security analysts' meeting. This is a good chart because it shows simply, at a glance, the various unit costs compared with the rate of inflation, thus illustrating productivity.

Another way to demonstrate declining unit costs is through a user-oriented charge-out system, as discussed under S-23. In that strategy, we discuss a method for allocating data processing costs based on relevant business transaction units (transaction pricing). For example, charges for demand-deposit accounting (checking accounts) might be based on the number of accounts processed. The pricing method accumulates costs in computer resource units and then converts them to business transaction units. The advantage is that data processing charges are put into more easily understood user terms. A secondary benefit is that this method can also be used to demonstrate data processing productivity gains. If, for example, the per account charge to the user this year was 50 cents per month and the next year it drops to 40 cents, a 20% productivity gain will have been demonstrated (assuming that all costs are charged out in the same manner as in the previous year).

Charging out DP costs in traditional computer resource units is not as effective in demonstrating productivity.

Service Measures   Perceived service is not a precise or statistical measure, to be sure, but it can be, nevertheless, an important measure of the success of the IM function. User service contracts (S-20) and user satisfaction surveys (S-14), discussed in Chapter 5, are two strategies for achieving service measures, as is the perception management (S-19) strategy. These are all techniques for demonstrating service levels.

Management Measures   Traditionally, most senior management has measured the effectiveness of the IM function through "soft" data; that is, user feedback, the opinions of trusted associates, judgments of the calibre of IM management, etc. While it is important to establish some "hard" measures of the IM contribution to the organization as previously discussed, it is also important not to underestimate the value of soft data to management, and to strive deliberately to enhance both the quality and the quantity of the soft data which reach senior management. For example, high user satisfaction through the strategies discussed in Chapter 5 can promote positive user feedback to management.

Participation in the corporate planning process as described in business information planning (S-10) can also be an important ingredient in success. CEO briefings (S-27) offer another opportunity to present positive soft data to management, and critical success factors (S-24) are another positive means of satisfying management's information needs. These, and other soft data measures, can be a vital part of any performance reporting strategy.

The lack of industry standards by which to measure themselves, top managers' limited knowledge of the IM business, and the increasing size of corporate IM budgets all combine to make it incumbent on every information manager to find ways to measure and demonstrate the value of IM's contribution to the organization. As a part of this strategy, we have presented a variety of measures used by successful organizations as a guide for our readers in developing performance-reporting measures appropriate to their own organizations. Beyond the hard measures of performance, however, the value of soft data in this exercise must not be overlooked. If user feedback and management perception of IM are positive, and if management is convinced that they have competent business-oriented professionals managing the IM function, they will be "believers," and the need to prove the value and contribution of IM to the organization will disappear as a critical success factor for information managers.

In the meantime, our next strategy deals with the development of an internal measurement and reporting system which, while used primarily by the information manager in monitoring the performance of the IM function, can also be used by the information manager in reporting to top management.

IM PERFORMANCE REPORTING AND EVALUATION SYSTEM

Another performance management strategy which can be useful to the information manager and to top management as a vehicle for measuring the performance of the information management function in the organization is our IMPRES strategy.

> **S-31   IMPRES**
>
> **An information management performance-reporting and evaluation system (IMPRES) for monitoring the efficiency and effectiveness of the IM function.**

Information managers manage in five major areas: planning, projects, human resources, technology, and money. Managing these requires information in the form of an internal management reporting system which tracks progress, reports deviations from the expected, and makes monitoring of the information resources easier. This is what IMPRES does. In fact, IMPRES could be viewed as a response strategy to the critical success factor (S-24) strategy. That is, under CSF we suggested that chief executive officers might measure the IM function by the quality of the staff, positive user feedback, and value for the EDP dollar. IMPRES is a strategy that can be used by an information manager to track how well the division is doing in the efficient use of resources and the effectiveness of user service levels, and thus, it contributes to managing critical success factors.

IMPRES stands for "information management performance reporting and evaluation system." It is the information manager's management information system. IMPRES is the accumulation of various performance reports into a monthly report to the information manager. It can also be used to communicate overall IM performance to management.

IMPRES measures and reports on five areas of IM efficiency and effectiveness as shown in Exhibit 6-8. On the efficiency side, it measures how resources are utilized (equipment and people). On the effectiveness side, it measures user service levels and systems project performance (user concerns). Finally, it measures overall financial performance.

Data Processing

From data processing, the two reports produced are the computer performance report and the user service report.

Computer Performance This report covers production and downtime, missed objectives, lost resources and the reasons therefore, resource utilization, throughput (jobs completed), response time problems, line outages, etc.

Exhibit 6-8   IM reporting system.

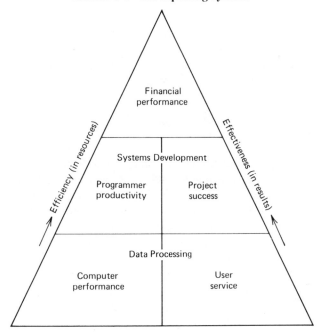

The data can be accumulated manually or with the aid of computer performance evaluation tools such as those described in Chapter 8.

User Service Levels   Four basic measures of user service levels are timelines, accuracy, cost, and reliability. This report covers systems availability, response times, timely delivery of reports (and the number having to be redone), chargeback costs, etc. This report can go not only to the information manager but to user managements as well. Objectives can be established with users against which performance can be measured. This subject was covered in detail under user service contracts (S-20) in Chapter 5.

Systems Development

From the systems side of the house, there are also two reports, dealing with programmer productivity and projects control.

Programmer Productivity   A project control system (S-60) can provide useful data to account for analysts' and programmers' time, but beyond knowing where the time has gone, we need to get a handle on the efficiency of the work. This is a bit more difficult. However, there are some useful measurements which can be employed to identify strong and weak performers. Four such measurements are discussed under the programmer productivity strategy (S-45) and can be used to prepare monthly reports to information managers.

Successful Projects   The proof of the pudding here is the successful implementation of large projects on time and within budget. This result requires good project management and a good project control system. A number of strategies that deal with this subject will be found in Chapter 11.

Financial Performance

Financial performance, the ability to plan and meet budgets, is a prime yardstick by which top management measures IM performance. Monthly budget variance reports are needed which measure actual versus planned expenditures, highlighting areas that require explanation and/or attention. A cost–benefit dilemma in the information management business is that the more that is automated, the more IM costs rise (equipment, operators, programmers), while the *benefits* of automation (jobs saved, productivity gains, added revenues) accrue to the users. If management sees only the cost side reflected in the IM budget, IM will be perceived as a necessary but high-cost overhead operation, rather than as the value-added, profit-contributing operation which it really is. One way to combat this cost–benefit dilemma is to record carefully the quantitative benefits of all major projects undertaken each year. At budget time, management can be presented with a list of the development costs of those projects matched against the expected benefits over the life of the systems. This approach helps immeasurably in establishing the real justification for the IM budget, which can easily be lost on management without this kind of relational strategy.

Good performance measurement can be extremely useful, but poor measurement techniques can be worse than none at all. Anyone can substantiate superlative performance even in the face of extreme user discontent by obfuscating measurement techniques; one can measure something other than what is purported to be measured, or measure nothing at all (or nothing meaningful).

Done properly, however, IMPRES can provide an information manager with useful monthly IM reports covering user service levels, computer performance, programmer productivity, project tracking, and financial performance, without expending a great deal of time or effort. These reports permit close monitoring of IM performance with a minimum of time demanded of all parties involved. Moreover, they can provide the information manager with good information for communicating IM performance to users and senior management. Because information managers are often frustrated by their inability to measure true IM performance, such communication is usually welcomed and can go a long way toward bridging the communications gap and building credibility between the information management function and senior management.

IM Effectiveness

Although *efficiency* and *effectiveness* are often used interchangeably, they are quite different in meaning. Efficiency is cost-oriented; it is concerned with internal performance, action without waste, doing things right. Effectiveness is results-oriented; it is concerned with the value produced, doing the right things. Efficiency and effectiveness should be twin goals, but over the years, many information managers have tipped the scale toward efficiency, often at the expense of effectiveness. We often hear systems described in terms of equipment utilization, throughput efficiency, run times, tight coding, etc., all technical (efficiency) considerations. But how often do we hear systems described in terms of the value (not the quantity) of the output, or of the value of the service to the user? It is perfectly possible to be efficient without being effective. An entire data center can be operating at optimal efficiency, but if the output is tossed in the wastebasket, what is the value? If there must be an emphasis of one over the other, the pendulum is swinging toward effectiveness, for to be efficient without being effective is to produce little of value; whereas effectiveness without efficiency may be costly, but it still has worth.

If information managers find it more difficult to concentrate on being effective rather than efficient, it is probably because they are used to working in a world of electronic efficiency where things are precisely measured. It is easier to measure equipment utilization, programmer productivity, and operating systems efficiency than it is to measure the value of output and of services to a user. How does one measure effectiveness? Because it is value-oriented, it is often hard to quantify. Somehow, it must be put into user terms (dollars, head count, return on investment, profit). Intangibles are hard to quantify, and it is hard to use qualitative benefits to back up a project that has no apparent cost justification. Yet, that is what must be done if automation is to move from clerical support to management support in coming years. Future management systems will be designed to produce better information that will help control and manage the business, information that will help the management decision process. Rarely will this kind of information have a payback in terms of people savings or lower transaction costs (productivity). Ways must be found to measure the effectiveness of such systems, based on the value of the information produced.

Efficiency was important in the years when everyone was busy automating clerical functions to squeeze labor out of labor-intensive operations. This goal has largely been accomplished in leading organizations today. Attention is turning more and more to automating managerial work, or at least to assisting managerial work. New systems are also needed to support new products and new services. These new systems must be tuned in to the problems of business if we are to meaningfully apply technology to the solution of business problems (effectiveness). This application will require a new awareness and a new role on the part of information managers—a tipping of the scale toward effectiveness as the primary motivation. One indication of top management's concern about effectiveness can be seen in the growing numbers of information managers coming from within the business rather than from the technical ranks. Scott Morton of MIT underscored this shift in an address before an SMIS conference in New York when he said:

> An informal survey as part of one of the C.I.S.R. (Center for Information Systems Research) studies showed that in 180 companies (mostly Fortune 500), 96 had had changes in the holder of the top DP or MIS position within the last 18 months. Of these 96 new appointees, 74 were user executives. That is, they had been in line or staff positions of real authority and had no significant previous training or exposure to computers.[13]

When three-quarters of new information managers of larger corporations are coming from the business side of the house, the message from top management is loud and clear: they want business managers who are effective in solving business problems more than they want technical managers who are efficient in solving technical problems. The information managers who do not carry off this role in the future will be replaced with business managers. Effectiveness will be the name of the game in the information era ahead.

Integrating for Effectiveness

In Part 2, we have presented a number of strategies for dealing with the people side of the IM integration stage of growth in the 1980s. Information management effectiveness requires the successful integration of three groups: (1) the information management group; (2) the user group; and (3) the top management group. No matter how able, competent, knowledgeable, or hard-working they may be, information managers in the era of distributed information resources who cannot bring these three groups together to *share* the management of information resources will not be effective and will continue to lose influence and power in the organization. IM effectiveness will be considerably enhanced by a strong and conscious effort to become integrated with the business and to work with user and senior managers as general business managers rather than as technicians set apart from the mainstream of the business.

This new association with management and the focus on business information needs will characterize the new breed of information managers. Information management is one of the few fields where one can cross all business disciplines and learn those disciplines while developing information systems. This is an opportunity to do more than evolve from data processing to information manager, or from information manager to chief information officer. It may well be the opportunity to move up from chief information officer of the firm to chief executive officer. An executive search consultant recently was quoted in *MIS Week* as saying, "Only about 10% of MIS and DP managers fully realize the potential they have for upward movement in the corporate organization."[14] Clearly, ways must be found to tap this potential.

At a recent Harvard seminar, attendees were told that with all of today's information tools available to them, chief executive officers of leading firms in the 1980s may well be the chief information officers of their firms. We doubt this. If we can assume that the chief information officer is involved not only with using information, but with managing information as well—that is, identifying, coalescing, consolidating, storing, and retrieving information; building technical delivery systems involving computers, systems, communications, and data bases—then we do not see chief executives managing these activities. Rather, we believe this is the job of information managers, and this is why we suggest that they should strive to become the chief information officers of the firm, serving the information needs of all.

NOTES

1 John F. Rockart, "Chief Executives Define Their Own Data Needs," *Harvard Business Review,* March–April 1979, p. 82.
2 A. Jackson Forster, "Power Strategies and Techniques for Obtaining Top Management

Input into MIS Master Plans," *SMIS Conference Proceedings,* Washington, D.C., September 1978, p. 57.

3 William Woodside, "A View From the Top," *SMIS Conference Proceedings,* Washington, D.C., September 1978, p. 21.

4 *Ibid.,* pp. 21–22, 24.

5 Rockart, "Chief Executives," p. 82.

6 *Ibid.,* p. 85.

7 Peter G. W. Keen and Michael S. Scott Morton, *Decision Support Systems,* Reading, Mass.: Addison-Wesley, 1978, pp. 229–230.

8 Joel Orr, as quoted in "Business Turns to Graphics," *Infosystems,* November 1980, p. 57.

9 "Corporate Chiefs Embrace Graphics," *MIS Week,* November 19, 1980, p. 1.

10 Richard L. Nolan, "Business Needs a New Breed of EDP Manager," *Harvard Business Review,* March–April 1976, p. 126.

11 William W. Marks, "Increasing Productivity," *SMIS Conference Proceedings,* Los Angeles, 1977, pp. 163–165.

12 Gerald Matlin, "What is the Value of Investment in Information Systems?" *MIS Quarterly,* September 1979.

13 Michael S. Scott Morton, "Organizing the Information Function for Effectiveness as Well as Efficiency," *SMIS Conference Proceedings,* New York, September 1975.

14 Scott Upp, as quoted in *MIS Week,* October 8, 1980, p. 26.

Information Resource Management

7

Human Resource Management

Our most valuable natural resource weighs three pounds and wakes up at six in the morning. The human brain.

THE PROBLEM

The number of systems professionals in the corporate information management function of one large multinational company has been 25% below the manning table for over two years. The director of systems and several of his senior managers spend hours each week in the search for and evaluation of potential systems professionals. Employment search firms are a primary source of new staff professionals at a cost of 20–25% of first-year earnings. The staff turnover rate is currently almost 30% a year. Managers in user divisions are concerned about the level of systems support that they receive. Some user divisions have employed systems professionals because of dissatisfaction with systems staff support from the corporate information management function. User divisions have purchased minicomputers and employed time-sharing services. Salaries of systems professionals have been bid up faster than the salaries of most other corporate staff employees. A sizable budget has been allocated for employee development. Management in this corporation's information management function must take time every day for staff assignments and training because of the percentage of inexperienced staff professionals.

We could continue the list of human resource problems confronting this director of corporate information services. The experience in this company is not unusual. The critical shortage of competent information specialists is a major factor in the creation of backlogs for information services, which are now two to three years or longer in most companies.

The 1979 *Datamation* survey reported that *DP employee turnover is now running at about 28% per year*. That's a big number; and at that rate, half the employees at an average DP site won't be there two years from now.[1]

The information revolution and the environmental problems described in Chapter 1 have created a condition in which the gap between the demand for information specialists and the supply of people with the required skills continues to widen with each passing year. The problem posed for information managers is twofold: strategies are needed for both the *acquisition* and the *retention* of these scarce human resources.

We have observed that the severity of human resources problems varies widely among firms. There are useful strategies for improving the effectiveness of human resource management in the corporate information function. The MBS strategies presented in this chapter are contributing to more effective information-resource management in a number of the country's best-managed companies. Let's begin our analysis of MBS options by examining the elements that ought to make up a company's staff management system.

STAFF MANAGEMENT SYSTEM

> **S-32   STAFF MANAGEMENT SYSTEM**
>
> **A set of integrated building blocks used to attract and retain qualified professionals that spans recruitment, skills identification, job assignment, staff development, performance evaluation, and remuneration.**

A staff management system involves the following capabilities:

Staff Recruitment

Staff recruitment may consist of a network of contacts with faculty and placement officers in universities with strong information sciences programs; working relationships with several executive search firms specialized in information professionals; the use of referrals from information function professionals and managers; recruitment brochures about opportunities in information staff positions in one's company (which may include several case studies of successful staff members); the use of "open house" programs to introduce prospective recruits to the organization and the work environment; attendance at job fairs aimed at matching jobs with job seekers; advertising in newspapers locally and in distant cities to attract people interested in the company's geographic area. Using a variety of ongoing recruitment methods is more likely to be successful than periodically jumping in and out of the job market when needs arise. In other words, good people should be hired when they are *found*, not just when they are *needed*. How does one identify good people? Good interviewing techniques are needed to determine real strengths, knowledge, and track records. But beyond that, testing can also be very helpful; that is, psychological, intelligence, and aptitude testing. For more senior staff positions, the cost of a professionally administered test is minor compared with the cost of hiring the wrong person for the job. For more junior positions, a simple programmer aptitude test can be used, provided it is first validated as a nonbiased test according to government requirements. A strategy for validation is covered later in this chapter under psychometricians (S-33).

Skills Identification

The corporate IM function is staffed by professionals who have a wide variety of technical skills and personality attributes. A good match between the technical skills and personality attributes of a staff professional and the job requirements is an important factor in both job performance and job satisfaction. The development of a skills inventory and an assessment of personality attributes for each staff position can contribute significantly to improved person–job matching. The skills inventory can be built from previous education and training courses taken as well as from aptitude tests, if given. These can then be matched against job requirements when one is filling a given position. The steps of the skills inventory are (1) defining the key results expected in the job; (2) identifying the skills needed to do the job; and (3) assessing the employee's skills. The completed skills inventory serves as a guide for further development needs. Personality attributes are a bit more difficult to define, except subjectively, and only *after* a period of observation. A strategy for developing a personality profile of individual staff members is the use of human motivation seminars (S-34), treated later in this section.

Staff Assignment

The high cost of recruitment, salaries, and staff development, plus the severe shortage of information specialists, provides a strong incentive for giving careful attention to the assignment of information specialists to jobs. Entry-level people, after a suitable training period, will very likely join a team of more experienced professionals and learn from their tutoring and supervision. A good strategy at this early point in the staff member's job experience is the assignment of a mentor (S-35), a further discussion of which follows in this chapter.

   Experienced recruits require a matching of their skills inventory with the specific needs of the job. Thus, both skills inventories and job descriptions must be in-place techniques before good matching can take place.

Staff Development

Staff development occurs through a combination of education or training opportunities and on-the-job learning. Most firms budget inadequately for education. Allocating 1–2% of DP budgets for training doesn't work, yet this is the percentage that is spent by most companies, according to industry surveys. Attendance at technical and management seminars should be carefully scheduled for those who would most benefit and should not be left to haphazard choice (such as when a seminar is being held in a city that a staff member wishes to visit). Also, the use of internal seminars should not be overlooked. Popular lecturers can be hired to give in-company seminars, often at a low cost per person (there are no travel costs). Another useful technique is videotape instruction. There are a number of companies with large libraries of rentable videotapes which can be particularly effective for the individual self-paced learning of missing skills. Many companies also pay tuition for staff members pursuing college degrees at night. However education and training are done, an adequate budget is necessary, and utilization of that budget should be carefully matched against individual staff member needs.

On-the-job training and development must also be carefully structured. A formal training program and a logical career path structure are useful in allowing the individual to see exactly how job progression occurs in the organization. Two strategies in this chapter dealing with this issue are systems interns (S-37) and career pathing (S-36).

Performance Evaluation

Evaluating performance is not just a matter of assessing how well a job is done. It also determines whether the individual is meeting his or her objectives. After all, doing the *wrong* things right is not as important as doing the *right* things right. Thus, an MBO contract should be established between boss and subordinate at the start (see Exhibit 2-3 for a further example of this point). With objectives established, the employee has something to shoot for and to be measured by. Actual measurement can be done informally, but it may be more effective with a written performance appraisal form, which can be discussed with the staff member. (If your company does not use formal performance appraisals, IBM has one which can be obtained from your IBM representative.) Some people's performance is so outstanding as to require special treatment to tap their strengths fully. Two such types of high performance are discussed later under the gatekeepers (S-39) and eagles (S-38) strategies.

Remuneration

The acquisition of technical skills, the meeting of job objectives, the rate of knowledge assimilation, interpersonal abilities, and management talents find their way into performance appraisals, and these, in turn, are used to guide salary reviews and promotion decisions. Written appraisals accompanied by salary and promotion data in an employee file are a necessary part of a career pathing plan, since they provide continuity on employees' progress as they work for successive bosses over time. One should conduct surveys from time to time to be certain salaries are in line with the market. Remember, you are competing not with other employees in your organization, but with competing companies in your geographic area looking for the same information specialists you are attempting to recruit and keep as employees.

Many companies have a number of these staff-management building blocks in place, but relatively few have brought them together into a cohesive strategy for the acquisition and retention of information staff professionals. Such a cohesive strategy is important because information specialists know that they are in high demand and therefore want to choose a company that is growing and that has a well-managed and up-to-date IM function. Where a formal program is in place that allows staff members to develop and maximize their skills and abilities and gives them the opportunity to apply those skills within a favorable working environment, the retention of good people will result, and turnover rates will decline from the 20–30% which is common in the industry today. A good staff-management system utilizes strategies for both the recruitment and the retention of qualified people. To attract people, one needs motivating strategies; to retain them, one needs job satisfaction strategies. In the remainder of this chapter, we present some strategies that address these issues of human resource management.

PSYCHOMETRICIANS

> **S-33   PSYCHOMETRICIANS**
>
> **A programmer-screening tool which helps identify good talent without bias or discrimination.**

Applicant testing can be a big help in recruitment. The use of programmer aptitude tests to determine a job applicant's aptitude and ability to succeed at programming and systems work can serve a real purpose. The logical mind, the reasoning ability, and the basic intelligence needed to succeed in technical work of this nature are not easy to perceive in advance through the interviewing process alone. However, job discrimination considerations caused the government to rule most such formal tests illegal several years ago. Since then, most DP shops have gone back to relying on interview results, school records, and the like. The problem is that often a fair amount of time and money is spent on the education and training of individuals who, in the end, are discovered to be unsuited to this type of work. This not only wastes the individual's time and the company's money, but results in further slippage in filling the pipeline with needed programming talent.

There is a solution to this problem: *psychometricians*. A psychometrician is a person possessing a double degree: one in psychology, the other in mathematics. The unique function that they can perform is test validation. The psychometrician can validate a test (such as a programmer aptitude test) so that it meets the nonbias requirements of the federal government and thus can once again be used as a tool in the applicant screening procedure. Here's how it works: the psychometrician first conducts job analysis interviews with a representative sampling of programmers currently employed in the organization. Supervisory personnel are also interviewed. Supervisors are asked to rate the people in the sample based on their experience with those employees. A rating, ranging from "marginal" to "excellent," is given on a number of job factors, such as technical knowledge, logical reasoning ability, quality of work performed, work organization and efficiency, ability to work with others, and conscientiousness. These ratings are converted into a numerical score for each person.

Next, a series of tests selected by the psychometrician is administered to each person in the sample. The test results are matched against the supervisor's ratings, and through regression analysis, a correlation between supervisor ratings and test results is established. The correlation, of course, must be sufficiently high to be predictable (and defensible). A composite test score is then produced for the battery of tests, and a range of "probability of success" on the job is established; that is, below a given score, the probability of success is predicted as being low. The entire procedure is documented and validated by the psychometrician so that it can be defended as a valid nonbiased test, if challenged.

The end result is that tests can once again be used as an added tool in screening entry-level people. We must caution, however, that the validated test can be used only for the specific job validated (e.g., programmer trainees at a specific location). It cannot be used as a screening device, either for other jobs or for similar jobs at other locations. Its use is very strictly controlled. Nonetheless, it is a worthwhile strategy for staff recruitment, particularly where few other indicators are available.

To learn more about this subject, one can talk to the company psychologist, if there is one, or with someone at any good psychological testing concern.

HUMAN MOTIVATION SEMINARS

> **S-34   HUMAN MOTIVATION SEMINARS**
>
> **A technique for guiding staff members to a better understanding of themselves and others to improve interpersonal work relations.**

Many companies use psychological testing to measure the intelligence, the emotional stability, the social skills, the interests, and the aptitudes of their managers in order to determine their suitability for specific jobs and/or promotion opportunities. Often, individual managers so tested are encouraged to discuss the test results with the company psychologist in the belief that such sessions are helpful in assisting individuals to learn their strengths and weaknesses and to prepare themselves to function more effectively in their jobs.

A related strategy not as widely used, however, is to have the company psychologist conduct seminars to teach the methodology used in evaluating personality types and human motivation. These human motivation seminars are intended to increase awareness about one's own personality and to teach one to recognize the behavioral characteristics of others and to apply this knowledge to achieve more effective performance from oneself and others. With a better understanding of their psychological profiles, employees are better able to understand, work with, and relate to the people with whom they must deal every day on the job.

Typical seminars are usually limited to 15–20 people and run two to three days (additional seminars can be run for larger groups). The aim of the seminars is not to try to change the participants but to help them understand different personality types and how to deal with and motivate them. Almost universally, the people we have seen go through these sessions come out charged up and excited about their newfound knowledge and understanding of what makes people tick, and human interrelationships on the job have improved markedly.

Following is an example of a personality profile theory, the Marston theory:

The Marston theory separates personality style into four major divisions: dominance, influence, steadiness, and caution (DISC). While everyone presumably has a bit of all, one usually dominates. The makeup of a person is the sum total of her or his DISC personality profile as determined through psychological testing.

Exhibit 7-1 illustrates a typical personality type (aggressive–persuasive) graphed on a DISC chart. This particular type is characterized by a high dominance orientation; he or she is reasonably persuasive, impatient for results, a fighter. We arrive at this particular personality type by determining, through psychological testing, where a manager fits in each of the four classes on the DISC wheel as shown in Exhibit 7-1. A dot is placed in the middle of each quarter circle of the wheel that corresponds to the individual's rating, on a scale of 1 to 10. When the dots are connected the individual's personality type is identified. The psychologist can then interpret this profile with the individual, listing typical wants and needs, possible pluses and minuses, and the motivational drives characteristic of each. Individual scores taken from previously administered psychological tests can be used to counsel each person attending the seminar as to his or her own personality type, with much more understanding and meaning.

Exhibit 7-1   Personality style.

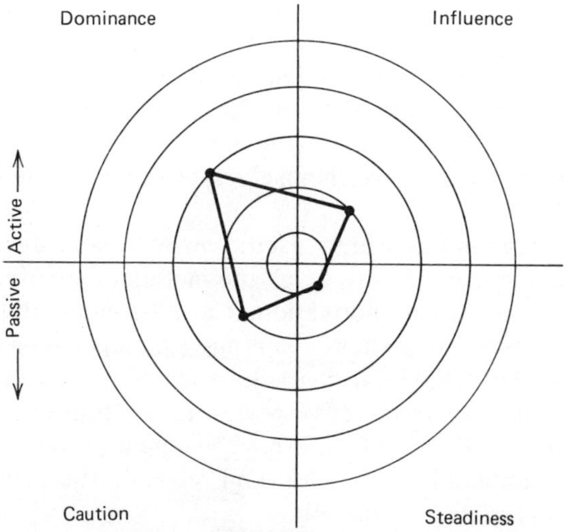

Through an understanding of the different personality types, individuals learn how to improve their own performance and how to deal more effectively with subordinates, peers, and superiors. In the simplest terms, for instance, one motivates a high D by challenging him, a high I by flattering him, a high S by winning him over as a friend, a high C by removing threats.

Since the majority of failures on the job are the result of personality problems, a strategy for improving a staff's effectiveness in human relations through a more thorough understanding of personality types and their motivational drives can benefit both the staff and the company. We know of one company president who felt so positively about the use of this strategy that he posted each individual manager's DISC graph on the wall for all to examine, in the belief that if all managers knew each other's personality type, more effective working relationships would result. If psychological testing is now done in your company, using the test results and personality typing methodology as the basis for a human motivation seminar could be a most rewarding strategy in human resource development. If it is not, engaging a professional psychologist to test key IM function managers might represent a good investment in human resource management.

MENTORS

> **S-35   MENTORS**
>
> **Experienced IM professionals assigned responsibility for the assimilation and early career growth of new IM staff members.**

The youth, inexperience, and limited knowledge of business of most entry-level information staff professionals has created the need for a strategy designed to foster the early career growth of information specialists. Mentors can provide an important source of professional growth and organizational assimilation in the early years of a young information specialist's career. A mentor assists inexperienced information professionals to learn and grow during the first one or two years on the job. Each mentor has responsibility for one or more trainees. This responsibility includes a wide range of support for the junior information specialist, including assistance in the following:

1 Development of technical skills—hardware, software, documentation.
2 Organizational assimilation—power, expectations, factors in performance evaluation, user characteristics.
3 Career path options.
4 Project management.

Gerald R. Roche,[2] CEO of Heidrick and Struggles, reported on his company's survey of the prevalence and importance of mentors in American business. His findings indicated that managers with mentors earn more money at an earlier age and are less mobile. They are much more satisfied with their jobs. Respondents to his survey were asked whether there was "a person who took a personal interest in your career and who guided you or sponsored you." This kind of mentor relationship occurs spontaneously with some frequency. The importance of this kind of mentor relationship in the volatile and tight labor market for information specialists makes the use of mentors in a formal program of human resources management a useful strategy for the IM function.

CAREER PATHING

> **S-36 CAREER PATHING**
>
> **Organized multipath structure within IM used to provide broad career-advancement opportunities for motivated staff members.**

In too many companies, the work dealing with career pathing in IM is concentrated on the development of technical skills. Often, management is neglected although the skills required of a manager are quite different from the skills required of a technician. But even more importantly, despite much talk about the desirability and need of career pathing along dual career paths (technical and managerial), mostly it remains just that—talk! Companies with formal career path programs in effect are still very much in the minority.

Channeling people where their strengths and interests lie, whether technical or managerial, accomplishes two important things: (1) competent people are retained through challenging assignments and job satisfaction, and (2) each individual's strength is put to work where it will do the most good for the company.

Without a career path program, advancement will be seen as an amorphous and chancy thing. Moreover, advancement may well be seen as a single path up a "managerial" ladder, resulting in the loss of good technicians and the promotion of poor managers. We once came across a study which suggested that only 1% of DP people make good managers. We couldn't help wondering if perhaps only 1% *want* to be managers! Technical and managerial roles are, in many ways, incompatible; one is thing-oriented and the other people-oriented. Each has different motivations. People with a managerial bent enjoy working with and through people and should be encouraged to progress up that ladder. Likewise, people with a technical bent enjoy technical challenges and personal accomplishment and should have the opportunity

Exhibit 7-2   Multipath career planning.

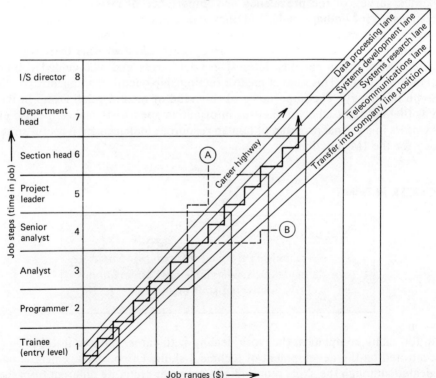

a Illustrates a sample progression path. Other paths would be similarly developed by department or various disciplines (e.g., systems, data processing, technical services, telecommunications).

to progress up a comparable technical ladder and should not have to default to a managerial position simply because it appears to be the only way up.

In Exhibit 7-2, we illustrate a career pathing strategy aimed at providing an IM staff a clear indication of where and how individuals in the organization can progress up the IM ladder. Let's review the various elements of this program in career path planning:

Job Steps

First, we establish a series of steps up the career ladder. In Exhibit 7-2, we identify eight steps up a typical systems department ladder. Other paths might involve more or fewer steps, but the important thing is to provide a logical succession of steps up multiple technical and managerial paths within the departments within IM. For example, parallel paths, by department, might run as shown in Exhibit 7-2. An individual starting up one path should not be limited to that one path but should be able to flow back and forth between departments during his or her career as needs and interests dictate, both laterally and vertically. Here we use the analogy of a career "highway," on which individuals can proceed in various departmental *lanes,* freely switching lanes as needs and interests arise, but continuing to flow forward and upward. In Exhibit 7-3, we show the hypothetical career path of

Exhibit 7-3   A hypothetical career path progression.

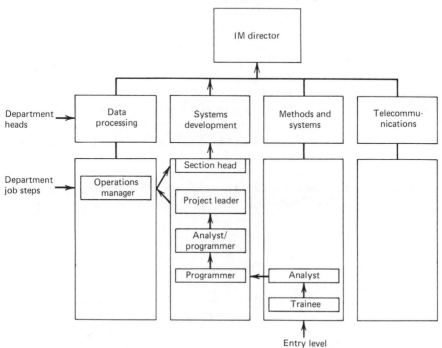

the systems department head, crossing over departmental lanes in progressing up the career ladder. This sort of multiple career-path opportunity is important for flexibility. It provides both the company and the employees multiple opportunities rather than a single, narrow path upward.

Job Grading

Once job steps have been established, job descriptions must be drawn up to make clear the responsibilities, skills, and educational requirements for each job step. From these job descriptions, job grades and, in turn, job salary ranges (part of every salary administration program) can be established. Normally, one could expect to receive two or three salary increases before one's skill, experience, and contribution warrant promotion to the next step. We have not attempted in Exhibit 7-2 to place a dollar value on the horizontal scale of our chart because this would obviously vary from company to company and from industry to industry and, in any event, would change over time. Suffice it to say that it is important that the individual stay on the career highway and not get sidetracked. There are two ways that an individual can stray from the career path, designated by (A) and (B) in Exhibit 7-2. (A) is what happens when individuals are overpaid for their positions, as sometimes happens when a company desperately needs to hold individuals in specific positions (because there is no replacement or the company does not want to lose their unique technical skills).

More often, companies, perhaps with poor working environments, are willing to overpay to lure individuals for their particular skills. Such individuals find they cannot get back on the career track because they are overpaid for the next rung up. Their only choice then is to stay with the small, shaky companies willing to overpay—a poor career choice. In our second illustration, (B), we see what happens when individuals allow themselves to become obsolete, or otherwise underperform on the job, causing salary increases to be slow and small, thus once again knocking them off the career path. Getting back on track in such a case can be a very difficult task. Good, steady performance should allow these individuals to continue to move up the ladder, from job step to job step, with appropriate salary increases that will keep them on the career highway, in a steady progression, providing that an effective career plan strategy is in effect in the organization.

Education and Training

Job descriptions, career counseling, and other sources should make it clear what skills and/or education are needed to achieve each successive step of the ladder. A good internal training program should provide entry-level, intermediate, and advanced training programs and education for applications programmers, computer operators, systems programmers, and teleprocessing people alike. The program should start with a skills inventory; that is, education and training, courses taken, familiarity with programming languages, hardware (vendor and models) experience, etc. Basic tests can also be administered, as appropriate, to validate proficiency level. Once technical skills have been determined, they can be matched against the technical skills needed for the job, and a custom-tailored curriculum designed to fill the voids can be put together for each individual. To minimize the need for a large training staff, some companies successfully utilize commercial videotape instruction programs and programmed-instruction texts, to allow individuals to move along at their own pace. Proficiency tests can be administered at the conclusion of each training module. A typical entry-level program of this type, consisting of a dozen or so modules, can usually be completed in three or four months.

It is a good idea to assign a mentor (S-35) to all trainees when they are hired. For example, a programmer trainee could be assigned an experienced person on the staff who will be his or her mentor throughout the training period, including both the formal training and the early on-the-job training, until the "trainee" designation can be dropped. This procedure eases trainees into the organization in such a way that they become productive faster and with less pain. Follow-up intermediate and advanced courses could be preceded in each case by a suitable period of on-the-job training. Since, at this point, it is too early to tell which career path an individual is likely to take, all entry-level staff usually start out along the same path within an assigned area: computer operations, systems and programming, etc. (Some companies, in fact, have everyone follow the identical job path in the early stages, regardless of his or her ultimate destination.) Eventually, the individual moves through a progression of technical jobs, such as trainee, programmer, and program analyst, as experience and ability grow. It is during this period that employees should be made aware of the different career opportunities open to them, and their technical and managerial interests and aptitudes for these career paths should be assessed.

Dual Paths

Aside from multiple departmental paths up the IM organization, there should also be clearly indicated and supported technical paths that allow people with a technical bent to achieve salary, title, stature, and responsibility equal to those on managerial paths. For example, if corporate titles are used (e.g., vice president—we prefer functional titles, such as systems officer or investment officer) and a department manager is an assistant vice-president of the firm, then the corresponding senior technician on the job ladder should carry the same title. The titles must carry similar responsibility, however, and must not just be empty labels; otherwise, they will be seen as a ploy and will not be effective as motivators. Titles and job responsibility must be real to be effective. In order to keep these equal, a move from one path to another, on an equal level, should be considered a lateral move, which is not accompanied by a raise or promotion. And, in fact, such moves could be encouraged, especially on the early rungs of the ladder, to help people to find their right niche in the organizational structure. This is what we call "stirring the pot." *Stirring the pot* means rotating people now and then as they move up in the organization, to help them experience different assignments and to determine where their real strengths and interests lie before they settle on a final career path. (Psychological testing is another effective way of testing interest and aptitude; this can be done either at entry level or before the employee chooses a long-term career path.) Lateral promotions are an important career policy because they let people see broader opportunities, as discussed earlier. The progression from systems programmer to computer specialist and computer consultant usually follows a period during which analysts have decided that the technical path is their "cup of tea" and have demonstrated their talents along these lines through a series of significant personal and technical contributions. Making these technical career positions compare favorably with managerial career opportunities is the real challenge. Few companies have been successful in doing so, and, in fact, we know of none that actually has a chief computer consultant who is equal in status and salary to the IM director. (IBM probably comes closest with its Chief Scientist designation.) It is important that we continue to work at this, however, for if skilled (and valuable) technicians decide that they are at a dead end in the company, they will pursue their careers outside the company. No company can afford to lose good people for the lack of an effective career path strategy.

Performance Appraisal

The evaluation of individual performance should be a formal process requiring written performance appraisals followed by a review of the appraisal with the employee. The purposes of a performance review are to determine whether company and personal objectives are being met, to review how successfully the various components of job performance are being addressed, to make sure that employees know what is expected of them, to examine strengths and weaknesses, and to learn where additional training may be needed. The characteristics of a good performance appraisal might include a list of job responsibilities, the results to be achieved in the coming period, the relative importance of each objective, the actual results achieved (with some kind of rating attached to each), other significant observations, and an overall rating of the individual. The counseling summary indicates employee strengths and weaknesses (i.e., suggested development). The interviewers summarize the significant points raised during the performance review, and the employees have the opportunity to record optional comments if desired (for example, agreement or disagreement) and to leave room for an optional management summary, if appropriate. Such reviews need not be done more than once or twice a year, but they can provide valuable feedback on employee progress, eliminate misunderstandings, and serve as input to salary review and promotion decisions. A career path strategy can be a valuable staff-management system in any MBS bag. Only a small number of leading IM organizations have adopted such a plan in a formal way. Here, then, is an opportunity to give prospective recruits what they are really interested in: a well-defined career progression path and continual feedback on their progress along the way.

The Boss–Subordinate Relationship

The success or failure of a career path plan can often be strongly influenced by a factor that is seldom considered. It is generally thought that people change jobs because of better compensation, career advancement potential, or job dissatisfaction. But another, less discussed, cause of a job change is often the desire of the employee to find a more satisfying boss–subordinate relationship. In a good relationship, respect, trust, and learning are exchanged between boss and subordinate. When one or more of these is lacking, the relationship tends to disintegrate. For example, if the employee does not respect the boss, the working relationship can become frustrating and unfulfilling. On the other hand, if the boss feels that she or he cannot trust the employee, the relationship is also strained. Or, when the employee feels that he or she has nothing to learn from the boss, the relationship can also be weakened.

The relationship may not be doomed by the absence of one factor if another of the factors is the primary one, or if a compensating substitute factor can continue to motivate the employee. For example, if the primary factor for a new employee in the relationship is one of learning from the boss, the mentor relationship may outweigh respect and trust. Or if the boss' character and interpersonal skills provide a warm and supportive work climate, an older employee may find adequate job satisfaction, even though the boss is ineffective as a mentor. Or perhaps the boss has a seat of power that can effectively sponsor an employee's career development, which may interest a fast-tracker, even though the boss can't teach the employee.

SYSTEMS INTERNS

> **S-37 SYSTEMS INTERNS**
>
> **A horizontal entry-level training strategy used to upgrade the quality of the IM staff and improve user service levels.**

Typical data processing trainees start at the bottom in a given job—say, auxiliary equipment operator—and rise on a vertical path through a succession of more complicated operations to senior computer operator or computer operations supervisor. Persons on the vertical training path must work a long time at each job to become knowledgeable about a lot of computer operations jobs. In addition, they may still lack knowledge and understanding of jobs in other areas of the data center: data entry, data distribution, scheduling, etc.

An alternative is the systems intern concept, a training strategy that follows a horizontal path rather than a vertical one. That is, trainees spend only one or two weeks on every job in the data center. In six months' time, they have a good understanding of the entire process, not of just a small piece of it. They are then more valuable as employees wherever they ultimately may be assigned. Moreover, this strategy allows a different concept of work flow. In the assembly-line process, work flows through stationary people; systems interns can flow with the work and be responsible for a given users' product delivery from start to finish. In this sense, horizontal-path followers are analogous to medical interns. They are not limited to treating only one illness; they handle every patient who comes along, regardless of the symptoms, with the careful supervision of resident doctors. In a similar sense, systems interns learn all of the jobs in the data center and then can be responsible for a particular user's work from beginning to end.

The main objectives of the systems intern strategy are (1) to upgrade the quality of the DP staff and (2) to provide improved user-service levels. This strategy involves the creation of a new and higher entry-level position because every trainee is expected to have the *potential* to become a DP manager, not just a printer operator. The strategy proceeds with a phased elimination of all entry-level positions by filling those jobs with systems interns as turnover occurs. Horizontal job training can then ensue along with the concept of following the work through the data center. The end result can meet the objectives of a better-trained, higher-quality staff, providing improved service levels to users.

Supplementing the on-the-job training could be an education program for acquiring the required technical knowledge. In that regard, we have found videotape programs to be an excellent way of providing relatively inexpensive individually tailored instruction. Firms such as Deltak, ASI, and IBM rent tapes which can be used selectively to fill technical voids or simply to build technical knowledge and skills. Systems interns can listen to the tapes whenever time can be conveniently scheduled, and they can self-pace themselves through the subject, repeating it as necessary until they have learned the material. An instructor–educator can then test the staff member to validate that the needed knowledge has been acquired. Thus, a single educator using a commercial videotape library can monitor the education of many systems interns at once, even though all are at different levels of progress.

The point is that there is always an unwritten, yet real, "psychological contract" between boss and subordinate.[3] Each party enters into a psychological, or career, contract on the basis of what he or she expects in exchange for participation. The subordinate has needs and expectations in the areas of salary, career goals, recognition, a supportive work environment, etc. The boss seeks hard work, initiative, dedication, and loyalty. Each enters the relationship tacitly accepting the expectations of the other. This tacit acceptance forms the basis of a psychological career contract. When either party breaks that contract (i.e., fails to meet the needs of the other), the dissatisfied party often severs the relationship. Often, this unwritten psychological contract is formalized into an MBO contract between boss and subordinate. The successful completion of MBO goals satisfies the boss's needs, and tying in the reward system to this accomplishment satisfies the employee's needs.

This career contract idea should be considered in any career-planning strategy. If respect, trust, or learning is not present to the degree necessary to motivate the individual to continue in a specific boss–subordinate relationship, attention must be paid to the problem before a valuable employee is lost. As in the old adage, recognition of the problem is half the solution.

EAGLES

Give the bird room to fly.

ANCIENT CHINESE PROVERB

> **S-38   EAGLES**
>
> **Identify, motivate, and effectively utilize the high achievers in the organization.**

Eagles are also known as *water-walkers,* or *supermen* who can leap tall buildings with a single bound and are faster than a speeding bullet. Information management is a field in which it is possible to be a virtuoso performer. Given a 5-to-1 or even 10-to-1 ratio between a high performer and the average information specialist, these high performers are extremely valuable. They make up probably 2% of the staff in the average IM function—but what an important 2%!

The key to a successful information management organization is a first-rate professional staff, and the key to a quality staff are the "eagles" in the organization. The eagles are those rare individuals whose contribution far outstrips the contributions of those around them by any measurement standard. They seem to have limitless talent, brainpower, leadership skills, and diverse capabilities. Their track records are filled with successes, not problems. They are called on when weighty problems need to be solved, not just in their own sphere of influence, but throughout the organization. They are, in short, the all-important *high achievers*. High achievers are self-starters. They not only perform their assigned tasks well, they also take on self-imposed tasks: they see a need not being filled and proceed to fill that need. They are self-motivated, dedicated, hard-working. They give new meaning to the Pareto principle that 20% of the causes create 80% of the effects. In fact, one needs far less than 20% eagles on the staff to generate 80% of the effectiveness; only a few are needed. Why? Because good people tend to *replicate* themselves; they tend to build their staffs in their own image. Excellence begets excellence. Before long, quality and professionalism permeate the organization—all born of a few eagles. In searching out eagles, look for unusual strength. Tap people's strengths, and effectiveness will be doubled and tripled; attack their weaknesses and you will be lucky to see a 10% improvement. You cannot change what people are, but you can change what they do. When you find real strength, put it to work where it will be optimally used. Tapping strengths in this way can double the effectiveness of the organization with the same staff. All it takes is a few capable eagles to produce a high-performance IM function.

Only a comparatively few people consistently perform exceptionally well. Many people work hard, have talent, and are educated and intelligent but still are not high achievers. High achievers have something else going for them. What? J. W. Newman Corp., a Los Angeles consulting firm, described 14 primary characteristics on which high-performance people persistently score high, which we summarize here as the things to look for in eagles:[4]

1 *Self-esteem.*   High achievers have the confidence born of a strong feeling of self-worth and capability.
2 *Responsibility.*   They are self-made people, accountable for their own success and failures.
3 *Optimism.*   They believe that things will always be better, because they are in charge of their own destiny.
4 *Goal-orientedness.*   Because they keep their eye on goals at all times, they motivate and direct their efforts automatically.
5 *Imagination.*   They dwell on the good and have a positive attitude. They focus on new experiences. They don't just cope with change—they cause it!
6 *Awareness.*   They absorb their environment, are alert to signals, cues, clues, opportunities to reach goals.
7 *Creativity.*   They believe there always must be a better way. They have fewer restrictions and preconceptions to block creative thinking. Ideas flow spontaneously.
8 *Communications skills.*   They understand that success lies in the communication of ideas—in both directions. They are emphatic communicators.
9 *Growth orientation.*   They know they can't stand still in a changing

world. They continually search for ways to grow, to prepare for the future, to lead change.

10 *Positive response to pressure.*   They thrive on pressure, which makes them function more smoothly and efficiently, putting talent, creativity, and productivity to work.

11 *Trust.*   They trust people, believe that they will try hard, delegate willingly, and foster good communications and cooperation.

12 *Joyfulness.*   They enjoy everything they do. They have contagious energy and enthusiasm, which rubs off on those around them.

13 *Risk takers.*   They weigh probable gains and losses in making decisions and are willing to take reasonable risks. Their objective is excellence, not perfection.

14 *Nowness.*   The sum of high achievers' characteristics make them now people. Decisions, actions are made now. They reflect power, action, accomplishment, enthusiasm—NOW!

GATEKEEPERS

> **S-39   GATEKEEPERS**
>
> **Identify individuals with unique technical talents and abilities who can be called upon by staff members with difficult technical problems.**

A gatekeeper is a special kind of eagle, or water-walker, who appears to know everything about one or more technical fields of knowledge. The role of gatekeeper was documented by Professor Thomas Allen of the Sloan School of Management at MIT.[5] Professor Allen studied communication patterns among R&D scientists and engineers. His studies showed that a very small number of gatekeepers were the primary source of information supplied to other scientists and engineers in their R&D laboratories. When communications about technical problems were measured by questions such as "When you need a technical question answered, whom do you ask?" a small number of gatekeepers in each R&D laboratory were identified by most of the scientists and engineers.

The corporate information manager's function is similar in many ways to that of an R&D laboratory, which invents new products. Using rapidly changing high technology, highly trained specialists invent products and services. A gatekeeper can save a systems professional days of unproductive work just by coming up with the right answer when systems design decisions must be made. Professor Allen has discovered that gatekeepers have information search practices which are statistically different from those of the majority of scientists and engineers. Gatekeepers read much more, they attend more seminars, and they place a much higher value on staying at the frontier of knowledge in their field.

Note the differences between mentors and gatekeepers. A gatekeeper serves the whole IM function as an expert in one or more fields of specialized knowledge. The gatekeeper is expected to be at the technological frontier, while a mentor may have only average technical skills. The mentor should have strong organizational rather than technical skills. Gatekeepers frequently work for mentors. Mentors should pass on to the trainee their knowledge about the importance of gatekeepers. Mentors are users of gatekeepers and introduce trainees to them.

Gatekeepers are an example of why an effective human resource management system is so important in the information management function. Needless to say, it is critical to recognize gatekeepers, who should be encouraged in every way to pursue their special interests and increase their expertise in their chosen specialties. Gatekeepers should also be recognized and rewarded for their special contribution to the productivity of other staff professionals. This includes monetary reward as well as recognition and stature in the organization and the respect of their peers.

CONSULTANTS

> **S-40   CONSULTANTS**
>
> **Management strategy for the effective utilization
> of consultants.**

Consultants can perform an important function, if used properly. If you need a specific expertise for a short period of time, it's often cheaper and wiser to hire that expertise in the form of a temporary consultant rather than a permanent employee. If you need to supplement your staff temporarily, a consulting firm can supply temporary analysts, programmers, and other technical staff. If you're looking for a new manager, a temporary consultant can fill in while the search goes on. And finally, if you need an objective outside opinion to substantiate something—the need for additional resources, validation of a long-range EDP plan, a solution to a major problem—an outside consultant can often provide the necessary objectivity and expert opinion to help convince management. (Be sure of your grounds, however. No good consultant is simply going to rubber-stamp your recommendation. But if you're right and they agree, they can help sell it.)

The correct strategy for using consultants, however, is always to *hire the person,* not the company! There are three types of consultants: individuals, small specialized firms, and large multifield firms. If you hire either of the first two, you will very likely get the individual you are dealing with; if you hire the latter, you should recognize that customer reps, partners, and managers do not usually do the actual consulting. Many people will hire a large consulting firm based on its reputation, assuming that whoever is assigned will be a professional. Not a good idea! First of all, the person assigned will very likely be whoever is available—this could be the newest kid on the block. Not everyone in the consulting firm will have the skills and experience you need. The person you need is, in fact, very likely to be on another assignment, from which he or she cannot be freed. Second, you may believe that the consultant's work and recommendations will be reviewed by her or his superiors, who will thus provide additional consultancy. Maybe, but unless the superiors have studied the situation, their input will be based on personal viewpoints and experiences. So, you are still basically dealing with an individual. This being the case, you should hire the individual, not the company. Be sure the person assigned has the credentials to do the job. Read his or her résumé, and learn his or her track record and experience; don't buy a pig in a poke.

The effective utilization of consultants requires a careful search effort. Has the proposed consultant worked with other clients on similar problems? Ask for references. Talk with "satisfied" clients. The consulting industry was one of the country's fast-growing businesses during the 1970s. Company executives, overwhelmed with the speed of change in business and technological conditions, have increasingly sought assistance from the "experts" in large consulting firms. How has the large consulting firm staffed up to meet this extraordinary increase in demand? Mainly through the employment of inexperienced young graduates from the better schools of management. Well over half the 1980 graduates of the MIT Sloan School of Management accepted employment in the consulting industry. The starting salaries of these students averaged over $30,000 a year. Double or triple that number, and you get the billing rate for these bright but frequently inexperienced young staff consultants. Know what you're buying. Don't put out $1,000 a day for an unknown commodity. At those prices, they should expect to justify their existence.

Once you've decided to hire a consultant, don't wait until he or she arrives before defining the problem. Save time and money by writing the problem out before the consultant arrives, so that he or she knows immediately what the problem is, where and how to get the facts needed to do the analysis, and, above all, what is expected on this assignment. Unless you do this, you may well be disappointed by getting the right solution to the wrong problem. Understanding the problem is half the solution, so be sure the consultant gets on the right track from the beginning—write out the problem and the assignment beforehand. No consultant will thoroughly understand the assignment unless you do.

This leads us logically to our final point. *Have a contract!* If you have a contract, both parties will know what is expected, what "deliverables" constitute acceptable completion of the assignment, the estimated costs of the assignment, etc. Don't just accept the boilerplate contract which is handed you. If they wrote it, it will be to their advantage, not yours. Be sure it covers everything you want, strike out sections you don't like, and be sure that protective clauses work both ways. Everything in a contract is negotiable—don't just accept it as is (see package programs, S-46).

The use of consultants can be an effective strategy to supplement resources, to buy temporary expertise, and to convince management of needed actions. But to use consultants effectively, hire the person not the company, define the problem in writing beforehand, and have a contract so everybody knows what's expected. Above all, be sure *you* do the hiring, not top management. When top management hires the consultant, it's usually bad news. They're either unhappy with something, don't know what IM is doing, or otherwise feel they need outside help. This is called "job insecurity." You could fall victim to the kind of consultant who simply tells management what it wants to hear, as described by one management consultant (who shall remain nameless for obvious reasons):

> . . . the consultant's survival instinct will cause him to side with the seat of power in the organization. Much to his relief, he will find that a number of proposed options can be discarded without endangering his 'professional integrity.' As for the remainder, they are reasonably sound so that at little risk, for the company or for him, he can choose to reject any of the options. It becomes a simple matter of redoing the analysis before picking the answer that most closely approaches the opinions of the influential members of management—and incorporating minor variances for good measure that reflect other opinions. So much for independence.

TIME MANAGEMENT

> **S-41 TIME MANAGEMENT**
>
> **Twelve tested time tips for getting more done in less time.**

No discussion of human resource management would be complete if we did not recognize the importance of managing the time of people efficiently. After all, making the most of our resources offers more potential than almost any other endeavor. Here, then, is a most unexploited strategy.

Probably the three most important principles of management are *planning, organizing, and managing time*. Of all the problems a manager faces, probably the most frustrating, if not the most difficult, is how to find enough time in the day to do everything she or he wants to do. Yet, surprisingly, relatively few managers spend any time developing a strategy for managing their time more effectively.

We offer the following time tips as a strategy for learning to use not only your own time wisely, but your staff's time, as well. You may be pleasantly surprised to find that a little time spent learning to manage time can sharply improve total productivity. If you can't get a 10% increase in staff, try getting 10% more out of yourself and your staff, with these 12 time tips summarized from "Managing a Manager's Time":[6]

Time Tip 1   Self-motivation is key!

You must have deep respect for time and be determined to spend it wisely. Advice won't do it. You must be self-motivated and you must make a conscious effort to build in time management as a permanent, unconscious part of your management style.

Time Tip 2   Time management is self-management!

You're probably used to managing other people, but how much thought have you given to managing yourself? That's what managing time is really all about. If you don't accomplish what you wish in a given period of time, time is not the problem—you are, because you're not managing yourself effectively.

Time Tip 3   Apply the basic principles of management to yourself!

To manage yourself effectively, apply the management principles of planning, organizing, directing, controlling, and, above all, delegating. If you do, you will be automatically managing your time effectively. As Peter Drucker points out, unless he manages himself effectively, no amount of ability, skill, experience or knowledge will make an executive effective.[7]

Time Tip 4   Set priorities.

Make a list of things that must be done each day. Do the most important first, then the next, then the next, etc. Then, no matter how much you are sidetracked, you will have done the most important things and will feel a sense of accomplishment rather than frustration.

Time Tip 5   Practice fire prevention, not fire fighting!

It has been said: "Any damn fool can plan, but it takes real genius to be able to jump from one crisis to another." When putting out today's fires takes priority over planning for tomorrow, all you do is ensure that there will be more fires tomorrow. Of course, you must pay attention to the flames licking at your feet, but you'd also better find some time for a little fire prevention, too. Planning gives you control; control buys you time—and you need time to plan. A nice fire-prevention cycle!

Time Tip 6   Organize your job, yourself, and then others—in that order!

Start with your job, do some soul-searching about what your job really is. What results are expected? How best can you achieve them? What are the priorities? Are you doing the right things? The successful executive is distinguished by the self-imposed tasks he or she assumes—those not called for in the job description and not required by the organization, but perceived and filled nonetheless. Such managers are opportunity-oriented initiators who avoid getting buried in daily fire-fighting problems. They try to spend their time on opportunities, not problems.

Organizing yourself begins with an assessment of your skills. Find your strengths and put them to work. It's a far more constructive use of your time to concentrate on putting your strengths to work than in trying to overcome your weaknesses. Also, know where your time is going. Try a time log for a week, recording what you do each day for later analysis.

The effect of managing others is like the effect of a finger on a pendulum: a small push at the top can have a great effect at the bottom. So, you had better push in the right direction, or a lot of everyone's time will be wasted. Mold your people together synergistically, balancing talents and personalities into effective working units. Tap their strengths and ignore their weaknesses. Motivate them with real challenges and responsibilities. Remember that the organization of your time, plus your staff's time, equals effective management—and increased productivity.

Time Tip 7   Delegate: Never do anything someone else should do!

The most powerful time saver of all, delegation, is not only your best time saver, it's also your best management development tool. Push decisions down to the lowest level, delegate both responsibility and authority. Your effectiveness as a manager will ultimately be measured by how well you have developed your subordinates; that is, how well *they* perform, not how well *you* perform. Remember, managers don't work, they get work done through others; managers are not doers, but managers of doers. Crossing the bridge from a technical do-it-yourselfer (thing-oriented) to manager (people-oriented) is successfully accomplished by probably no more than 1% or 2% of the systems population. So, remember: technical is doing, managing is delegating.

And finally, be wary of reverse delegation, that is, your subordinates' passing the buck back to you. Always be careful to keep the monkeys on the right back. William Oncken suggested asking yourself constantly, "Who's got the monkey?"[8] If you collect 1 monkey a day from each of five subordinates, by week's end, you will have 25 screaming monkeys on your back requiring care and feeding, and you'll be the victim of upward delegation. Keep the initiative always with the subordinate. Assign work on a completed-job basis. Don't get into the nuts and bolts. Spend your time managing. Be a delegator, not a delegatee!

Time Tip 8   Communications will eat up two-thirds of your time—so be good at it!

Verbal communications can be ambiguous. (When I say, "Fish," do you think of eating or fishing?) Ask for "instant replays," instructions summarized back to you, and remember that direct communication is always better than indirect communications. Verbal communication is faster, so is the telephone; so, try to keep written communications to a minimum. Your aim should be to say the most with the fewest words. Why? Two reasons: (1) Clear writing requires clear thinking. A short, well-thought-out memo is likely to be more effective, clear, and unambiguous; (2) other people are busy too—the shorter the communication, the more likely that it will be read and acted on immediately. If you can call, don't write. And don't handwrite letters. Learn to dictate, which is six times faster. Be informal. Write short notes instead of typed replies. Every minute saved through efficient communications can be rechanneled into creative work. If you're spending half your time communicating and only 10% on creative work, a 20% cut in the former will double your time on the latter. That's worth working at!

Time Tip 9   Avoid meetings!

Most group meetings last an hour and a half (Synnott's law). When they end sooner, attendees tend to hang on; when they last longer, people start fidgeting and checking watches. An hour and a half is too much time to waste, so be sure you should be there in the first place. Don't get caught in the prestige trap: everyone's invited so as not to omit anyone, not because they all need to be there. It's seldom necessary for more than two levels of a hierarchy to be at a meeting. (Example: a project manager may call a meeting to which he invites the systems department head, who, in turn, invites his division head, etc.) If you're not needed for a decision, perhaps someone else should attend and simply brief you later. A 10-minute briefing could save an hour and a half of your valuable time.

Time Tip 10   Read smart!

Be selective in what you read and how you read. Would you like to know how you can read 50,000 words per minute? Easy! Just decide in one minute that a book of 50,000 words does not suit your purposes and decide *not* to read it. The point is, be selective in what and how you read. Scan, preview, skim, speed-read, but don't read every word unless necessary. Skimming, for example, involves reading the opening sentence, skimming for key points, reading the beginning of each paragraph (in 70% of all paragraphs, the main idea is expressed in the opening sentence). Intense word-for-word reading should be reserved for technical material, textbooks, and editing. Systems specs must be read; a magazine is skimmed. Did you know that the average adult reads about 300 words per minute? With a little effort and attention to types of reading skills, this rate can be at least doubled. The point is, don't read everything, and for what you do read, choose the most appropriate method. With just a little effort, you'll find that your reading productivity can jump several-fold.

Time Tip 11   Increase your planning and thinking time!

Most people put so much time into communicating, attending meetings, reading, etc., that very little is ever left over for the important creative thinking and planning that gives real direction to all activity. Perhaps this statement suggests that the office is no place to work. Most managers, in fact, do most of their thinking and planning at home, at night and on weekends, commuting to and from work, or before and after regular working hours. We all do this, of course, but the point is that you should constantly try to increase your office thinking and planning time by borrowing time from other areas, like reading, writing, and communicating.

Time Tip 12   Identify the time thieves in your life!

"Are you a decisive person?" "Well, yes and no!" Is this poor decision-making ability, or just the unwillingness to make decisions? Either way, it wastes time. Try to find the time thieves that eat up your productivity. Are you a good decision maker, or do you spend all kinds of time waiting for more results to come in (decision paralysis)? Do you make good use of exception management, or are you flailing away at detail? Do you follow through by having a formal system for remembering, or do you simply depend on your memory? Do you establish priorities at the beginning of each day so that the most important things will be done first? Do you practice wastebasketry, or file everything away because of destruction anxiety? How do you handle interruptions such as the telephone or an unannounced visitor? (Try standing up to greet him, and stay standing; stand-up meetings never last long!) Do you have to work unreasonable hours to get your job done? Maybe you're not delegating or managing your time wisely. In short, develop the habit of spotting time thieves and develop a system for eliminating them. Ask yourself how many are robbing you of time, and then begin knocking them off, one by one.

The manager who recognizes the value of time management is already on the way to becoming a more effective manager. Planning your time each day may well be the most important thing you can do to increase productivity. Stretching time stretches resources—an important human resource strategy.

IMPLEMENTATION PLAN

Lenin is alleged to have said shortly after the Bolshevik revolution, "The peasants are starving. Therefore, they cannot work. That is why they are starving." And so it is with human resource problems. When an information management function is grossly understaffed, when huge amounts of management time are committed to recruitment interviews, or when management time is badly managed, rarely are there sufficient management resources to implement the strategies presented in this chapter.

As a first step in the implementation process, it may be useful to take an inventory of the current status in your company of the human resources strategies offered in this chapter. Given only limited resources for innovating improved management practices, priorities must be established. Some improved practices will take more management time in calendar months to implement than others. Some will have a faster payback or a higher benefit–cost ratio.

NOTES

1 R. A. McLaughlin, "That Old Bugaboo, Turnover," *Datamation*, October 1979, p. 97.

2 Gerald R. Roche, "Much Ado About Mentors," *Harvard Business Review*, January–February 1977, pp. 14–16.

3 This notion of a psychological contract is based on a note prepared by Professor R. Roosevelt Thomas, Jr., *Managing the Psychological Contract*, Harvard Business School 9-474-159, January 1978.

4 Pamphlet prepared by J. W. Newman Corporation, Los Angeles, *PACE: High Performance Characteristics of People*, undated.

5 Thomas Allen, *Managing the Flow of Technology*, Cambridge, Mass.: MIT Press, 1978, pp. 161–180.

6 William R. Synnott, "Managing a Manager's Time," *Association for Systems Management Conference Proceedings*, Washington, D.C., 1977, pp. 131–145.

7 Peter F. Drucker, *The Effective Executive*, New York: Harper & Row, 1967, p. 169.

8 William C. Oncken and Donald L. Wass, "Management Time: Who's Got the Monkey?" *Harvard Business Review*, November–December 1974, pp. 75–80.

8

Hardware and Software

The single factor most affecting how companies will be managed in the 1980s will be technology.

James Martin[1]

If technology had changed the airplane as much as it has changed computers, we could now fly around the world in 45 minutes at a cost of $1.50 in an 18-inch airplane. Of course, we would have to find a way to miniaturize people, as we have chips, in order to fit them into 18-inch airplanes, but with computers, *smaller, cheaper,* and *better* have been the watchwords of the industry since its beginning a little over 25 years ago.

The driving reason for the growth in minicomputers and the accompanying trend toward distributed processing is largely economic. To be sure, there are users who want their own computers in order to have more control over their own destiny and to get out from under unresponsive centralized support, or because they believe they can satisfy local needs better. But, we suggest, none of these reasons would even be considered if costs were not now so low as to make distributed processing *possible.* It is safe to say that each new advance in computing power and memory density in future years will be reflected in an additional capability to distribute an additional set of applications. Cheaper computing means that applications previously not cost-justified become so, and cheap computers also mean that users can cost-justify their own systems and that many will opt to do so.

The driving engine which will continue to fuel this trend in the years to come is the *chip.* The chip revolution continues to produce bigger and better cost–performance improvements, improvements that have seen computers evolve from the multi-million-dollar room-sized monsters of the 1950s to today's desk-top computers selling for a few hundred dollars. Hardware cost performance has, in fact, been dropping by a factor of 10 every five years. Similarly, memory costs have been halving every two years. Increased speed and memory, at lower cost, is the contribution of *chip technology* to the advancement of computing, minicomputers, and distributed processing (see Exhibit 8-1). Until quite recently, it was common for small systems to be

Exhibit 8-1 Cost–performance consequences of progress in semiconductor technology.

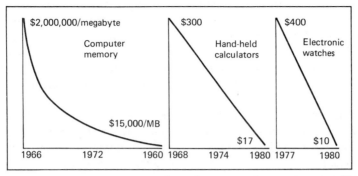

Source: *The Monosson Review*, American Computer Group, Boston, November, 1979.

limited to memory sizes of a few 10s or 100s of kilobytes. That barrier is now broken, and as a result we can expect to see huge advances in the 80s. The recently announced IBM E Series exemplifies this trend. The number of components on a chip should continue, as in the past, to double every year, continuing right through the 1980s. The result will be very powerful computers housed in desk-sized cabinets at prices almost everyone can afford. Some even say that hardware will be giveaway items in the 1980s, with profits generated from the sale of software (very much the way Gillette gives away razors in order to sell blades). The use of chips in computers, known as *large-scale integration* (LSI), has not only caused prices to drop dramatically, it has made possible a reduction in size and power requirements to the point where one can put a minicomputer on a single chip of silicone. Thus, in the future, the cheapest way to update software may be simply to replace a semiconductor part, making the semiconductor device a throwaway item.

In the 1980s, LSI will be replaced by VLSI (very-large-scale integration). The impact of VLSI on computers will be threefold: first, costs will again decline for equivalent functions and performance (several boards replaced with one); second, the lower cost per function performed will make it possible to acquire a larger set of functions for the same cost; third, new functions, mainly in programming and maintenance, will be implemented, lowering the operating cost of computers. The large increase in main memory space made possible by VLSI will also impact on virtual memories. It will not eliminate virtual memory, but it will increase page size, allowing a high percentage of programs to reside in a single page in the computer. Beyond these advances, there are emerging technologies such as Josephson junction devices, charge-coupled devices, and bubble memories (bubble memories with 1 million bits per square inch first appeared in minicomputers in 1980; 100 million bits per square inch are predicted for mainframe computers by 1985).

There is, of course, a limit as to how far costs can decline. Note, for example, that a computer system is only about 50% in the CPU and memory; the other 50% is in peripherals. Although excellent strides have been made in tape and disk densities and printer speeds, these have not begun to parallel the gains from chip technology. Moreover, even if a product could be manufactured for *free* (e.g., Perrier water), it would still carry marketing and service costs, general and administrative overhead expenses, and a profit margin. Hence, the cost would drop only by the manufacturing cost ingredient.

Nonetheless, we can expect to see continuing and dramatic cost–performance improvements in 1980s computers driven by chip VLSI technology. These will provide the opportunity to automate more and more functions, squeezing the labor out, and helping managers to run and control the business better.

PRODUCTIVITY MANAGEMENT

> **S-42   PRODUCTIVITY MANAGEMENT**
>
> **IM role in the planning and implementation of new information technology to improve the productivity of business operations.**

What does all this mean to information managers of the 1980s? It means PRODUCTIVITY! We are one of the few industries today successfully fighting inflation. Information managers can use that fact to apply advancing technology to increase the productivity of the firm in the years ahead.

One of the country's biggest problems today is inflation. Many factors are responsible for inflation, of course, but one of the most important is the nation's declining productivity growth. Declining productivity means that we are all struggling to share what income there is, driving up inflation. In 1979, the inflation rate in the United States rose to 13%, the dollar eroded in world markets, and the country moved toward a recession. In 1980, we were in a recession. Yet, even in a recession, inflation persisted as one of the country's most pressing problems. Inflation persisted because one of our fundamental economic problems is collapsing productivity. In the last 10 years, U.S. productivity (output per man hour) has been up about 1½% per year compared with 3% from 1947 to 1967. U.S. productivity is now behind that of most of the nations with whom we do business. Productivity growth is important because without increases in output, our standard of living declines as we pay higher prices for fewer goods, and as increased wage demands cause our companies to raise prices in lieu of offsetting productivity.

A partial answer to declining productivity is increased capital investment and R&D. Similarly, a productivity strategy for an information manager is one which results in *increased investment in automation* and systems research, to exploit technological gain by applying technical capabilities to company needs. Computing capability has been improving at a rate of some 15–25% per year, memory costs are dropping 30% per year (halving every two years), and communications costs are dropping 11% per year. Personnel costs, on the other hand, are rising inexorably, with inflation, by 7–10% per year. What is the inevitable conclusion of this trend? Users will be motivated to seek more computing power and more communications capacity in order to hold down growing payroll costs. Computing will continue to replace labor because *automation equals productivity*.

Information managers need to perceive each coming change, recognize its impact on their business (and products), and exploit it to their advantage. The success of a productivity strategy will depend on the ability to perceive change and exploit it. To use emerging technologies and products successfully will require (1) an awareness of business needs and (2) an awareness of technological capabilities.

Business Needs

The information manager will need to seek out new automation frontiers where computers can replace labor or can make possible the processing of increased volumes with the same labor. As the cost of computing and communications continues to decline, these opportunities will unfold in areas and functions that could not previously be automated. To find these opportunities will require active product planning, as described in our proactive change agent (S-4) and business information planning (S-10) strategies. Technology itself could be considered a solution looking for a problem. To find the problem, information managers need to learn the business they are serving—its needs, problems, and goals.

Technical Capabilities

Along with learning business needs, information managers must also stay abreast of technological developments in order to recognize products, ideas, concepts, and trends that can be successfully applied to the served firm. The spread of low-cost minicomputers into user areas will create a need for control over distributed information resources—a new role for information managers. Microprocessor developments will permit the automation of smaller and smaller functions within a business, which will need to be actively sought out. Office automation represents another opportunity to increase productivity in an area which has experienced continued growth, which is today a large part of every organization (especially service industries), and which has experienced few or no productivity gains until now.

These and many other trends will represent opportunities for alert information managers to exploit emerging technological trends by matching them to company needs and thereby increase the productivity of their companies, which translates directly into bottom-line performance through better cost control. Cost savings are every bit as important as income generation; both impact profit the same way. Information managers can affect both through the continued spread of automation, that is, through new revenue-producing services and through cost control from increased productivity.

HARDWARE MANAGEMENT

The spread of automation means that much behind-the-scenes work must be done to ensure that the necessary technical resources will be on hand when needed to provide these services. That is, resources must be matched against expected needs long in advance. Because of the long lead times in technical evolution, in equipment delivery, and in system development, hardware/software migration planning must necessarily be fairly long-range. Hardware migration planning involves matching up resources against needs. There are at least four major steps in this process:

Keeping Abreast of Technology   As noted earlier, the technological evolution is almost a revolution, with cost–performance gains accelerating by geometric proportions. Not to plan well in advance could well mean having bought a multi-million-dollar machine which is made obsolete in short order. Keeping abreast of hardware evolution means *research*. Many companies cannot afford research staffs of their own, of course, but there are many research organizations which provide excellent research services for very reasonable prices. These include commercial research organizations like International Data Corp., academic research groups such as the Center for Information Systems Research at MIT, and consulting groups such as A. D. Little, to mention a few. The dollars spent for such research is money well spent, considering the cost of mistakes in large computer acquisitions. For example, in July 1980, an 8-megabyte IBM 3033 could be bought for approximately $3.7 million. Various research outfits speculated about where IBM's impending Series "H" cost–performance announcement would impact on that price (see Exhibit 8-2). It is crucial that information managers have the best information available to help the company's hardware needs over the next five to seven years. Information should pertain not only to equipment selection but also to acquisition options (i.e., purchasing, leasing, or renting from manufacturer or used-equipment dealer or lessor). IM organizations which do not subscribe to research services and lack access to this information may be doing their companies a disservice in terms of prudent hardware planning. (See user roundtables, S-48, at the end of this chapter for another research strategy.)

Exhibit 8-2   IBM computer price–performance improvements in the 1970s.

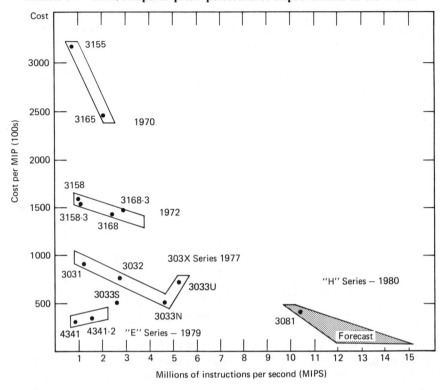

Forecasting Company Needs   This goes back to business information planning (S-10). New computer applications must be projected, and projected volumes must be forecast for existing applications. Likely candidates for minicomputer applications which will affect the work load must be identified (i.e., new applications that will be developed for minicomputer processing, and existing applications which might be off-loaded from the mainframe computers to a mini). It may be helpful to plot applications and volume growth over the past two years and then project it two years ahead. This procedure will indicate whether the trend line will accelerate or decline and will serve as an information source to management as to data center growth.

Knowing Resource Utilization Levels   A knowledge of current use is necessary to project the impact of added business. IBM's Systems Measurement Facility (SMF) provides raw data such as this, as do other vendor systems, but considerable analysis is necessary to convert such raw data into meaningful planning information. This conversion can be done through a formal process of capacity planning, discussed in the following section.

Keeping Management Involved   The knowledge gained from technology research, business information planning, and capacity planning can be distilled, encapsulated, and presented to management in such a way that they are able to be involved in the hardware planning decision-making process. This requires summary nontechnical explanations which show what resources are needed to do what at what cost. Emphasis should be placed on demonstrating increased productivity as the reason for computer upgrades, not just having "the latest new toy," as is sometimes suspected. Two ways this can be done are through the year plan (S-28) and CEO briefings (S-27), presented in Chapter 6.

CAPACITY PLANNING

> **S-43   CAPACITY PLANNING**
>
> **Management procedures for the balancing of existing IM work loads and the forecasting of future work loads through analytical modeling.**

We suggested that capacity planning can be an important activity for information managers. Capacity planning has both a today and a tomorrow benefit. Today, it helps balance existing work loads (fine tuning) to get the most efficient use of resources and the most effective user-service levels. For tomorrow, it helps forecast the needed resources in advance of demand so that the right "horses" are there when needed. Without capacity planning, information managers can only do one of three things: (1) wait until they run out of gas (this spells job insecurity as service levels disintegrate); (2) buy more equipment than can possibly be needed (bringing in an $80,000-per-month computer 6 months earlier than needed is pretty costly to the company); and (3) simply guess what resources will be needed and when (this will very likely result in high costs or poor service levels, or both).

Unfortunately, too many managers wait until they are out of capacity, or suffering from systems bottlenecks resulting in poor service levels, before taking action. This approach often results in a crisis leading to management reaction, a quick performance evaluation, some frantic fine-tuning to carry the system until an equipment upgrade can be effected, a management decision, and then a wait for the next crisis. Needless to say, this kind of situation is annoying to senior management, who have to begin to wonder why the information manager runs the data center by crisis rather than by advanced planning. As a result, they sometimes institute a little performance measurement of their own—not of computers, but of the information manager.

Let us look at what is needed in capacity planning. Planners must foresee capacity problems well in advance and come up with a hardware upgrade plan with enough lead time to assure that the right equipment is in place precisely when needed. The equipment must have enough, but not excessive, capacity to do the job. If next year's work load is vague and uncertain, this planning gets to be difficult. Ideally, the planner would identify various potential equipment configurations and then estimate the resources that would be used by each of several work loads over a range of possibilities. From the information thus obtained, the planner could calculate performance figures (resource utilization, throughput rates, response times) to determine the optimum configuration needed to deliver good service. In practice, this has not been very easy to do.

There are various methods for doing this job: (1) the *rule-of-thumb* method, which is really a guess based on past experience; (2) the *linear projection,* or "eye-balling," method, which simply extrapolates trend lines into the future based on past performance (OK if everything is simple and going in a straight line, but not very reliable for erratic work loads or increasingly complex on-line systems); and (3) *bench-marking,* which requires an analytical model that converts guesses into precision, and allows the capacity planner to forecast accurately what resources will be needed and at what time so as to optimize service levels and costs. Because it can use aggregate rather than detailed data, and because all queueing theory is built in, bench marking is easy and fast to use. An overview of an analytical model is presented in Exhibit 8-3.

From the performance data analyzed, capacity planning charts such as those shown in Exhibit 8-4 can be constructed for management reporting purposes. The capacity chart for batch work tracks equipment capacity in

Exhibit 8-3   Analytical modeling process for computer hardware capacity loading.

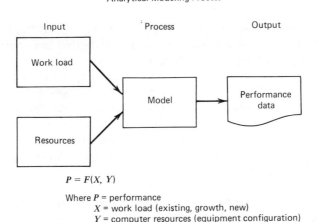

Analytical Modeling Process

$P = F(X, Y)$

Where P = performance
X = work load (existing, growth, new)
Y = computer resources (equipment configuration)

Exhibit 8-4   Computer hardware components–resources chart.

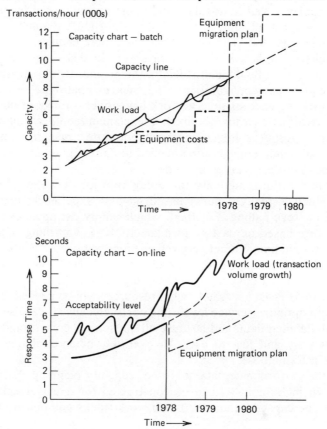

terms of transactions processed per hour (based on the data center's current
multiprogramming factor), current and projected work load (accompanied by
a listing of new automated applications and growth in existing applications),
and current and projected costs over time. The dotted line representing the
equipment migration plan shows the effect of planned equipment upgrades on
lifting the data center's capacity to meet the expanding work load. The
simplicity of this chart gives a manager the total picture at a glance. The
work-load trend line shows when capacity will run out, the equipment line
shows when and what upgrades are planned to expand capacity, and the cost
line shows the productivity–cost ratio of these planned actions. This analysis
allows the placement of protective equipment orders far enough in advance
to be ahead of equipment delivery lead times.

The capacity chart for on-line work tracks response time in seconds as
work load increases and projects when response time will become unacceptable. The effect of planned new equipment on response time is again shown
by the equipment migration line.

COMPUTER PERFORMANCE EVALUATION

> ### S-44   COMPUTER PERFORMANCE EVALUATION
> **New tools and techniques used to effect management control over computer performance.**

The role of computer performance evaluation (CPE) has gained increasing attention from information managers in the last 10 years because of the development of new and better tools and techniques that can be used to evaluate computer performance. For this strategy, we describe four useful CPE tools, three of which are unique products for the management and control of computer operations.

Hardware/Software Monitors

The first tool used by most installations getting into CPE is usually either a hardware or a software monitor. Monitors are not a new tool; they have been around for years. Nevertheless, no discussion of CPE tools would be complete without a consideration of the role of monitors in the task.

Briefly, *software* monitors are relatively easy to use (easier than hardware monitors), are inexpensive ($10,000 range), and are less disruptive to computer operations since they reside in the operating system. They collect and measure data which are used to examine work-load characteristics and actual equipment utilization. This process provides the information needed to optimize the equipment configuration and to improve response time, turnaround time, and job throughput. These monitors can also provide data for system modeling such as that described earlier. Popular software monitors include Comten's Alert, Boole & Babbage's CUE, Applied Data Research's LOOK, and Cosmic's Slacmon.

Hardware monitors attach probes to the hardware itself. Their major advantage over software monitors is that they don't impose any additional load on the operating system (software monitors produce somewhat distorted data since they are part of what they are measuring). However, they can be considerably more expensive than software monitors. This disadvantage can be overcome, however, by the hiring of consultants with their own hardware monitor to do a one-time monitoring job for any installation. They provide the expertise, and the cost is considerably cheaper than that of purchasing a monitor. Popular hardware monitors include Comten's Dynaprobe, Tesdata's MS Series, and Computer Performance Instrumentation's DSP.

Best/1

This tool is a mathematical, or analytical, model and not a simulator model as a software monitor is. Best/1 (BGS Systems, Lincoln, Mass.) can be used to model computer performance as well as for capacity planning. By inputting changing work loads against the current equipment configuration, performance results can be projected before problems arise. Altered configurations can then be tested for appropriate solutions to performance bottlenecks. For a further discussion of analytical modeling, see capacity planning (S-43).

MICS (MVS Integrated Control System)

This is a new product developed by Morino Associates of Vienna, Virginia, to address the complexity, reliability, performance, and day-to-day management control problems of MVS installations. MICS provides a single, common analytical process to analyze the many unlike-measurement sources. It provides an integrated data base to store unlike-measurement data in a common storage and retrieval format. An on-line inquiry facility enables the user to operate on, and analyze, the data interactively, as through IBM's Time Sharing Option (TSO). Management reports provide graphic illustrations of the installation's performance against predetermined objectives. Exception reports, a generalized report writer, and statistical analysis capabilities enable the user to access the data base for special report requirements. An array of measurement products, including TSO/MON, RMF, SMF, and SAS (Statistical Analysis System from SAS Institute, Raleigh, N.C.), are used by the system. The data base and many of the reporting capabilities utilize the features provided by SAS because of its unique ability to handle the high volume and the random nature of measurement data, its extensive inventory of reporting capabilities, and the flexibility and ease of use of the SAS language. Here is a description of three such reports developed by Morino Associates for one of their clients; two of the reports, a management control report and a technical-control recap report, have the same format.

   The management report is a one-page recap of the day's activity related to system availability, effectiveness, TSO service, batch service, and system load. The technical report runs up to three pages and contains more detail, including MVS activity, batch and TSO loads, and MVS, batch, and TSO peak processing periods. The report provides management and performance personnel with a daily overview to identify any installation objectives that missed their target. This identification requires first establishing a range within which everything is considered on target. For example, let us say that a performance objective for TSO users is a 5-second response 85% of the time. A low and high objective could be established so that whenever services fall below a 5-second response 85% of the time or is providing a 5-second response more than 90% of the time, a control exception would be reported. In the first instance, corrective action is needed to restore good service levels. In the latter case, the manager might want actually to "tune down" the system so as not to raise user expectations to a service level which cannot be maintained over the long run. The incident control report provides exception reports of the following critical incidents for the day and time of occurrence: system IPL, CPU varied off-line, real memory loss, TSO response degradation, JES2 shutdown, and critical work packs varied off-line.

The combination of the missed objectives in the technical control report and the critical incidents in the incident control report provides the information manager with an action list for computer performance control.

Reliability Plus

Here is a unique product that addresses equipment maintenance efficiency. The reliability of computer hardware has been increasing as we have progressed through generations of machines. However, as systems grow more complex, small failures can have greater impact on service levels. Increased dependency on real-time on-line systems, data management systems, and complex operating systems, and the greater scheduled use of all these resources, increase the probability of failure. Availability is often confused with reliability, but there is an important distinction: reliability is the measure of failure of a device. For example, a job in its fourth hour of processing gets a tape-drive data-read failure. There are plenty of alternative tape drives which are available, but the unreliability has caused a four-hour rerun. It is straightforward to increase the availability of the system by adding hardware, but the reliability of the devices impacts the work processed through the installation. It's this facet of the operation which, if measured, tracked, and managed, will distinctly contribute to the timely processing of the work load.

Each hardware failure of a CPU, channel memory, tape, or disk device is logged by the operating system on the computer mainframes. But until now, only the vendor's customer engineers used these data for fault diagnosis on these devices. Reliability Plus is a software package from Reliability Research, Inc., which can be run daily against these data, and the results can be formulated in a manner designed specifically for operations management to track and measure the reliability of every single device recorded on the error file. The reports are produced on an exception basis only, and they give a history of the device over the last five days as well as the record of the previous month. Thus, the current failure as indicated in the exception report is put in the context of the history of the device. This procedure allows operations to manage, for the first time, the effort and direction of the engineers performing preventive maintenance (PM) to attend to specific devices which are shown to be weak, or, in the case of excessive failure, to replace the device, if it is on rental.

Two types of failure are recorded: hardfail and softfail. Hardfail is a device failure which causes a job executing in the CPU to fail. Softfail is a failure from which the device or operating system has recovered, but it will have caused degradation of the device and will also cost some CPU time. Softfails are particularly important in predicting the next hardfail, because frequently a hardfail is preceded by many softfails. Thus, these reports can be used to direct the attention of an engineer to a device that can be scheduled for maintenance at a time convenient to the operation, so that it won't cause a problem and consequent loss when the hardfail hits. Reliability Plus has algorithms which decide whether a failure can be ascribed to the media or the device. This is a very important distinction to draw, as in the past much effort was expended by the customer engineer on a tape drive, for example, when in fact the tape *reel* should have been discarded as defective.

Monthly reports are produced which compare each device in its class (for example, all IBM Model 7 tape drives form one class, all STC tape drives another), rating the drives into one of four quartiles. The aim here is to ensure that devices in the fourth quartile of a class do not appear in the next month's fourth quartile. If this procedure is maintained, the general level of reliability of devices within the class will rise as weak devices are either weeded out or get good preventive maintenance. In addition to the monthly summary report, subscribers send to Reliability Research monthly tapes of the device records, and this information is entered in the data base of over 250 other large installations. The individual company's performance of devices can then, class by class, be rated and compared with that of other users, providing for the first time an indication of the extent of reliability problems as compared with those of other installations. These statistics are also useful in comparisons of competing vendors' equipment.

For a one-time charge of around $10,000, Reliability Plus can provide invaluable help in tracking and managing device failure and increasing the reliability of the hardware through directed maintenance. When one considers that equipment maintenance runs to 5% or more of the installed value of equipment, such a program will go a long way toward getting value for the maintenance dollar as well as reducing the time and cost of hardware-related job reruns.

SOFTWARE MANAGEMENT

While the cost of hardware continues to drop, the cost of software continues to climb, as depicted in the chart reproduced in Exhibit 8-5. In the 1950s, the ratio of hardware to software costs was 4 : 1; in 1980, it was 1 : 4. The cost of a line of code rose from $4 in 1960 to $10 in 1980. The reasons for this rise are a combination of lower hardware costs (automatically raising the software part of the ratio), higher labor costs (fueled by inflation), and the greater sophistication and complexity of today's systems. The investment in software by the average organization today is probably several times the value of the hardware installed.

Ironically, probably the biggest barrier to automation in the 1980s will be *programmers!* The shortage of skilled programmers coupled with an ever-

Exhibit 8-5 Trend in the percentage of MIS budgets spent for hardware and software.

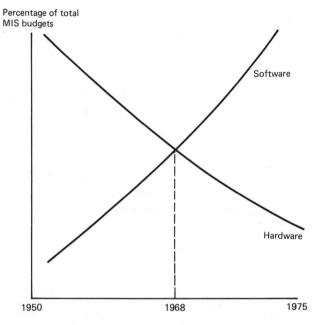

increasing demand for applications programs is creating a widening gap between what is needed and what can be delivered, as conceptualized in Exhibit 8-6. The demand comes from two sources: new development and modifications to existing systems (otherwise known as *maintenance*). In December 1978, a survey conducted by Dean Witter Reynolds of 95 DP managers (mostly Fortune 500 companies) revealed that most managers felt that they were only halfway toward full automation (i.e., of what *should* be automated). When asked when they thought they would be at or near 100%, the majority opinion was 10 years. If the industry is going to do as much in the next 10 years as it has in the past 25 years, the gap between supply and demand is obviously going to become even greater. On the maintenance side, Charles Lecht[2] suggested that most shops already have some 65% of their programming resources devoted to existing systems, and that this amount will grow to 80% in 1982. Now, when we see that the average life of a system today is shortening because of fast-changing business, competition, and regulatory changes, it is easy to see that the burden is being increased by the necessity to rewrite systems already automated every five to seven years. The upshot of all of this is that in the 1980s, there will not be enough programmers to use the power of the computers produced!

What is the answer, then? There are many answers, of course, and all will be used to one degree or another. Let's consider the following:

1 *Programmer productivity.* If one of our strategies for dealing with advancing technology is productivity management (S-42), software is an

Exhibit 8-6   Demand, supply, and gap in programmer resources.

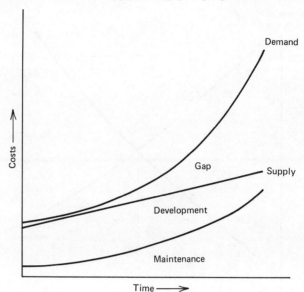

area where greater efforts must be made to increase productivity. Based on present trends, it appears that programmer productivity will double in the next 10 years. This rate is not nearly high enough. We must find new ways to increase this productivity rate. Some thoughts on this problem are covered under the programmer productivity strategy (S-45) following.

2 *Contract programming.*   Although this item now takes up only a small part of most IM budgets, we believe that there will be a continuing increase in the use of outside resources to supplement the shortage of in-house staffs. Ultimately, of course, this is only an interim answer because the shortage of programmers will eventually dry up this source also.

3 *Package programs.*   Constituting only 1–2% of most IM budgets today, package programs should enjoy significant growth in the 1980s as good, flexible, modular programs become more available and are well supported by professional software vendors. A package that "fits" a need can cost a fraction of the cost of development. It should be noted that most package programs today are systems software. Systems software does the same thing in every shop, unlike applications programs. But what is already working for systems software will eventually work for much applications software. For more on this subject, see package programs (S-46).

4 *Automatic program generators (APG).*   Interest is growing in the use of programs that create programs (Data/3, APG/7, AMS), but these are still in limited use. As they become more perfected and sophisticated, they will grow because "automating" programming is a natural way out of the programmer shortage. Watch for APGs really to come to maturity in the 1980s.

5 *Firmware.*   With hardware expected to shrink from 40% to 20% of DP budgets in the next five years, how will manufacturers stay in business selling hardware? The answer: *firmware!* More and more software will become firmware. Floppy disks and programs on a chip will certainly spread in the systems software world. Teleprocessing monitors and data base systems of the future will be separate microprocessors—software turned into hardware. Operating systems by the end of the 1980s will be firmware. There will be fewer systems programmers (but they will probably be more highly skilled). Progress in moving applications software to firmware will be slower because of differing demands and other problems, but the move to firmware will be an important long-term solution to the software problem.

6 *Move the mountain to Muhammad.*   The most promising answer of all is to increase direct end-user interface with machines, bypassing programmers, especially for maintenance operations (which are often report-generation activities). What will make this possible? The use of very-high-level languages (VHLL) coupled with data-base management systems. Query languages and report writers are already in wide use, but their use will increase as more and more companies move into data base systems (see data-base management system, S-47). We are rapidly moving toward the day when most people will be programming. They won't recognize themselves as programmers because they will be using VHLLs (comfortable, easy to use, computer-prompted), but they will be doing what programmers now do, thereby reducing the amount of maintenance programming necessary. By 1985, James Martin[3] has said, there will be one terminal for every five employees doing this kind of work. Our goal, as an industry, for the 1980s should be to reach the "50% automation level," that is, to eliminate 50% of programming by pushing it out to end users. This solution is not simply shifting the burden. VHLLs will enable unskilled clerks to do the work instead of programmers. Thus, the programming burden will have, in effect, been automated.

All of these solutions address the growing supply–demand gap in programming. The use of more package programs will reduce development work; the use of VHLLs will reduce maintenance work. Automatic program generators and more firmware will automate programming. Solutions will be found, but they will require time and a lot of work. Meanwhile, we offer three software strategies dealing with the problems of software management.

These deal with programmer productivity, the use of package programs, and data base management.

PROGRAMMER PRODUCTIVITY

> ### S-45   PROGRAMMER PRODUCTIVITY
>
> **A carefully prepared menu of programmer productivity tools and aids can result in dramatic gains in applications software development with the existing staff.**

For years, we have been automating labor-intensive processes. With computer costs dropping and people costs rising, it's time to apply this approach to the IM function itself. A premium is being placed today on reducing the time and the cost involved in systems development. This premium will put increased pressure on us to find ways to improve programmer productivity. Many of today's new programmer productivity techniques have been given impetus by this pressure. These and other techniques will continue to be applied more and more because programming resources will continue to become more scarce, and development costs will continue to rise. Earlier, we suggested that we are only halfway toward full automation. Automation demand will continue because there is a current backlog of justified projects, inflation is squeezing real dollar costs, the expanding world economy is generating increased volumes of transactions, and on-line requirements are growing in all areas of automation. As the need for programmers grows, people-related costs will demand an increasingly high percentage of the budget.

We indicated earlier that in our opinion, the long-term solution to the supply–demand gap in programming lies in *automating programming,* that is, the use of application-program generator packages, moving software into hardware (firmware), and very-high-level end-user languages to bypass programming. But a short-term answer, other than buying software, is to improve programmer productivity. A programmer productivity strategy should involve the use of various tools and techniques to speed up programming, and ways to measure it, which can include:

High-level languages.

Interactive programming.

Structures technologies.

Software aids.

Report writers and query languages.

Productivity measures.

High-level Languages

"Programmer productivity may be increased as much as five times when a suitable high-level language is used."[4]

The most obvious productivity tool is the use of high-level languages like COBOL, PLI, and Pascal. These provide increased productivity and faster debugging. Debugging is faster because English usage reduces syntactic and semantic errors, and compiler diagnostics make them easier to find. The old objection that COBOL programs are too big and inefficient no longer holds because today's compilers are efficient, COBOL optimizer programs can reduce size and improve speed, and memory is cheap. One cannot imagine why any shop today would not be using a high-level language, and, indeed, most are.

However, a much less used high-level language strategy is the use of nonprocedural languages. Nonprocedural languages—for example, Ramis (Mathematics Inc., Princeton, N.J.)—can be licensed for use for around $10,000, a tremendous bargain considering what can be gained in programmer productivity. Training time is usually measured in days, and a great many programs which might normally be done in COBOL are adaptable to a nonprocedural language which can produce programs in far less time. Sometimes, veteran programmers, accustomed to working with a high-level language such as COBOL, are reluctant to work with a nonprocedural language. To overcome this reluctance, a small group of programmers could be trained in the new language to act as an information center (S-22) group, or a single individual on each team could carry that responsibility. In any event, having a nonprocedural language in one's bag of programmer productivity tools can be a great asset which should not be overlooked.

Interactive Programming

Today, the most popular tool for improving programmer productivity is interactive programming. There is a computer overhead cost, of course, but with the cost of hardware dropping, and the cost of programmers rising, it's a good trade-off because productivity is directly related to the test time available. For example, one IBM contract programming manager gave an IBM 3032 to 25 programmers on a contract job for a manufacturer. He reported that six trainees coded 55,000 lines, a threefold productivity increase over his previous experience (of novice lines per day). The trainees were given skeleton programs written by a chief programmer. The project came in early and below costs. The manager's conclusion was that test time is more important to productivity than the quality of the programmers doing the coding. Proponents claim productivity increases of 25%, 50%, 100%, and more. These gains, however, are difficult to prove. So, how does one convince management to spend the necessary money for terminals and computer overhead? The best way is the same way many user systems are cost-justified: through promised people savings! If you have a department of 100 programmers, promise to *reduce* staff by 10 if interactive programming is introduced. That's very conservative, and it's something senior management will certainly understand. Telling them you're going to get more work done in less time is all very well, but it leaves management wondering if, indeed, that has been accomplished. They have no way of measuring it. Reduced staff is measurable. This was effectively demonstrated recently by an information manager who, as we walked through his programming section, pointed out the empty desks and informed us that he had reduced his staff from 60 to 45 as the result of the introduction of interactive programming. He could not have said anything more convincing than the impact of the empty desks.

Structured Technology

Much has been written about structured design and programming, so we will not belabor the merits of this technology. Suffice it to say that top-down development and its aids, HIPO (Hierarchical Input Processing Output—a graphic documentation technique that aids top-down development) and structured design (breaking down requirements specifications into hierarchical modular programs), provide an effective technical discipline which can produce better systems design, fewer design and logic errors, fewer integration problems, higher-quality work, and faster development. Structured programming, with its emphasis on top-to-bottom logical code flow (avoiding "go-to" and label statements), likewise makes programs easier to read, maintain, and change.

In addition to the use of structured technology, two team aids can also be used to advantage: chief programmer teams and walkthroughs. Chief programmer teams are based on the principle that a few top-level programmers working closely together can accomplish more in less time than a large heterogeneous group with varied experience. The team is usually composed of about five or six people: a chief programmer, a backup programmer, two or three other experienced programmers, and a documentation librarian. This is an especially useful technique when time is of the essence; that is, when an early target date has been arbitrarily set by management, or circumstances require high productivity by a small group of people over a short period of time. (The chief limitation is that there are not that many good chief programmers around.) Walkthroughs—a group of experienced people reviewing design and coding at various project milestones—are helpful in avoiding wasted time (lost productivity) by uncovering design and coding errors early; thus, a walkthrough is a *team* quality-assurance tool. Some companies use inspections instead. An inspection is similar to a walkthrough, except that it's more formal and involves management; thus, it's a *management* quality-assurance tool.

Software Aids

Program optimizers and analyzers are also useful in preventing wasted resources. Optimizers process source or object codes and apply changes directly to user programs to reduce run time and memory requirements. Analyzers collect statistical data as a program is run and report on the most heavily used sections of the code for optimization by the programmer. These aids should be used primarily for big, daily systems that use up the bulk of resources. They are available from vendors such as Boole & Babbage and Capex and are generally in the $10,000–$15,000 range.

Programmer aid packages also help programmers to get the most out of their time by eliminating much of the detail work associated with programming. Packages include debugging tools, job control language (JCL) generators, test data generators, and the like. Examples are Applied Data Research (Autoflow), Management and Computer Services (Datamacs, JCL Macs), Boole & Babbage (Dump Formatting), Tomard (Abend-Aid), and Synergistics (Pro Test). There are a great many useful software aid packages on the market today, and most sell for a few thousand dollars or less.

Report Writers/Query Languages

These products permit English-language specification of the parameters and contents of an ad hoc query or of the contents and layout of a report. Some of the packages now available are the forerunners of the high-level natural programming languages of the future. They offer a first step to the development of a user-programming capability. Some product examples are Mark IV, Easytrieve, Inquire, Ramis, IBM's GIS, and Focus.

An interesting example of a home-grown system is one developed by Continental Bank of Chicago, called *CARL* (Continental Automated Report Language). CARL takes a user's English-language report request, translates it into a technical programming language, submits it for computer run, and displays the resulting report to the requestor via a CRT or directs it to a high-speed printer. Access is via a time-shared terminal to the computer complex anytime, day or night. Average turnaround time runs about 15 minutes per request. Another way to use report writers and query languages is through the use of a quick response report group (see information center, S-22) within the IM function, which does the work of users instead of their doing it themselves.

Productivity Measures

Four measurements of programmer productivity reviewed in *EDP Performance Review* are summarized here (the first two were borrowed from

Gerald Weinberg's *Psychology of Computer Programming*).[5] Note that just two types of input are required. The first is normally provided by the installation's job accounting system (or, in its absence, console logs). This system includes, by programmer and project, the number of runs made, the computer time used, the reasons for termination, the job type, etc. The second input comes from the programming staff and consists of time allocated, by programmer, to program modules (including program size) and to projects.

1 Computer usage rate $= \dfrac{\text{computer resources used}}{\text{machine instructions completed}}$

This equation measures the efficiency of computer usage by the programming staff, computed by individual and for the whole staff. The number of instructions completed requires project leaders to estimate the number of instructions when each program module is complete. Programs with results consistently higher than norm should be watched for.

2 Production rate $= \dfrac{\text{machine instructions completed}}{\text{man-months expended}}$

This measure of overall programmer productivity provides the instructions produced per man-month of programming effort. It should be used to compare the work of different individuals and for overall trends. Candidates with consistently poor results are candidates for replacement.

3 Debug efficiency $= \dfrac{\text{number of test shots}}{\text{machine instructions completed}}$

Similar to computer usage rate, this measure focuses on a programmer's debugging efficiency *off* the computer. It is an indicator of the quality of the original code, desk checking ability, and ability to get maximum results from each test. A poor showing here may be due to poor analytical ability or to laziness (letting the computer do all the work).

4 Error analysis
This measure is a tabulation of job-termination reasons, by programmer and for the entire staff. It helps to highlight the errors repeated too often. For TSO users, IBM's Interactive Problem Control Program (IPCP) can also be effective in tracking programmer failures. Such an analysis could indicate when further training or better programming standards are needed.

Not all of a programmer's performance, of course, can be measured quantitatively. But these simple measurements, coupled with subjective judgment, can be very useful in identifying the strong and weak performers on the staff and can lead to increased programmer productivity and a narrowing of the supply–demand gap in software development.

PACKAGE PROGRAMS

> **S-46   PACKAGE PROGRAMS**
>
> Search and evaluation steps for acquiring package programs which are a good "fit" for the organization, as well as service tips on contract negotiation.

As noted under programmer productivity (S-45), systems development costs are continuing to rise dramatically. Aside from increasing programmer productivity, a good alternative to internal development is to buy the software, which is usually available at a fraction of the cost of building it oneself. This is especially true of systems software (i.e., technical programs which improve hardware performance and/or special-purpose programs such as data base systems, teleprocessing monitors, and programming aids). The scarcity of systems programmers often makes writing one's own systems software prohibitively expensive in comparison with purchase.

There are at least five good reasons to consider buying software today, when feasible, rather than building it: (a) rising development costs; (b) scarce resources; (c) time pressures; (d) increasing demand for automation (rising work load!); and (e) increased package availability. Some systems, of course, probably should continue to be built; for example, systems that are the "guts" of the business; unique services which cannot be satisfied with package programs; systems that give a competitive advantage; and systems that change so rapidly (for marketing or regulatory reasons, for instance) that maintenance and modifications are easier when the systems are developed internally. In general, the pros of building are the cons of buying, and vice versa, as shown in Exhibit 8-7.

Package programs are available today from a variety of sources, including software vendors, software brokers, the federal government, the academic world, computer manufacturers, common-bond groups (user groups and trade associations), and individual companies. Software brokers, like stockbrokers, serve as middlemen between buyers and sellers; they do not sell programs per se. However, they often provide advisory services and/or do software package evaluations. *All* produce software directories of available packages. A few of the more widely known are International Computer Programs (ICP), Datapro, and Auerbach.

Two indicators of leading packages on the market are the ICP Million-Dollar Awards and the Datapro Software Survey. The ICP awards are an annual ceremony held to honor those software vendors who have sold more than $1 million of their product. In 1971, only 29 packages made the list; by the end of the decade, there were 363 packages on the list. Besides sales volume, packages with the largest number of installations are also honored, again reflecting the most popular packages.

Exhibit 8-7   The pros and cons of building and buying software.

Pros	Cons
Build	Buy
Get custom-tailored product	Modifications often extensive
Get state-of-art system	System may not be state-of-art
Integration with other systems possible	Integration with other systems more difficult
Familiarity with system makes maintenance easier	Foreign systems more difficult to maintain
Buy	Build
Lower cost	Higher cost
Less development time	Longer development time
Frees scarce resources for other work	Hard to get needed resources
System proven and tested	More debugging needed

The Datapro Software Survey is a survey of "User Ratings of Proprietary Software," conducted annually among some 30,000 *Datapro* and *Datamation* magazine subscribers, who are asked to list and rate their purchased packages. The highest-rated packages are listed in Datapro's Software Honor Roll.

Finally, software brokers also publish lists of literally thousands of available package programs in software directories, which can be an excellent starting place to search for a program to fit one's needs.

When buying a package program, be wary of the distinction between a package and a program. The word *package* means "a packaging together of goods." That's exactly what differentiates it from a program. Package programs are a combination of flexibly built general-purpose programs, backed by complete and easy-to-understand documentation and supported by a vendor dedicated to helping install and maintain a system. The successful software vendors understand this; the rest do not. Many companies are still trying to recoup costs by selling basically "as-is" programs designed for their own use, which are poorly documented and without support. With proper marketing and sales support (selling expense, profit margin, documentation, training, installation, support), a package can cost 5 or 6 times the cost of original development. Nonetheless, it can still cost less to the buyer, because the buyer is a shared user; that is, a $20,000 program, costing $100,000 as a package, can still sell for $5,000 based on an expected market of 20 sales over the life of the product. Software vendors, in fact, claim it is 7–10 times cheaper to buy than to develop software.

In evaluating a package program, one is really evaluating three things: oneself (one must know one's own needs); the package (is it a good fit?); and the vendor (strengths and weaknesses). Here is *a twelve step package-*

program search strategy taken from a presentation by one of the authors before a 1977 banking conference:[6]

1 *Determine your requirements.* Prepare a requirements document outlining your needs, report requirements, configuration restraints, etc.

2 *Research the available packages.* Start with the software directories, and research package evaluations and user ratings.

3 *Develop knockout factors.* These include things like upper cost limit, extent of modifications necessary, equipment constraints (hardware, operating system, language), number of installations, vendor reputation. Drop a package if it fails on any knockout factor.

4 *Develop evaluation criteria.* The criteria used in the Datapro Survey cited earlier are throughput/efficiency, ease of installation, ease of use, documentation, vendor technical support, training, and overall satisfaction. You can even weigh the criteria according to what is important to you.

5 *Call the software brokers.* Get specific information on the remaining packages and vendors.

6 *Call the vendors.* Get brochures and other information describing their package, as well as a list of users.

7 *Call the users.* Get their experience and opinions and the names of other users not furnished by the vendor (these could be dissatisfied users, the most important to contact).

8 *Invite vendors to bid.* Invite the remaining few vendors in for a presentation, matching their package against your requirements document.

9 *Study the candidates.* Go over your "shopping list," review the documentation and sample program listings (judge quality, not quantity), and develop a matrix-comparison form to compare the features of competitive packages.

10 *Visit other users.* Visit several companies using the package in which you are interested.

11 *Credit check.* Get a credit check on the vendor. How strong is the vendor? Will it be around in five years? How good are its guarantees and support capability?

12 *Select the package.* If you have followed the above steps, the final package selection (or rejection) should now be relatively easy.

Software Contracts

We could not leave the subject of package software without considering contracts. Contract negotiation means just that: negotiation. There is no such thing as a standard contract. Everything is negotiable. And the contract constitutes the complete and total agreement between the parties. If it isn't in the contract, it doesn't exist!

Many people simply leave the contract to their lawyers. This is a mistake. Obviously, a lawyer should review the contract once it's put together, but most lawyers know as much about EDP as you know about the law. *You must carefully read the entire contract yourself and look for "what if"* problems (What if the vendor doesn't perform as stated? What is my protection? remedy? penalties?) Things to look for in contracts include terms (lease, license to use only, or purchase), extent and cost of modifications needed, all deliverables which come with the package, rate of payment, restrictions as to use (multiple computers? multiple sites?), protective clauses and nondisclosure agreements, warranties against patent–copyright infringement, "bugs," support services, and maintenance agreement and terms.

The Independent Computer Consultants Association has developed a standard consulting contract which covers the services to be performed, the rate of payment, reimbursement for expenses, the invoicing method, the treatment of confidential information, the soliciting of client employees, ownership and use of the product, the client's contract responsibilities, liabilities and warranties, a statement that the contract constitutes the complete agreement and is in accordance with the laws of the state in which the consultant lives, the scope of the agreement, the procedure for contract amendments, notice address, and assignment rights. Get a copy of the ICCA contract and use it as a guide in contract negotiation.

In summary, there are many good packages on the market today, well supported by competent vendors. The cost of acquiring and installing these packages can be many times cheaper than writing one's own. Therefore, this can be an excellent strategy for stretching software development resources. For these reasons, we believe the use of packages will increase dramatically in the 1980s.

DATA-BASE MANAGEMENT SYSTEMS

> ### S-47   DATA-BASE MANAGEMENT SYSTEMS (DBMS)
>
> **A prudent strategy for moving into data base systems.**

By all signs, the DBMS promises to be one of the most dynamic developments of the 1980s. Data base management merges the user's need for easy, but sophisticated, data manipulation with the technological capabilities of computers. The corporate data base is on its way as the replacement of today's multiple-application data files. Yet, in spite of its promise, the movement to the DBMS has been slow. There seem to be as many reports of problems as of successes. It is estimated that only about 20% of today's automated data are stored in data bases. Why? Because installing a data base system can be a complex, difficult, and costly process. Yet, sales of DBMSs are growing rapidly, indicating that the trend will probably accelerate in the 1980s, especially as DBMSs become hardware (as in IBM's System/38, a progenitor of such systems). But a movement to a DBMS is not a trivial undertaking. It is a conversion of at least as much magnitude as converting from second- to third-generation computers, and everyone remembers what a traumatic experience that was. This is because large organizations today have data bases measured in billions of characters. In a move to a data base system, all existing programs and data files must be converted, a huge job. Not only is it big, it is complex, and if done improperly, it can be an utter disaster. *You can make a mess with a DBMS!* So the best advice is take it slow and easy.

There are many advantages to a DBMS. As a shared resource, it offers easy access to data, a single data-entry and -edit system, the use of query languages for on-line user ad hoc requests, minimal data redundancy, and easier applications systems development since the data are already defined. Moreover, not only does direct user access lead to faster response to information needs, but bypassing programming also lowers programming maintenance costs. The power and advantages of the DBMS make it not a question of whether, only of *when* to go. Nonetheless, it's a big job, and a move today, to any DBMS, will be only an interim step. One will convert from whatever system is chosen to another in time, because today's data base systems are not the final answer. The evolution of the DBMS is going through a variety of models to determine what is best—Codasyl, hierarchical, relational? Moreover, future data base systems are likely to be built into the hardware, as indicated earlier. Thus, if one is going to evolve from one system to another, one must plan carefully and in such a way as to make future conversions easier. Our suggestion for a data base strategy, then, is to move slowly and follow a phased conversion approach, starting with the following action steps:

1 *Start with a data dictionary.* Install a data dictionary before attempting any data-base application. Corporate data must first be put in order. The tool to do this is the data dictionary. The dictionary puts the data in order by defining data definitions and data relationships for all data elements in the data base. A few of the more well-known data dictionaries are Data Catalogue (Synergistics), Datamanager (MSP, Inc.), IDD (Cullinane), and Lexicon (Arthur Anderson).

2 *Buy a DBMS package.* When ready, buy it, don't build it. There are a number of good commercial DBMS packages available today: Cullinane's IDMS, Software AG's ADABAS, Infodata Systems' INQUIRE, to name a few. Judging by the rapid growth in sales of DBMS software, we will see more extensive use of such packages in the 1980s. So don't

attempt to build your own system. The job will be complex, big, and unnecessary. You will spend more time and money to get less satisfactory results. When you are ready to put your data base scheme together, look into the use of automated data-base design packages. These tools can be a big help in reducing the considerable manual effort needed to create the data structure. One such package is DBSYN (Data Base Synthesizer) available from DMW Group, Ann Arbor, Michigan. DBSYN receives input source data, translates the logical relationships of the data according to prescribed rules, and designs the initial data base.

3 *Acquire a query language/report writer.* Most DBMS packages have these as options (for additional money). They can be used by systems personnel to respond to ad hoc queries of users, or the users themselves can use them without going through programming (reducing maintenance programming, which often involves report generation work).

4 *Appoint a data base administrator (DBA).* A really competent full-time person will be needed to control the data dictionary. The DBA's job is to develop corporate standards for data definitions and data relationships, to review application data-base designs for consistency in a shared environment, and to assure design integrity through control of the dictionary's contents. He or she should also guide the conversion effort, preferably in a phased approach, which is easier to control and more likely to succeed.

5 *Plan long-range.* Whatever DBMS is selected, it is not likely to be the final answer. Plan in advance to convert from one data base system to another. Because large corporations have thousands of application programs and a sizable investment in them (probably several times the cost of installed hardware), this investment must be preserved. Thus, conversion to the DBMS is often done over several years, as systems are rewritten, rather than all at once. The goal is a single data base structure that can interlink many individual data bases, not a single massive data base.

6 *Involve top management.* A high level of management understanding, acceptance, and support is necessary for an undertaking of this magnitude. Management needs to understand both the costs and the benefits of the DBMS. This is important because when dealing with the organization's data resources, one is dealing with the heart of management. This requires education—a lot of it.

DMBSs of the future will be standardized. Our guess is that *relational* (two-dimensional flat-file form) data base models will win out as the way of the future. And data bases will very likely be in hardware, not software. The conversion problem from today's data base systems to a hardware relational system would not be inconsequential.

The best way to prepare is to get the data into logical and flexible form, to make future conversions easier. Also, not all data bases will be centralized. Distributed data bases are harder to control, but they are coming. No manufacturers have them yet, but Computer Corp. of America has a working distributed data-base system called SDDI. If the data base is to be distributed, even more caution and careful planning are needed.

In summary, data base systems are big and complex, the final answer has not yet arrived, and conversions from one data base to another must be expected. So take it slow and easy. Build small data base systems in short time frames to build credibility and user confidence and to increase the chances of success.

INFORMATION EXCHANGE GROUPS

Earlier, we suggested that hardware and software planning required considerable research: reading, attendance at conferences and seminars, schools and courses, membership in research organizations, etc. An extremely useful research strategy in this regard is participation in user roundtable groups, in which several companies have some commonality of interests. These may be companies in the same city, or in a similar industry, using the same type of equipment, sharing common problems, or having any number of common interest bonds. By meeting periodically to exchange information on each others' research experiences, problems, and solutions, they can obtain considerable valuable information to help in the management of technical resources.

User Roundtables

> **S-48 USER ROUNDTABLES**
>
> **Participation with a small number of other organizations in a program of information exchange on issues of common concern.**

To illustrate the use of user roundtables, we will review a few examples of such working groups with which we are familiar.

Case 1   Most major banks in the United States belong to one of several user-roundtable groups which meet periodically (usually annually) to exchange views and information on what they are doing in various areas of banking activity, ranging from lending to trust business, to operations and personnel management. One of these, in which we have participated for years, consists of 15 major banks from as many large U.S. cities; it meets annually for a three-day conference, usually in a remote resort-type atmosphere (which tends to keep the group together throughout the conference), for a general exchange of information. A subgroup from these banks also meets annually for a technical electronics conference dealing with computers, communications, and systems issues. In addition, the banks exchange "letters" twice a year reporting on their experiences; their projects and plans dealing with finance, operations, personnel, and automation; and other subjects which are of general interest to all. The host bank at each conference generally researches the member banks in advance of the meeting to determine which topics are of greatest interest and solicits speakers on each subject from conference attendees. Sometimes, the subject is simply left for open discussion, or each bank is canvassed for a short report of its status on the subject. Either way, the result is a valuable exchange of information on many subjects of mutual interest. The value and popularity of the roundtable is attested to by its endurance through several decades and the establishment of many longtime friendships in the groups.

Case 2 The rapidly growing international banking business, coupled with technological advances in recent years, has led to a corresponding interest and growth in international systems planning and development. As a consequence, some of the leading U.S. international banks recently banded together to form an international systems working group (user roundtable) which meets twice a year for three days to review each bank's activities, plans, and progress in international systems development. In this case, a professional firm handles all of the arrangements and logistics of each meeting. The meetings usually start with an update from each bank on its major activities since the last meeting. A variety of specific subjects are presented by member banks during the course of the conference. Detailed presentations are made by selected banks about the status of their overseas systems developments, and the meeting usually ends with a vote on subjects for discussion at the next meeting. The considerable amount of information exchanged and the sharing of experiences by the attending banks provide more intelligence on the subject of international systems than any one bank would probably ever assemble on its own without such a user roundtable.

Case 3 A simpler and less formal user roundtable was recently formed in Boston for the purpose of exchanging research and information on office automation planning. In this case, the information manager of a large Boston company simply contacted several of his peers in other local companies to determine their interest in forming a special-interest group on the subject. The group meets for lunch periodically to discuss plans and progress in office systems development and provides a useful exchange of what is going on in the immediate area in different industries. This type of user roundtable is simple to form and requires no advance planning or preparation.

The above examples of user-roundtable groups are merely illustrative of the many such special-interest groups that exist around the country to provide information research on industry trends, company experiences, and personal observation and opinions of peer-group members. User roundtables can be an excellent and inexpensive strategy for finding out what others are doing in the hardware/software area of information management.

SECURITY

Information resources are the most valuable category of corporate physical assets. Human resources are the only category of asset that has a higher value. The importance of information resources as a corporate asset has been recognized only in the last few years. The historical neglect of information resources as an asset has exposed many companies to the risk of serious losses. In addition, of course, assets which are not valued tend to be poorly managed.

There is an emerging recognition by senior executives that their corporations would be out of business if they lost the information resource base of data, computers, and programs. Electronic information resources are easily destroyed. Despite this obvious fact, many companies continue to have woefully inadequate security for information resources. Frequently, attention is limited to security for physical information resources, such as computer hardware. It is time for corporate executives to make a full study of the security of their information resources. This is a challenge which has not been adequately met by the executives in most U.S. companies.

Physical Asset Myopia

Companies spend hundreds of thousands and even millions of dollars on the development of their computer-based information systems. All of this investment in computer programs and information systems is usually maintained in electronic form in the company's computers. In such form, it can easily be lost, stolen, damaged, or destroyed if not properly controlled. It can be read onto a tape and carried out of the company in an employee's briefcase. Or it can be transmitted from one company to another, computer-to-computer, in a matter of minutes. Thus, corporate strategic plans, information on competitive products, customer lists, salary data, and all sorts of sensitive information stored electronically can be more easily stolen than most kinds of physical assets.

As companies have become more and more dependent on their computer systems to provide their daily information, process their transactions, and maintain corporate records, more attention has been paid to the physical security of information management. The attention, however, has largely centered on what can be seen; that is, the computers themselves. Thus, considerable work has gone into the physical protection of computer systems. Computer room access is controlled by guards, mantrap entrances, coded badges to open doors, and the like. Protection from fire is provided by smoke detectors, water sprinklers, CO_2 extinguishers, and halon gas. Power protection takes the form of internal generators, or automatic power supply (APS), and uninterrupted power supply (UPS) in many organizations. Computer room environments are closely controlled by temperature and humidity control devices. Backup is effected by schemes ranging from internal backup (multiple computer systems) to external alternatives through agreements with local computer sites (companies, service bureaus), contracts for environmentally prepared space, shared emergency-computer sites (such as the Sunguard Service), or split (multiple) data centers. Likewise, remote storage of production programs and master files has been a widely accepted practice for years.

While we do not want to minimize the importance of such physical security, a preoccupation with the protection of physical assets could, in fact, lead to physical asset myopia. It has been demonstrated many times that when computer sites have suffered fire or flood damage, companies have been able to get replacement equipment shipped in, often within a few days, to reestablish the data center. After all, IBM continues to make computers, and they can probably have the next machine off the assembly line shipped to a disaster location with a little juggling of priorities. More important is having the key people, programs, and master files available to reconstruct the operation. In other words, it is the vital *information resource* that is most critical—not the computers per se. This recognition of the value of information resources has led in recent times to a greater concern about data security.

As distributed processing spreads, one would expect that the all-eggs-in-one-basket problem of physical security would begin to solve itself through the dispersion of resources. On the other hand, higher storage densities, satellite communications, and distributed intelligent terminals are likely to make information resources, especially data security, even more vulnerable. Who will be responsible for assessing these risks and for providing control over these risks? We believe it is the responsibility of the information management function to assume leadership over the control of the company's data resources. If it does not, it is likely that corporate management, user management, auditors, and security people will ultimately force the issue. We have already seen ample evidence of this in a number of leading companies, in governmental privacy legislation, in transborder data-flow restrictions by a number of countries, and in a variety of concerned groups in the private sector. *We believe that data security will become the number one security issue in the 1980s,* transcending even the age-old concern with physical security. For this reason, we suggest that information managers begin now to develop the data security appropriate to their company's needs, before it is forced on them by others.

Control over Data Security

S-49   SECURITY

An access control strategy over a company's vital
data resources.

The increasing interest in data security comes about from the growing realization of the value of the firm's information resources. The concerns take several forms:

1 *Fraud and dishonesty.*   The ability to manipulate electronic files in ways which managers trained in basic accounting systems and controls do not understand is causing corporate managers to be extremely nervous about the potential of computer crime in the company, a nervousness that is being continually fanned by reports of computer crimes (often not computer crimes at all) from security consultants anxious to sell their services.

2 *Malfeasance.*   Willful alteration and/or destruction of files by disgruntled employees is another concern. We have all heard the story about the programmer who put a self-destruct routine in his program that, under a given circumstance, would change all binary 1s to 0s, thus wiping out the program. (Of course, stored copies can protect against such happenings—if these are not destroyed as well.)

3 *Mistakes.*   Honest errors can do damage to data files and often have, necessitating reruns with generation data sets. Compounding errors can, in fact, wipe out all generation data sets, leaving the company without a critical master file. We know of one user with a minicomputer system that wiped out all copies of the master file *and* the programs while trying to recover from hardware/software problems.

4 *Trade secrets.*   Valuable company data can be given or sold to competitors. Such a sale can seriously damage a company's business.

5 *Privacy.*   Personal-data privacy (salary data, personal credit files, and the like) is also becoming a major issue. The U.S. Privacy Act of 1974 was aimed at the protection of sensitive consumer information. Transborder data flow (TDF) laws in various countries (Sweden, West Germany, France, et al.) are looming large in the international use of personal information and threaten to hinder international trade and the use of advanced technology for information management. The concern here is that personal data about citizens of one country will be transmitted and stored in another country with little control over their use. Restrictions prohibiting the transmission of personal data outside a country could, for example, kill the business of international credit-card transactions.

These are some of the concerns being expressed by more and more corporate managers and users interested in protecting their valuable information resources. As these concerns grow in the 1980s, there will very likely be an increased demand for more secure operating environments. Vendors will be prompted to add security hardware features to processors, peripherals, and terminals. Auditors and security officers will step up their audits of data security controls. Information managers with data security programs in place will be leading the way to information resource control rather than being pushed and harassed to a greater sense of responsibility for this important aspect of information management.

The following three-part data security program consists of (1) an assessment study, (2) an access control system, and (3) the issuance of data security standards.

Risk Assessment Study   What is it we want to protect? And from what or whom? Before one can decide on a solution, one must first identify the problem. A good way to begin is to determine, with the help of corporate and user management, who are the *owners* of the information resources that we seek to protect. Production files may have multiple users, but each should have only one owner. In some cases, the owner will be obvious (finance owns the company's general ledger; personnel owns the payroll file; manufacturing owns the inventory control file). In other cases, the owner will not be obvious simply because multiple departments use the same file as part of their business activity (the deposit accounting system is used by practically every department in a bank). In such cases, corporate management should decide who the owner is. If the owner of each file is designated, responsibility can be fixed as to what protection is needed over each file so that an appropriate security system can be put into place.

Once the owners of the information resources have been determined, the next step is to review with each owner the sensitivity of the files, the controls already in place, and the additional controls needed. For example, the owner should understand the internal systems controls (balancing, cash totals, audit trails, transaction logs, etc.) which were built into the system during system design. In addition, external management controls must be reviewed (settlement procedures, output control, access methods, dual approval processes). Access controls over terminal usage, data entry, programming, use of user ID/password control, key locks on terminals, and other base-level security features should be understood. With this understanding, the user or owner is in a position to determine the adequacy of the controls in place in terms of the sensitivity of the data. Highly sensitive files may require additional controls; less sensitive data may require fewer controls. Each file must be examined from the point of view of which information resources are valuable and need protection, and what are the threats to those resources (internal fraud, external stealing, destruction, privacy)? The risk assessment study can be done through a series of interviews and user–owner questionnaires to determine where the risk is that must be protected against. From the results of this study, we learn where to focus attention on security control.

Access Control   It is the responsibility of the IM function to provide base-level access security over the company's production programs and production data files, regardless of the sensitivity of the various files.

Program security controls are designed to ensure that unauthorized changes cannot be made in production programs. Basic controls to this end

Exhibit 8-8 Production program cataloging procedure.

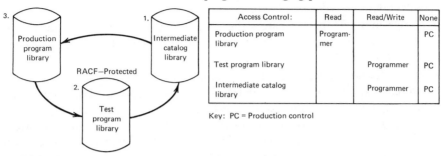

Access Control:	Read	Read/Write	None
Production program library	Program-mer		PC
Test program library		Programmer	PC
Intermediate catalog library		Programmer	PC

Key: PC = Production control

include access to production programs, changes in production program libraries, separation of responsibilities so that no one person has complete control, dual-control procedures, and protection of backup copies.

Data-file security controls are designed to ensure that unauthorized changes cannot be made in data in production files. These controls include access to on-line data files such as through TSO (time-sharing option), authorization of data file usage, physical security over production data files, separation of duties, dual-control procedures, and the use of job control language (JCL) and utility programs against these files.

The following describes an access control program over production programs and production data files instituted at one large company:

An independent and objective security officer, reporting directly to the IM function head, was appointed to carry out and monitor the data security program. This person's first duty was to develop a data security plan, which was reviewed with and approved by IM management, the audit department, and the risk management department. This plan formed the basis for the subsequent data security program.

An access control system was next developed to provide a base-level security program covering access to production programs and production data files. This program concentrated on four key elements: access to production programs, access to production files, changes in job control language, and user access.

Access to Production Programs A dual-control procedure using IBM's RACF (Resource Access Control Facility) software was instituted for cataloging production programs as follows (see Exhibit 8-8):

1 Programmer A copies an application program out of the production program library (which is "read only") into his or her test program library (the log-on procedure records A's user ID/password).

2 After the program is modified, tested, and compiled, Programmer B (a different authorized programmer on the same application) reviews the changes made (software packages are available that can readily identify

changed, added, or deleted lines of code). This procedure provides spot-checking dual control.

3   Programmer B then transfers the program into the intermediate catalog library under control of production control personnel in data processing (this procedure records B's user ID/password).

4   The intermediate catalog library contains a table of authorized programs for each application. The user ID/passwords of both Programmer A and Programmer B are checked to validate that both are authorized programmers on that application and that the modifier (A) and the authorizer (B) are not the same person. (Note in Exhibit 8-8 that production control could not alter the programs, since they have no access to the test library and can read only the intermediate catalog library.)

Access to Production Files   Production files are accessed by users (transaction data entry, on-line inquiry) as well as programmers (correcting program and production problems). Under certain circumstances, they might also be accessed by outsiders. Access by users was controlled as described in the next section. Outsider access was largely negated because no dial-up telephone-line access was in operation (all access was by dedicated leased lines or internal microwave). Programmer access to production files was controlled in different ways:

Physical separation of TSO program testing and production processing was accomplished during the normal working day (i.e., on-line programming was confined to testing on a dedicated machine, having no access to production files).

After normal daytime working hours, an automated facility was put in place that permitted programmers to "read only" a production data set from a TSO terminal and then only through dual control. When a production data set was requested to be read, two users' ID/passwords were prompted by the system: the first from the requesting programmer, the second from an authorized person in data processing. After the "reading" of a production file in this way, if a repair was needed, it had to be submitted under dual control using the cataloging procedures discussed earlier. (Note: In the early morning hours, a data processing supervisor performed the work of Program B to get the job done. In the morning, Programmer B verified the work performed after the fact, thus preserving the dual-control aspect of program cataloging.)

Certain sensitive files were RACF-protected with a description of the user, so that even "read only" operations could not be performed on the production files. In such cases, any problem occurring in the middle of the night had to be left for correction the next day. Needless to say, this was an option of the user–owners (which, we might add parenthetically, was seldom exercised).

Job Control Language (JCL)   Control over JCL consisted of batch and on-line (TSO) control. *Batch control* was achieved through the simple process of instituting a procedure of accompanying all JCL changes with a "speedy" letter which outlined the changes made and was signed by an authorized JCL *initiator*. This letter was delivered with the JCL changes to a JCL *executor*, who verified the work, countersigned the form, and executed the JCL change. The form was delivered to the data processing staff supervisor, who initialed and retained it to match the following morning against all logged JCL changes made during the night (or day). This procedure assumed that no JCL changes were made bypassing the dual-control procedures. All forms were forwarded to an authorized application programmer (and the audit department) each day. *On-line* (TSO) control was achieved in a very simple way through the cataloging procedure, which required that two different and authorized user ID/passwords were submitted with each JCL change, thus preserving the dual-control feature for on-line changes.

User Access   Users require access to production files for the purposes of both processing transactions and maintaining their business records, as well as for information inquiry purposes for customer dealings, decision making, and control purposes. The internal systems controls and external management controls described earlier helped to control the process. But, in addition, base-level physical security was presented in three parts:

1   Physical terminal access was controlled by terminal ID; that is, a person in Department A could only access physical files authorized for that department. No "master" access was permitted.
2   User ID/password control was used to allow individual authorized users to access files or to perform only certain limited functions within these files.
3   Key-lock devices were installed on terminals in particularly sensitive areas or where sensitivity-file access took place.

This four-part data security program has satisfied the dual need for good service and sound data security, and may provide readers with some thoughts on establishing their own data-security programs.

Security Standards   Once the base-level data-security control program has been devised, the next step is to establish the program formally, beginning with user interviews to acquaint users (and user–owners) of data files with the base-level security provided. The risk assessment initially set the groundwork for what was sensitive and needed protection. The access control system establishes the what and how of the basic protection afforded. The user interviews determine what further protection, if any, is needed to complete the security program. Once this program has been put in place, the final step is to document the data security program in the form of corporate security standards. These standards can specify security issues and problems, the ownership of corporate information resources, and the protection afforded (over those resources), including the responsibilities of user–

owners for the care of the information resources entrusted to them. (This responsibility would also include physical security over the physical resources—e.g., minicomputers—under their care.)

A corporate policy (see S-65) could be issued to establish and fix the responsibility for security within the company. This is a useful strategy to set the stage for the subsequent issuance of security standards within the company.

In summary, establishing an effective data-security system takes considerable effort because it must be done without sacrificing good service for the value of security. Both are important, but good security and good service are usually conflicting objectives. The ultimate in security would be to lock up the data processing operation so that no one could get at it; the ultimate in service would be to allow everyone easy and quick access to all data in the corporate data base. Obviously, these aims are at cross-purposes. The key to an effective data-security strategy is to achieve an optimum balance between good service and effective security.

NOTES

1   James Martin, *The New DP Environment and How to Design for It*. James Martin Services, Toronto, 1979.
2   Charles Lecht, *Waves of Change,*
3   James Martin, *ibid.*
4   Frederick P. Brooks, Jr., *The Mythical Man-Month*, Reading, Mass.: Addison-Wesley, 1975, p. 94.
5   Gerald Weisberg, *Psychology of Computer Programming*, New York: Van Nostrand Reinhard, 1971, pp. 56–64.
6   William R. Synnott, "Software: Buy or Build," *ABA National Operations/Automation Conference Proceedings*, New Orleans, May 1977.

9

Telecommunications: The Enabler

To see a World in a Grain of Sand, . . .
Hold Infinity in the palm of your hand.

William Blake, Auquries of Innocence

The glue that will hold all of the information resources together in the 1980s will be telecommunications. This "enabling" technology will be the force that allows information managers to integrate computers, systems, networks, distributed processes, and office systems into an effective integrated-resource management capability. Moreover, advances in telecommunications are accelerating rapidly, and costs are dropping. Telecommunications is likely to build into an explosive force in this decade, making possible automation, communications, and information movement heretofore not even dreamed of by information managers. In this chapter, we review some of the advances in telecommunications that are creating these enabling capabilities.

NEW TECHNOLOGIES

Microwave Systems

Microwave links, which were considered exotic 10 years ago, are today becoming much more common for business, medical, and other communications needs. The First National Bank of Boston, for example, has used a microwave link between its head office in Boston and its operations center four miles away since 1970. It consists of a 1.544-megabit system, of which they are using 7 channels of 56 each. These handle all data transmission between the two points at speeds ranging from 4800 to 19,200 bps. A video channel also makes possible signature verification from customer signature cards located at the operations center which can be displayed at teller stations uptown. The system was also designed to service videoconferencing located at headquarters and the operations center. A zoom lens enables documents at one end to be read at the other. The system paid for itself in one year in terms of equivalent line costs.

Bankers Trust in New York has a similar microwave link between its uptown and downtown offices. The Massachusetts General Hospital uses a microwave link to Logan airport in Boston for the practice of telemedicine. Patients at the airport have audiovisual contact with doctors at the hospital, who can direct various tests by trained technicians and/or nurses at the airport medical facility. The system is now being extended to nursing homes throughout the area as a way to bring top medical care to patients who might not or cannot come to the hospital for treatment.

Satellite Communications Systems

A major trend in the use of satellite communication systems is forecast for the 1980s. Today, a typical communications satellite weighs a few hundred pounds and is about 8 feet in diameter. The Space Shuttle in the 1980s, with its 60-foot cargo body, will enable huge satellites, weighing tons and spanning hundreds of feet, to cast communications "footprints" covering one-third of the world. Consider this statement by James Martin:

> The combined population of the United States and Canada is about 240 million. Let us suppose, for the sake of this illustration, that every person makes substantial use of computer terminals. If the average working person uses them one hour per day and the average nonworking person one half hour per day, the total terminal usage would be about 160 million hours per day. Let us suppose that in the peak hour of the day the usage is three times the daily average. The total data rate in the peak hour is then
>
> $$\frac{160 \text{ million} \times 3 \times 10}{24} = 200 \text{ million bits per second}$$
>
> In other words, one satellite could have enough transmission capacity to provide every man, woman, and child in the United States and Canada with a computer terminal.[1]

Three such satellites, in geosynchronous orbit some 25,000 miles in space, would cover the entire world. But even today, satellite communications are in cost-effective use by a number of companies. Western Bancorp, in Los Angeles, uses 56-kilobit satellite paths to connect four data centers in Portland, Oregon; Seattle, Washington; Phoenix, Arizona; and its corporate data center outside Los Angeles. The system is used to support a bankwide teller-transaction processing system consisting of some 5,000 terminals in 700 banking offices covering 11 western states. The cost is around $10,000 per month per line, and WBC claims it is saving $300,000 a year over the cost of terrestrial lines. Another example is the *Wall Street Journal*, which is printed by satellite communications to several remote printing sites, allowing timely distribution of news to subscribers in distant cities.

Arthur C. Clarke, author of many books on space, feels that satellites will have at least the same impact on the populace as telephones. With the advent of new protocols replacing the existing bisynchronous and asynchronous protocols, propagation (the 220 milliseconds or so it takes to get 23,500 miles up and back) will truly have a minimal effect on response time. IBM's SDLC protocol, for example, will send several blocks of data at a time and check errors while retransmitting, making data communications quite conducive to satellite transmission.

Of equal significance, most major U.S. telecommunications companies (e.g., AT&T, GTE, Southern Pacific, and IBM) have launched or will launch their own vehicles. Australia, Brazil, Indonesia, the European Common Market, and others have done or will do the same. Future Systems, Inc., projects that by 1995 there will be a worldwide need for 120 transponders for data, 1,000 transponders for voice, and 8,000 transponders for video conferencing. Our limited resources, our shrinking world, and our need for fast, economical facilities capable of carrying millions of bits of data per second will make the satellite one of the stars of our emerging communications technology.

Cable TV

In 1980 some 15 million households in the United States subscribed to cable TV. The advertising agency Young & Rubicam estimates that this number will grow to one-third of U.S. households (over 24 million) by the end of 1981—and that's just the start. When cable TV and satellite communications marry in the next few years, cable TV should really take off. Communications Satellite Corp. (Comsat) recently announced plans to offer a private pay-TV service beamed from satellite directly into the home by 1983, eliminating even the need for cable. Comsat intends to beat the high cost of receiving antennas with cheap antennas made in Japan for $260 each, which they believe they could rent to homeowners for about $15 a month. The telephone industry also wants to get into the act by feeding television signals through telephone wires rather than cables. Although present telephone wires do not have enough capacity to carry such signals, the telephone industry plans to get that capacity when fiber optic cables begin replacing copper wires in the 1980s.

Optical Fibers

AT&T's terrestrial answer to satellite communications is fiber optics, although AT&T will also be launching satellites. Optical fibers work by bending and bouncing light waves through tiny strands of glass about the size of a human hair, which are embedded in cables and carry communications on a beam of light (LED or laser) at 1,000 times greater a capacity than today's copper wire pair. Fiber optics will lower terrestrial communications costs dramatically for decades because they are inexpensive (they are made from one of the world's most common substances—silicon, the main ingredient of sand), and because of their dramatic communications capabilities (one half-inch fiber optic cable can carry 8,000 phone conversations). Benefits include higher bandwidth, less noise interference (because it's nonelectrical), greater security (can't be tapped), and suitability for digital transmission (light pulses lend themselves well to binary notation as used by computers). While still more costly than copper cable, fiber optics (now $1.00 per meter, soon will be $.10) will continue to drop in price and will eventually be cheaper than today's copper wiring. There are about a dozen experimental applications today; for example, GTE has a small telephone installation outside of Los Angeles, and AT&T has replaced a small portion of the Chicago telephone network. Progress will be slow, however, because of the enormous investment which AT&T and others have in copper wire in streets and buildings. But in the 1980s, we will see rapid growth as the telephone industry replaces copper wire, and as fiber optics spreads in use for such things as cable TV and computer coaxial cable, and in government and industry installations.

Infrared

Another technology of the 1980s and 1990s will be infrared transmissions. Infrared is an optical transmission system which uses the infrared spectrum of light-emitting diodes. One such system, designed by Jack Baud at the University of Colorado and called *Lite-Link,* is marketed through Newport Data, Inc. It operates at as high as 500 kilobits per second or can, through the use of multiplexers, be segmented into 2,400, 4,800, 9,600, or 19,200 bits per second. Like microwave, it is "line of sight," which makes it most useful for building-to-building data communications up to 1 kilometer, but unlike microwave, it requires no Federal Communications Commission licensing. It replaces local loops, which tend to be the weakest link in any system, and is cost-effective at less than $20,000 per unit.

Digital PABXs

Private automatic branch exchange switches (PABX) will represent another technical evolution in the 1980s. Voice and data will be merged and transmitted over the same lines. Today, 95% of all switches are analogue, but the trend toward digital networks is already strong. Digital networks are faster, of better quality, lower-cost, and computer-compatible, and they will allow all terminals, computers, telephones, and other data and voice communications systems to hook up to the same physical lines, eliminating the need for special cables and modems to translate from analogue to digital and back again. Some companies, like Northern Telecom of Canada, are already selling such systems, although on a modest, low-speed basis. Integrated voice and data switching on the same wiring is offered today as an option on Northern Telecom's LS-1 telephone system.

Digital PABXs, already in production by Exxon, Datapoint, and others, will provide a 56-kilobit capability for each telephone, enabling both voice and data capability over 3 or 4 pairs of wires, replacing the current 25 or 50 wires for large multitelephones. Code conversions, speed conversion, protocol conversion, and error checking are some of the features that will be integral to this emerging genre of switches. They will have the capacity to connect directly to satellites, microwave, or networks such as Xten and SBS. In effect, a PABX could become the local switch wired to every point in a building, through which all data, voice, and facsimile can be transmitted with the enhancements of high speed and transparency. Any terminal, facsimile machine, or word-processing device will be able to communicate with any other, regardless of the peculiar characteristics of different devices.

Digital technology will have a profound impact, not only on business communications, but for consumers as well, as the *Wall Street Journal* reported in a front-page article on May 25, 1979:

> At home, your telephone will dial numbers at the touch of a single button, your stereo will play music of concert-hall quality, your television set will flash pictures of lifelike color. In your automobile, the engine will automatically keep emissions of pollutants to a minimum and fuel economy to a maximum. Your dashboard will spew forth facts and figures about how long it will take to reach your destination. At work, your telephone will keep your appointments, and your facsimile machine will transmit documents in seconds rather than in minutes. Products such as these, some of them already appearing on the market, will be the staples of the future because of an important change in electronic technology: a change to what engineers call digital circuits from analog circuits.[2]

NEW NETWORKS

Consider the following developments in new communications networks.

ACS

AT&T's much-touted advanced communication system (ACS) promises to greatly simplify data communications between customers by providing the software to eliminate protocol problems. The system reportedly will do data switching (store and forward) and data management (connect to all kinds of equipment—all transparent to users. Customer use of ACS could include connecting between: host for data base access, intercompany host, host for order entry, customer control terminals, message-switching terminals, inquiry terminals, clustered data-entry terminals, remote printers—without regard to different vendor protocols. The attractiveness of ACS is that it will be a Bell System standard, well managed, ubiquitous, reliable, fast, and flexible (access anywhere). Perhaps because it is all these things, it is extremely complex, and AT&T has announced that it will be delayed in offering this service. This probably means it will not only take longer but will very likely be brought up experimentally in one or two small areas to be shaken down before it goes into widespread use. This could take several years. Nonetheless, the system offers the promise of a much needed communications interface which could save customers much headache and frustration from trying to tie together nonstandard networks.

SBS

IBM's answer to ACS is their Satellite Business System (SBS), a joint venture between IBM, Aetna Insurance, and Comsat. The first SBS satellite was launched in 1981. When fully operational, it will offer very broadband communications. The satellite will have a capacity of 430 million bits, consisting of 10 channels of 43 million bits, the equivalent of some 120,000 voice-grade telephone lines. It will be inexpensive because it will be distance-insensitive (after traveling 47,000 miles up and back, a few thousand miles on the ground will be inconsequential). It will be 100 times more reliable than telephone lines because there will be no local loops involved. It will cover the entire United States, reaching down to rooftop antennas and providing a private communications network for corporate high-speed long-

Exhibit 9-1   A comparison of proposed satellite telecommunications networks.

	ACS	SBS
Type of Net	Intercompany	Intracompany
Link Technology	Land lines except where imbedded in the public network	Satellite, local loops provided on demand
Transmission	Analog and digital	Digital
Maximum Speeds	56 kbps	6.3 Mbps
Customer Set	Small Medium Large	Large (need for 20 or more stations)
Features	Store-and-forward Customer access to stored data	Dynamic allocation
	Broadcast capability (multipoint) *least likely* to be used	Broadcast capability (multipoint) *most likely* to be used
Good for	Data, message	Voice, data, message, fax, video

Source: Distributed Processing Newsletter, November 1978.

line traffic. SBS also plans to share this facility through commonly accessed earth stations. Further, it is looking to compete along with MCI, SP Communications, IT&T and others in providing off-net access to the AT&T network. What these companies are doing is building their own backbone networks using microwave, satellite, or AT&T leased lines between major cities and allowing users to go off-net into the local areas. Most major U.S. cities are now covered by one or the other, offering long-distance telephone service at a 15–25% discount. These services may be accessed from the home, from the office, or on the road. The only real disadvantage is that they now cover and will probably continue to cover only the major population areas.

Xten, before it was scrapped was a satellite network which would carry signals from rooftop transceivers to a city node to an earth station to the satellite and round-trip to another city. Services contemplated were document distribution (facsimile), data transmission, and teleconferencing. Xten sought to find a niche for itself between SBS's large customers and AT&T's small customers, as illustrated in Exhibit 9-1 comparing these two services. Unfortunately, Xerox could not make it go, and cancelled the project in early 1981. They are now concentrating on making Ethernet, their local network, the standard for interoffice communication.

NEW SERVICES

Packet Switching

An integral part of telecommunications in the 1980s will be packet switching, which involves the use of value-added carriers using Bell System lines to buffer messages at each switch point (store and forward) and uses a time-slotting technique instead of traditional analogue; that is, dividing the bandwidth by time rather than by frequency. Visualize a highway; cars are flowing down different lanes, which divide the highway, as in frequency-division multiplexing, except they do it on the basis of time. Now imagine a railroad: as people arrive, they fill a rail car and it leaves, another is filled and it leaves. Only one car at a time is using the track, as in time-division multiplexing. Packet switching takes highway traffic and turns it into railroad traffic, as shown in Exhibit 9-2, at a considerably lower cost—about one-tenth of the cost of the regular telephone. This is so because unlike telephone conversations, a conversation between a terminal user and a computer does not usually require continuous transmission. Rather, data flow in short bursts of information with long periods of nonuse in between. Using our railroad track analogy, visualize one car leaving on the average every 10 minutes and traveling at 100 mph. You can see that the actual utilization of the track is going to be pretty low. Now visualize a high-speed telephone transmission link of 1.5 million bps. A burst of data would run the link in less than a millisecond. The operator at the terminal sends a burst of data down the line,

Exhibit 9-2   Telecommunications multiplexing.

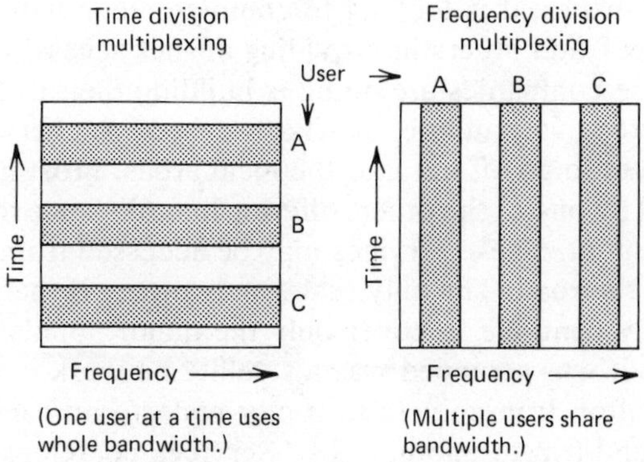

then thinks for a while—say, 15 seconds—then sends more data. Utilization of the line is going to be pretty low, allowing a lot of people to be interleaved on the same line. That's what packet switching is all about: the bursts of data are packets (our railroad car) and the technique of buffering and switching each arriving packet is called *packet switching*. ACS will be a packet-switching network. There are a number of major packet switchers today, including Telenet and Tymnet in the United States, Euronet in Europe, Transpak in France, Datapak in Canada, and IT&T's recently announced international version of ACS, called *UDTS* (Universal Data Transmission Services). When one realizes that two-thirds of all mail is projected to be electronic mail by 1985, using packet switching, it is apparent why the post office wants to be in the electronic mail business.

Packet networks need not be public or shared. GTE/Telenet is exploring the feasibility of providing private networks for large data-communications users such as banks. They will install nodes at key locations, allowing a company to connect its own private or switched lines to it. The major advantage is, of course, control and service in low-density population areas that are not now covered by the public networks. Like the public networks, this service could provide speed, code and protocol conversion, alternate routing, redundancy, store and forward capabilities and all of the features inherent in the public networks.

Packet networks employing ×.25 protocol could very well become the international standard for data transmission. GTE Telenet and Tymshare are operational domestically. Transpac in France is partially complete. England, Germany, Japan, Argentina, and other countries are either building their own or have signed contracts with packet suppliers. The ×.75 standard is already set, providing interconnection between domestic networks.

The next step will be packetized digital voice and facsimile. Digital PABXs will fold very neatly into this system, thus providing a total voice, data, and facsimile network.

Electronic Mail

Electronic mail is growing on a variety of fronts: the post office's proposal for electronic communication of mail (ECOM) is their effort to stay in business in the 1980s; communicating word processors are spreading around corporate offices; message-switching systems are growing; facsimile transmission for physical document distribution is getting faster and cheaper; and banks are providing electronic-mail lockboxes to speed corporate cash flow. Electronic mail will increase steadily as more users are found for this new mode of communication. This is discussed further in the next chapter.

Teleconferencing

Teleconferencing is being pushed as an alternative to person-to-person communications. Xten was to have included teleconferencing. Xerox obviously thought the world was ready for this alternative in light of today's energy shortages and the high costs of travel. And AT&T now has an experimental teleconferencing service in operation in 10 major U.S. cities, called Picturephone Meeting Service. For $6.50 per minute, you can hold a meeting in Bell's meeting room in Boston with another group in Bell's meeting room in Los Angeles. Documents used at the meeting can be easily displayed and copied at the other end. The system connects two groups in separate cities so that they see, hear, and interact audiovisually with each other as if they were in the same room. A $400-per-hour meeting could save several thousand dollars in travel costs when the meeting does not require person-to-person contact. The Lanier Company used teleconferencing to launch a new line of office products with a three-hour sales meeting to 11 cities broadcast via satellite. They estimated that they saved $300,000 in transportation, lodging, and meals.

The real future in teleconferencing will be international. Several companies are now using slow-scan or freeze-frame video, but there is no common carrier providing AT&T-equivalent service on an intercontinental level. However, as satellites proliferate and energy costs increase, the capability will be only a matter of time.

TELECOMMUNICATIONS MANAGEMENT

These new technologies, services, and networks are examples of the dramatic changes that we can expect in the world of telecommunications. These changes will give information and telecommunications managers both the challenge and the opportunity to put this new technology to work for the corporation. Economic pressures argue even today for replacing labor and transportation costs with computing and communications costs.

New and emerging technologies such as satellite communications systems and fiber optics should cause the telecommunications industry to explode in the 1980s. New networks will come into being (e.g., IBM's SBS, AT&T's ACS), and new services will grow (e.g., document distribution, electronic mail, teleconferencing, packet switching, and digital switches—PABXs). Computers and communications are rapidly merging into a single industry. Authorities are unable today to say where one ends and the other begins. The growing cost of telecommunications services in the company will receive increasing attention from management as we move into the interlinked information world of tomorrow. All of this will need management, a more sophisticated management than perhaps has been necessary heretofore. The following strategies are aimed at more effective communications management in this increasingly complex environment.

COMPUTICATIONS

> **S-50   COMPUTICATIONS**
>
> **Merger of data processing and telecommunications within the IM function to achieve single-mind planning and implementation of tomorrow's communications-based computer systems.**

Computications is our word for describing the merger of computers and communications, which has been occurring in recent years and which will be complete in the 1980s. Computications is an important coalescence strategy for information managers. The logic of placing the responsibility for both computers and telecommunications (voice and data) under the same management lies in the fact that these industries have now become technological Siamese twins. Computers used to run without communications, and communications used to get by without computers, but that has all changed. All advanced computer installations today have communications requirements, and the communications industry is rapidly changing from electromechanical switching to electronic computer switching with broadband capabilities. Industry experts predict explosive growth in communications-based computer systems as intelligent networks and distributed processing spreads, as office automation takes hold, as minicomputers proliferate, and as communications costs drop dramatically through fiber optics technology and satellite communications.

Communications are rapidly taking computers into a new dimension of information processing—the *movement of information*—in addition to storing and processing, cheaply and instantaneously, in any part of the world. The purpose of communications is, in this sense, to bring the computer to the customer wherever he or she may be. Recognizing the potential of the movement, both IBM with its satellite communications system (SBS) and AT&T with its terrestrial network (ACS) are aiming at capturing this huge market.

It is not a question of whether telecommunications merges with DP or vice versa. Both are today part of a bigger function, that of information resource management. Information must be processed (data processing) and must be communicated (telecommunications) to be useful; thus, both computers and communications are an integral part of today's information management function, and they will be even more intertwined tomorrow, as communications-based systems continue to spread. Voice and data communications have merged, often using the same lines and facilities. As voice is digitized and/or packetized, there will be little sense in separating networks. Computers and communications have merged, each being part of information management. It is time for data processing and telecommunications to merge, not one into the other, but both into the larger function of information management. This coalescence process has already taken place in many forward-looking companies. In the future, this merger will not be merely desirable, it will be required, as Paul Strassmann of Xerox suggested, "the need for integrating telecommunications (voice and data, facsimile, administrative messages, teleconferencing, planning) is an absolute requirement for achieving any semblance of cost effectiveness."[3]

Now, let's look at two strategies aimed at more effective management control over both voice and data communications.

NETWORK CONTROL: VOICE COMMUNICATIONS

> **S-51   TELEPHONE NETWORK CONTROL**
>
> **Computer-controlled telephone accounting and control systems used to reduce telephone costs and improve service to telephone users.**

The amount of money spent on POTS (plain old telephone service) in most companies is becoming sizable, usually in the area of 75–95% of the communications dollar. Therefore, a strategy for dealing with the control of corporate telephone networks through the application of the computer to the telecommunications function can realize significant benefits to the company. There are two types of systems that can be used for controlling telephone expense: passive systems and active systems.

Passive Systems

Early telephone-expense control systems were passive systems. In a passive system, a data collection device monitors lines to capture a record of each call placed or received (internal and local, as well as long-distance). Reports are generated for management use in configuring a proper line network and in controlling abuse of facilities. Savings are entirely dependent on the proper use of these data by management, however. The system functions as follows:

1   The caller dials exactly as at the present time, routing his or her own calls, that is, through WATS, tie line, or direct distance dialing.

2   Data on each call made are recorded on tape; calls are recorded by the telephone extension used.

3   Periodically, the tape is processed on the company's mainframe computer to produce a series of reports for management use in configuring a proper line network and for controlling the unauthorized use of facilities. Report data include time of day, number called, duration of call, approximate (based on average) cost, routing, "proper routing" if a wrong routing was used, and "proper" cost savings which could have been realized. Reports are generated by telephone exchange, department, division, etc. Traffic is reported by area code and exchange, WATS bank, DDD, etc.

4   Managers use the reports to control abuse and to determine the actual need for equipment in their sections. Telecommunications uses traffic reports to continually monitor network configuration for optimum benefit.

Passive systems are sold by companies such as ESE, Vidar, Telaid, and Phonetel.

Active Systems

In more recent years, telephone-expense control systems began to incorporate minicomputers. The value of a computer in network management is its ability to control a variety of simultaneous events. In an active system, a long-distance call is analyzed for destination and code, and the least expensive route is chosen from a routing table (WATS, tie lines, DDD, etc.). If all routes are busy, the call is queued until a route is available. When the call is completed, all data concerning it are captured. Scheduling and queueing calls in millisecond time packs calls more closely and uses the facilities more efficiently. The result is usually fewer WATS lines needed, producing immediate hard dollar savings. Better service also results because fewer busy signals are encountered. Moreover, priorities can be established to allow high-priority callers to go ahead of low-priority callers. An active system functions as follows:

1   Each employee who is allowed access to long-distance usage is issued a unique ID number of five or more digits, known only to the employee and the assigning authority.

2 On other than local calls, the caller dials a three-digit miniaccess code, plus his or her ID number, and then the telephone number to be called. Example:

Access	ID	Area	Number
224	65464	201	673–1000

3 The computer places the call via the least expensive route—WATS, tie line, direct distance dialing, etc.

4 If the least expensive route is busy, the call will be queued for, say, 30 seconds, and then, depending on the restrictions placed on an individual's ID number, the call is busied out (i.e., you get a busy signal), or completed via another routing. Example: Ms. Jones is programmed to have her calls go through 100% of the time after queueing, by whatever route available. Mr. Smith's calls are restricted to the least expensive routing, which, if busy for the entire queueing period, will give him a busy signal.

5 Key individuals may be programmed always to go to the head of the queue.

6 Remote locations can be tied into the system. Also, calls can be placed from an individual's home.

7 Reports are generated by individual department or division, itemizing each long-distance call made. Report data include the time of day, the number called, the routing, the duration, and the cost.

8 Managers use the report data to control long-distance abuse.

Active, or minicomputer-based, systems have been around for about seven years. The first one introduced was WATSBOX from Action Communications Inc. in 1973. Other vendors introducing active systems since then include TDS (Telemax) and Datapoint (Infoswitch/LDCS). Also, AT&T recently announced their Electronic Tandem Switching (ETS) service, which will also provide accounting and control information similarly to an active system. Other companies, such as Northern Telecom and Rolm, have also begun to incorporate limited least-cost routing and accounting capabilities in their PABX systems.

The trend is clearly toward PABXs providing all of these features as part of the telephone system itself. With this approach, no special access has to be dialed; nor do any special identifier codes need to be pulsed. This system will know what telephone is making the call. It will provide other features; if, for example, a WATS line is busy, it will ring the caller back when the line is available, obviating the necessity to queue up for a line.

Further, such systems will provide self-diagnostics, printing out when there are component, line, or trunk failures; similarly, vendors will be able to use continuous polling for preventative maintenance of their system.

Another highly useful aspect of these systems is that they will provide statistics on trunk or telephone usage, busy-hour usage, telephone feature usage, and on the maintenance status of any service attached to the system, such as WATS lines. The obvious advantage of these features is that the user can determine how well the system is working, where to add or cut back on facilities, and how to engineer the system as a whole.

In summary, passive systems are giving way to computer-monitored active systems today. Although passive systems generally cost half as much as active ones (because there is no minicomputer involved), savings are all soft in that they depend entirely on management action to control abuse and to configure equipment optimally. Savings from active systems are both hard and soft. Hard savings come from actual dollars saved by a reduction in WATS lines, a reduction in the number of DDD and message-unit calls, and the elimination of telephone operators' console equipment and keypunching toll tickets. Soft savings come from an increase in the number of calls carried over the same or fewer lines through more efficient line utilization, management control of long-distance calls through the monitoring of monthly call listing, and the elimination of abuse (e.g., Dial-a-Joke) through 100% call billing and call blocking.

Yet, despite the apparent advantages of active telephone control systems, there are only about 500 companies in the U.S. with active systems installed. Thus, only a small fraction of the potential users have adopted these systems to date. The $200,000–$300,000 price tag is probably one reason; another is the newness of the concept. But the payoff is great. Most systems pay themselves back in one to three years in terms of reduced communications costs. According to Action Communications (which recently introduced a more advanced WATSBOX II), the return on investment on their systems averages 30%. Here is a strategy, then, that can make a significant impact on rising telephone expenses while concomitantly improving telephone service. A strategy with that potential should not be ignored.

The larger strategy is whether to use Bell or others to provide these services along with basic telephone service. Traditionally, it has been an industry adage that "No one ever got fired putting in a Bell system;" however, as other companies provide demonstrated performance, including maintenance (maintenance is always 51% of any consideration), the opposite may be the case. Digital voice, significantly lowered costs, and customer access to the system, including the wiring and enhanced features, are making it mandatory to consider alternatives. Estimates as high as 35% have been used to describe future competitive inroads into this traditional Bell System domain.

With IBM, Exxon, and Datapoint looming on the horizon, the competition will intensify. Bell will answer through its to-be-formed unregulated subsidiary. The net effect is that the PABX decision will require greater telecommunications, business, and financial skills on the part of the user than has ever been the case in the past.

NETWORK CONTROL: DATA COMMUNICATIONS

> ### S-52   DIAGNOSTIC CENTER
>
> **A centralized capability for communications-systems failure diagnosis and maintenance in a complex multivendor data-communications equipment environment.**

Today's fast-growing on-line systems, distributed processing, and extensive terminal networks require increasingly sophisticated network management. The characteristics of 1980s data communications networks will be that:

They will be large, in terms of the number of terminals supported.

They will be widely dispersed geographically.

Near 100% availability will be demanded.

The multiplicity of vendors will complicate fault isolation.

A quick diagnosis and correction capability will be required.

Central-site control will be needed (i.e., there will be no remote-site technical personnel).

Once the network is installed, a key consideration in network management is service level. How do managers minimize outages and maximize system availability? There are three ways: (1) by paying vendors to keep their equipment operating at top performance; (2) by engaging an equipment service company to maintain the network; and (3) by buying a diagnostic center and doing it themselves. For most companies, the latter approach is probably best. One needs a diagnostic center for efficient network management today for three reasons: (1) there are too many vendors involved when a problem occurs, as depicted in Exhibit 9-3; (2) the technology is becoming too complex to track manually; and (3) repair in a minimal time depends on calling the correct vendor the first time.

A communications diagnostic center is composed of two parts:

The Technical Center.   Data traffic is monitored in real time using patch panels and analogue/digital test equipment to run line-parameter tests in a high-speed point-to-point data network. The center uses limited diagnostic instruments such as a datascope, a decibel meter, a data test set, and an audio signal.

The Diagnostic Center.   Intelligence is spread throughout the network by the use of intelligent modems. The host-computer controller sends addresses and command information to the remote modems and receives results. Troubles are thus isolated to the correct vendor. No operator intervention is needed at the remote end because the central site operator performs

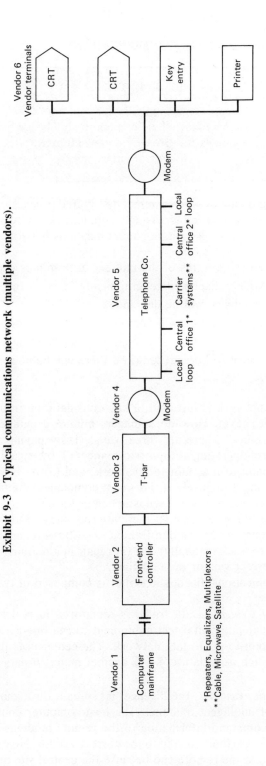

Exhibit 9-3 Typical communications network (multiple vendors).

*Repeaters, Equalizers, Multiplexors
**Cable, Microwave, Satellite

all tasks and remedial actions. Network polling provides continuing central-site monitoring of network performance and any line degradation that is occurring.

The function of a diagnostic center is to assist the operator in maintaining maximum network availability by providing early-warning fault trends, rapid and correct fault isolation when it occurs, remedial and restoral capability from a central location, and statistical data on network activities. Diagnostic centers, like telephone network control systems, also come in two versions, passive and active.

The passive system has a small line capacity that can be extended by switching. The diagnostic tests that it performs are driven by the operator, who has been notified by an external event (e.g., a user reports that a terminal is malfunctioning). The tests are the same on both active and passive systems and consist mainly of checking the electronic levels on the line and in the modem. The active system, on the other hand, is again a minicomputer system. It samples all lines in real time, records all exceptional events, and signals alarms as they occur. Both systems employ a side channel technique whereby the diagnostic unit sends signals in this channel in parallel, but independently of the data stream. These signals are processed by special circuit boards in the modem and are retransmitted to the diagnostic center. Thus, for either an active or a passive diagnostic center to function, circuitry has to be placed in the remote modems. For most vendors, this means that the modem must be from the same supplier as the diagnostic center. In some cases, however, there is a separate box which attaches to a manufacturer's modems. No manufacturer of a diagnostic center, to date, can provide diagnostic capability to terminals with integrated modems. These systems work only with stand-alone modems.

To speed the diagnosis of telephone line faults and to provide automatic dial backup for a failing line, a network diagnostic controller that is used in conjunction with diagnostic modems is needed. The diagnostic control system provides a central point of control over distributed data communications networks. It provides immediate, automatic notification of network problems, noninterruptive automatic status testing of critical network functions, and thorough diagnostic testing to isolate faulty components. Once a fault has been isolated, service can be restored by means of a dial backup (if available), or by notification of the appropriate vendor for service. Some problems, such as degraded conditions, can be detected before they interrupt service, and downtime can be prevented by repair of the condition during off-hours. A centralized system for notification, testing, restoral, and monitoring provides a powerful tool for optimizing network performance by reducing downtime.

Diagnostic modems can replace existing modems in the network (assuming they are not integrated with the terminals). The diagnostics are run over the line on a secondary channel in parallel, but not interfering with, the data stream. This procedure provides the ability to constantly monitor the integrity of the line, to determine at once whether there is a line fault or a terminal fault, to switch off malfunctioning remote modems from the central site, and to perform automatic dial backup to a remote site, thus providing maximum system availability to the individual terminals. Some of the leading suppliers of diagnostic center equipment are Codex, Data-Comm Industries, Intertel, and ICC-Milgo. All of these suppliers have installed major diagnostic systems and have reputations as vendors of quality equipment. There are certain differences between them, however; for example, Codex does not support 1200-baud asynchronous; Data-Comm has an active monitor which will work with any manufacturer's stand-alone modem, providing it is Bell System–compatible; Intertel makes only a passive monitor but fully supports IBM 3600 series star and remote loops; ICC-Milgo makes active and passive diagnostic units but currently can handle only IBM 3600 series star configurations and not the remote loop concept.

All suppliers offer a "turnkey" package for a technical center, a diagnostic center, and a marriage to your existing equipment. Costs can range from $10,000 to $1 million, depending on the type, size, and sophistication of the system. For example, one might select a passive diagnostic unit alone at a cost of $10,000, or an active diagnostic unit for $80,000. A separate technical center for each network could cost another $10,000. In a sizable network, most of the cost will be in the diagnostic modems ($1,000–$2,000 each). Since a fully integrated diagnostic center only speeds the diagnosis of line faults, in a low-value terminal system the high cost of the diagnostics could become prohibitive. In a system where the terminal value is high, however, the cost of diagnostics becomes low (as time is of the essence)—not only for speeding the diagnosis of line faults, but for enabling automatic invocation of dial backup at remote sites without intervention at the remote site. This is important in maintaining the high level of uptime required in such a network. Control and diagnosis of the network are thus left in the hands of the central site, where the telecommunications expertise is located.

In the 1980s, we should see more sophisticated programmable equipment offerings that are easier to operate and that have more built-in self-diagnostics. Improved troubleshooting capability over multivendor networks will be required as networks expand and proliferate. Providing a company with diagnostic center capability now will build needed expertise and provide insurance for better network management and improved availability in the on-line world of the future.

It is becoming increasingly apparent that in the future, companies will have to rely more and more on their own expertise not only to diagnose, but also to repair failures; or, at the very least, to take an active hand in the repair activity. There is no supplier in the business today that can conform to the standards required for relatively uninterrupted data-communications activity. Talent for this increasingly sophisticated operation will be very difficult to recruit; perhaps the best approach is an in-house training program or even a consortium of similar businesses' setting up training classes for trade school graduates.

Most voice and data communications users have designed their networks intuitively; however, with the increasing complexity and variety of alternatives available today, one is now able to move to at least a semirational state. Computers and PABXs will feed statistics on volume, distribution, speeds, busy-hour loads, and accuracy. The problem is the sheer bulk of the information. Even if we know the statistics, what do we do with them?

Several vendors supply network tools that will, to some extent, "design" voice and data networks. AT&T, IBM, Burroughs, and others can also perform such service for customers. Neither approach is all-inclusive, as it cannot handle all architectures; take into account all protocols, speeds, etc.; and consider every tariff (for example, SBS, GTE, and AT&T). Nor does any tool combine voice and data. However, companies such as DMW Group, Inc., Network Analysis Corporation, and perhaps even AT&T, on a time-shared basis, are moving to this end. What is clear is that for an effective, economical, and responsive network, some software design tool will be needed. Perhaps more importantly, the user will need the in-house talent to employ it and interpret it to its best advantage.

THE REGULATORY AGENCIES

Unlike computers, telecommunications has been regulation-driven. To understand telecommunications, one has to understand the regulatory environment. Domestically, all common carriers must obtain the approval of the state public-utility commission or the Federal Communications Commission for rate increases and new services. Although the prospect for the future is likely to be a trend toward less regulation, these agencies will not disappear. Regulators tend to be far more liberal in granting increases for business services than for residence services, making it imperative for businesses to be at least informed, if not active. Government decree can either foster or impede technology, as we have witnessed since the Carterfone decision in 1968, which allowed competition in the telecommunications industry for the first time.

Internationally, telecommunications is governed by a postal, telephone, and telegraph authority (PTT) or some equivalent group. As a body of the International Telecommunications Union, the CCITT (Consulating Committee on International Telephone and Telegraphy) sets standards such as $\times .25$. It is impossible to understand international telecommunications without also understanding the profound impact that the PTTs and the CCITT have on what can or cannot be done. Monopoly, rather than competition, is the usual result of governmental control of the telecommunications industry. For these reasons, voice and data communications systems almost have to be designed on a country-by-country basis with a thorough knowledge and understanding of the regulatory climate in each country. This kind of knowledge of technology and regulation is hard to find. If it is not available in-house, the only real alternative is to hire outside telecommunications consultants to lead one through the difficult path from telecommunications planning through implementation.

NOTES

1   James Martin, *The Wired Society,* Englewood Cliffs, N.J.: Prentice-Hall, 1978, pp. 144–145.
2   Liz Roman Gallese, "Electronic Switch," *Wall Street Journal,* May 25, 1979, p. 1.
3   Paul Strassmann, *The Future Direction of Information Systems to Impact the Bottom Line,* unpublished Xerox Corp. paper.

The Office Automation Frontier

There is nothing more difficult to take in hand . . . than to take the lead in the introduction of a new order of things.

Machiavelli, The Prince

The office will be one of the most exciting frontiers for major automation in the 1980s. Very little automation has been brought to bear on this vital activity of every firm, although it is the backbone of information generation and management. Actually, most of today's office equipment was invented prior to 1900, including typewriters, mimeographs, dictation equipment, and adding machines. (By contrast, IBM's plans for its new Displaywriter are for eventual support of up to a megabyte of memory. That's like have a 370/138 on a typewriter!) New tools for office productivity are certainly long overdue. Productivity improvement in the office provides an extraordinary opportunity for information managers to increase their influence and effectiveness in the organization by leading the development and spread of office information systems (OIS).

It is an axiom of economics that the only real way to reduce inflation is to increase productivity. White-collar workers today outnumber blue-collar workers, and their number is growing at the rate of 7% a year: a large percentage of the work force will be knowledge workers by 1990. Yet, we spend only $2,500 in equipment to support an office worker today, compared with $25,000 to support a factory worker and $50,000 to support a farm worker. It is obvious why the increase in office productivity has been at a relatively flat rate (3% over the last 10 years compared with 84% for factory productivity). Along with rising administrative costs, we are also faced with a growing shortage of skilled secretarial (500,000 short by 1985) and administrative personnel. Office automation will be the key that unlocks the productivity potential of this important area of business activity.

The office revolution is not just coming—it is here! The rapidly rising interest in office automation has been given impetus by the continuing increase in the proportion of office administrative costs to total costs, coupled with the technology that has begun to make some real inroads toward increased *productivity* on this largely untapped automation frontier. The Yankee Group estimates that the $800 billion spent on office operations (direct and indirect) in 1979 could reach $1.6 trillion by 1990. If so, this will truly represent an office revolution.

Why all this interest in office automation? The office is a labor-intensive area of the firm. It is also where managers and executives get the vital information they need to control the business, make decisions, and move the company forward. It offers the opportunity for increased productivity, not only by clerks and secretaries, but by the managers and executives that consume the majority (70%) of the salary cost in most companies. Automation can accomplish office tasks more cheaply, faster, and more effectively. It can reduce and control labor costs by computerizing routine functions and enhancing those portions of the administration function that require mundane, repetitive tasks. Secretaries and administrators will experience job enrichment by doing more work in the same time or by replacing routine work with more advanced work that can be taken over from managers, in effect, establishing viable career paths. To managers, this means freeing their time for more planning and creative work, and increasing their span of control (so fewer supervisors are needed). Office productivity can probably be doubled through automation. Technology is the key to major office productivity in the 1980s.

STAGES OF GROWTH

As in Nolan's stages of EDP growth, OIS will also very likely evolve through stages of growth. Michael Zisman, while at MIT, described his corollary of office automation stages, which we summarize as follows:[1]

Stage 1: Initiation.   Emphasis will be on mechanized efficiency as the way to increase productivity; that is, improved paperwork management, text processing, etc., primarily through extension of the word-processing concept.

Stage 2: Expansion.   Rapid expansion of electronic office concepts will follow growth in the use of such tools as electronic mail, electronic filing, and administrative glossaries. There will still be reliance on secretaries, but they will use more tools to increase productivity.

Stage 3: Formalization.   There will be a proliferation of separate, nonintegrated systems, with an increasing need for systems integration. There will be a shift from devices to processes, from mechanizing tasks to automating functions, beginning to deal with *managers,* not just secretaries.

Step 4: Maturity.   Individual solutions will be integrated into a cohesive office system. A shift from the mechanization of tasks to the automation of functions (processes) will become the primary focus. As automation increases, the integration of functions increases.

The main distinction which Zisman made between mechanization and automation is that under mechanization, people initiate and control office processes, whereas under automation, these functions are turned over to the computer. Under mechanization, separate nonintegrated systems are developed; under automation, these systems are integrated into a total office system.

Strassmann made somewhat the same case when he characterized the four stages of growth as (a) mechanization of tasks; (b) computer-aided instruction; (c) work redesign; and (d) work enlargement.[2]

The history of the evolution of technology would seem to support the hypothesis that office automation is likely to proceed as a series of phased systems, some building on others, and some standing alone. A long-range OIS plan, then, should identify the various phases of automation growth and provide for an integration plan which will link separately implemented systems into a unified whole.

OFFICE INFORMATION SYSTEMS

> **S-53   OFFICE INFORMATION SYSTEMS STRATEGY**
>
> **IM leads the firm into the office of the future through proactive leadership and phased planning to increase office and managerial productivity in the organization.**

A good office information systems (OIS) strategy, in our opinion, would embody:

Leadership.
Organizational planning.
Phased implementation.

Leadership

There is no doubt that *someone* must take charge of the direction, implementation, and coordination of office information systems if they are to progress in an orderly, systematic, and integrated fashion. The experience needed for this leadership includes data processing, telecommunications, and administration (office work). Thus, the principals usually considered for this leadership are:

The administrative services manager.
The telecommunications manager.
The EDP manager.

Administrative services managers usually have backgrounds in administration, that is, in secretarial/administrative support, general services, building properties, purchasing and supplies, and the like. Thus, they often lack the technical expertise needed to combine data processing, word processing, and communications.

Telecommunications managers most often have backgrounds in voice communication and, of late, data communications, but they often lack computer systems knowledge and experience.

DP managers have heavy computer backgrounds and usually some telecommunications knowledge as well, but they have seldom had adequate exposure to the human dimension of office and administrative processes.

Most firms that use computers heavily are either involved in office systems projects or planning to implement them in the next one or two years. Very often, data processing is identified as the driving force behind the office systems projects.

Michael Zisman has stated:

> It will be interesting to see who manages this evolution in organizations. Office automation requires information processing in a much broader perspective than traditional data processing, general administrative services, or telecommunications. The leadership for the office automation effort will come from one of these areas, but a successful effort will require the involvement of all groups. Each group will have to widen the scope of its mission to include the office of the future: the group which does so most quickly will emerge as the leader and catalyst.[3]

Finally, the Diebold Research Group, in a special survey an office automation, reported:

> 22 percent of respondents indicated that control of all office automation services is vested in one individual. These organizations have taken the first step toward integrating office automation tools. 20 percent of the individuals are administrative executives, 70 percent report to Data Processing and MIS organizations, and 10 percent are in general management.[4]

We have seen the leadership come from all of these sources, with perhaps the edge going to data processing managers, when they have been alert to the opportunities of office information systems. We also see—in major corporations, at least—a growing tendency to establish a new position, an office information systems manager, reporting in many cases directly to a senior company executive other than the three named above. The subject is apparently becoming important enough in many companies to warrant the appointment of an OIS manager who is *on a par* with the data processing, telecommunications, and administrative managers.

We suggest that if, in fact, DP managers move themselves up in the organization to achieve the broader role of information managers, then it would be entirely appropriate for *all of the above* to report to the information manager, since all of these activities constitute the management of the firm's information resources. Given that the IM function would provide technical staff support services across organizational lines, would have the technology and systems skills needed to plan and implement OIS, and would be managing the resources into which office systems must ultimately fit (mainframe host processors, telecommunications links, corporate data bases), there would be no function other than IM that could better assume this responsibility. The opportunity unquestionably is there, but leadership and direction are clearly needed. The IM mission, then, should be to actively apply to office automation the systematized planning approach applied to other areas which have been automated—to bring the same productivity gains to the office that have been brought to other areas of the organization over the past 20 years.

Organizational Planning

The success or failure of an OIS strategy will probably depend more on human factors than on anything else. People often resist change, especially when it involves technology that threatens their jobs or the way they do their work. Therefore, to be successful, *technology must adapt to users,* not the other way around. Don't scare them, don't heap it on them. Implement slowly. Learn their fears and their skepticisms. This approach will help to implement office systems more successfully. Technology must be made nonthreatening, and job enrichment must result from the application of office systems. People must *like it;* otherwise, no matter how much potential benefit it has, office automation will fail. Automation will require that people learn new skills to perform jobs that are dependent on automated information processing. The training has to be made easy. Hardware engineering has to make the users comfortable. The IM function should make the technology appear as transparent to the user as possible. User-friendly systems are the key to office systems because the office environment is not a data processing environment. Office workers are not technically oriented, as are programmers. OIS design, to be successful, must reflect this fact. A manager or a clerk is not paid to understand how the system works and should not have to in order to use it. Office systems will succeed only if they are designed to process information in a manner that conforms to the user's understanding of the business process, not in a manner designated by a systems design that optimizes the technical capabilities of the system. People tend to fear what they don't understand or perceive it as too difficult to master. Thus, in the selection of equipment, in the development of software, and in the training of office personnel, an emphasis on the human dimension of OIS acceptance will probably be critical to success.

In addition to providing users with "friendly" easy-to-use equipment, organizational acceptance also involves implementation with the least possible disturbance of the total work environment. To attempt to reorganize office workers, to disrupt their environment for the sake of technology, would go exactly contrary to our earlier admonition that technology must adapt to users rather than users' adapting to technology. Thus, we would not advocate an attempt to reorganize administrative personnel into a different corporate arrangement. One can simply leave everything as is and add technological aids to the existing environment. This approach minimizes threat. We know of a major southern bank that removed all secretaries from their managers by having them report to a new administrative services division. They would continue to work for the same executives, but administratively (work assignments, salary reviews, promotions, career orientation), their allegiance would obviously be elsewhere. Neither the secretaries nor the executives took kindly to the proposed reorganization. The president backed the administrative manager, however, and forced the planned office automation into place. The result was a major morale problem, as well as considerable turnover of scarce human resources—not just secretaries but executives as well, including a senior vice-president of the bank. That seems a high price to pay to force users to adapt to technology.

As far as the role of information management is concerned in the leadership of OIS, we believe it, too, should continue in its traditional role as a staff-support function of the company. That is, IM can be responsible for such staff functions as long-range planning, technical decisions, and systems implementation; line-operations responsibility can remain with users (i.e., the secretaries and other office workers operate the terminals but continue to report to their line managers). As suggested earlier, the biggest hurdles to office automation will probably not be technology but political (authority) and behavioral (acceptance) considerations. If one does not attempt to wrest responsibility for administrative staff from present organizational arrangements, one of the biggest resistance factors may be effectively removed. Paul Strassmann, at Xerox, has functional responsibility for some 18,000 administrative people around the world—but none of them report to him directly. They report to their organizational units. He has responsibility for the *function,* not the resources. Similarly, an IM function can effectively control office automation implementation without having physical control over people or machines. This is leadership with minimal organizational or human disturbances, designed to manage *information* resources, not people or machines.

Phased Planning Implementation

Working with the stages-of-growth hypothesis, we have developed a four-phase approach to office information systems which can serve as a useful background to planning for the office environment of the future. This four-phase implementation plan for OIS is diagrammed in Exhibit 10-1. Each phase builds on the former; that is, each successive phase is dependent on

Exhibit 10-1 Phased office information systems strategy.

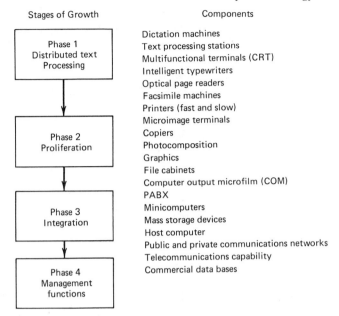

Stages of Growth

Phase 1
Distributed text
Processing

Phase 2
Proliferation

Phase 3
Integration

Phase 4
Management
functions

Components

Dictation machines
Text processing stations
Multifunctional terminals (CRT)
Intelligent typewriters
Optical page readers
Facsimile machines
Printers (fast and slow)
Microimage terminals
Copiers
Photocomposition
Graphics
File cabinets
Computer output microfilm (COM)
PABX
Minicomputers
Mass storage devices
Host computer
Public and private communications networks
Telecommunications capability
Commercial data bases

the previous one and would not be viable without it. These four phases of OIS implementation are:

Phase 1: Distributed text processing.
Phase 2: Proliferation.
Phase 3: Integration.
Phase 4: Management functions.

Phase 1: Distributed Text Processing Word processing is not new. It has been around for some 15 years, beginning with the IBM magnetic tape days of the late 1960s. Early shared logic systems, however, were built around centralized typing pools to justify the cost of the equipment. These proved to be unpopular with both typists and secretaries. In attempts to make them more acceptable, they were given euphemistic titles such as *secretarial services* or *administrative services*. They were still resisted, and even though many companies still use central typing pools, they are still unpopular.

Distributed text processing, on the other hand, works on the philosophy discussed earlier of not disturbing the organization. Text processing machines, terminals, and printers are put in place where the people are, as added tools to help them do their jobs better and faster. These machines may be harder to cost-justify, but it has been our experience that they are better accepted, and managers soon become convinced of the increased productivity which they make possible. This acceptance, in turn, makes cost justification of less concern.

At The First National Bank of Boston, for example, a lot of time was spent initially developing numbers that would cost-justify the first few installations. This report involved the usual calculations of displaced typists or secretaries, and the value of freed-up time of principals and secretaries based on estimates of hours saved through increased productivity. At best, such calculations are suspect because, with the exception of displaced people, the numbers are all soft and difficult to prove. What the bank found, however, was that the managers of the first few installations became enthusiastic supporters of their text processing systems, not because of economics, but because they became convinced of the ability of the systems to dramatically improve productivity. The law department, for example, saved many high-salaried lawyers hours through eliminating the need to reread contracts, agreements, and the like when changes were made, because the system was able to make the changes and reprint the documents without introducing typographical errors requiring proofreading, as would be the case if the documents were retyped in the traditional way. The finance department similarly saved many valuable CPA hours through the use of the "math" feature of their text processing system, which automatically cross-footed all financial statements as changes were made, avoiding the necessity of constantly having to readd columns of numbers. The division heads of these two important areas of the bank not only became convinced of the value of their system but also became very supportive of the implementation of additional systems throughout the bank, as members of the banks' equivalent of the information resources management committee (S-29), without having to cost-justify each installation over and over again. In other words, having demonstrated the productivity value of OIS in two important areas of the bank to the satisfaction of the senior managers involved, the IM function was able to proceed with implementation in many other areas of the company, without having to further cost-justify individual installations. The moral: make the first sale right and the product will sell itself.

Having selected the equipment and a "friendly" application through the survey process, it is probably a good idea to start with a pilot program. Starting small with a positive user will help ensure success.

Positive feedback from the user will spread by word of mouth in the organization. Other potential users can be brought around to see OIS in operation, and to see the user's acceptance of and enthusiasm about the system. Other installations can follow, again where interest is high. In this way distributed text processing can spread throughout the organization in a nonthreatening, nondisruptive way. Its own success will breed upon itself, and soon OIS will be in place, ready for Phase 2.

Phase 2: Proliferation   Phase 2, the proliferation of OIS in the organization and the adding of functionality and capability to existing OIS, would not be possible without Phase 1. Each phase thus builds logically on its predecessor. Whereas text processing replaces typewriters, Phase 2 begins to replace other office components, such as paper and file cabinets. Once distributed text processing takes hold, users will find all sorts of innovative administrative functions to add to the system as they discover its capabilities for themselves. Keeping a glossary of these applications for dissemination to other possible users will help to increase OIS usefulness. One of these capabilities is electronic mail (message sending and document distribution); another is electronic filing (storage and retrieval of information).

There are at least four types of electronic mail devices in use today: (a) teletype (telex/TWX) machines, which are fading out; (b) facsimile transmission devices, which are expected to show big growth in the 1980s as they become faster and cheaper; (c) computer-based message systems, which are still rather expensive and thus in limited use; and (d) communicating word-processing machines, the latest of which is OCR word processing—that is, a typist creates the hard copy, and an optical character reader reads it into a word processor for editing. Satellite communications and cheap rooftop antennas (e.g., SBS) will provide the impetus for the growth of electronic mail systems of the future. Electronic filing (information storage and retrieval), involving both microimagery and image processing, will grow to provide extensive indexing and hard copy capability. CRTs will interlink with distributed text-processing stations and mainframe computer data bases. Portable terminals accessing such data bases by dial telephone from anywhere in the world will be in common use. The machines of the future must have multifunction capabilities, combining into one machine several functions that are now separate. Copier-printers will be combined with computer output microfilm and document transmission, for example. A multiplicity of different components will make up tomorrow's office systems.

Message-switching will prove popular as people learn its advantages. Much time is wasted today simply trying to *reach* people by phone. Electronic messages, stored in the recipient's electronic "in-basket" until noted and responded to, are especially useful when simultaneous communications are not necessary. The following five advantages of electronic mail were identified by the Yankee Group at their 1980 Electronic Mail Symposium in New York:[5]

1 Users can handle up to 30 pieces of routine correspondence in an hour (compared with the ability to make five or six phone calls in that time, or to hold one face-to-face meeting, or to write three letters).

2 Problems can be handled according to their importance (prioritized, as compared with the more common last-in–first-out, or LIFO, method).

3 Electronic mail will sharply reduce the delivery time of the 90% of *intracompany* mail that now takes more than a day to deliver.

4 Since 70% of all phone calls are not completed on the first try, electronic mail will reduce the time lost in repeated call attempts (telephone "tag").

5 Since 80% of Fortune 500 companies have or are considering electronic
   mail systems, intercompany communications with these firms will be
   easier and faster.

Teleconferencing will save time and the costs of travel, but ingrained habits
will have to change before it gains widespread acceptance. Facsimile transmission (document distribution) is already the most prevalent form of electronic mail today. It has the distinct advantages of requiring no rekeying and
of being able to transmit anything on paper: pictures, drawings, letters, etc.
This system will be begun between departments in the same building, then
will be extended to different geographic locations of one company, and finally to customer locations. All of these OIS tools will proliferate in the
organization because they all spell *PRODUCTIVITY*. Postage for a first-
class letter is 18 cents, and delivery takes days; electronic mail will cost
pennies and take seconds.

Electronics will be the force that finally brings productivity to the neglected office. Information managers will need to monitor progress of new
products and new capabilities in order to achieve a well-managed proliferation of OIS in the organization. This will build on itself slowly, however,
because changing old work habits will take time.

Electronic mail and filing will very likely coexist with paper and filing
cabinets for some time to come. But as people become more accustomed to
the new, the old will, like old soldiers, "just fade away." More and more
office tasks will be done by computers or computer assistance. People will be
freed from mundane tasks, and the result will be greater job enrichment.
Managers will be able to spend more time doing what computers cannot do:
creative thinking and planning. It will be the job of information managers to
actively spread text processing and to add capabilities such as administrative
functions, electronic mail and filing, facsimile transmission, teleconferencing, and the like so that OIS proliferation will occur in a controlled and
integrated manner.

Phase 3: Integration   Most organizations today are in the first one or two
phases. In Phase 3, information managers will need to keep a watchful eye
on the need for integration of office system components in order to avoid
creating a nightmare of unrelated, uncoordinated systems that leads to con-
fusion rather than to integrated order. The office of the future must consist of
a single, integrated office *system,* not systems. This does not mean one piece
of hardware. There will very likely be many machines of different vendors,
and many office processes will be automated. But the machines must be
coordinated for system compatibility so as to become an integrated office
system. It will be important to have a long-range plan to assure compatibility
of these separate system components in order to unify them into a cohesive
whole. This will include, of course, planning for the merger of text processing and data processing as well as telecommunications planning, the glue that

will hold it all together. Telecommunications will connect all the various office machines, word processors, copying machines, printers, and host computers—and will be the underlying technology for systems integration. The office of the future will need to communicate information as much as process it. Once information is captured in a machine it will be in electronic form, and be capable of being moved about from machine to machine without ever having to be printed. Manufacturers are already beginning to introduce multifunction machines to replace separate devices (e.g., a printer, a copier, a COM, and a facsimile transmission machine all built into a single unit). Synthesizing independent systems into a single office system will mark the difference between indiscriminate use of new products and services and an integrated office system. The list of office system components is lengthy. It includes:

Text processing.
Administration functions.
Electronic mail and filing.
Data processing interfaces.
Output devices.
Reprographics.
Optical character recognition.
Teleprocessing.
Personal time management.
Telecommunications networking.

This is only a partial list. Moreover, each of the components listed can be further broken down into subcomponents. For example, administrative functions might include the development of various lists sorted in different orders, contract preparation aids, marketing information, assistance in filling in forms, budget report comparison, correspondence tracking, pricing schedules—an almost unlimited list of possibilities. Similarly, electronic mail and filing applications might include facsimile transmission, telex/TWX interface, mailgrams, in-house and external terminals, telephone answering services, and store and forward messages. Personal time management could include personal calendars, meeting schedules, diaries, itineraries, bulletin board announcements, and task tickler (reminder) functions. Telecommunications networks might cover dial-up, leased lines, packet switching, ACS, videotext, coaxial cable systems, fiber optics, lasers, satellite systems, and other options. A comparison of various data and word processing applications that can be found in various departments of many large corporations today is shown in Exhibit 10-2. These application areas are prime targets for office automation.

Probably the most dramatic form of OIS integration in the 1980s will be the evolution of the *work station* concept. This is something that information

Exhibit 10-2 Data and word processing applications in various departments

Accounting	Invoicing Payroll Cost accounting Order entry Inventory control Accounts receivable Accounts payable General ledger	Quarterly reports Annual reports Security exchange Committee reports Collection letters Audits Memos
Advertising	Lead tracking	Brochure copy Press releases Advertising copy Customer newsletters Correspondence Memos
Corporate Education		Lesson plans Training schedules Educational material Memos
Legal	Time accounting Docket control Document indexing	Letters of opinion/advice Pension plans Profit-sharing plan Leases Contracts Mergers Articles of incorporation Minutes of meetings Correspondence Memos
Marketing	Sales analysis Sales product Sales industry Customer data base	Marketing plans Product releases Competitive profiles Correspondence Memos
Personnel	Personnel records Employee benefits Benefits administration Affirmative action Skills inventory	Lists/directories Job acceptance letters Job refusal letters Job descriptions Open job posting Reviews Training manuals Policy manuals Memos
Publications	Inventory Project control	Operating manuals Training manuals Data sheets Product bulletins
Purchasing	Purchase orders Reorder notification Part number verification	Vendor file maintenance Spec writing Correspondence/memos Bid request memos
Sales	Sales analysis Forecasts Customer file maintenance	Proposals List/directories Promotions/contests Correspondence

managers will need to promote as the new way offices will function. The office work-station concept envisions a merger of text processing, data processing, and telecommunications into a single, compact, multifunctional, intelligent terminal in the hands of the information worker. A work station will be *one* terminal (instead of four) on a shared system, with easy access to data bases, wherever located; it will perform information management (storage, retrieval, manipulation); it will be programmable, with an internal diagnostic capability, and inexpensive. The office work station could become the universal office utility of the future. Many companies are working on this: IBM, Xerox, Wang, Digital Equipment, Raytheon, Data General, Prime Computer—all the big names in the industry. Xerox's 8000 Network system, for example, includes an electronic office-file (electronic filing and mail) base printer and communications devices that link, through communications "servers," its own and other (IBM protocol) vendors' equipment into an integrated office network. The 8000 system is aimed at the larger market segment (Fortune 500 companies) because of its cost ($15,000–$30,000). The system works in conjunction with the Ethernet communications system, which in turn was developed jointly by Xerox, DEC, and Intel Corporation as a communications system that would enable computers, terminals, and other office products to communicate with each other within one office or with other Ethernet offices. Thus, it is sure to evolve as an integral office system in the 1980s. One of the most interesting things about Ethernet is its "information outlet," whose purpose, in effect, is to provide a plug-in-the-wall information utility like telephone and electronic outlets. For example, if an information outlet were desired in an office without a plug, building properties could be called to install one, giving access to the Ethernet service: *information* power instead of electrical power! Information managers must continue to research developments in this area and plan the gradual addition of OIS components, working with vendors on equipment interface requirements, the establishment of needed standards, and the development of enabling software in the absence of compatibility standards.

Phase 4: Management Functions   The growth of OIS in the organization and its integration as a single office information management capability will affect not only clerical and secretarial people, but managers as well. Here will be the real payoff in office automation: when we finally begin to automate the *functions* performed by managers, rather than just the clerical tasks. Management, after all, is really a process of analyzing, synthesizing, and disseminating information, much of which can be automated. When we are able to automate the administrative functions performed by *managers,* we will really begin to strike at the productivity potential of office automation (perhaps more aptly called *officer automation* at this point). When managers are relieved of routine office procedures, they can spend more time on true management functions. The work station concept, using intelligent desk-top terminals (microprocessors), will also be designed to serve managers at their desks, and executives will be able to drive these terminals by voice command and touch-sensitive screens, not just by typing onto a keyboard. Harvey Poppel, of Booz, Allen, and Hamilton, has said that the automated office of the future may not work because of the failure to move it into managers' offices. Poppel is conducting a study of what's wrong with the office of the future for the benefit of people with a stake in it, like IBM, Xerox, IT&T, and AT&T. Poppel's study postulates that the office of the future has to be moved into professional and managerial suites: "What we found was that we were really dealing with the wrong problem. The real problem is helping managers and professionals do a better job."[6]

Today's college graduates and MBAs have some familiarity with computers and are more inclined to use them in their work. As they move up into the executive ranks, so will computer-assisted management systems. But this will take time. We need to put computers to work for managers and executives today, because that's where the bulk of office services and costs are. Providing good, accurate, and timely information to managers for control and decision-making purposes is the *raison d'être* of the office. It will not be enough to have others get the information out of the OIS for executives; we want to enable them to do it themselves. How are we going to accomplish this role for OIS when we all know what an aversion most top managers have to using computers directly (fear of the unknown?) and typing on keyboards (won't or can't?). We believe the answer lies in *ease of use*. Executives use telephones because they are easy to use. They don't need extensive specialized knowledge or training to use a phone, but they do to use a computer terminal. They don't want to type or to struggle to get information. They want to ask for it. It follows that office systems must be designed to make the technology transparent to the executive. The executive terminal must:

Be user-friendly—simple commands, English messages, menu-driven.

Require minor training in a few hours, not days or weeks.

Provide "soft" entry—no typewriter keyboard needed.

This kind of executive terminal will have a lot of inherent hardware/software compatibility. The use of simple English words and simple push-button commands, as well as the elimination of typing, requires that all the technology be self-contained. Let us consider *soft entry* as an example. Alternatives to typewriter keyboards include entry pads, touch screens, voice systems, and digital pens.

Entry pads usually have a series of function buttons and numerical keys that allow commands to be made by the simple punching of a button or entering of a number (as a menu selection). Touch screens are divided into a series of rectangular touch points (like rows of post office boxes). As the menu appears on the screen, the manager touches the item desired (one of the programmed points) to get the desired information.

Voice systems have been around for quite a while on the output side (e.g., audio response systems in banks for balance inquiry) but are much newer on the input side. Now that "talking chips" are coming into use (e.g., Texas Instrument's Speak and Spell toy, talking dolls, replacements for auto instrument panels, home appliances), we can expect to see them used more as computer output, especially for executive systems. Voice input is also improving. Matsushita and Xerox are both rumored to be coming out with voice input typewriters by 1983 (do you think IBM put a 50,000-word dictionary in its Displaywriters just to help people spell?). Machines that recognize a limited number of words are around but need to be "trained" for each person's voice. Recognition of different voices or continuous speech is still a long way off, although Dialog Systems of Belmont, Massachusetts, has developed a system that can recognize simple words and digits spoken by any person over a telephone (used for bank-by-phone bill paying). Further breakthroughs are needed before voice commands become practical as input for executive systems. Digital pens involve writing on a pressure-sensitive pad on a desk, which is read by an OCR-like matrix device which displays it on a terminal screen.

The point is, there are alternatives to typewriter keyboards, and we need highly specialized knowledge that can be employed to get executives to use OIS directly. If we are going to be successful in automating the office and delivering increased productivity to the firm, we must extend OIS to managers and executives directly, and not just to secretaries and clerks. Thus, the automation of management functions and the delivery of information management work stations into the executive office represent the final goal of OIS and the culmination of the fourth phase in the evolution of office automation.

SUMMARY

These developments will take a number of years to implement—perhaps the whole decade of the 1980s. That is why a *phased* OIS approach, such as is depicted in Exhibit 10-1, can be a practical strategy. Word processing is already here. Electronic mail and filing are in the embryonic stage, trying to find logical applications and users. Systems integration will be a product of advanced planning, the merger of text and data processing, and multifunction developments in the years ahead. The automation of management functions and the direct use of office work stations by executives is still only a glimmer in the information manager's eye. Yet it must be planned for if we are to get to the integrated office of the future. Office systems must not be allowed to evolve as unrelated pieces. The pieces must be linked together as part of a total OIS plan. The most important action for an information manager to take today regarding an OIS strategy is to create a long-range OIS plan that leads to the integrated office system of the future through phased development. It must be integrated to tie together the entire company. It must be phased because you can't get to Phase 3 from Phase 1 without going through Phase 2. They are building blocks.

Building efficient systems, which contain the logic of office processes and functions, in order to transfer work and control from people to technology, will be the challenge to information managers in the years ahead. The processes involved are not unlike traditional DP in one sense; that is, they involve the logical processes of input, processing, and output. An office system must receive input, analyze the input to determine the appropriate processing, generate some required output, and store the data needed to trigger follow-up actions, as appropriate.

The real productivity gains in the office will come from the synergism of a total systems approach, rather than from individual solutions. The office information systems strategy suggested in this chapter has the following objectives:

1 *Increased productivity:* reduce and control office costs by getting more work done with fewer people; that is, organizational efficiency.
2 *Increased effectiveness:* improve the work quality of the administrative staff, as well as work satisfaction, through increased emphasis on creative and innovative work.
3 *Integrated systems:* unify multiple local systems into a single office management system.

Leadership in the coalescence of diverse office systems and products into a truly coordinated office information system could bring significant productivity improvements to the company. We believe that the IM organizations that lead this effort, that demonstrate the needed leadership, and that realize the productivity potential of office automation will extend their function and increase their influence and effectiveness in the organization enormously. The opportunity is there for those with the imagination to use it as a logical extension of the IM function in the organization.

NOTES

1 Michael D. Zisman, *Office Automation: Revolution or Evolution,* CISR Report 34, Sloan WP 986-78, MIT, April 1978, pp. 5–13.
2 Paul Strassmann, personal communication.
3 Zisman, *Office Automation,* p. 20.
4 *Organizational Trends and Issues in Office Automation,* Diebold Research Group, 1979.
5 *Electronic Mail Symposium,* Yankee Group seminar, New York, 1980.
6 Harvey Poppel, as reported by Connie Winkler, "Office of the Future May Not Work," *Computerworld,* May 21, 1979, p. 12.

CHAPTER

11

Project Selection and Management

An enormous number of contradictions and broken promises have been created in project management.

F. Warren MacFarlan[1]

LAWS OF PROJECT MANAGEMENT

1 A project not worth doing is not worth doing well.
2 A carefully planned project will take only twice as long to complete as expected.
3 A project will progress to 90% completion, then remain 90% complete forever.
4 If project content is allowed to change freely, the rate of change will soon exceed the rate of progress.
5 When things appear to be going better, you have overlooked something.
6 Any attempt to debug a system will simply add new bugs.
7 No major project was ever developed on time and within budget; your project will not be the first.

THE PROBLEM

Systems projects *can* be successfully managed! If this is true, why are cost overruns and missed target dates more the rule than the exception? Why have so many DP shops lost their credibility, with management questioning cost justification, control, efficient use of resources, and the ability of managers to manage? There are many reasons, of course, for poor project management and for project overruns. Four major contributing culprits are that:

1   Project management is not an exact science.
2   Cost estimates are generally made prematurely.
3   Too many projects suffer from loose management control.
4   Poor definition by users results in bad specifications, leading to frequent requests for changes.

Mix together, stir well, and you have all the ingredients for a project overrun.

Inexact Science

Commercial computing is 25 years old—a Johnny-come-lately compared with sciences like engineering, architecture, and construction. Moreover, computer technology has been changing so rapidly that it has outpaced the ability of people to keep up. The theory that 50 programmers can write a given program 50 ways is even truer when applied to systems designers. As a result, systems development and project management need all the help they can get—in the form of formal guidance through installation standards for systems and programming, through support resources, and through project management tools and strategies.

Early Estimating

Systems people are often required to estimate project development costs too early to possibly be accurate. Moreover, the scope of the project being estimated is often much too large, which contributes to a bad estimate. This is like trying to judge the size of an iceberg by its tip: one needs to see much more of it come out of the water before one can judge with any accuracy. To compound the problem, many estimating techniques are inherently poor because of three primary factors:

1   There are no standard guidelines in the industry. Estimates are often unscientifically arrived at and indefensible (which is why many systems people won't stand by their estimates).
2   There is inadequate accounting for uncertainty. Large systems projects involve a complex set of interrelated variables, including people, technology, support resources, and management. The uncertainties created by these variables must be properly accounted for in the estimating process. To assume that all will go well is to invoke Murphy's law: "Whatever can go wrong, will."
3   Management tries to underbuy and systems managers often undersell, because they are unsure of their estimates, because they assume that all will go well, because they desire to accommodate, or because they are just plain optimistic. Whatever the reason, the "undersell syndrome" is a common failing, which increases with project size.

Loose Management Control

This brings us to the management control process. The qualities that distinguish technicians are not necessarily the qualities required for management. A technician is a doer; a manager is a manager of doers! When project managers allow themselves to become so immersed in the technical aspects of the project that they are no longer managing the effort, then the basic principles of management—planning, organizing, staffing, directing, and controlling—are not being addressed. Making the move from technician (thing-oriented) to manager (people-oriented) is often a most difficult task. Effective project management doesn't just happen by itself. It takes formal and disciplined management and control techniques—from start to finish. Too often the instinctive response to a project overrun is to throw more people in, a response that either smothers the project or has people bumping into each other, but seldom helps; for as Brooks' law says, "Adding manpower to a late software project makes it later."[2]

USER/IM PROJECT MANAGEMENT

Systems projects are usually funded by the users, who have authorized the expenditures for new or improved computer applications. A systems development project is usually devised for users in one or more functions or divisions, and an important test of performance on a systems development project is whether these users are satisfied with the usefulness, timeliness, and costs of their new or improved system.

Users only rarely have a clearly detailed idea of what they want from a systems project. The front end of a systems project requires significant amounts of time from users if the project is to be well specified. The assessment of the users' needs requires the ability to understand both the current and the future user business activities to be supported by a new or improved system. The identification and involvement of all key users is critical to the success of a systems project.

Two- and three-year backlogs for systems projects are common in large companies today. Forecasting of the future business activities of users to be served by new systems projects is a very difficult task. Changes requested by users partway into a systems project are a major source of project cost and time overruns. The failure to specify user needs correctly is one of the most serious sources of project failure. A systems project is a management change activity. The two-cultures problem of technical systems professionals and users who have little knowledge of systems must be managed if work on systems projects is to achieve high standards of performance.

A new or improved system usually involves the management of change in one or more user functions or divisions. One might expect that organizational development specialists would play an active role in a process which brings together technical systems professionals and various users with business knowledge but little systems experience. Unfortunately, in most companies, specialists in the management of change have only rarely been involved in systems projects.

In this chapter, we address the problem of project management with some specific strategies aimed at the various management processes involved. The judicious use of a combination of these project management strategies can result in real progress toward proving the premise that systems projects can be successfully managed.

The acid test of successful systems projects is, of course, the overall *satisfaction of the users* with the results of these projects. Therefore, the principal strategy stressed in this chapter deals with the role and responsibility of the users working with IM professionals in the *shared* management tasks of systems delivery; hence, we begin our management by strategies (MBS) discussion of project management strategies with a discussion of the user/IM role in the project life cycle.

PROJECT LIFE CYCLE

> **S-54 PROJECT LIFE CYCLE (PLC)**
>
> **The systems-development life cycle, from project selection to postaudit, as a shared systems/user process.**

An effective program of systems project selection and management must begin with an overview of the project life cycle. Systems projects can fail because of errors along the complex path which begins with the planning needed for project selection and concludes with a postaudit of the system implemented. The project life cycle provides the overview to manage this complex process.

The steps of the project life cycle are fairly standard in the industry. Many books have been written on the subject. Few, however, have defined the roles and responsibilities of both systems and user people involved in the systems development process throughout its life cycle. The shared management process described here has been used for more than a decade at The First National Bank of Boston as a way of ensuring the success of the systems development process. The process begins with business information planning (S-10) and then proceeds through a six-step process as follows: (1) proposal, (2) functional design, (3) detail design, (4) programming, (5) implementation, and (6) postaudit.

Overview of the Project Life Cycle

Exhibits 11-1 and 11-2 provide an overview of the key elements in the implementation of the project life cycle for effective project management. A

Exhibit 11-1   Project team organization.

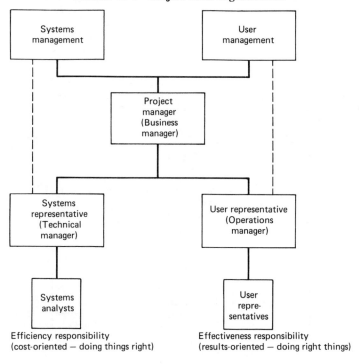

Efficiency responsibility
(cost-oriented — doing things right)

Effectiveness responsibility
(results-oriented — doing right things)

careful study of these two figures will communicate the essence of the PLC strategy about to be described.

Implementation of PLC Strategy

Phase 0: Business Information Planning   This phase is described in detail in BIP (S-10). Preliminary search, project identification, definition, and scope are the elements of this activity. Once a project has been approved for a feasibility study, it can be turned over to systems development (Phase 1).

Phase 1: Proposal Phase   The proposal phase (also known as the *feasibility study*) has as its main objectives an understanding of the user's problem; an appropriate computerized solution; a report for management, complete with a cost–benefit analysis in sufficient detail for an intelligent judgment to be made as to the desirability and justification of the project; and the allocation of the necessary resources (staff and dollars) for its undertaking. Once all this is done, the first task is to select an overall project (business) manager, from either IM or the user department. The project manager's responsibilities throughout the project include overall project management, coordination, and control—monitoring time, costs, and quality, as well as communicating progress to management at scheduled milestones. Next come the

Exhibit 11-2   Systems and user responsibility by stage in the project life cycle.

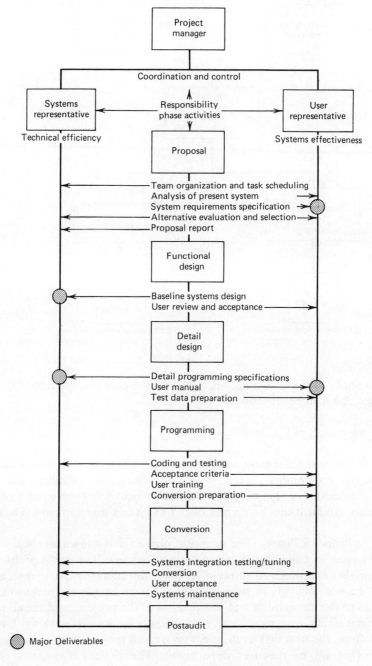

selection and organization of the project team, beginning with the project manager's two arms: the systems representative (SR) and the user representative (UR). The SR should be responsible for the technical efficiency of the system throughout the project and is assisted by other systems personnel assigned to the project. The UR should be responsible for the system's effectiveness (results) and is assisted by other specified user personnel. This team organization is illustrated in Exhibit 11-1.

A critical decision in this strategy is the selection of the key user representative. *This must not be a junior-level person.* The UR must be high-level, thoroughly knowledgeable about the user's business and needs, and committed full time to the project for its duration. The desired person is probably the one who will have to make the new system work once installed; hence, his or her involvement in its creation is vitally important. This person is probably now the department head's right-hand assistant. You will know if you have the right person when his or her name is suggested for this long-term full-time assignment: the department head will scream at the very suggestion. If so, you have the right person; if not, you have the wrong person.

After the SR and the UR have been designated, the rest of the team can be put together. It's important to know exactly the talents and experience of each team member, both to ensure good estimating and to know that the necessary talent is on the job. (Incidentally, the larger the team, the more difficult will be the communications: 3 people have 6 communications relationships; 10 people have 90!) Once the team is organized, project orientation can begin with a review of the project definition prepared by the BIP group. A task schedule can match the tasks with the manning requirements by project in simple calendar form, in Gantt chart form as in Exhibit 11-3, or in PERT/CPM form. The UR in this phase can conduct a thorough analysis of the present system (work flows, problems) and develop the requirements for the proposed system. This task will involve extensive data gathering, user interviews, analysis of needs, and the trading off of costs against the value of the desired systems features. The SR can participate in this activity, but it is primarily a UR responsibility. The SR should have primary responsibility for evaluating alternative system solutions and selecting the best alternative. The SR and the UR can then write the proposal report, describing the problems, the alternative solutions investigated, the solution recommended, and the new system (files, data elements, controls, volume estimates, etc.). The report could also include a rough cost–benefit analysis (S-57), which at this point should be only a ballpark estimate because it is still a bit premature. A fixed-cost estimate, however, would be expected for the functional design phase to follow.

Phase 2: Functional Design   The objective of this phase is to describe the new system in terms that the user can understand and accept. The functional design document is a major deliverable prepared by the SR. It should be formally approved by user management before the next phase begins. The document might contain a general system definition, list of all files, hardware requirements, output reports, controls, backup and security considerations, estimated run times, etc. The user's role is to review and accept the report. Involvement comes in the form of review and acceptance. Users must understand that this specification defines the system; this is what they will get—no more, no less. Sign-off (formal approval) at this point freezes the system—an important milestone. To avoid project overruns, any future change, regardless of reason, must become an addendum to the project, with added costs and a revised target date.

Phase 3: Detail Design   Whereas the functional design describes *what* is to be done, the detail design describes *how* it is to be done. The modules that make up the system can now be defined in precise detail (detailed systems flow, file descriptions, input/output procedures, forms requirements, etc.) This and the succeeding phase (programming) should be primarily an SR responsibility, with little or no user involvement. Nonetheless, the UR should be involved during technical development to the same extent that the SR was involved in the functional specifications phase—to review the work done by others and to continue to balance off the cost of information (an SR responsibility) with the value of information (a UR responsibility). Users have several other tasks to perform in this phase. They must begin work on a user operations manual, another important deliverable, and prepare test data in preparation for systems testing. The user operations manual should contain detailed user operating procedures—in effect, all of the input and output operations and procedures which surround, support, and control the new system. The test plan should enumerate all factors to be considered for the testing and acceptance of each module in the system. Test transactions must be prepared, not only to cover normal, expected transactions, but for all conceivable abnormal and bad input possibilities and error conditions. The objective is to try to make the system fail, to uncover missing logic. Test conditions also extend to all reports: regular, periodic, and special.

Phase 4: Programming   Detailed design results in each element of the system's being designed, detailed, and accepted by systems management. Programming can proceed rapidly from this point, giving real visibility to the system for the first time. Program flowcharts, coding, and unit testing can proceed from the detailed design specifications. The SR can monitor the accuracy, efficiency, and completion of all program codes. Following progress and target dates closely, ensuring that needed computer time is made available and that common routines and data descriptions are communicated properly to team members will reduce test time, computer runs, and general inefficiency. Concomitantly, the UR can develop the acceptance criteria for the system (e.g., one week's parallel operation with no more than two minor errors noted, production of month-end reports in balanced condition). Conversion preparation can begin (including site preparation in the case of a minicomputer system); this requires much coordination among the user department, data processing, and systems development. Schedules must be developed describing the arrival and control of input, the preparation of customer statements and internal reports, the availability and use of forms, and numerous control factors concerned with systems cut-over and parallel operations. User training in the use of terminals or other data entry procedures, system settlement and controls, and distribution and use of output reports also must be completed before implementation begins.

Phase 5: Conversion   The SR and the UR begin to work more closely together again as conversion nears. The SR conducts systems integration testing and tuning to ensure that all the pieces fit together and work as a system. Acceptance testing is done based on the acceptance criteria agreed upon with the UR. Conversion to the new system takes place in parallel, in phases, or all at once, again depending on the method agreed upon with the UR. After the system is successfully converted, the project can be closed, and a maintenance project can be opened to handle ongoing support, the resolution of "bugs," minor system enhancements, etc. (Note: Major system enhancements should become a new project.)

Phase 6: Postaudit   The postreview is an important, but often overlooked, follow-up activity, especially for major projects. Probably fewer than half of all IM functions perform it routinely (perhaps because project management is not always filled with successes). Project managers who are successful encourage postaudits; those who are not avoid them. Postaudits are important because without them, opinions of success or failure will be formed and spread anyway, perhaps erroneously, to IM disadvantage. The principles of the project life cycle are based on control, which operates on feedback. Evaluation after the fact has several important benefits: (1) we learn from mistakes; (2) the quality of future work is improved; (3) evaluation leads to better future utilization of resources; and (4) the success of projects is communicated to management (good public relations). The post-audit report should go to information management, user management, and the information resources management committee. (For more on postaudits, see S-63.)

Benefits of Project Life Cycle

Project life cycle standards, with heavy user involvement, can be invaluable to successful project management. Benefits include easier program maintenance (due to good documentation); easier transferability of work and people (movement of people from one team to another, from systems development to production); consistent management review of checkpoints, which is ensured by standard project structure; and easier training because the standards become part of the in-house education program. In short, PLC standards can lead to better project control by establishing a series of short-term objectives and then measuring progress against those objectives. Each phase can be a separate entity, planned in advance and reviewed in progress. The scheduling of tasks within each phase between the SR and the UR guarantees strong user involvement throughout the project, assuring a high probability of success. The systems implementation plan described in Exhibit 11-3 can help in estimating time and resource allocation, both of which are frequently underestimated. Team members can see the purpose of each activity and how it contributes to the whole, because all facets of the project are focused on achieving phase goals in a logical and structured order. Each phase plan can be standardized, making the job of allocating resources more precise. Project progress is then easier to follow because the scheduling of deliverables combined with management review and approval checkpoints throughout make project progress easier to follow. Coupled with a formal project tracking system, as shown in Exhibit 11-4, management monitoring can be virtually automatic. The project manager will benefit from the disci-

Exhibit 11-3   Project work schedule form.

No.	Activity	Mo. 1 2 3 4 5 6 7 8 9 10 11 12 13 14 15 16 17 18	
0.0	Management review checkpoints		
1.0	PROPOSAL PHASE		
1.1	Team organization and task scheduling		PM
1.2	Analysis of present system		UR
1.3	Systems requirements specs.	Typical project manning curve through project life cycle	UR
1.4	Alternative solutions (evaluation/selection)		SR
1.5	Proposal report		PM/SR/UR
2.0	FUNCTIONAL DESIGN PHASE		
2.1	Base-line system design		SR
2.2	User review and acceptance	Time	UR
3.0	DETAIL DESIGN PHASE		
3.1	Detailed programming specs.		SR
3.2	User manual		UR
3.3	Test data		UR
4.0	PROGRAMMING PHASE		
4.1	Coding and unit test		SR
4.2	Acceptance criteria		UR
4.3	User training		UR
4.4	Conversion preparation		UR
5.0	CONVERSION PHASE		
5.1	Systems integration test/tuning		SR
5.2	Conversion		SR/UR
5.3	User acceptance		UR
5.4	System maintenance		SR
6.0	POSTAUDIT		PM/SR/UR

▲ Checkpoints   ● Information systems

● User   O Management approvals
management approval

Exhibit 11-4   Control over activities and milestone dates in a project-tracking system.

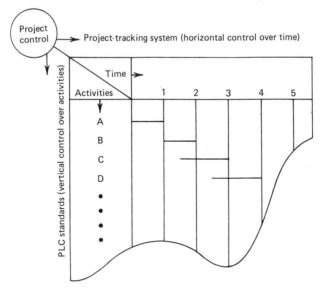

pline, which provides improved control over the entire effort. The project can be controlled so as to uncover exceptions for early corrective action. The structured approach of this PLC strategy makes the project manager's role easier and ensures successful project management.

PROJECT INITIATION

> ### S-55   PROJECT SELECTION
>
> **A process for identifying and selecting new systems projects.**

Searching for and identifying projects and giving birth to new needed systems was covered in business information planning (BIP) (S-10) in Chapter 4. Once a project has been identified through this process, there should be a series of steps to move it along the preliminary investigation and approval process. This process constitutes our project selection strategy.

Project Selection

The project selection process described here is really a series of prescreening steps. Our project selection strategy suggests a three-level screening process consisting of coordinators in user areas, an IM screening process, and a high-level management review.

Level 1: Project Coordinators In the Trojan horse strategy (S-9), we presented the concept of transferring systems specialists into user departments to further the application of technology to user business problems. Project coordinators are also user-based. These are individual users who have been designated to serve as liaison between the IM function and the users. They help to present a "single face" to IM by collecting, coordinating, and screening all systems requests from their division. In some cases, they are, in fact, the Trojan horses. Most of the time, however, they are not transferrees from IM, but simply resident users who have been given a project coordinator's role as an added duty. The coordinator's role as the single focal point between the user and information management allows the latter to limit the number of interactions within the company, making the communications process considerably easier.

When coordinators receive a request for systems services from anyone in their area, they investigate the nature of the request, assess its suitability and need, and establish the priority; in effect, they do a preliminary prescreening to assure the legitimacy and priority of the request before forwarding it to the IM function. All systems requests, no matter how large or small, should be accompanied by a formal request-for-services form such as the one illustrated in Exhibit 11-5. This form contains basic information about the requester, the purpose of the request, the anticipated benefits, and other pertinent comments, and it is usually signed by the requester and the designated project coordinator. The form can be used by IM to initiate appropriate action on the request. Requests for minor modifications to existing systems (which probably represent 90% of the requests and 50–70% of the work of most IM organizations) can then be accepted for implementation under a preapproved level of maintenance programming activity for that division. All others can be followed up by the business information systems group for proper project definition and scope, as well as rough cost–benefit analysis.

The project coordinator should keep a copy of all open project requests, in priority order, and should work closely with the BIP group, IM, and users to coordinate all interface requirements among them. Thus, *the number of people in the company with whom IM deals can be minimized to just one person per division, the project coordinator.* This arrangement makes it easy for people anywhere in the company to request IM services, yet it keeps the project selection process simple, though structured, for increased effectiveness. Periodic meetings of the project coordinators can also be an excellent way of communicating systems developments of interest to users, of allowing users to learn of each other's activities and problems, and of providing a free flow of information between all interested parties. Yet, the time which project coordinators must devote to this role usually amounts to a small percentage of their overall time, and thus this responsibility can easily be added to almost any line job.

Level 2: Information Management The second level of screening, which we have aptly named the *mutual protection association* (MPA), consists of a

Exhibit 11-5 Sample request for systems services.

Request for Services of the Information Management Division		

From: Division: Department: Date:

Purpose of Request:

Anticipated Benefits:

☐ Cost reduction/avoidance of $ _____ annually

☐ Increased revenue of $ _____ annually

☐ Regulatory or other requirement

☐ Other _____

This request has priority over the following outstanding requests: _____

_____

Has this been discussed with anyone in IM   ☐ Yes   ☐ No

If yes, explain: _____

Additional comments, if any: _____

_____

Requested completion date	Contact personnel for preliminary discussion	
Dept. to be charged	Requestor (Dept. Mgr.)	Approved by (Division Head)

To Be Completed by IM Division:

Status of request:

☐ Project opened & assigned to: _____

☐ Project being evaluated

☐ Project declined (see reverse for explanation)   IM Division
                                                          (Dept. Head)

weekly meeting of key IM function managers to review project requests and keep each other informed about what is going on in all areas of IM activities. Most requests will be for maintenance and enhancements to existing systems. All such requests can be handled by the MPA without having to be passed on to the information resources management committee. This committee can have preallocated a given amount of systems resources to each division for maintenance work. For example, it may be decided that no more than 60% of all systems resources ought to be dedicated to the maintenance of existing systems, while the other 40% goes into new development. The 60% would then be allocated among the various divisions on the basis of past need, experience, and priority. Thus, all maintenance requests reviewed by the MPA would simply be prioritized by the user to be done with the assigned resources. If the work becomes excessive, a backlog would be built up and an appeal would have to be made to the information resources management committee to increase the maintenance allocation for that division, if the request is warranted.

New development requests can be screened by the MPA in preparation for presentation to the information resources management committee. All supporting material can be gathered, covering summary letters can be written, and requests can be passed on the committee.

Level 3: Information Resources Management Committee   Finally, requests for new development (a dollar limit is usually appropriate, so as not to bog the committee down with minor projects) can be screened by an information resources management committee (S-29). At this point, the project request can be approved or rejected, or a feasibility study can be commissioned (standard operating procedure for major projects).

This formalized three-level process of project screening acts as an effective discipline to ensure that all systems requests are adequately researched, that a genuine need exists, and that appropriate benefits are considered as the project request moves its way up the approval ladder. The object is not to kill off systems requests but to make sure that unnecessary, trivial, and unjustified requests are held to a minimum, so that the important work gets the scarce resources on the basis of what's best for the company as a whole.

PROJECT ESTIMATING

> **S-56   PROJECT ESTIMATING**
>
> By combining experience-based with research-based estimating techniques, better project cost estimates are possible leading to fewer project over-runs.

One of the important aspects of project initiation is the estimating process that goes into project approval. In considering project costs, we are concerned with two factors: development costs and return on investment. Our next strategy deals with estimating development costs, and the strategy that follows that addresses return on investment through a standard cost–benefit analysis.

In the early stages, "ballparking" the project's scope and costs is an inexact science. Therefore, a technician is needed to help estimate the costs of the project within certain boundaries without having to be too precise. One way to do this is to use our project-estimating strategy.

Much project estimating is done the way some backwoods people weigh pigs: by balancing a porker on a teeterboard with rocks and then, when the board is even, estimating the weight of the rocks.

A major reason for project overruns is underestimation; a major reason for underestimation is estimating too early in the process. To get around this problem, we offer this three-part project-estimating strategy.

Phased Estimating

Most project estimates are made too early, usually after a limited feasibility study. Estimates given before the facts are known are less than worthless, because they can be permanently damaging to a systems professional's reputation. In fact, estimates that understate systems requirements are cause to fire systems managers. Accurate estimates (especially for large projects) cannot be made until the functional specifications have been completed. It has been estimated that the feasibility study equals about 5% of a project, and that detailed functional requirements equal about 15%. *Thus, 20% of the work is needed before a good estimate can be made.* To combat this problem of early estimating, we suggest the adoption of phased estimating based on specific deliverables using the following 50–20–5 rule: The Phase 0 deliverable is a written problem definition which produces a rough-cut estimate of the project which has an accuracy expectation of no more than ±50%. At this early point, that's good enough to decide whether to approve a feasibility study. A fixed cost could be allowed to conduct the feasibility study. The Phase 1 deliverable is the feasibility study, or the proposal phase. The feasibility study makes possible an increase in precision because it develops more and better information on the proposed project, though still no functional specifications. The analyst's estimate after the feasibility study should be accurate to within ±20%. (Some use a range estimate here, i.e., pessimistic, optimistic, most likely. We think ±20% accomplishes the same purpose.) A fixed cost could be given for development of the functional specifications at this point.

The Phase 2 deliverable should be a written, signed-off, functional specification of the system. It can be detailed enough to give a fixed cost for implementation, which should be accurate at this point to ±5%.

The 50–20–5 rule based on these deliverables gives the analyst some breathing room, but at the same time, it gives the users and the information resources management committee enough to make commitment decisions at several "go—no-go" commitment points. (Incidentally, we suggest that estimates always be rounded; e.g., $172,514.20 is unwise since it suggests a precision that simply does not exist in estimating.)

The 50–20–5 rule can work for all but multi-million-dollar projects. The accompanying unknowns and uncertainties make the costs of such large projects too difficult to predict. They must be broken down into smaller subprojects. The problem is that if 20% of the project's budget has to be spent before one arrives at functional specifications on which to base good estimates, the price tag is already big by the time costs and benefits can be reasonably estimated. A decision not to go on a $2.5-million project at that point would see $500,000 in costs down the drain. (One way to get around this problem is discussed later under the iceberg strategy, S-59.) In some cases, of course, the big picture will still have to be considered because some subprojects can be cost-justified not on their own, but only when combined with other subprojects. In such cases, the big picture might still be treated with the 50–20–5 rule while the subprojects are looked at in closer detail. Another technique which can be used is the *benefits- ×-4* rule. Let's say that a project is so large and vague at the outset that even an accuracy of ±50% cannot be given. However, the benefits may be easier to determine than the costs. Then, the benefits-×-4 rule provides an order of magnitude, which is that potential benefits will support a project costing 4 times the projected savings; that is, a savings of $1 million will justify a $4-million project and still provide a decent return on investment (benefits-×-4 is based on a payback of the original investment in something over four years). Costs–benefits using this rule-of-thumb in the feasibility stage might justify a $500,000 functional specification study. After functional specifications, one can return to the 50–20–5 rule and give an estimate for implementation which is ±20% accurate.

Experience versus Research-Based Analysis

The estimating process is usually either experience-based or research-based. Experience-based estimating involves comparing the proposed system with an existing system of similar size and complexity, then adding a "fluff" factor (10–20%) for the unknowns. Research-based estimating involves estimating the number of man-months involved based on size, then adding something to cover management and support activities.

If estimates will be required after the feasibility study, there is little choice but to use experience-based estimating because there is little else to go on. However, if one can follow the 50–20–5 rule and provide increasingly accurate estimates after detailed specifications, then one has enough information to use the research-based analysis described in Appendix A at the end of this chapter.

Walkthroughs

If the experience-based estimate after the feasibility study is four people for six months (24 man-months), and the research-based estimate after functional specification is 21.4 man-months, one can feel reasonably comfortable with the estimate. But if the two estimates are wide apart, another useful technique at that point is an estimate *walkthrough*.

Walkthroughs are usually associated with system design and programming. However, the concept can also be used effectively in estimating. In this case, the estimator "walks" the review team through the estimating process. The team walks through both the experience- and the research-based processes to validate or adjust the estimates, providing a final check on the estimating process.

The combination of these three estimating techniques can considerably improve the project-estimating process, can minimize overruns, and can increase the credibility of the IM function with management and users.

COST– BENEFITS ANALYSIS

> S-57   COST–BENEFITS ANALYSIS
>
> A practical guide for determining the value of investments in information systems.

Development costs, of course, are only half the equation. Benefits are the other half. A cost–benefits analysis (CBA) considers both development costs and ongoing operating costs and benefits over the life of the system. This analysis should not be left to the choice of style and presentation of every analyst. The CBA worksheet should be a standard, formal document, and return-on-investment calculations should always be based on present value accounting over the life of the system. Not only does a standard structure make the job easier for the analyst, but the information resources management committee has an easier time passing on projects which are all calculated in a like manner; that is, ROI means the same for every project. So long as resource constraints require project selection among alternative opportunities rather than simply completing every request made, a standard is needed to provide the funding-approval committee the data to compare all project investment opportunities on the same basis.

Without a standard method, there is a temptation to justify projects solely on the basis that future benefits will pay back the original investment. This approach is not very different from a bank's proposing the purchase of bonds at $100,000, provided there is a good chance that the bank will get its $100,000 back in a few years. Merely getting back the original $100,000 investment in five years falls short of the assumed investment objective of obtaining a decent return on the investment.

The strategy suggested involves the use of a standard costing summary for all major systems projects beyond some dollar limit, such as $50,000 or

$100,000. (Instructions for completing the standard CBA worksheet described here are detailed in Appendix B at the end of this chapter.)

The CBA strategy recommended involves an eight-step process as follows:

1 *Present operation.*   The first step is to document the costs of the operation as it is now performed and then to estimate how these costs will grow with inflation, work-load increases, salaries, space, equipment, etc., over the number of years equal to the life of the new system, if the proposed project is *not* undertaken.

2 *Proposed operation.*   Next, do the same for the proposed system. That is, determine requirements for staff, equipment, space, etc., for the new system and the operating costs. Again, these should be extrapolated over the life of the new system.

3 *Projected gain or loss.*   The above process will result in a projected gain or loss, from an operation-cost point of view only. But this is what illustrates the savings to be gained from the proposed system.

4 *Project costs.*   Now that we have the benefits, we need the costs. These are the up-front, one-time costs of developing or acquiring the new system, including software costs and people time, but not capital investments, which are treated separately below.

5 *Cash flow.*   The after-tax cash flow from these calculations is then determined for each year over the life of the proposed system.

6 *Capital investments.*   All capital expenditures (equipment, etc.) involved in the new system are next added.

7 *Total cash flow.*   All cash flows are now discounted on a present-value basis to take account of the value of money over time; that is, benefits that will be obtained in a number of years are not worth as much as benefits obtained today.

8 *Return on investment.*   The calculation of ROI is the final step in determining the project's worth. Does it cover the company's cost of capital or internal "hurdle rate" for investments? In other words, is it cost-justified?

A word of caution: there is a danger in emphasizing cost–benefit as the sole justification for a project. It can knock out worthwhile, but not easily quantified, projects such as management information and control systems, or quality improvement systems (better customer service, more support for decision makers, etc.). In such systems, benefits may be difficult to quantify, yet they are there just the same. It becomes important in such cases to have a statement of qualitative benefits in addition to the standard CBA form. The statement will carry more weight if prepared and defined by user management.

A useful device in this regard is the "value-of-information" approach; that is, determining the quantitative benefit that would be necessary to cause the project to pay back or the ROI to be acceptable, then inserting that amount in the CBA as the quantified value of the qualitative benefits. For example, if it is determined that added revenue of $50,000 annually would cost-justify the project, include this amount as if it were real revenue, and explain: "If you believe that the qualitative benefits of this system are worth $50,000 a year, then the project is worth doing." You will be surprised how often this procedure sells a project which cannot otherwise be cost-justified. (At The First National Bank of Boston, we add a summary sheet to the CBA, listing the original investment, operating costs, and benefits over the system's life and the return on investment. If the benefits have not been fully quantified, we add the following statement: "In order to achieve an after-tax return of x within seven years, the nonqualified system benefits must have a value of $_____$ annually.")

A cost–benefits analysis strategy such as this can be a useful and effective tool for helping the IM function, the user management, and the company's information resources management committee to conduct a consistent and standard evaluation of major proposed systems projects. The above-described cost–benefits analysis could also be automated, so that the analyst could simply fill in the appropriate data in the designated categories. This procedure would allow running a number of trials based on changing data without excessive manual work.

PROJECT DEVELOPMENT

The project development process was described in some detail under project life cycle (S-54), so it will not be necessary to repeat it here. However, two additional strategies which fit into this process of project management are the use of in-company standards and the iceberg rule.

Installation Standards

> **S-58   STANDARDS MANUALS**
>
> **Help to assure success in IM management by consistently applying past successful practices to future activity.**

Every IM organization should have a standard systems development methodology; one that provides consistency, makes tracking project progress easier, and builds on success. A set of standards can also be a powerful productivity technique. Standards are simply a guide to what has been successful in the past and thus will tend to ensure success in the future. They can also be an effective way to ensure consistency and communication between IM and users. User involvement should be part of this standard. User involvement in systems development is probably the most important key to success. User involvement means that users are designing their own systems. Users will accept change far more readily when they have been involved in making it, and customer satisfaction is practically guaranteed.

It is not necessary to write one's own standards. Many books and courses on the subject will serve the purpose, such as IBM's publication on project methodology, available from any IBM representative. The methods described usually apply to larger (multiyear) projects whose size requires more formal management to control. However, the basic underlying principles apply to all projects, regardless of size. A number of project management packages on the market today covering the project life cycle can also serve as the basis for a systems development standards manual. Installation standards should probably include data processing standards, systems standards, and programming standards.

1 *DP standards.*   These cover the operation and control of computers, whether they are in a mainframe data center under IM control or are minicomputers in user locations. Users particularly need guidance on security and control matters because of their inexperience with computers. For further discussion of such a manual, see the distributed processing standards strategy (S-8).

2 *Systems standards.*   These cover the various phases of the project life cycle, from the initial business information planning (S-10) process through the steps of system proposal, functional design, detail design, programming, conversion, and postaudit. A technical appendix might include detailed guidelines concerning interviewing techniques for data gathering and analysis, cost–benefits analyses, project-estimating techniques, package program search and evaluation steps, structured design methodology, documentation standards, and general control standards. This subject is also described in detail under project life cycle (S-54).

3 *Programming standards.*   These, of course, must be unique to each organization but might include standard naming conventions; the languages used, including the preferred procedure; use of TSO for program creation and testing; program cataloging procedures; access control methods; JCL standards; printing specifications for different printers; description of standard subroutines; software aids; the tools and utilities in use; and debugging tips.

A method must be devised for keeping this manual, in particular, updated because of the many and continuing changes that occur within a programming environment.

Whether one uses a package program or develops one's own, the important thing is to *have* installation standards as a strategy to ensure consistency, a standard of quality and control, and successful IM management. Once developed, standards shouldn't just gather dust on the bookshelf. The IM function must be committed to the value and use of installation standards, must see that they are kept current, must make them part of the internal training program for new staff members, and must enforce their use. Standards are not an insult to creativity. In other professions (e.g., accounting, medicine), extensive guidelines cover every facet of practice. A well-written standards manual will leave plenty of room for creativity while ensuring consistency and success in IM management and control.

Project Scope

Much of the poor performance in systems development in the past—and probably most project slippage—can be attributed to oversized projects. The reason for such failure is obvious: such projects are too complex to grasp. As a result, there is more likelihood of underestimating the project's scope, of forgetting certain activities, or being fuzzy about requirements. Over time, many changes occur because of changes in business, competitive considerations, or new regulations; and turnover occurs, both in IM and in user departments (turnover increases in relation to elapsed time—20% is not uncommon on larger projects). Perhaps a new user department head wants the system completely changed; an inadequate project-tracking system lets things get out of control; the impatience of users waiting for results causes the project to be scrapped; or finally, given enough time, Murphy's law is bound to take hold. To combat this, try our Icebergs strategy.

> **S-59   ICEBERGS**
>
> **The one-year iceberg rule can be effective in breaking down large tasks into easy-to-manage subprojects.**

One solution to these problems is our iceberg strategy. The first law of icebergs is: "Seven-eighths of what is there cannot be seen." Nearly all experts in project management agree that projects should be broken down into small, manageable tasks. Larger projects are like icebergs: they are big, mainly hidden, and risky.

As Exhibit 11-6 illustrates, an iceberg can't be judged from its tip (is it A? or B?). The same is true of systems projects. A big leap forward is more easily taken in small steps. The iceberg strategy deals with breaking down an iceberg into many smaller icebergs—big projects into smaller subprojects. The one-year iceberg rule says that no project will be undertaken unless it

Exhibit 11-6   The hidden iceberg problem in estimating systems development costs.

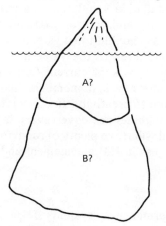

can be brought out of the water within one year. If it will take longer, it must be broken down further into free-standing subprojects. Building smaller icebergs is not very difficult. Almost any task can be broken down into smaller pieces. That is one reason minicomputers are making such inroads. When they're not big enough for the job, the job is broken down to the size of the mini (or more minis are added).

An IBM publication illustrates the point by noting how people work (Exhibit 11-7). In theory, work moves in a straight line from project start to project end. In practice, long elapsed times cause the project's progress to sag. As the project nears completion, slippage creates a crisis, and a major effort is made to pull the project back up to the original schedule. Perhaps more people are added and Brooks' law takes hold: "Adding more people to a late project will make it later."[2] The result is usually less than successful, and the project overruns.

When a project is broken down into subprojects, shorter goals can be established, minimizing the "sag" phenomena. The benefits of the one-year iceberg rule are that:

The project is easier to comprehend and, therefore, can be planned more accurately.

Scheduling is easier with the use of short intervals.

There are few gaps in system design (better detail, less likelihood of omitting activities).

There are fewer changes in requirements specifications during development.

There is less turnover to affect project progress.

Management sees results faster (promise–deliver is better than promise–wait-and-wait-and-wait-and-wait!).

Exhibit 11-7   Little iceberg strategy in project management.

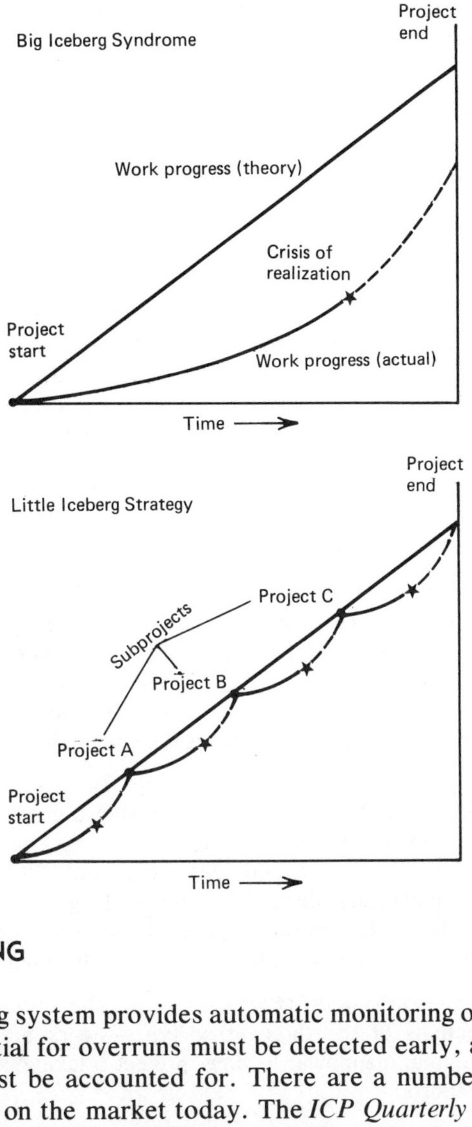

PROJECT TRACKING

A project-tracking system provides automatic monitoring of the project's life cycle. The potential for overruns must be detected early, and staff time and project costs must be accounted for. There are a number of good project control packages on the market today. The *ICP Quarterly* software service, for example, lists a number of them, which by and large, are fairly inexpensive; hence, no DP organization today should be without one.

> **S-60   PROJECT CONTROL SYSTEM**
>
> **Four types of project control systems are options for assuring project target dates and avoiding overruns.**

Before buying a project control system, however, first decide what kind is needed. There are four kinds, according to Clayton Harrell, Jr., project manager for Xerox:[3]

Manual structured systems.

Project tracking systems.

Project networking systems.

Pull project management systems.

Manual structured systems. These are the systems that impose a standard structure on all projects, generally involving from 8 to 12 phases. Each phase has its defined work products and defined documentation. Management checkpoints specify when project progress is reviewed, when revised estimates on remaining costs and expected benefits are presented, and when to decide whether to proceed. Approval to proceed applies only until the next checkpoint. This process has been given the name "creeping commitment." In general, these methods involve no computer assistance. The current phase for each project is carefully controlled and any project may be terminated if costs start getting out of control or if expected benefits are disappearing.

Project tracking systems. These systems provide no particular facilities for project planning. Instead, they accept whatever list of activities for a project is developed and whatever time and cost budgets are assigned to those activities, and then track actual times and costs against these budgets. The reports show actual schedule realization and cost accumulation. [Sample reports produced by a typical project tracking system are illustrated in Exhibits 11-8 and 11-9.]

Project networking systems. These systems develop a critical path network for a project, determine which activities fall on the critical path, and what the "heat" or "slack" is for the other activities. PERT and CPM are well known examples of two networking disciplines. Networking, used effectively on large construction and defense projects, is best suited for planning and controlling schedules and is not particularly convenient for controlling costs.

Full project management systems (PMS). These are the systems that perform most of the functions of the three other types—work breakdown, time-estimating, scheduling, manpower loading, project tracking, and providing a wide variety of reports.

Harrell went on to point out:

Over half of the full PMS installations have been failures—the customer ends up not using the package. . . . A full PMS is no panacea. It will not bring order out of chaos. It cannot be used as a solution for the other ills, such as poor system design procedures or poor programming practices. . . . If an organization does not have a project management system . . . start with a manual structural system or a project tracking system. . . . Installing a PMS

Exhibit 11-8   Project status report.

Period ending——————

Project No. ———— Name ————————— Priority ——— Cost Center ————

Date Opened ————— Target Date————— Rev. Target Date——— Auth. by ———

Project Leader ————— Project Description —————————————

————————————————————

Activity No.	Start Date	Completion			Hours		Cost		Activity Description
		Est. date	Actual	Pct.	Est.	Act.	Est.	Act.	

	Manhours	Cost	Overall Project Completion Pct. ———
Actual to date	———	———	
Est. to date	———	———	
Difference	———	———	
Total est. for project	———	———	
Rev. est. for project	———	———	

Personnel reporting on project: ————————————————

————————————————————

Exception items: ————————————————————

————————————————————

297

Exhibit 11-9   Personnel and project time analysis report.

Personnel Time Analysis   Period Ending _____

      Staff No. L_____ , Name _____

Project No.   Project Name   Hours Charged   Cost   Description

_____

_____

_____

      Staff No. _____ Name _____

Project No.   Project Name   Hours Charged   Cost   Description

_____

_____

_____

Project Time Analysis   Period Ending _____

      Project No. _____,   Project Name_____,   User L_____

      Staff No.   Staff Name   Hours Charged   Cost   Description

_____

_____

_____

               Project Totals _____   _____

      Project No. _____   Project Name _____   User _____

      Staff No.   Staff Name   Hours Charged   Cost   Description

_____

_____

_____

               Project Totals _____   _____

needs commitment, encouragement, and endorsement by management. . . . Management must support the system by actually using the reports.[4]

Why do so many of the full project management systems fail? We believe that project failure is caused by commitment and complexity factors. The former is needed to cope with the latter. Top-down commitment is needed to get bottom-up support, because the amount of time consumed in a project management system can be substantial. Managers get the benefit, and analysts get the work; hence, the motivation must come from the top. The organization must also be of sufficient size to warrant this kind of commitment.

Cost is another consideration: total installation costs can be double and triple the package cost, not to mention the ongoing operating cost, which is not inconsequential. Beyond the cost is the impact on the organization. Add it up! It costs, it upheaves, it's a lot of work; hence, a high failure rate. Therefore, one has to determine whether the problems experienced in systems development may not occur in project control, as much as in other areas of project management. In which case, a simple project-tracking system may be sufficient.

In any event, some kind of project tracking is desirable for better project control. A manual structured system should probably be used only by very small organizations. Conversely, project networking systems are probably best suited to very large projects of the iceberg variety. A project-tracking system may be sufficient for most others, unless the more sophisticated and extended planning and reporting functions of a full PMS are desired. Know which type fits your needs, then look for a suitable package.

QUALITY ASSURANCE

> **S-61   QUALITY ASSURANCE**
>
> Quality assurance in the IM function is all too rarely used, yet it can be an excellent early-warning system for the information manager.

The manufacturing industry learned long ago that because of the complexity and speed of the assembly line, it was necessary to implement a quality control department that reported directly to management and ensured that the product was up to established standards. The line managers were not given responsibility for quality assurance because they were too involved in getting the product out of the door.

In the same way, it is a good strategy for the IM function to establish its own independent quality assurance (QA) function to make sure that development and operations are timely and complete, as well as within budget and accepted performance standards. Incorrect or late work will affect the success and profitability of the company; hence, an independent monitoring of the quality of output is just as appropriate to an information management function as it is to a manufacturing function.

In most companies, this job can be done by one or two people, depending on the scope of the function. For example, QA could be limited to project assurance only, monitoring systems development through the project life cycle and calling management's attention to potential problems and/or slipping targets. Or it could be involved more extensively in systems design through participation in design walkthroughs. QA could also be applied to DP operations, monitoring reruns, downtime, the timely delivery of reports, etc. The breadth and scope of QA are a matter of the individual information manager's needs and desires. Whatever its scope, however, it is important that the function of QA *exist*. It can play an important role in providing objective and impartial checks and balances for IM activities, alerting the busy manager to early-warning signals requiring corrective action which might otherwise be missed.

A minimal type of QA activity for any organization might consist of the following:

Service assurance.
Project assurance.
Management reporting.
Postaudits.

Service Assurance

A customer service center (see S-21) could be part of the QA function. Its job could include the tracking of user service from IM operations. Problems in the quality control of work delivered to customers could be overseen and complaints handled by a single source. Beyond present customer service, however, is future customer service, so QA might also participate in or review capacity planning, security planning, the issuance of operations standards, and other functions designed to assure the continuation of stable and quality service.

Projects Assurance

As noted, QA activities in systems development can range from a minimal role of project monitoring and review to a broader participation in systems design, programming design, project milestone review, and the issuance of concurrence reports, depending on the desires of the information manager. Simple project monitoring involves establishing a working relationship with each project team for the purpose of assisting a project manager in achieving objectives. If project managers need resources or other help, QA helps them to get it. If they are falling behind on a project, QA helps to resolve the problem, if possible, while also bringing the problem to the attention of management. QA can track milestone reviews to be sure they are not overlooked, review all major deliverable documentation, review project control reports, check adherence to systems and programming standards, and ensure that DP standards are being met before new systems are accepted for production. In short, QA calls the information manager's attention to any and all potential problems requiring attention. A broader QA role would include counseling on any facet of systems design and development, including design review through participation in walkthroughs and review of major project deliverables.

QA should be able to call on resources, both in-house and outside, if needed, to carry out its function. Its responsibility is to help the project manager and the IM function to achieve their common goals of delivering a quality product on time and within budget. QA is, therefore, a support resource, not an auditor. It functions to help, not to hinder, project progress. Thus, to be effective, the individual heading this function should be highly respected; that is, she or he should be technically competent, have solid successful project management experience, and be at least of equal stature with the project managers with whom he or she must interact.

Management Reporting

This involves seeing that the information manager receives the information needed to run the IM function effectively. This information might range from monthly project status to production problems, performance measurement, budget variance reports, and/or oral reports on potential problems, user complaints, etc. The reports produced in our IMPRES strategy (S-31) are examples of the kind of information management reports that could be the responsibility of QA.

Postaudits

QA should be responsible for commissioning postaudits on every major project at an appropriate time following project completion. It should put together the team and lead the effort to review the project and produce the postaudit report to management as described in our postaudit strategy (S-63).

These examples are simply a guide to how a QA strategy can provide additional control for an information manager in overseeing the many activities that might be tracked to prevent potential problem areas from slipping through the cracks, either by oversight or by design. A busy manager needs such checks and balances. The manufacturing business discovered quality assurance many years ago; its time has come for the information industry as well.

PROJECT IMPLEMENTATION

> **S-62   PROJECT IMPLEMENTATION**
>
> Standards and procedures for *full* implementation of new systems capability, including postsystem propagation.

The typical project produces a new or improved computer system which processes data. The funding of a systems development project is authorized on the expectation that there will be benefits when the new or improved system is implemented—benefits in the form of more effective management practices, savings in clerical costs, or other improved practices or expense savings.

We have observed that only a minority of companies have an adequate postaudit procedure. In the typical company, project tracking occurs through the project life cycle until the project is "completed." A project is defined as complete when a new or improved system is implemented and utilized; that is, fully operational. If the new or improved system appears to work as expected, the project is considered completed and project tracking is terminated.

We believe it is important to extend the project life cycle through a follow-up stage—even when responsibility for implementation lies primarily with a user department rather than with the IM function. The postaudit review, especially for major projects, should include experience of the utilization of a new or improved system over a period of 6–12 months or longer. The full implementation of large systems frequently requires a multiyear program. By *implementation,* we do not mean simply *converting* to the new system. We refer rather to the implementation of a system based on a *full* utilization of all of its features, report capabilities, etc., by *all* potential users in the company. Most of the time, only part of a system is fully utilized, or its use is restricted to one department or group, and no attempt is made to extend the system to other people in the company who would benefit from it.

Clerical versus Management Systems

It is not uncommon for millions of dollars to be authorized for systems design, programming, the purchase of computer software, and even the purchase of computer hardware, whereas only tiny amounts are budgeted for full implementation of the total system for all prospective users. In the old days, when new systems were funded primarily with the expectation of improved clerical productivity, such implementation was not as critical an issue as it is today.

Systems projects set up to achieve clerical savings are easy to implement in comparison with systems projects authorized to improve the effectiveness of management. It has been our experience that systems which affect management practices frequently take one or more years before users are fully trained to use the total system. Moreover, many users who could benefit from the system do not take full advantage of its capabilities or, worse, do not even know of its existence. The following examples will illustrate the point.

A portfolio management system that was installed in 1970 took several years to win over some of the "old-school" managers who preferred working with traditional methods (pencil, paper, calculator) to working with computer terminals. Moreover, the slow acceptance of this computer tool by some managers resulted in their learning only partial features of the system, and they were therefore not receiving the full benefits of its capabilities even 10 years after its initial installation, as evidenced by this example: a portfolio manager who had been using the system for a number of years was talking one day to another portfolio manager about certain capabilities of the system and proceeded to demonstrate a few things that he had recently done for a client customer. The second manager said, "Gee, I've been using the system for years and didn't know you could do that."

In another example, a management information system was developed and introduced to a variety of potential users. Terminals were installed in various key locations to provide easy access. One day, in discussing the information needs of one of the department heads (who, it was assumed, was a key user of the MIS system), the information manager discovered that this department head was seeking information which existed in the MIS and was accessible by a terminal just outside his office, but which he had never used. The problem was not so much that the manager did not want to use the terminal (his secretary could have done that), it was that an inadequate marketing job had been done in teaching all potential managers of the system just what was available to them and how to get it. The systems people trained the first group of users, but instead of going on to market the system to all potential users, they left the users to do that themselves. They did not.

A final example deals with a minicomputer-based system for financial analysis which was installed in a bank credit department to calculate financial ratios and cash flow projections from historical data supplied by individual corporate customers. A pro forma capability was added to the system to allow managers to ask "What if?" questions based on changing assumptions (sales data, interest rates, debt burden, etc.) to see what effect such conditions would have on the financial condition and cash flow of the company five years ahead. The credit department was trained in the use of the system, and the project was closed. Some time later, during the building of a support management information system, it was realized that many managers who could have been making good use of the pro forma capabilities of this system were not using it simply because they were not aware of its existence. It was then decided to further implement the system, by adding more terminals in more areas of the bank, and to train additional users in the full capabilities of the system. Once again, an existing system turned out to have considerably more use to the organization when it was not limited to the original installation user.

Resources for Implementation

There are many examples of systems that have simply not found their true potential in the organization. A concerted effort has to be made to tap the full potential of these existing systems.

If a project is considered complete when a new or improved system is first utilized, then it is unlikely that adequate resources will be allocated for further promulgation or full implementation. The total cost of a new or improved IM project should therefore include expenditures for thorough training and propagation to all prospective users. The full benefits of an IM project are realized only if and when this is done.

However, since implementation occurs at the end of the project life cycle, there is a natural reluctance to add implementation costs to a project budget. Therefore, responsibility for the full implementation of a new or improved IM capability is often left unassigned. A new management information system may require organizational changes and new skills, yet the organizational development or human resources departments are usually not involved in the implementation process. Perhaps this is why in most organizations many management information systems are not extended to all potential users: no one assumes the responsibility for "marketing" the system throughout the organization.

Given the importance of the systems implementation stage of the project life cycle, it follows that resources for implementation must be budgeted, and an implementation reporting system with the following capabilities must be utilized:

1 Responsibility assigned for implementation.
2 Objectives, budget, time horizon, and tasks/milestones for implementation specified.
3 Reporting procedures and relationships specified.

An implementation reporting system can be an ongoing process that monitors the full implementation of a new system. There is probably no easier or less costly way to extend systems capabilities to the firm than to promote the extended use of *existing* systems to other users throughout the company.

POSTAUDITS

> **S-63 POSTAUDITS**
>
> **The comparison of actual capabilities developed in a systems project and the actual costs with project objectives and budget.**

The implementation of some systems is never really "complete." But at some point in the project life cycle, management must decide that active monitoring of further implementation is no longer needed. As part of the completion stage of the project life cycle, it is useful to do a final evaluation of the success of the project, or postaudit (S-63).

There are a number of reasons that a postaudit is beneficial. First, if there are weaknesses in a system, they can be discovered and corrected while the project team members are still available. Second, opportunities for later enhancements may be discovered in a postaudit. Third, the time of expensive IM professionals and of users has been expended to produce a new or improved systems capability. The contributions of these people to the project and the competence of scarce systems professionals can be evaluated. Finally, the experience of introducing new and improved information capabilities can be assessed through a postaudit.

As we pointed out in our discussion of the project life cycle (see p. 281), there is nothing to be gained by *not* doing a postaudit—it is futile to hope that an unsuccessful project will pass unnoticed. Thus, it's better to take a positive approach to postaudits. These after-the-fact evaluations offer several important benefits:

1 We learn from mistakes.
2 The quality of future work is improved.
3 Evaluation leads to better future utilization of resources.
4 The success of a project is communicated to management.

This last point is an often underutilized strategy. Very often, the benefits of a successful automation effort are substantial and impressive. The benefits cited in the original project proposal are projected benefits; the benefits cited in the postaudit are *real*—hence, they have much more impact. There is no better way to advertise a good systems job than to communicate how good it is to management through a postaudit.

If the postaudit is to have credibility, however, it should not be solely an IM undertaking. A postaudit team ought to be composed of several outside, objective third parties as well. A good representation might consist of the systems project manager, a high-lever user representative, someone from the controller's office, an audit representative, and perhaps a quality assurance person. The object of this postaudit team is to find out if the project succeeded in what it started out to accomplish. Were the objectives realized? Were expected savings realized? Did the project come in on time and within budget? And if not, why not? The resultant report should be distributed to information management, to user beneficiaries of the system, to the information management resources committee, and, on a major project, to top management.

Postaudits of all major projects will work best if made a matter of corporate policy rather than choice. The IM organization that is doing a good job will benefit greatly from the good press; the IM organization that is not will benefit greatly from the lessons learned.

Appendix A: Research-Based Estimating

The following estimating process was developed from work done by Aron[5] and Pietrosanta[6] at IBM, based on their extended experience in managing many large projects. This is not a precise method, but it is offered as an aid to estimators working in unfamiliar areas and as a verification of estimates obtained through experience or other estimating methods. The steps involved are to:

1 Break the system down into modules.
2 Calculate man-months, by module.
3 Adjust for higher-level languages.
4 Extrapolate for the total project.
5 Adjust for risk.

Step 1 Break the System Down

Break the system down into subsystems, then subsystem modules. The problem definition document (see project life cycle, S-54) should contain a list of all modules in the system, which can be used for estimating purposes.

Step 2 Calculate Man-Months

1 Choose the appropriate level of difficulty for each program based on the number of interactions expected. Easy modules have very few interactions; that is, they communicate only with the operating system and I/O-type programs (e.g., most application programs are easy). Medium modules have some interaction (e.g., utilities and compilers). Hard programs have many interactions (e.g., TP monitors and operating systems).
2 Estimate the size of each program by estimating the core size of each

Exhibit 11-10   Man-day estimating table

| (1) | (2) Estimated Project Duration (Months) | | | | (3) Total Core Size of | (4) |
Level of Difficulty	0–6	6–12	12–24	>24	Load Modules	Man-Days
						(2)*(3)
1	—	20	500	10,000	600,000	30,000
2	—	15	375	7,500	300,000	20,000
3	—	10	250	5,000	80,000	8,000
4	—	7.5	188	3,250	—	—
5	—	.5	125	1,500	—	—
		Instructions per				58,000
	Not applicable	Man-day	Man-month	Man-year		

load module. (Enter this figure in Column 3 of the man-day estimating table, Exhibit 11-10). Our example uses 600,000, 300,000, and 80,000 statements for Levels 1, 2, 3, respectively.

3 Calculate total programming man-days, -months, or -years by selecting the appropriate project duration (adjust for the learning curve on larger projects).

Step 3   Adjust for Higher-Level Languages

Since we used load module size in our example, we have assumed object code programs. Alternatively, we could have estimated the number of COBOL or assembler language statements. To adjust for higher-level languages, we need to convert by an object/source ratio as follows:

If load module size was used: divide by 20 if COBOL; by 10 if assembler.
If COBOL source statements were used: divide by 2.
If assembler source statements were used: no adjustment.

So, in our case:

$$\frac{58,000}{20} = 2,900 \text{ man-days}$$

Step 4   Extrapolate for Total Project

The estimate thus far has covered the project life cycle (S-54) phases of functional design, detailed design, and programming. We now need to add something for conversion (system integration testing and conversion). One author[7] suggested that one-quarter of the total systems effort should be allowed for systems testing. Applying this rule of thumb, we next get:

$$2{,}900 \text{ man-days} \times 1.25 = 3{,}625 \text{ man-days}$$

The estimate also assumes a 100% effort by all. To account for time lost to vacations, holidays, education, etc., 70% productivity is more realistic, so our calculation becomes:

$$3{,}625 \text{ man-days} \times 1.30 = 4{,}713 \text{ man-days}$$

$$\frac{4{,}713 \text{ man-days}}{22 \text{ workdays/month}} = 21.4 \text{ man-months}$$

Step 5   Adjust for Risk

Two variables, uniqueness and environment, can add considerable risk to a project. *Uniqueness* means the extent of the familiarity of the project team with the hardware, the software, and the application; *environment* means working relationships, organization, programmer abilities, and physical facilities. Should any of these be unfavorable, a risk factor must be added to the project. An interesting weighting set in this regard is one suggested by John Toellner.[8] He adjusts for a number of environmental factors, including the size and the experience of the project team, the application's complexity, the sophistication of the user, turnaround time, user availability, and interruptions to project work. The actual adjustment is necessarily a subjective judgment on the part of the estimator. In essence, it's a fluff factor based on the amount of risk attached to the project.

Appendix B: Cost – Benefits Analysis Worksheet

The sample CBA form shown in Exhibit 11-11 can be completed by means of the following procedures in our eight-step process:

Step 1   Present Operation

List annual revenue and expenses of the present operation (assuming no new system is introduced) over time. Use as the time frame the life of the proposed new system in order to show the correct return on investment. In cases where the payback will be rapid, however, it may only be necessary to carry out the calculations for a few years to demonstrate justification. Systems life generally spans a 5- to 10-year range; we have used 7 years in our illustration. In calculating income and expense for Steps 1 and 2, either list all in both steps, or list only items which change. For example, if equipment costs are unchanged, these items could be omitted from both steps. The net

Exhibit 11-11 Information systems and services cost-benefits analysis

	Pe-riod 0	Year 1	Year 2	Year 3	Year 4	Year 5	Year 6	Year 7
1. Present Operation								
Income								
Expenses								
Net operational result								
2. Proposed Operation								
Income								
Expenses								
Net result								
3. Projected Gain (Loss)								
4. Project Costs								
(One-time)								
IM charges								
User time								
Computer develop-ment								
Package cost								
Consulting fees								
Site costs								
Other								
5. Cash Flow								
Less taxes @ 55%								
Less tax return on depreciation								
Less ITC								
Net cash flow								
6. Capital Investments								
7. Total Cash Flow								
Discount factor (6.5%)	1.000	0.939	0.882	0.828	0.777	0.730	0.685	0.644
Present value								
Cumulative net present value								

8. Return on Investment
(ROI)
(Check one)
☐ Net benefits discounted at 6.5% after taxes produces a payback
   in _____ years and a return on investment of _____ %.
☐ In order to achieve a 6.5% after tax return over the life of the system, the
   non-quantified system benefits must have a value of $_____
   annually.

operating gain (or loss) from the present operation is projected over the period used.

Step 2   Proposed Operation

Repeat the same procedure for Step 2. Obviously, since the new system does not yet exist, a benefits analysis must be done first. Only quantitative benefits are included in the CBA form, so every effort should be made to quantify qualitative benefits. Those which cannot be quantified should be described in a separate statement of qualitative benefits. Quantitative benefits may involve increased income, reduced expenses, or both. The income side is normally the responsibility of the user; the cost side is done primarily by systems. Cost reductions come from many sources (people savings, increased productivity, changed function, avoidance of losses, etc.) and thus must be thoroughly and carefully estimated.

The use of probability (Bayesian analysis can be useful here) involves estimating a probable range of outcomes and then calculating the resulting estimate. Exhibit 11-12 presents two examples, one estimating cost reduction, the other increased profit.

In these examples, estimated savings of $27,500 and $16,875, respectively, would be used for the proposed-operation section of the CBA. Probability analysis can be used to estimate likely people savings, reduction in costs, improvements in revenue (any area where a range of probable outcomes is likely), or to quantify benefits thought to be nonquantifiable.

Step 3   Projected Gain (Loss)

This is simply the result of Steps 1 and 2. So far, we have examined only the ongoing operating benefits of a new system. We now look at how long it will take to recover the initial investment.

Exhibit 11-12   Probability analysis

Estimated Cost Reduction			Estimated Increase in Sales		
Range of Possible Cost Reduction	Probability of Occurrence	Probabilistic Savings	Range of Possible Sales Increases	Probability of Occurrence	Probabilistic Savings
10% or $10,000	10%	$ 1,000	5% or $250,000	70%	$175,000
20% or $20,000	25	5,000	10% or $500,000	25	125,000
30% or $30,000	50	15,000	15% or $750,000	5	37,500
40% or $40,000	10	4,000	Total probability of new		
50% or $50,000	5	2,500	revenue		337,500
Total probabilistic savings		$27,500	Profit margin (@ 5%)		$ 16,875

Step 4   *Project Costs (One-Time)*

Here we list the nonrecurring costs of developing or acquiring the new system. Since all these occur prior to the new system's operation, we list them in the Period 0 column. These costs include internal IM charges (see project estimating strategy, S-56), the cost of full-time users assigned to the project (fully burdened; i.e., salary, benefits, overhead), computer time for program testing, package cost (if purchased), consulting and professional fees (if any), space and renovation needs, and any other one-time charges. (Note: Do not include equipment and other capital investments here, as these are taken into consideration in Step 6.)

Step 5   *Cash Flow*

Total project costs for Period 0 are carried down from Step 4, as are the projected gain (loss) dollars from Step 3 over *n* years. Next, deduct federal and state taxes at the company's effective tax rate (in the example, 55%). (Note: Since depreciation is not a cash flow, it should not be included under expenses in Step 2. However, the tax savings on depreciation do reduce taxes and must therefore also be deducted from cash flow.) Having done all this, we arrive at net cash flow after taxes.

Step 6   *Capital Investments*

Investment in equipment or other capitalized items should be listed in Period 0 for cash flow purposes, even though recovery through depreciation is taken in Step 2.

Step 7   *Total Cash Flow*

So far, we have calculated gross cash flow over the life of the system. Now we take into account the time value of money; that is, a dollar tomorrow will not be worth what it is today. To overcome the shortcomings of the straight dollar payback, our CBA discounts future benefits to what they are worth in offsetting the original investment; for example, at a discount rate of 6.5% after taxes, each dollar returned two years later offsets only $.882 of the original investment. (The discount for each year is the reciprocal of the compound interest rate, e.g., 1.00/1.065, 1.00/1.134 . . .) When the total of the present values of future years' benefits is equal to or exceeds the initial investment, a return on the investment equal to or greater than the hurdle rate has been achieved. The more a systems project is expected to exceed the hurdle rate, the more attractive it is as an investment for the company.

The CBA worksheet in this illustration shows total cash flow discounted at 6.5% after taxes. This rate provides the annual present value and the cumulative present value of the cash flows over time. (The discount factor used in your own calculations should always be your company's hurdle rate; that is, your company's average rate of return on capital, after taxes.)

Step 8 *Return on Investment* (*ROI*)

Our final step is to calculate the return on investment. The net present value (NPV) of the investment is the cumulative amount of money earned *after* discounting. If the NPV is positive, the rate of return is greater than the discount factor used; if the NPV is negative, the rate of return is less than the discount factor used. The payback period (in present value terms) is indicated, to show how long the new system will take to recover the original investment. The return-on-investment percentage can be calculated either by formula or by interpolation; for example, try a higher discount factor and interpolate the results. If the NPV is negative (i.e., the project's return does not cover the hurdle rate), skip to the last box and use the value-of-information approach discussed earlier to determine what the nonquantified benefits would have to be to cover the company's hurdle rate.

NOTES

1   F. Warren MacFarlan, "Management Audit of the EDP Department," *Harvard Business Review,* May–June 1973, p. 139.

2   Frederick P. Brooks, Jr., "Why Is the Software Late?" *Data Management,* August 1971, p. 21.

3   Clayton Harrell, Jr., quoted in "Project Management Systems," *EDP Analyzer,* September 1976, pp. 1–13.

4   *Ibid.*

5   J. D. Aron, *Estimating Resources for Large Programming Systems,* unpublished paper for IBM, 1971.

6   A. M. Pietrosanta, *Management Handbook for Estimating Computer Programming Costs,* IBM TM-3225, 1966.

7   Brooks, "Why is the Software Late?", p. 20.

8   John Toellner, "Project Estimating," *Journal of Systems Management,* May 1977, pp. 6–9.

CHAPTER 12

Managing Distributed Processing Resources

The next ten years contain the opportunity for the corporate computer executive to become obsolete. He is controlling dinosaurs while the ants are swarming over his world.

Alvin Toffler[1]

COMPUTER TO INFORMATION ERA

We suggested earlier that the 1980s will mark the transition from the computer era to the information era, a reorientation from data processing to information management and from central control over all resources to shared control over distributed resources. Information managers will have particular difficulty adapting to the latter changes.

Distributed processing is one of the most potent and pervasive forces in the information management industry today. Technically, the engine driving this movement is a combination of "chip" technology and telecommunications advances. The packing of more and more components onto chips has resulted in the birth and the rapid growth of minicomputers, and the improvements in communications capabilities and declining costs have enabled the linking of computer networks in ways that until now were unaffordable. The result is that computers are moving out of computer rooms and into user habitats. From a management standpoint, however, the driving engine is not just technology. It is also that distributed processing seems to offer the best of both worlds: the advantages of centralization and decentralization without the disadvantages of either; that is, a means of effecting corporate coordination and control without disturbing local autonomy, and of allowing an organization to pattern its information systems after the organization's structure, to follow the business as it is really conducted.

In the early days of the computer revolution (only 25 years ago), computers were large and difficult to operate, and their vacuum tubes generated tremendous heat. The operating environment of these early computers had to be carefully controlled, within close humidity and temperature ranges. The writing of programs for these early computers was a high-level specialized skill. Early computers did not have time-sharing or multiprocessing capabilities. Batch processing meant that a large computer was dedicated to one user at a time, usually through reading in a program punched on 80-column cards. As noted previously, it is now possible to lease for $200–$300 a month computers that perform at a higher level than the computers of 25 years ago, which were leased at $50,000 a month or more.

Almost any manager of a division or a function can now afford his or her own computer. Teleprocessing and remote terminals have made it cost-effective to input data into centralized computers from various parts of the world. Networks of computers and remote data-entry terminals have created the 1980s environment of distributed data processing. The big jump from the large, centralized, batch-process computers of 25 years ago to the net-worked, distributed computers and remote terminals of the 1980s has solved some problems and created others.

Planning will be a major key to the successful transition from data processing to information management in the distributed environment of this information era that is now beginning. In this chapter, we examine some strategies for effecting this transition in the management and control of distributed resources.

TECHNOLOGICAL FORECASTING FOR DISTRIBUTED PROCESSING

In Chapter 4, we suggested the use of technological forecasting as an important input into corporate planning. It can also be a useful strategy for evaluating the impact of distributed processing on the business and for developing strategies appropriate to the management and control of distributed resources. Let's go through the five-step process:

Step 1   Trend Identification

In the 1980s, effective management will require the monitoring of important technical trends, such as distributed processing, and the assessment of their likely impact on the organization. The extraordinary rate of technical change is just too powerful a force to treat casually. A few companies have futurist experts on the staff who continually monitor technical trends for their likely impact on the organization. This kind of monitoring could also be a responsibility of the business information planning group (S-10) discussed in Chapter 3. But for those who cannot afford the luxury of such staff specialists, a number of research organizations (International Data Corp., Diebold Research Group, MIT's Center for Information Systems Research, and others) study these trends and report on them to subscribers or sponsoring organizations, as reported in Chapter 8. Private organizations, government organizations, and professional societies like the World Future Society; magazines like *The Futurist;* and books like *The Wired Society* (James Martin), *The Third Wave* (Alvin Toffler), and *Waves of Change* (Charles Lecht)—all deal with future forecasting. Each of these can be a rich resource for the information manager who wants to evaluate the impact of technology on the business environment. These sources of information can provide a useful framework for planning, for spotting future problems and opportunities, and for suggesting possible strategies which the company can follow to take advantage of coming technologies. Failure to take advantage of technological forecasting could result in a company's handicapping its corporate effectiveness, and jeopardizing its future survival and return on investment. The commitment of IM resources to this task provides protection from obsolescence as well as from competition.

Step 2 *Industry Impact*

Having identified a trend such as distributed processing and the spread of minicomputers, the forecaster next needs to analyze its likely impact on his or her industry. For example, one must ask, "Is it a fad, or is it here to stay?" Our assessment is that distributed processing and minicomputers are here to stay and are likely to mushroom over the next five years in all industries. Economics is the driving reason. Minicomputers are becoming so inexpensive that they can be justified almost anywhere. Thus, users see at least the potential for lower-cost solutions to their problems, quicker response to their needs, and control over their own operations. These are appealing advantages, especially to widely dispersed geographic units that have difficulty getting corporate attention and resources.

Step 3 *Company Impact*

Next, the forecaster assesses the likely impact on his or her company. Depending on the company's size, geographic spread, organizational style, and many other factors, this impact will range from none at all to a complete decentralization of data processing. Consider the ways in which one multinational company might use minicomputers: (a) for automation of the domestic branch network; (b) at international offices; (c) in interlinked minicomputer systems, and (d) for special purposes in user departments of the main headquarters. The company would keep a central data center for large data-base applications, high-volume transaction systems, and heavily interdependent systems, which still run best on big mainframes. But regional data centers would serve international offices, and a minicomputer-based distributed international-branch system would be in place in smaller foreign offices. Domestic branches would be automated and linked to the bank's mainframe computer data-base. Several satellite links would be operational, as would a wide variety of special-purpose and single-application minis in user locations.

Step 4   IM Role

At this point, the forecaster needs to examine the appropriate role of the IM function in the application of the trend to the specific company served. Here, we see a shift in responsibility. IM will very likely have less control over *physical* resources, but *increased* control over the function of information resource management. Thus, a coordinated master plan for integrating diverse systems needs to be developed, and management must be brought to recognize the need for such control by the central IM group. Thus, management will have to become educated about the problems of distributed processing as well as the benefits, and establishment of a distributed-processing controller (S-64) must be considered.

Step 5   Strategies

Finally, once the trend has been identified, and its impact on the industry and the company have been assessed, strategies must be developed to manage the controlled growth of minicomputers in the corporation. What is essential at this point is a long-term strategic plan based on such strategies as those suggested in Exhibit 12-1 and discussed in more detail in the remainder of this chapter.

Exhibit 12-1   Example of situation analysis of the consequences of distributed processing in a large commercial bank.

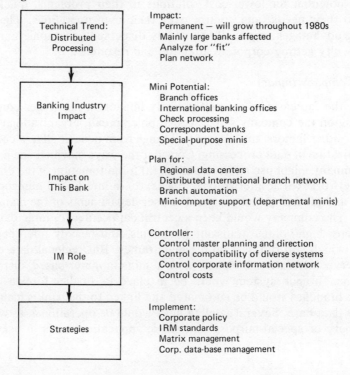

PLANNING FOR DISTRIBUTED RESOURCE MANAGEMENT

Early batch processing, mostly controlled by accounting departments, was centralized. At that time, computers were used in business almost exclusively for the more efficient processing of transactions. Clerical savings in the processing of accounts payable, accounts receivable, inventories, costs of goods sold, and other such accounting transactions were the primary justification for early corporate investments in computers.

The early use of computers was frequently called *automatic data processing* (ADP), which referred to the replacement of manual clerical labor by automation. Accounting managers, who were responsible for ADP functions, tended to be interested in cost reduction. Management uses of computers were neglected, and division and function executives became increasingly unhappy with centralized ADP functions managed by corporate accounting departments.

This dissatisfaction led to decentralized information systems. In some cases, divisions being served inadequately by centralized information management partially decentralized this function. There is frequently little coordination or integration between the corporate and decentralized IM functions.

The need for the action plan for centralized management control over distributed resources recommended in this chapter is demonstrated by the extraordinary rate of growth of distributed data processing in the last 10 years.

As noted in a *Fortune* magazine advertising supplement:

A few years ago, distributed processing was just a hazy gleam in the eyes of all but a few hardy pioneers; today, it is a fact of life;

Shipments to the distributed processing marketplace from component industries will total $900 million this year, grow to $3 billion by 1983;

Every one of the nation's largest companies have evaluated the concept; over half are in the process of implementing it to at least some degree;

Supplier product lines have gained breadth so that users now have plentiful equipment selections and upgrade possibilities.[2]

This *Fortune* advertising supplement was financed by the companies producing distributed data processing equipment and services. The equipment and services selection process is difficult for corporate management because of the large variety of vendors, the speed of change, the need to integrate equipment and services from different vendors, and the organizational problems created by the implementation of change.

Distributed processing is the most recent in a series of major "improvements" in information resources and practices which must be managed. The need for a wide range of skills to manage this new information resources capability can be observed by evaluation of practices in different companies. For example, John L. Kirkley, editor of *Datamation,* wrote:

Ours is an industry given to brief but intense enthusiasms. Still enthralled by our technology, we seek easy answers and instant solutions at the drop of an acronym. Each new engineering triumph promises the user fast relief from the corporate heartburn brought on by being the collector, keeper, massager, and disseminator of the company's vital information.

Distributed processing is our latest panacea. Sanctification is usually followed by initialization and we have now added DDP (distributed data processing) to an over-flowing bowl of alphabet soup.

But all this euphoria aside, just what is it? And what does DDP mean to the DP professional?—the man in the organization who has to respond to innovation while simultaneously keeping existing corporate systems functioning smoothly (a juggling act comparable to changing engines on a 747 while en route from Los Angeles to New York).

The point of all this is that it's a waste of time trying to pin down a definition of distributed processing. Instead of asking "What is it?"—it's more productive to ask "What does it allow me to do?"[3]

FACTORS IN DECENTRALIZATION/DISTRIBUTED PROCESSING DECISIONS

Many researchers have documented the advantages and disadvantages of centralized, decentralized and distributed information processing. A typical list is presented in Exhibit 12-2. We do not intend to provide an exhaustive list of all the factors to consider; rather, we wish to demonstrate the complexity of choosing among the three modes. The speed of change in information resources technology and practices often encourages the following two entirely inappropriate management responses. The emphasis in centralized IM is on corporate efficiency. In decentralized IM, it is local effectiveness that is emphasized. A blend of corporate and local effectiveness and efficiency is the product of distributed IM.

Exhibit 12-2 A comparison of the advantages and disadvantages of centralized, decentralized, and distributed EDP functions.

Centralized IM		Decentralized IM	
Advantages	Disadvantages	Advantages	Disadvantages
Economies of scale	Less responsiveness	Responsiveness to local needs	High costs (redundancies)
Central control	No local accountability	Accountability	Controls/standards needed
Depth of expertise	Complexity (bigness)	Autonomy	Local DP expertise missing
Standardization		User control	
Data consolidation			Weak consolidated reporting
Internal backup			Loss of integration option
Integration possibilities			

Exhibit 12-2 (*Continued*)

Distributed IM	
Advantages	Disadvantages
Responsiveness to local needs	Technological complexity
Corporate/user shared control	Higher telecommunications costs
Accountability	Greater management problems
Local data entry and management	
Shared data bases and programs	
Hardware efficiency	
Depth of expertise	
Standardization	
Integration Option	

Vanishing Problem Syndrome

A full evaluation and implementation of issues in centralized/decentralized/ distributed information processing decisions often involves several years. The work includes, among other things, the identification of the need for a network of information processing capabilities, the writing and approval of proposals, and the selection of vendors. Too often, by the time such a solution has been implemented, as suggested by Hal B. Becker, "The initial problem has either vanished or changed so dramatically as to make the [information processing network] configuration of little value to users."[4]

Short-Term Fixes

The opposite side of the excessive evaluation problem is the frequent practice of making big decisions with a short-term mentality. The speed of change in information processing and practices has been made possible by new technology and problems that increase the requirements for improved information-processing capabilities. As Becker correctly observed, much of the change in information processing practices "has occurred in the form of short-term solutions produced under pressure to solve immediate, real problems. Frequently, and in many cases predictably, the short-term solution has become the long-term problem."[5]

DIMENSIONS OF THE CENTRALIZATION/DECENTRALIZATION ISSUE

As we will demonstrate in the following section, distributed information resources are significantly more difficult to manage than decentralized infor-

Exhibit 12-3   Dimensions of centralization–decentralization in an illustrative division of a large decentralized company.

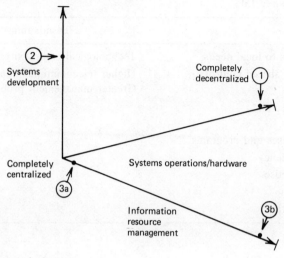

Decisions illustrated above

1. Hardware and systems operations decentralized. Computer hardware uncon- nected to corporate computer system.
2. Some cooperation between corporate and division management in systems de- velopment and sharing of systems and programming resources.
3a. Management of information systems highly centralized on such issues as hardware purchases, security, documentation standards.
3b. Management almost completely decentralized on such issues as priority setting for division and function needs and user relations.

Source: Adapted from John F. Rockart et al., "Centralizing versus Decentralizing: Your Application," Datapro Research Corp.: Delran, NJ, November 1979.

mation resources, which are more difficult to manage than centralized re- sources. The trend is clearly toward an increase in the difficulty of informa- tion resources management.

On the other hand, the increased difficulty of management can be cost- effective by virtue of the very sizable improvement in the efficiency and effectiveness of well managed distributed information resources.

In Exhibit 12-3, the options for the centralization/decentralization of in- formation resource management are illustrated along three dimensions. The range of activity is from completely centralized to completely decentralized for each of the three dimensions. Thus, Exhibit 12-3 illustrates a large decen- tralized company with:

1   Hardware almost completely decentralized.
2   Some cooperation between corporate and division management in sys- tems development and the sharing of human resources.

3a Management of information resources highly centralized on such issues as hardware purchases, security, and documentation standards.

3b Management of information resources almost completely decentralized on such issues as setting priorities for division and function needs and user relations.

As we have noted, if well managed, distributed processing can offer a major increase in the efficiency and effectiveness of information resources. But the promise of improved efficiency and effectiveness has often encouraged a rush of ill-conceived efforts.

Distributed processing involves three basic functions:

1 *Information processing:* processing of data by application programs to produce needed information.
2 *Network processing:* control of data and information movement among different locations in an information network.
3 *Data-base processing:* the storage of data and information in such a way that they are available to different users in various locations in the information network.

Too often, companies rush into distributed data processing with imperfect knowledge of the technical complexities of managing these integrated functions. In addition to the technological complexity, rapid change in the field, and the large number of vendors with products that may or may not be compatible with each other, serious organizational problems are frequently experienced in efforts to implement distributed data processing.

STRATEGIES FOR DISTRIBUTED RESOURCE MANAGEMENT

The diffusion of minicomputers networked by teleprocessing does not mean the end of large central data centers. These will still exist, but many minicomputers, whether stand-alone or linked, will coexist with them. Information managers themselves, however, will need to change. That is, the role of information manager will change in a distributed world, as discussed in Chapter 3. One of the roles the information manager will assume will be that of the information controller, or stated more aptly, perhaps, controller over distributed information resources. With reference to Nolan's stages of growth, we believe that distributed processing has begun implementation in the pattern of growth stages shown in Exhibit 12-4.

Most well-run EDP organizations today are now in or approaching Nolan's fourth stage of EDP growth. Others are only in Stage II. Responsible information managers have the opportunity in the 1980s to draw on their experience with EDP growth to help their companies compress the period

Exhibit 12-4   Stages in the growth of distributed processing in the typical company.

Staff	Planning/Control	Activity
I Initiation	Lax	Introduction of minicomputers in early 1970s.
II Contagion	More lax	Everyone gets a mini. Many vendors, service problems, chaos mid to late 1970s.
III Control	Formalized planning/central	Authority to purchase minis centralized. Corporate/division relationships set by policy rather than by needs assessment.
IV Integration	Tailored planning/central	Evaluation of shared EDP resources. Larger time horizon for planning and information resources. Initiated in best-managed companies in late 1970s.

between Stages II and IV by initiating control strategies for the effective management of distributed processing resources in their companies.

Before going into distributed-processing control strategies, however, we should first discuss why there is a need for such control. Distributed processing has both benefits and pitfalls. Some advantages and disadvantages of decentralization were outlined in Exhibit 12-2. The point is that a computer system is just that: a system, not a box. One doesn't just plug in a computer, as one plugs in a copying machine, and expect it to work. A computer of any size is still a computer, and today's minicomputer is more sophisticated that yesterday's mainframe. Therefore, it needs management, and it needs professional staff to run it. Before they are aware of what's happening, user managers may find that they have become DP managers, enmeshed in myriad DP problems instead of running their business. We have found that most organizations do not want to set up DP staffs at user sites. They would prefer to have users concentrate on running their own businesses and not get into the technical esoterica of data processing. If this does happen, what has been effected is pure decentralization, not distributed processing. The distinction is important. Under decentralized processing, everything is distributed, including management control; under distributed processing, everything may be distributed *except* management control. Few companies, in fact, opt for distributed control. The majority want distributed processing, with some form of *central management control*.

Donald T. Winski, manager of management advisory services at Price Waterhouse, had this to say at a recent banking conference:

> In a number of banks we are seeing a balance between distributed and consolidated computer equipment with the responsibility for the data processing

functions still within a centralized MIS group. . . . In almost all cases there is either a formally defined or implied management policy of centralized control [over] such factors as cost–benefit justification, adherence to necessary standards and proper interfacing between adjoining application systems. . . . An MIS organization will be reshaped by DDP, transformed into a higher quality, less populated elliptically shaped MIS organization. All operational responsibilities and much of the programming as well as the maintenance will revert to the user; the MIS department will have a greatly expanded technical support and quality assurance function, becoming an internal consulting organization.[6]

This need for control is a common thread emerging from considerable research conducted at such places as MIT's Center of Information Systems Research, Harvard Business School, Diebold Research Group, and International Data Corp. There has been a developing consensus that while hardware (and even software) may be distributed, management control must not. *To give up central management control is to move not to distributed processing but to distributed incompetence!* Implicit in the definition of distributed processing is the existence of a central site from which resources are distributed and from which some level of control is exercised. If we don't want to make the mistakes of second-generation computing all over again, we must take responsibility for the control of distributed data processing. Information

Exhibit 12-5 Some pitfalls of distributed processing.

Incompatibility. Proliferation of incompatible systems makes integration difficult, if not impossible.

Inefficiency. Poorly designed programs use the computer inefficiently and incur high maintenance costs over the life of the system.

Corporate ineffectiveness. Remote computing serves local needs well but not overall corporate information needs.

Amateurs doing professional work.

Redundancy. Duplication of effort occurs as the same functions are programmed over and over again in different company areas.

No corporate data base. Failure to take advantage of data-base technology.

No corporate consolidation. Since data are represented in different ways in different systems, it becomes impossible to consolidate them into meaningful information for corporate management.

Weak security. Inadequate control can exist over physical site, hardware, and media.

Escalation. The Xerox syndrome occurs as machines proliferate and expand at user sites.

High costs. These and other pitfalls can result in higher (not lower) costs for the corporation than if distributed resources were under central management control.

Source: Adapted from the James Martin seminar, "The New DP Environment and How to Design for It," Technology Transfer, Inc., December 1979, p. 589.

managers should be *information* controllers in the same way that every company has financial controllers. The company can benefit in three ways: (a) central support and expertise would continue to be available to ensure efficient and effective use of the computer facilities operated by users; (b) standards, controls, and security considerations would be in place and monitored; and (c) the need for DP skills at remote sites would be minimized, so that users can concentrate on the running of their own businesses without having to become DP managers to boot.

Corporate managements must be made aware of the potential pitfalls of distributed processing, such as those shown in Exhibit 12-5. These are not steps forward, they are steps backward! When corporate management understands *both* the benefits and the pitfalls of distributed processing, they will also understand the need for an information controller for distributed information resources.

THE INFORMATION CONTROLLER

> **S-64 DISTRIBUTED-PROCESSING CONTROLLER**
>
> **Centralized management control over corporate information resources which are distributed throughout corporate divisions and functions.**

The responsibilities of an information controller would include:

1 Automation master planning—coordination and integration of all distributed information resources.
2 Major software development—could be done by, or managed by, central IM group, or distributed regionally under installation standards control.
3 Major spending—for equipment, software contracts, consultants, outside computing services.
4 Standards—for equipment selection (compatibility), software languages, distributed-processing policy, security and control, and data base management.
5 Communications networking—all network services and interface requirements.
6 Corporate data resources—for compatibility and consistency, retrieval and consolidation, data base architecture.
7 Quality assurance—consulting, advising, monitoring, auditing of distributed processing activities.

For the distributed-processing (or information) controller to have the portfolio to carry on these responsibilities, he or she must have the necessary authority to go with them. A minimum strategy for achieving this authority could be put together from several of the MBS strategies, discussed elsewhere in this book; for example:

1 *Corporate policy (S-66)*. Management can issue corporate directions outlining the functional responsibilities of the controller over distributed-processing resources.

2 *Distributed-processing standards (S-8)*. Authority to issue distributed-processing standards governing common hardware and software, communications protocols, security, and data can be given to the distributed-processing controller. These standards could then be used by the internal audit staff to monitor conformance.

3 *Matrix management (S-65)*. Organizationally, a dotted-line (functional) relationship could be established between the distributed-processing controller and all remote computer operations.

4 *Data base management (S-47)*. If a data dictionary has been selected for use in the organization as a first step toward establishing a corporate data base, it can be used to effect compliance to a standard data structure and thereby control all informational data bases, wherever they may reside in the firm.

In summary, companies that fail to recognize the need for central management control over distributed processing may well find themselves moving up Stage II of Nolan's stages of growth, with escalating costs, inefficiency, incompatibility, and loss of control over distributed-processing activities. It is the information manager's responsibility, as the *distributed-processing controller,* to make management aware of the problems as well as the benefits of distributed processing and to lead the company toward *controlled* growth through an effective information controller strategy.

MATRIX MANAGEMENT STRATEGY

> **S-65   MATRIX MANAGEMENT STRATEGY**
>
> **Multidimensionality of large complex organizations is recognized through the assignment of shared responsibility for specializations which cross divisional or geographic borders.**

The implementation of strategies such as coalescence planner (S-5) and chief information officer (S-7) involves a perception of information in the organizational structure which is radically different from current practices in most companies. Matrix management is another important strategy for effective implementation of this new perception of the management of information resources. In Exhibit 12-3, we illustrated the degrees of centralization and decentralization of information management. In that context, matrix management will vary with the amount of distribution. The more the push out from the center, the more matrix management.

In matrix management, each operating division and functional group has a coordinated plan for the processing and utilization of information. The several levels of information management in most large companies have some characteristics similar to the finance/accounting organizational structure. Exhibit 12-6 is an adaptation of some findings from the research on MIS centralization/decentralization of John Rockart and his associates at the MIT Sloan School (Center for Information Systems Research). Rockart's evaluation of trends in hardware size and effectiveness, teleprocessing, and the effectiveness/efficiency issue in MIS has led him to conclude that computer hardware and software development in large companies will be decentralized, but that a number of facets of MIS will be centralized. We have adapted Rockart's work to include the concept of a chief information officer,

Exhibit 12-6 Matrix management for information processing and utilization. A = other functions or divisions; B = a function or division

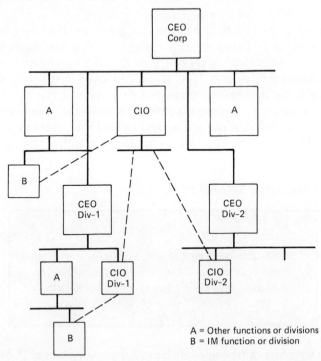

A = Other functions or divisions
B = IM function or division

Source: Adapted from John F. Rockart et al., "Centralizing versus Decentralizing: Your Application," Datapro Research Corp., Delran, NJ, November 1979.

who will have a greater breadth of responsibility than is currently the practice in most companies.

The information processing and utilization functions in this example are decentralized in various functions and divisions (labeled "B"), with direct reporting relationships to functional and division management (labeled "A"). However, there is a strong dotted line between the chief information officer (CIO) and the decentralized information resources. The shared management responsibility, with essentially two bosses for the managers of decentralized information resources, is a current practice in only a few large companies. It is our expectation that during the 1980s, this condition of relatively uncontrolled and uncoordinated decentralized information resources will be restructured in many companies into an organization like the one diagrammed in Exhibit 12-6.

Effective management of the rapid progress in information technology requires the assignment of responsibility for keeping current in the variety of specialized fields of knowledge comprising information sciences and technology. Decisions will frequently involve three, five, or even more specialized fields of knowledge (such as teleprocessing, support software, operating systems, terminals, application software, and data storage). This breadth of specialized knowledge will rarely be available in decentralized divisions and functions. Therefore, the corporate centralized information-resources function should include staff professionals who are at the frontier of these specialized fields of competence.

The systems people in the decentralized divisions could be responsible primarily for user needs assessment and systems planning. The centralized expertise at the corporate level would be a resource for decentralized systems people working directly with users in the divisions and functions. This kind of coordination is an important facet of good matrix management.

The specification of responsibilities in a matrix management organization is also essential for the success of this kind of complex organizational structure. Decentralized systems staffs are assigned to user divisions and functions to provide the following:

1   A knowledge of user needs and situational factors.
2   Communications with users.
3   Coordination at the user level of systems development and implementation.
4   Linkage with the corporate centralized IM resources.

Example of Matrix Management

There is value to having a coordinated automation master plan throughout an organization, especially if it is decentralized. Data base architecture, communications networking, and distributed processing all require an overall plan, standards, and, to some degree, shared systems. In fact, as a company's operations become more widely scattered, the need for coordination and control over automation activities becomes more important, if not more difficult. One way to provide this control is through matrix management. Through matrix management, control can be exercised over dispersed operations without upsetting a decentralized organizational structure. That is, individuals continue to report to their local organization while having a functional, or dotted-line, responsibility to some staff person at the head office as well. Exhibit 12-7 illustrates a matrix arrangement in an international, dispersed firm covering several specialized staff functions such as finance, audit, and data processing. In this example, the controller in London would be responsible for financial and accounting controls in his or her office and would report directly to the London manager. He or she would also have an indirect reporting responsibility to the head-office controller, to comply with and adhere to corporate financial policy, reporting requirements, and other corporate needs. Similarly, the data processing officer would provide services to the London office but would do so within general company standards relating to hardware, software, communications, and security and control, as established by the central IM function. The value of a matrix reporting arrangement is that general standards and controls can be kept in place and a corporate overview can be maintained without undoing the autonomy of decentralized offices. Local managers are free to pursue their main line of

Exhibit 12-7   Corporate–division sharing of responsibilities in a matrix management organization.

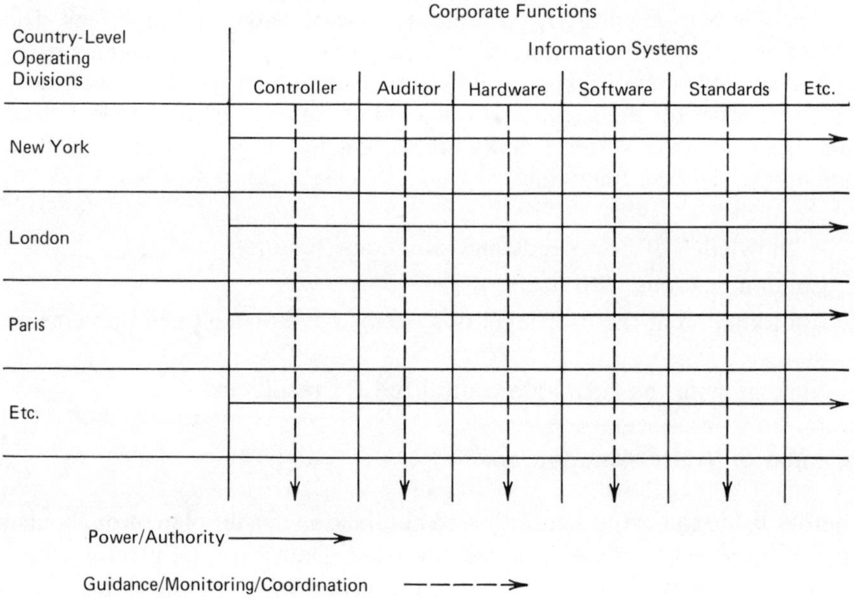

business without being encumbered by the needs of various corporate line and/or staff divisions, and, at the same time, they do not need to be experts in all lines themselves, since the matrix arrangement provides corporate guidelines in specialized areas of the business.

Generally, a company uses matrix management or it doesn't—it's a matter of management style. A matrix arrangement is not going to work for information management if it is not used for other staff functions. If it *is* used elsewhere, a case can probably be made for information management's also using this style of shared management.

CORPORATE POLICIES

The issuance of corporate instructions, which include corporate policies, standards, procedures, operating manuals, etc., is an information service of the organization which falls logically within an information management function. The issuance of corporate policies, particularly, can be a good control strategy in a distributed-resource environment.

> **S-66   CORPORATE POLICY**
>
> **Issuance of corporate policies is an appropriate information service of the IM function.**

In management by strategies (S-1), we suggested that one of the environmental factors to consider when looking at the *company* being served is the political environment. We stated that political strategies were basically of two types: those intended to influence and those that directly control. A corporate policy strategy is an example of the latter type. Corporate policies, of course, can cover a wide variety of subject matter affecting all areas of the company. The ones which can particularly work for IM, however, deal with the control of corporate information resources, automation development, and major spending on computer and computer-related activities. Responsibility for the issuance of corporate policies is not a prerequisite for effecting these controls. It can be done through management agreement, whether formal or informal. On the other hand, if the IM function actually has the responsibility for writing corporate policies, for obtaining the necessary approvals, and for disseminating them through the firm, it will not only be performing an information service, but it will have the opportunity to *originate* the policies needed to achieve control over automation activities.

Senior management creates policies, of course, but these must be translated into formal corporate instructions. Why is this an appropriate IM responsibility? Because it is an *information service*. Corporate policies are a form of management information. They cut across divisional lines; they relate to management control; they relate to corporate procedures; in fact, corporate policies *are* information. This is an IM role in the corporation—if it has the right identification. And that's the key. It would make no sense to have corporate policies issued through data processing, but it makes good sense to have them issued through an information management function. Having the right identification is the key to gaining the right responsibilities.

If the issuance of corporate policy is a proper information management responsibility, then one of the policies which the IM function should promote is the firm's computer policy with regard to distributed processing, or distributed information resources. Distributed processing is a new world that must be *managed,* and not simply allowed to grow on its own. In our distributed data-processing standards (S-8), we suggested some ways this can be done, including the issuance of corporate policies governing the acquisition and use of computers, as well as the development of DDP standards.

Start by issuing a corporate policy establishing the ground rules for the use of distributed computers in the organization, indicating the conditions under which computers can be acquired and the approvals necessary, and referring to any standards to be adhered to. Next, prepare a DDP standards manual to be issued to each user who proposes to acquire a computer. These standards are meant to assure that distributed-processing resources will be compatible with corporate long-range planning, will be secure, and will be used efficiently and effectively throughout the corporation. DDP standards sometimes serve as guidelines (e.g., contract negotiation) and sometimes serve as "thou shalt not's."

Somewhere in the standards, specify such things as the responsibility of IM over automation master planning and coordination, the criteria for an application's going on a minicomputer as opposed to centralized mainframes, and the responsibility of users for the operation and control of minis in user areas. Cover such things as hardware and software selection criteria, security over physical facilities (site, computer, media), contract negotiation guidelines (especially for "turnkey" development), data communications network protocols, corporate data standards, organizational issues, use of outside resources (time-sharing, service bureaus, consultants, contract programmers), and systems implementation guidelines. A list of typical DDP standards is shown in Exhibit 12-8.

The standards should be prepared by the IM function and approved by designated key management personnel (e.g., information manager, security officer, auditor, comptroller). Once issued to every minicomputer user, they should be tested for adherence as a routine part of the internal audit of a user's operations, with copies of audit comments relative to standards forwarded to the information manager.

The use of corporate standards governing DDP within the organization will become increasingly important as the trend toward distributed processing accelerates in the years ahead. The company that gets control over these diverse resources early in the game will ensure that its future information

Exhibit 12-8   DDP standards.

Introduction
Distributed-processing overview
Equipment selection/acquisition
Systems software selection/acquisition
Application software selection/acquisition
Feasibility studies
Requests for proposals—software development
Contract negotiations—general
Contracts—hardware acquisition
Contracts—hardware maintenance
Contracts—package program acquisition
Contracts—package program maintenance
Contracts—systems development
Organizational issues
Use of consultants/contract personnel
System/program implementation
System/program documentation
System/program controls
System/program testing
System/program changes
System (control) program changes
Use of text processing/administrative terminals
Computer operations control
Data security
Physical security—site
Physical security—equipment
Physical security—media
Software security
Backup and recovery
Insurance
Use of outside computing services
Data communications protocols
Planning/installing voice communications systems
Planning/installing data communications systems
Corporate data standards
Data privacy
Software protection
Personal use of computers

network will function as a fully integrated set of systems able to pass information around the firm easily and quickly for improved management information and control. A strategy of developing and disseminating distributed-processing standards *before* distributed processing goes too far will eliminate the diverse, uncoordinated, and incompatible systems which plagued the company in the example related earlier.

VENDOR POLICY

> **S-67   VENDOR POLICY**
>
> **Centralized IM control over major hardware and software acquisitions, as well as vendor contacts and contracts.**

For control and efficiency purposes, it can be a sound strategy to have a corporate policy of centralized control over certain vendor contacts and contracts. This control is easier to effect in a highly centralized organization, but even in a decentralized company, there are advantages to having central IM control over vendor dealings. Let us cite a few:

More effective vendor management.
Control over major spending for equipment, software, and services.
Better equipment research.
Expertise in contract work.
Improved vendor service and support.

Effective Vendor Management

A single contact point between a vendor and a company is highly desirable, to prevent the waste of a lot of many people's time. Many vendors still attempt to contact anyone and everyone who will listen to them in their zeal for sales. However, impressive numbers of company executives are beginning to realize the importance of a single contact point and are working toward this end. Vendors are also attempting to organize themselves around this goal as much as possible in the belief that, in the final analysis, it will lead to more effective use of marketing personnel, better service to the customer, and more sales. From a company standpoint, a single contact point gives the company more "clout" with a vendor than contact through diverse users throughout the organization. Single-point contact will not be completely feasible in geographically dispersed companies, but it can work.

As an example in another field, a number of major international banks have recently established multinational corporation groups at their headquarters to serve the worldwide banking needs of major firms doing business with their various branches around the world. In these offices, a headquarters lending officer, with a thorough knowledge of the financial activities of the customer corporation, works directly with the corporation's treasurer or financial vice-president in arranging loans, letters of credit, deposit accounts, and other banking services wherever needed. Depending on the degree of central control desired by the customer corporation, of course, this can be a more effective way of serving multinational corporations than expecting individual business units to do business with local banks or branches, leaving the problems of cash and credit management and control to a headquarters treasurer to pull together throughout the corporation.

The same principle can be applied to vendor dealings. For example, a company dealing with IBM or Xerox could establish corporate policies and work out all business arrangements for all locations between a single contact at the headquarters office and a single vendor representative. One of the authors did just that working with IBM to install a distributed processing network. IBM was instructed not to call on individual foreign branches because all automation planning, equipment selection, and software development would be controlled through the head office. The branches knew that a standard hardware/software system was being developed because they had participated in setting its functional requirements through regional operating committees. Yet, they were spared the burden of having to get involved in technical decisions and were able to concentrate on defining their business needs.

In other cases, vendor contact could be left to individual offices, but even then, at least a list of approved vendors could be provided based on previous experience, research, or standards for equipment selection. Proposals could also be forwarded to the head office for review and comment, if not outright approval.

Control over Major Spending

It can be company policy to have all purchase orders go through a central purchasing department, which would ensure control over spending for equipment, software, and other automated services. If, for example, corporate policy states that some central body must approve all expenditures above a given amount, the purchasing department can make sure that such approvals have been obtained before issuing the check in payment, thus assuring that nothing major will slip through the control process.

Equipment Research

When vendors call on users, they are there to sell products. Users not only get a biased presentation but may be completely unaware of alternative competitive products. Equipment evaluation, in such cases, is a hit-or-miss proposition. A centralized equipment-research group, on the other hand, can be in constant touch with the technology, the leading vendors, and new product announcements. They can do comparative product evaluations, serving as an internal research consulting group for all potential users within the company. Knowing that such a central research group exists, vendors will find it easier to arrange presentations and demonstrations, with less disruption and wasted effort. If a user *does* schedule a presentation or a product demonstration, the central research group could be represented to prevent later having to duplicate the effort. The research, incidentally, could include evaluating the vendor itself, its financial strength and credit rating, the size and age of the company, the principals' strength and depth, and the general viability of the company. It is a good idea always to run a credit check on vendors with whom the company is dealing for the first time, especially if they are expected to give ongoing service and support.

Expertise in Contract Work

Some sort of central expertise is essential when it comes to vendor contracts. Contract negotiation and contracts per se should not be left to every Tom, Dick, and Harry in the organization. Contract work is a highly specialized and important part of dealings with vendors. A central group can develop contract standards; can assist users in negotiating contracts; can review contract forms for needed provisions, protective clauses, etc.; and can assist in the preparation of requests for proposals (RFP) to vendors for software development. These are all areas where experience and expertise can avoid many pitfalls, and where a highly specialized central group can perform best. Contracts should not be left entirely to the company lawyers, either. They don't know the computer business. Terms and conditions, acceptance criteria, warranties of software "bugs," and many other technical considerations should be reviewed by technical personnel in IM *before* the contract goes to the company lawyers.

Vendor Service and Support

A central group monitoring and recording the general service level and response of vendors to service problems can provide a total corporate picture not otherwise possible. As a result, the full weight of the company can be brought to bear on a vendor where overall service is unsatisfactory or slipping, with much greater efficacy than through individual user complaints. A central vendor contact for new products, demonstrations, and presentations also enables the IM research group to exert pressure (through potential new business) on the vendor's marketing area to keep service and support levels high.

These are some of the reasons that some central IM control over vendor contacts and contracts makes sense, even in an otherwise decentralized organization. It is a strategy designed to get the most from the vendors who serve the company. Considering the amount of money spent on equipment, software, contract consulting, etc., a policy of vendor control in the organization can pay off handsomely—as another controlled resource.

HOME INFORMATION SYSTEMS

We could not leave this chapter on distributed information resource management without commenting on the burgeoning home information system movement and the accelerating rate of growth and use of personal computers in the home *and* the office. Minicomputers today contain chips with 18,000 components capable of executing a million instructions per second (MIPS). By the late 1980s, the rate is predicted to be up to 100,000 components per chip and over 10 MIPS. Industry sources predict that greater power for less money will cause microprocessors to grow by a factor of 150 in the next 10 years. Thus, the home computer market is expected to explode in the 1980s. Radio Shack, Texas Instruments, Apple Computer, and others are already selling home computers for a few hundred dollars. Over half a million were sold in the last two years alone.

Originally, these minis were conceived and marketed for hobbyists, programmers, and engineers. Then the industry went after the consumer market with great expectations and growth forecasts. However, they soon discovered that consumers were not yet ready for the revolution, probably because the home computer was still a "solution looking for a problem." These problems—educational courses, bill paying, personal finance, home management, budgeting, investment aids, etc.—need "canned" software to make home computers attractive and easy to use. In the 1980s, the software should catch up, and then the personal computer market will really take off. People in all walks of life will use computers and computer terminals routinely for their work, for education, for personal money management, and for just plain fun and games. More and more of the routine work of humans—mathematics, engineering, medical diagnosis—will be computerized, providing everyone with more and better information. When canned software and firmware make computers easy and comfortable to use, then everyone will use them.

Meanwhile, computer makers have moved into the small-business market. This is not a new frontier; it just means doing the same for less money. Today $2,500 buys for a small business a small microprocessor with perhaps 32K random access memory (RAM), some read-only memory (ROM) and a keyboard terminal; for a few thousand more, the keyboard can be upgraded to a CRT terminal and a line printer can be added. This lowered price tag is appealing to thousands of smaller businesses that can now afford their own computers. Small functions in departments of large corporations are also being automated for the same reason, giving further impetus to decentralized processing.

Another home information system which is rapidly gaining interest is the marriage of the television set and the telephone in what is commonly called *videotext,* which will create a whole new and exciting information medium. An example of the use of such a home information system was discussed in our technology forecasting (S-11) strategy in Chapter 4.

Videotext service can provide subscribers with access to millions of pages of information which can be called and displayed on the subscriber's TV set—information such as weather forecasts, stock market reports, and shopping, travel, and entertainment information. Computer programs can be accessed which provide computer-aided instruction in languages, mathematics, cooking, tax return information, encyclopedia data, and computer games. Through an attached keyboard, the system becomes interactive, allowing any subscriber to enter data into the videotext files. Hence, stores, ad agencies, and others can use this aspect of the service to publicize products and services. Newspaper and magazine publishers could use it as a new publishing medium.

Videotext systems are fast entering the Canadian and U.S. markets and are providing the first impetus to the development of widely used home information systems. A recent book on the videotext revolution had this to say:

> There are as yet only glimpses in the United States of this new world of videotext, or TV-transmitted information, but developments are coming pell-mell in countries like Britain, France and Canada. There, information retrieval systems with names like CEEFAX, Viewdata, Prestel, Antiope and Videotex are moving from labs and research centers into homes and offices. By mid-1979 several experimental services had been announced in the U.S. as well.[7]

The book went on to list 99 organizations, both in the United States and abroad, that were involved with videotext, in one way or another, by 1980. The list has since grown. Here is an example of one such videotext system in operation today. "The Source" is a videotext system which is available from Telecomputing Corporation of America. *Autotransaction Industry Report* described this service as follows:

> Subscribers to the service will need a modem and a dumb terminal (which they can buy or lease from TCA) for access. By dialing a toll-free number, users gain access (through key wording) to the U.P.I. and N.Y. Times data bases, the Dartmouth College educational library (which offers a myriad of courses at many levels), Consumers Union information, reservation services for entertainment and travel, dozens of games, financial advice and more. Additionally, TCA's data base now has over 3,000 programs with five more being added daily.
> Customers will pay the aforementioned $100 initial hook-up fee plus $2.75/hour for non-prime time use (6:00 P.M. to 7:00 A.M.) and $15/hour for

prime time (7:00 A.M. to 6:00 P.M.). Unlimited storage is also provided for "a very low cost" (3.3¢/2,048 character block/day). The billing mechanism will be direct charges to credit card accounts timed to the nearest minute. TCA plans to spread the word through a franchise matrix of about 200 nationwide. Franchises will pay TCA 40¢/maildrop (business or residential) and in return will get $30 of every subscriber's initial $100 hook-up fee plus 7% of the line charges. Also netted will be 33% of the profits from equipment rentals or sales. Salesmen will be trained to go door to door demonstrating the "information utility," a novel approach for the data processing industry.[8]

What will be the implications of home computers and videotext systems for information managers? Perhaps we will need to think in new dimensions. Could we solve the shortage of programmers by using part-time housewives working at home? Could we increase the supply of programmers by running programming courses on home TV sets? Could we attract programmers, secretaries, and other workers in distant places if they could work at home or in regional distributed-work centers instead of commuting long distances to the city to work? Perhaps this form of distributed processing will have an impact in ways that are not even dreamed of today. The "wired society" described by James Martin will be a vastly different world to live and work in than today's environment and will offer new and exciting challenges to information managers now and into the 21st century.

SUMMARY

In this chapter, we attempted to examine distributed processing as a technological trend which will impact most IM organizations to one degree or another in the 1980s. Using technological forecasting, one can predict the likely impact of this trend on the industry and the company. The information manager can then decide on appropriate roles and strategies to adopt to exploit its potential to the advantage of the firm.

It is clear that the 1980s will usher in the *information age*. A great variety of new products, services, and applications will emerge, made possible by computer and communications advances. These innovations will find their place in the business and personal lives of almost everyone. Teleconferencing, voice message storage and retrieval, electronic banking, document distribution, satellite communications, optical fibers, microcomputers, and home information systems are all examples of the rich potential of 1980s technology.

There will be many challenges. If everyone is to be able to use computers and computer terminals, they must be not just cheap and available but easy to use (comfortable, self-prompted). To make software transparent to users, very sophisticated systems will be needed, systems using very high-level languages, relational data-base structures, and firmware. To move from a stand-alone world of computers to a wired world of communicating computers will require standards. Industry standards or, alternatively, "black boxes," will be needed for communications protocols, vendor interfacing, and data base access. These are sadly lacking at the moment. ×.25 is an international telecommunications standard now being adopted by U.S. firms such as AT&T (ACS) and others. Standards will represent one of the major challenges of the interlinked world of the 1980s.

Certainly the problem of management control will become much greater as processing and communications are distributed throughout the firm. Diverse systems must be linked, overall planning and coordination will become vital, and availability and reliability will need to be near 100% in a real-time wired world.

All of this supports our thesis that the role of Information Managers in the years ahead will be vastly different from that of the DP managers of the past. We need to understand these new roles, understand the impact of the technical trends going on around us, and lead the firm into a new, higher level of productivity, progress, and information utilization in the information era.

NOTES

1   Alvin Toffler, interview in *Software,* January 1981, p. 24.
2   "Distributed Processing from Buzzword to Byword," *Fortune* advertising supplement, May 4, 1979, p. 23.
3   John L. Kirkley, "Happiness Is Distributed Processing," *Datamation,* March 1978, p. 79.
4   Hal. B. Becker, "Let's Put Information Networks into Perspective," *Datamation,* March 1978, p. 81.
5   *Ibid.,* p. 81.
6   Donald T. Winski, *ABA National Operation/Automation Conference Proceedings,* New Orleans, May 1977.
7   Efrem Siegel (Ed.) *Videotext: The Coming Revolution in Home/Office Information Retrieval,* White Plains, N.Y.: Knowledge Industry Publications, 1980.
8   *Autotransaction Industry Report,* published by International Data Corp., Framingham, Mass., July 9, 1979.

13

Management by Strategies in Action

We shape our tools, then they shape us.

The information management era is now a major factor in the practice of management. The revolution in information technology has created opportunities for improving the effectiveness of management. There has been a proliferation of innovations in data processing, office information systems, and telecommunications in recent years. The computer era is over. Traditional data processing is now relegated to cost-effective transaction processing. The vision of information managers in the 1980s should be focused on executive information systems, office information systems, and the integration of information resources and corporate communications through teleprocessing.

Management in an era of revolutionary change requires strategic planning and a program of management by strategies.

The development of information management strategies as a way of coping with the rapid pace of change in the information revolution is a strategic planning process which we have called *management by strategies* (MBS). Many of the individual strategies presented can be effective in helping information managers address the challenge of the information era and the transition from data processing to information management, with its increased emphasis on the shared management of information resources and the integration of the IM function with the user and senior management of the organization. In this final chapter, we return to the MBS concept, this time viewing the synergistic effect possible from a cumulative MBS program of information management.

> ### S-68   MBS SYNERGISM
>
> **A program of management by strategies produces a synergistic effect that can greatly increase the overall effectiveness of individual management strategies.**

An MBS program of innovation in information management represents an investment to achieve more effective IM capabilities and utilization in the future. The stronger the IM capabilities, the less prone a company will be to a management-by-crisis syndrone.

Each additional strategy implemented will increase IM effectiveness, thereby making further investment in the management program easier, as this commitment is reflected in the synergism of successfully implemented strategies. Commitment, careful planning, and follow-through on strategy implementation are the critical first steps in ending the vicious circle caused when management by crisis consumes much of a manager's time.

The strategies introduced in this book are not exhaustive by any means. The particular strategies discussed represent a cross section of successful strategies which have been used by a number of leading companies. A more exhaustive search of the best practices in leading companies would result in a much expanded list of IM management strategies, and the dynamic change occurring in IM capabilities will doubtless result in the development of many additional strategies for improving the effectiveness of information management and utilization during the 1980s. In other words, there are an infinite number of proven strategies for improving the effectiveness of information management and utilization. The problem is the failure to recognize that an investment in time and resources is necessary in order to achieve the benefits of management by strategies. The implementation of an MBS program can be viewed as an investment in management with a multiyear time horizon. The early strategies implemented, if successful, will tend to be perpetuated, so that over time, a portfolio of successful strategies will be built, each in turn adding to the effectiveness of the IM function in the organization. A program of MBS therefore becomes cumulative over time, as illustrated in Exhibit 13-1. This "value-added" process is in itself a strategy, a strategy that builds MBS synergism.

A portfolio of strategies for increased IM effectiveness can be built following a simple four-step process, which can be repeated as often as necessary for each problem.

Step 1: Identify the problem.

Step 2: Select problem-solving strategies (see Appendix A).

Step 3: Develop an action plan.

Step 4: Implement MBS.

Exhibit 13-1   Cumulative effect of strategies for improving IM effectiveness implemented in a typical company.

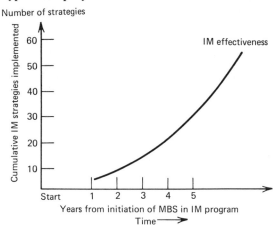

In Step 2, the selection of appropriate problem-solving strategies, a number of variations can be successfully employed, depending on the circumstances. That is, a single strategy can be repeatedly applied to a problem in general in different parts of the company, or a combination of related strategies can be applied to a specific problem, or a number of unrelated strategies can be applied to a specific problem. We can perhaps best illustrate this process with some case studies taken from our experience at The First National Bank of Boston. Let us consider, for example, a common problem faced by many IM organizations: *how to achieve greater user automation penetration.*

Case 1   User Penetration

Solution 1   In this solution, a *single* strategy is applied to the problem in general. One of the more successful techniques utilized by The First National Bank of Boston to achieve greater user penetration in the application of technology to business problems has been the Trojan horse strategy (S-9) described in Chapter 5. Properly employed, this can be a most effective strategy for achieving user penetration for needed automation projects. Its success, in fact, has often resulted in the building of a small staff of system planners in the user area to carry on and support on-going automation planning.

Having had good success with this strategy in the early days of data processing, the IM function at the bank in the early 1970s resolved to use it in an attempt to bring the computer into service in some of the high-profit contribution areas of the bank where little technology was, at that time, being employed. As in many institutions in the early 1970s, the computer had been successfully applied to the labor-intensive operational areas, but very little attention had been paid to other important areas of the bank. In fact, a comparison of the allocation of systems resources to the profit contributors of the bank showed that only 15% of the systems resources were devoted to divisions contributing 75% of the profits of the bank. Target divisions for Trojan horses were selected, and one by one—over a period of several years, to be sure—capable systems personnel were successfully moved into these divisions. Senior management support was enlisted, where necessary, to convince top user management of the value of adding a *senior* systems person to their staff if they were not convinced of the need themselves. Over time, 14 of 16 bank divisions have been staffed with one or more systems people. These people do no technical work as such (e.g., systems design or programming), but they do systems *planning* for the users once they learn the users' business and can identify the places where computer systems can be intelligently applied to those business activities. In the process, they, the user management, and the bank all benefit by the increased application of up-to-date technology for increased cost control—a no-lose situation all the way around. The Trojan horse strategy is just another way of educating management to the promise of computers. But at the bank, it has proved to be a superior way to "win friends and influence people in the corporation" and to achieve high user penetration with a minimum of consternation and political upheaval.

Case 2   User Penetration

Solution 2   This solution is an example of the application of *related* strategies to a specific area of the company. The bank also successfully applied the concept of Trojan horses in its commercial finance (factoring) division, which resulted in early and heavy utilization of computer-based systems. A strong integration between IM and the commercial finance division soon developed. Among the strategies utilized to bring this about were heavy user involvement in the project life cycle (S-54) and ongoing business information planning (S-10). Systems efforts resulting from these strategies led to the development of a leading-edge, on-line, real-time factoring system led by a business manager from the commercial finance division. Together with a project leader from the IM division, he was instrumental in leading the project to a successful conclusion, giving the bank one of its leading-edge computer-based systems, which has stood the test of time for a decade of industry leadership.

The resident systems-planning group (Trojan horses) in the user division has continued over the years to plan new systems features and additions through ongoing business information planning efforts with the systems people and by staying closely involved during systems development. Other strategies aided automation penetration in this case, but the key ones were the Trojan horse, user penetration, business information planning once the Trojan horse was in place, and extensive user involvement in the project life cycle of projects. These user-relations strategies were combined to produce high user automation penetration and a winning product that produces good market share, profits, and good customer satisfaction for this major bank division.

Case 3   User Penetration

Solution 3   In this solution, *unrelated* strategies were applied to a specific area of the company. In 1973, the information management division made a comparison of the allocation of systems resources to the contributing profit sources of the company. It discovered that the company's fastest-growing area, the international division, was also one of the lowest users of IM resources. Because of the far-flung nature of the company's banking activities, however, achieving automation penetration here was going to require considerable advanced planning.

Adopting a proactive change-agent role (S-4), the information manager went to work to learn as much as possible about the bank's international operations. Interviews were conducted with senior management and visits were made to other major multinational banks to learn how they were managing their information resources overseas. As a result, a foot-in-the-door proposal (see S-16) was prepared and presented to senior management, outlining what was perceived to be a growing problem of expanding, splintered overseas operations with no standard plan to control redundancies, incompatibilities and inconsistencies. Minor funding for a feasibility study to address the problem further was sought from and approved by senior management. During the course of that study, technology forecasting (S-11) was employed to match emerging technology with company needs. The result was a proposal to develop a distributed processing system which would use standard and common hardware and software as the system base in each remote facility, modified as necessary to fit local needs. The system would utilize an on-line, real-time processing minicomputer in each overseas location. The system proposed has since been installed in a number of overseas locations, and plans continue to automate the remaining facilities over the next few years.

Meanwhile, the need to control the rapid proliferation of minicomputers, both in the United States and abroad, was addressed through the development and issuance of a corporate policy of distributed-processing standards (S-68) governing the user's responsibilities with regard to computer acquisitions, systems development constraints, major spending on hardware, operations, security and control, etc. A matrix management (S-65) arrangement was also established between overseas data centers and the headquarters IM division. The result? A combination of diverse strategies applied to a single problem has brought the international operations of the bank to a high level of computerization, with increased control and productivity, with better and faster information flow throughout the firm, and most of all, with planned and controlled automation growth to handle the rapid expansion taking place in the company's global business activities.

It is clear from the above examples that the technique of management by strategies can be employed in a variety of ways to add cumulative strength to the solution of problems and the attainment of objectives. The most important point to be made, however, is that *getting started with a deliberate program of MBS is the most critical decision.* If no objectives are established in the first place, then strategies cannot be adopted to reach those nonexistent objectives; and if situation analysis is not employed to determine what strategies will work best in the environment in which they are meant to work, then a less effective program of innovative management to reach objectives will result.

The strategies presented throughout this book are not the be-all-and-end-all of effective information management. They are merely illustrative of strategies that have been used successfully by many leading-edge IM functions in solving problems and meeting objectives unique to their own environments. They may or may not work in a different environment. Our attempt here has been merely to stimulate the reader to begin the process of environmental analysis, role analysis, and strategy formulation that will result in more effective information management and increase the influence of the IM function in the organization.

Clearly, there is not a shortage of strategies for improving the effectiveness of information management. The case studies presented in this chapter illustrate, however, the cumulative effect that MBS synergism can produce in a program of management by strategies. There is a natural sequence of automation penetration in most organizations. For example, senior executives often support the early concentration of IM resources on projects aimed at reducing operating costs (i.e., record-keeping clerical systems). It is easier to implement automation on such routine clerical processes than to implement changes in management practices. Yet only when the former has been largely achieved can the latter be successfully attempted. When companies have largely automated their labor-intensive clerical process, they are more ready to consider information systems for improving the practice of management. In other words, the situational factors making that shift in emphasis possible are then in place. This is true in most better-managed companies today. Thus, information managers in the 1980s will have greater opportunities to contribute research-based management information systems for the improved practice of management than ever in the past because most clerical processes have now been automated. The more exciting and challenging work of putting computers to work for managers can now begin.

INFORMATION MANAGEMENT IN THE INFORMATION AGE

What would our future business be like if there were no constraints on how we responded to opportunities and problems? What would the Wright brothers or Thomas Edison do if they were suddenly returned to life? They would probably look with awe at the extraordinary inventions of the last 30 years. We are perhaps too close to the revolution in information technology and management to appreciate fully the opportunities offered by the information age.

The apparent continuity in data processing tends to hide the information revolution that is occurring around us. John Diebold has urged executives to recognize that data processing technology is not information technology.[1] As we proceed into the information age, it will be important to cast aside obsolete ideas about data processing. Momentum toward the penetration of information management into non-record-keeping tasks became visible in the 1970s. The application of this technology to aid the practice of management is now ready to come of age in the 1980s.

Some of the key emerging trends which will impact business managers in the 1980s follow.

Research-Based Management

Decisions of major consequence will be made by teams that include experience-based line executives (who have a "feel" for the key factors) and specialized staff professionals (who have the training to do thorough analyses of the information relevant to a decision).

Investment in Management

Companies will invest in information management depth and competence in a relationship appropriate to the consequences of the activity to be managed. The high dependence on computers, technology, and information services of most companies, coupled with their high investment in these resources, will cause chief executives to devote time, money, and attention to this activity commensurate with its potential impact on the organization.

Distributed Processing

The distribution of data processing activities will spread dramatically in the 1980s. But the advantages of improved effectiveness and responsiveness of distributed processing will, in our opinion, best be realized under conditions of central management control.

Coalescence of Information Activities

The many areas of information activity will be integrated in the future firm of the 1980s. Data processing, word processing, telecommunications, and other information activities will be integrated through the adoption of corporate information policies, standards, and procedures.

Information Resource Management

Market, customer, competitor, field service, quality control, manufacturing, regulatory compliance, financial, budget, R&D, and other sources of data will be managed more as a whole when data bases, mainframe computers, distributed minicomputers, terminals, graphics, and telecommunications are put in place and managed as a system of information resources. The total cost of these resources will be measured, and programs will be implemented to improve the return on investment and the productivity of these valuable corporate resources.

Executive Information Systems

The information required for the effective management of the factors critical to the success at the top and at each successive level of an organization will be monitored as a more formal practice of management. Concepts for determining executive information needs (see critical success factors, S-24, and business information planning, S-10) will help information managers to better address the top-down information needs of senior managers as the computer is applied increasingly to the support of management.

Chief Information Officer

The responsibility for information management will be separated from the management of other activities through the increased utilization of matrix management. Each company will ultimately need a corporate information officer with high-level responsibility for ensuring the efficient and effective use of information in the organization.

Decision Support Systems

The speed of change and the increased complexity of decisions have increased the need for computer-based decision support systems to assist decision makers to evaluate the consequences of alternative decisions. As we learn more about how to design such systems and as the success of present decision systems is demonstrated, this discipline should find greater application in management.

The above are only a few of the techniques and standards of information management, which we expect to expand as information management becomes more deeply entrenched in management suites. Better information management is an idea whose time has come. It is a new way of looking at the practice of management. Technology is now making it possible to get good information faster and in more useful ways than ever before. Until now, the information revolution occurred in bits and pieces, with little integration. But change is taking place all around us, every day, in every way. We need to learn to recognize it and to pull it together more effectively. Management by strategies can help, because it offers a new way of thinking about how to improve information management as we evolve into the information age.

THE CHALLENGE OF THE 1980s

The practice of management is essentially only the processing of information by people. Who will take the leadership position in the information age of the 1980s to lead information management? Historically, people who controlled specialized kinds of information have risen to top management positions. Is the information manager's time coming? We believe that the 1980s will be the decade of opportunity for information managers (see Exhibit 13-2). Whether the opportunity is realized in a transfer of power in the 1980s will depend on how well information managers manage the transition from EDP to IRM. Today's DP managers and MIS directors *do* have a chance to get to the top, not by being EDP experts, but by becoming businessmen, learning the business, managing the information that is the life's blood of the business, and becoming very much a part of the mainstream of the business instead of ancillary technicians.

In the 1980s, the business world will become more complex, and the need for good information in the practice of management will become vital to the new management. Technology will be a most important factor in the management of enterprises. The challenge to information managers will be to take the offensive to shape their environments and their roles within those

Exhibit 13-2   Dominance of corporate management by function: the 1960s, 1970s, and 1980s.

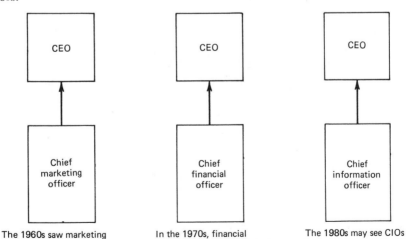

environments rather than merely allowing changes to happen. They must lead change, they must control information resources, and they must integrate themselves into the businesses they serve. Today, our companies are vitally dependent on computers. By the end of the 1980s, our whole society will be totally dependent on computers and communications for their recreation, their work, their very survival. Today's information managers and information specialists are in one of the most exciting, dynamic, and quickly growing industries. The opportunities and challenges of this decade will be almost limitless for those who proactively seek new responsibilities with enthusiasm, courage, intelligence, and imagination.

NOTE

1   John Diebold, foreword to the Diebold Group Special Report, "IRM: New Directions in Management," *Infosystems,* October 1979, p. 41.

Index

Strategies are identified by number; pages of main discussion of strategies are in bold type. Page numbers in italics indicate presentation of exhibits.